LANGUAGES AND LITERATURE

OF THE

SLAVIC NATIONS.

HISTORICAL VIEW

OF THE

LANGUAGES AND LITERATURE

OF THE

SLAVIC NATIONS;

WITH A

SKETCH OF THEIR POPULAR POETRY.

BY TALVI.

WITH A PREFACE BY

EDWARD ROBINSON, D.D. LL.D.

AUTHOR OF "BIBLICAL RESEARCHES IN PALESTINE," ETC.

NEW-YORK:
GEORGE P. PUTNAM, 155 BROADWAY.
M.DCCC.L.

JOHN F. TROW, Printer,
49, 51 & 53 Ann-street.

PREFACE.

The present work is founded on an essay, which appeared in the Biblical Repository for April and July, 1834, then conducted by the undersigned. The essay was received with favour by the public; and awakened an interest in many minds, as laying open a new field of information, hitherto almost inaccessible to the English reader. A few copies were printed separately for private distribution. Some of these were sent to literary men in Europe; and several scholars of high name among those acquainted with Slavic literature, expressed their approval of the work. Since that time, and even of late, inquiries have repeatedly been made, by scholars and by public libraries in Europe, for copies of that little treatise; which, of course, it was impossible to satisfy.

These circumstances, together with the fact, that in these years public attention has been more prominently directed to the character and prospects of the Slavic nations, have induced the author to recast the work; and to lay it anew before the public, corrected, enlarged, and continued to the present time; as a brief contribution to our knowledge of the intellectual character and condition of those nations, in the middle of the nineteenth century.

In its present shape, the work may be said to supply, in a certain degree, a deficiency in English literature. It is true, that the literature of the Russians, Poles, Bohemians, and some others, is treated of under the appropriate heads in the *Encyclopædia Americana*, in articles translated from the German *Conversations-Lexicon*, though not in their latest form. The Foreign Quarterly Review also contains articles of value on the like topics, scattered throughout its volumes. Dr. Bowring, in the prefaces to some of his Specimens of Slavic Poetry, has given short notices of a similar kind. The Biblical literature of the Old Slavic and Russian has been well exhibited by Dr. Henderson;[1] while an outline of Russian literature in general is presented in the work of Otto.[2] Valuable information respecting the South-western Slavi is contained in the recent work of Sir J. G. Wilkinson.[3] But beyond this meagre enumeration, the English reader will find few sources of information at his command upon these topics. All these, too, are only sketches of separate *parts* of one great whole; of which in its full extent, both as a whole and in the intimate relation of its parts, no general view is known to exist in the English language.

Yet the subject in itself is not without a high interest and importance; relating, as it does, to the languages and literature of a population amounting to nearly or quite seventy millions, or more than three times as great as that of the United States. These topics embrace, of course, the history of mental cultivation among the Slavic nations from its earliest dawn; their intellectual development; the progress of man among them as a thinking, sentient, social being, acting and acted upon in his various relations to

---

[1] See *infra*, p. 45. [2] Page 100. [3] Page 121.

other minds. They relate, indeed, to the history of intellectual culture in one of its largest geographical and ethnological divisions.

In this connection it is a matter of no small interest, to mark the influence which Christianity has exercised upon the language and literature of these various nations. It is to the introduction and progress of Christianity, that they owe their written language; and to the versions of the Scriptures into their own dialects are they indebted, not only for their moral and religious culture, but also for the cultivation and, in a great degree, the existence of their national literature. The same influence Christianity is even now exerting upon the hitherto unwritten languages of the American forest, of the islands of the Pacific, of the burning coasts of Africa, of the mountains of Kurdistan; and with the prospect of results still wider and more propitious. Indeed, wherever we learn the fact, whether in earlier or more recent times, that a language, previously regarded as barbarous, and existing only as oral, has been reclaimed and reduced to writing, and made the vehicle of communicating fixed thought and permanent instruction, there it has ever been *Christianity* and *Missionary Enterprise* which have produced these results. It is greatly to the honour of Protestant Missions, that their efforts have always been directed to introduce the Scriptures and the worship of God to the masses of the people in their own native tongue. In this way they have every where contributed to awaken the intellectual, as well as the moral life of nations.

The present work has been prepared with great care; and with the aid of the latest and best sources of information, so far as they were accessible. The author, however, would be the last to desire, that any one should regard the volume as comprising a full or complete history of the literature of the seven or eight Slavic nations. Scholars familiar with the subject, and especially intelligent Russian, Polish, or Bohemian readers, will doubtless discover in it deficiencies and errors. Limited to the resources of a private library,—for the public libraries of the United States and of Great Britain have as yet accumulated little or nothing in the Slavic department,—and without the privilege of personal intercourse with others acquainted with Slavic literary matters, the author desires to be distinctly understood, as aiming only to present a *sketch*, an *outline*,—a work which may fill its appropriate place, until it shall be supplanted by something more perfect.

The preceding remarks have reference especially to the first *three* Parts of the volume. In the *fourth* Part, containing a Sketch of the Popular Poetry of the Slavic nations, the author is perhaps still more at home; and the reader, it may be hoped, will receive gratification from the views and specimens there presented. Similar views, and a few of the same specimens, were given in an article from the same pen, in the North American Review for July, 1836.

In conclusion, it may not be inappropriate to remark, that circumstances have combined to secure to the author some qualifications for the preparation of a work of this kind, which are not common to writers in the English language. A residence of several years in early life in Russia, first in the southern provinces, and afterwards at St. Petersburg, presented opportunity for a personal acquaintance with the language and literature of that country. At a later period, this gave occasion and afforded aid for an extensive study of the Servian dialect and its budding literature; the results of which were given to the public in a German translation of the very remarkable popular songs and ballads of that country.[4] The field was new; but certainly that can be regarded as no barren soil, nor that as a fruitless labour, which at once drew the attention, and secured to the translator the friendship and correspondence, of scholars like Goethe, von Humboldt, J. Grimm, Savigny, C. Ritter, Kopitar, and others. Similar researches were subsequently extended into the popular poetry of the Teutonic and other nations; a portion of the results of which have likewise been given to the public.[5]

I may venture to commend this volume to the good will and kind forbearance of the reader, in view of the difficulties which must ever press upon the writer of such a work. The enterprising publisher has done his part well; and I would join him in the hope, that the book may prove an acceptable offering to the public.

E. ROBINSON.

NEW-YORK, April 10, 1850.

---

[4] *Volkslieder der Serben, übersetzt von Talvj,* Halle 1825–26, 2 vols.

[5] *Versuch einer geschichtlichen Charakteristik der Volkslieder germanischer Nationen, etc. von Talvj,* Leipzig 1840.

CONTENTS.

INTRODUCTION.

Part First.

HISTORY OF THE OLD OR CHURCH SLAVIC LANGUAGE AND LITERATURE.

Part Second.

EASTERN SLAVI.

CHAPTER I.

HISTORY OF THE RUSSIAN LANGUAGE AND LITERATURE.

CHAPTER II.

HISTORY OF THE ILLYRICO-SERVIAN LANGUAGE.

SECTION I.

Language and Literature of the Illyrico-Servians Proper.

Servians of the Greek Church.

Servians of the Romish Church.

SECTION II.

SECTION III.

CHAPTER III.

LANGUAGE OF THE BULGARIANS.

Part Third.

WESTERN SLAVI.

CHAPTER I.

CZEKHO-SLOVAKIAN BRANCH.

SECTION I.

History of the Czekhish or Bohemian Language and Literature.

SECTION II.

Language and Literature of the Slovaks.

CHAPTER II.

HISTORY OF THE POLISH LANGUAGE AND LITERATURE.

CHAPTER III.

LANGUAGES OF THE SORABIAN-VENDES IN LUSATIA, AND OF OTHER VENDISH TRIBES NOW EXTINCT.

1. Vendes in Upper Lusatia.

2. Vendes in Lower Lusatia.

Part Fourth.

SKETCH OF THE POPULAR POETRY OF THE SLAVIC NATIONS.

EASTERN SLAVI.

WESTERN SLAVI.

NOTE.

On the Orthography and Pronunciation of Slavic proper names, see the note on p. 151; also the note under the letter V in the Index.

HISTORICAL SKETCH.

INTRODUCTION.

The earliest history of the Slavic nations is involved in a darkness, which all the investigations of diligent and sagacious modern historians and philologians have not been able to clear up. The analogy between their language and the Sanscrit, seems to indicate their origin from India; but to ascertain the time at which they first entered Europe, is now no longer possible. Probably this event took place seven or eight centuries before the Christian era, on account of the over-population of the regions on the Ganges.[1] Herodotus mentions a people which he called Krovyzi, who lived on the Ister. There is even

[1] See Schlegel's *Sprache und Weisheit der Indier*, Heidelb. 1808. Von Hammer's *Fundgruben des Orients*, Vol. II. p. 459 sq. Murray's *History of the European Languages*, Edinb. 1823. F. G. Eichhoff, *Histoire de la Langue et de la Literature des Slaves etc. considerées dans leur origine Indienne, etc.* Paris, 1839.—Frenzel, who wrote at the close of the seventeenth century, took the Slavi for a Hebrew tribe and their language for Hebrew. Somo modern German and Italian historians derive the Slavic language from the Thracian, and the Slavi immediately from Japhet; some consider the ancient Scythians as Slavi. See Dobrovsky's *Slovanka*, VII. p. 94.

now a tribe in Russia, whose name at least is almost the same.[2] Strabo, Pomponius Mela, Pliny, Tacitus, and several other classical and a few oriental writers, allude to the Slavic nations occasionally. But the first distinct intelligence we have of them, is not older than the middle of the sixth century.[3] At this period we see them traversing the Danube in large multitudes, and settling on both the banks of that river. From that time they appear frequently in the accounts of the Byzantine historians, under the different appellations of the Slavi, Sarmatæ,[4] Antæ, Vandales, Veneti, and Vendes, mostly as involved in the wars of the two Roman empires, sometimes as allies, sometimes as conquerors; oftener, notwithstanding their acknowledged valour and courage, as vassals; but chiefly as emigrants and colonists, thrust out of their own countries by the pressing forward of the more warlike German or Teutonic tribes. Only the first of the above mentioned names is decidedly of Slavic origin;[5]

---

[2] *Krivitshi.* The Greek is Κρόβυζοι, Herodot. 4. 49. Comp. Strabo VII. p. 318, 319. Plin. H. N. IV. 12.

[3] The first writers, who mention the Slavi expressly, are Jordan or Jornandes, after A. D. 552; Procopius A. D. 562; Menander A. D. 594; and the Abbot John of Biclar before A. D. 620. See Schaffarik's *Geschichte der Slavischen Sprache und Literatur,* Buda, 1826. Dobrovsky's *Slovanka,* V. p. 76–84.—Schaffarik, in his more recent work on *Slavic Antiquities,* 1838, and in his *Slavic Ethnography,* 1842, supposes he has found the first Slavi already three centuries B. C. in the Veneti or Wendi on the Baltic. But as every connecting link between them and the *historical* Slavi is wanting, the fact seems of little importance.

[4] Schaffarik in his work on *Slavic Antiquities* attempts to prove that the Sarmatæ were no Slavi, but a Perso-Median nation; remnants of which, he thinks, he has discovered in the Alanes and Osetenzes in the Caucasus.

[5] The name of the *Slavi* has generally been derived from *slava,* glory, and their national feelings have of course been gratified by this derivation. But the more immediate origin of the appellation, is to be sought in the word *slovo,*

the second is ambiguous; and the last four are later and purely geographical, having been transferred to Slavic nations from those who had previously occupied the territory where the Romans first became acquainted with them.

It results from the very nature of this information, that we cannot expect to get from it any satisfactory knowledge of their political state or the degree of their civilization. In general, they appear as a peaceful, industrious, hospitable people, obedient to their chiefs, and religious in their habits. Wherever they established themselves, they began to cultivate the earth, and to trade in the productions of the country. There are also early traces of their fondness for music and poetry; and some circumstances, of which we shall speak in the sequel, seem to justify the supposition of a very early cultivation of the language.

All the knowledge we have respecting the ancient history of the Slavic race, as we have seen, is gathered from foreign authors; the earliest of their own historians did not write before

---

word, speech. The change of *o* into *a* occurs frequently in the Slavic languages, (thus *slava* comes from *slovo*,) but is in this case probably to be ascribed to foreigners, viz. Byzantines, Romans, and Germans. In the language of the latter, the *o* in names and words of Slavic origin in many instances becomes *a*. The radical syllable *slov* is still to be found in the appellations which the majority of the Slavic nations apply to themselves or kindred nations, e. g. Slovenzi, Slovaci, Slovane, Sloveni, etc. The Russians and Servians did not exchange the *o* for *a* before the seventh century. See Schaffarik's *Geschichte*, p. 5. n. 6. The same writer observes, p. 287. n. 8, "It is remarkable that, while all the other Slavic nations relinquished their original *national* names, and adopted *specific* names, as Russians, Poles, Silesians, Czekhes, Moravians, Sorabians, Servians, Morlachians, Czernogortzi, Bulgarians; nay, when most of them imitating foreigners altered the general name *Slovene* into *Slavene*, only those two Slavic branches, which touch each other on the banks of the Danube, the *Slovaks* and the *Slovenzi*, have retained in its purity their original national name."

the second half of the eleventh century.[6] At this time the Slavic nations were already in possession, partly as masters, partly as servants, of the whole vast extent of territory, which they now occupy; and if we assume that at the present time about seventy or eighty millions speak the Slavic language in its different dialects, we must calculate that at the above mentioned period, and in the course of the next following centuries, before the Slavic was by degrees supplanted in the German-Slavic provinces by the German idiom, the number of those who called that language their mother tongue was at least the fifth part greater. Schlözer observes, that, with the exception of the Arabians, no nation on the globe had extended themselves so far. In the South, the Adriatic, the range of the Balkan, and the Euxine, are their frontiers; the coasts of the Icy Ocean are their limits in the North; their still greater extent in an Eastern and Western direction reaches from Kamtschatka and the Russian islands of the Pacific, where many of their vestiges are to be found among scattered tribes, as far as to the Baltic and along the banks of the rivers Elbe, Muhr, and Raab, again to the Adriatic. It is this immense extent, which adds greatly to the difficulties of a general survey of the different relations and connections of nations, broken up into so many parts. The *history of the language* is our object, not the history of the people; we therefore give of statistic and political notices only so much, as seems to be requisite for the illustration of our subject.

The earliest data for the history of the civilization of the Slavic race, we find in their mythology; and here their oriental

---

[6] The earliest Slavic historian is the Russian monk Nestor, born in the year 1056. See below, in the History of the *Old Slavic* and of the *Russian* languages. The reader will there see, that even the authority and age of this writer has been in our days attacked by the hypercritical spirit of the modern Russian Historical school.

origin again appears. The antithesis of a good and evil principle is met with among most of their tribes; and as even at the present time in some Slavic dialects every thing good, beautiful, praiseworthy, is to them synonymous with the purity of the white colour, they call the good Spirit *Bielo Bôg*, the white god; the evil Spirit *Tcherno Bôg*, the black god. The *Div* of the old Russians seem to be likewise akin to the *Dev* of the Hindoo; the goddess of life, *Shiva*, of the Polabae, to the Indian *Shiva;* as the names of the Slavic personification of death, *Morjana, Morena, Marzana*, evidently stand in connection with the Indian word for death, *Marana*. Strabo describes some of the idols of the Rugians, in which we meet again the whole significant symbolization of the East. The custom prevalent among many Slavic nations, of females burning themselves with the corpses of their husbands, seems also to have been brought from India to Europe.

There are, however, other features of their mythology which belong to them exclusively, and which remind us rather of the sprightly and poetical imagination of the Greeks. We allude to their mode of attributing life to the inanimate objects of nature, rocks, brooks and trees; of peopling with supernatural beings the woods which surrounded them, the mountains between which they lived. The *Rusalki* of the Russians, the *Vila* of the southern Slavic nations, the *Leshie* of several other tribes, nymphs, naiads, and satyrs, are still to be found in many popular tales and songs. If, however, we have compared them to the poetical gods of the Greeks, we must not forget to add, that their character has less resemblance to these gods, (who indeed appear only as ordinary men, with higher powers, more violent passions, and less limited lives,) than it has to the northern Elf, and the German Nix and mountain Spirit—without heart and soul themselves, but always intermeddling with intrusive curiosity in human affairs, however void of real interest in them;

revengeful towards the most trifling offence or the least neglect; and beneficent only to favourites arbitrarily chosen.[7]

The earliest historians mention the Slavi as divided into several tribes and as speaking different dialects. There are no very ancient remains of their language, except those words or phrases, which we find scattered through the works of foreign writers; and these mostly perverted by their want of knowledge. Besides these we have the names of places, of festivals, partly still existing, and of some dignitaries, *Knes*, *Zupan*, etc. There are, indeed, among the popular songs of the Bohemians, Servians, Russians, and several other tribes, many which are evidently derived from the pagan period; but as they have been preserved only by tradition, we must of course assume, that their diction has been changed almost in the same proportion as the language of common life. Hence, national songs, before they have been fixed by letters, are always to be considered as much safer proofs for the genius than for the language of a people.

It is, however, probable that at least *one* Slavic idiom was cultivated to a certain degree in very ancient times; for from the single circumstance, that Cyril's translation of the Bible, written in the middle of the ninth century, bears the stamp of uncommon perfection in its forms, and of great copiousness, it is sufficiently evident, that the language must have been the means of expression for thinking men several centuries before. There is, indeed, no doubt that the state of the language, as it appears in that translation, required no short interval of preparation.

---

[7] See Görres' *Mythengeschichte der Asiatischen Welt,* Heidelb. 1810. Kayssarov's *Versuch einer Slavischen Mythologie,* Götting. 1804. Dobrovsky's *Slavin,* new edit. by W. Hanka, Prague 1834, p. 263–275. Durich *Bibliotheca Slavica,* Buda 1795. J. Potocki's *Voyages dans quelques parties de la Basse Saxe pour la recherche des antiquités Slaves,* Hamb. 1795. J. J. Hanusch, *Wissenschaft des Slavischen Mythus.* Lemberg, 1842.

The first attempts to convert portions of the Slavic race to Christianity were probably made before the seventh century; but it was only at the beginning of the ninth that their partial success became of importance to their language and literature. It is true, that by the last investigations of the late great Slavist, B. Kopitar, the fact has been ascertained, that a portion of the Slavic race was already in possession of an alphabet *before* Cyril;[8] but as this fact appears to have had no further result, we must still consider the ninth century and Cyril's translation of the Gospels as the beginning of their literary history, the dawn at least of a brighter day.

Before we enter upon our examination of the different branches, we must not neglect to direct the attention of the reader to the whole great trunk, which in the most ancient times appears to have ramified into two principal stems.

A boundless confusion indeed reigns in the classification of the Slavic nations among the earlier historians and philologists. It was the learned Dobrovsky of Prague, who first brought light into this chaos, and established a classification, founded on a deep and thorough examination of all the different dialects, and acknowledged by the equally great authority of Kopitar. Adelung, in his Mithridates,[9] has adopted it. The specific names, however, Antes and Slavi, which Adelung applies to the great divisions, and which were first used by Jornandes, are arbitrary, and less distinct than those adopted by Dobrovsky, Kopitar, and Schaffarik; who divide all Slavic nations, according to certain philological affinities and differences, into the *North-Western* and *South-Eastern* Stems.[10]

---

[8] *Glagolita Clozianus*, Vindob. 1836.

[9] Vol. II. p. 1610 sq.

[10] Schaffarik in his *Slavic Ethnography*, published nearly twenty years after his "History of the Slavic Language and Literature," omits the word "North," and divides the Slavi into the "*Western*," and "*South-Eastern*" nations. He must mean the *Western*, and the *Southern* AND *Eastern*.

Far better would have been the terms 'Northern *and* Western,' 'Southern *and* Eastern,' divisions; which indeed can be the only proper meaning of those appellations. The Slovaks in Hungary, for instance, who belong to the first division, can in no way be called a *North*-Western people; and the Russians, who belong to the second, still less a *South*-Eastern nation. The *origin* from the South is common to all the Slavic tribes; hence the appellation of Northern and Southern can be applied to them only in a relative sense; and that portion of the Slavic race, which inhabits Russia, is not known to have ever lived in a more southern region than their Bohemian brethren. We adopt, therefore, the division of the Slavi into EASTERN and WESTERN Stems; which seems indeed to be the only strictly proper one.[11]

The following enumeration of the still existing distinct nations of the Slavic race, may serve to give a clearer view of them.

A. EASTERN STEM.

I. RUSSIAN BRANCH.

1. RUSSIANS. The Russians of Slavic origin form the bulk of the population of the European part of Russia. All the middle provinces of this vast empire are occupied almost exclusively by a people of purely Slavic extraction. The numerous Slavi who are scattered through Asiatic Russia, are of the same

[11] We acknowledge, however, that even this latter appellation admits of some restriction in respect to the Slovenzi or Windes of Carniola and Carinthia; who, notwithstanding their rather Western situation, belong to the Eastern race.

race. They belong to the Greek Church. To ascertain the exact numbers of the different races of one and the same nation, is exceedingly difficult. The statistical tables of the government afford little help; since it is the policy of the latter to annihilate as much as possible the difference of races. Schaffarik, in his Slavic Ethnography, gives the number of the Russians proper at 38,400,000. We follow him, as the most diligent and most consistent investigator of this matter; but we also feel bound to remark, that his statistical assertions have occasioned surprise, and met with contradiction.

2. Russniaks or Ruthenians, also called *Russinians* and *Malo-Russians.* These are found in Malo-Russia, the South of Poland, Galicia, Ludomeria or Red Russia, the Bukovina, also in the north-eastern part of Hungary, and scattered over Walachia and Moldavia. The Kozaks, especially the Zaporogueans, belong chiefly to this race; while the Kozaks of the Don are more mixed with pure Russians. Their number is given at more than thirteen millions. They all belong to the Oriental Church; though a portion of them are Greek-Catholics, or adherents of the United Church.

II. ILLYRICO-SERVIAN BRANCH.

1. The Illyrico-Servians proper, frequently called *Rascians* or *Raitzi*, comprising five subdivisions.

a) The Servians in Servia, lying between the rivers Timock, Drina, Save, the Danube, and the Balkan mountains; and, as a Turkish province, called Serf Vilayeti. Their number is at least a million. In earlier times, and especially at the end of the seventeenth century, many of them emigrated to Hungary; where even now between three and four hundred thousand of them are settled; exclusive of their near relatives, the Slavonians, in the kingdom of Slavonia so called.

2*

b) Bosnians, between Dalmatia, the Balkan mountains, and the rivers Drina, Verbas, and Save; from four to five hundred thousand in number. Most of them belong, like their brethren the Servians, to the Greek Church; about 100,000 are Roman Catholics. There are of late many Muhammedans among them, who still retain their language and most of their Slavic customs.

c) Montenegrins (Czernogortzi). These are the Slavic inhabitants of the Turkish province Albania, among the mountains of Montenegro. They have spread themselves from Bosnia to the sea-coast as far as Antivari. This remarkable people the Turks never have been able to subjugate completely. They enjoy a sort of military-republican freedom; their head chief being a Bishop with very limited power. They amount to nearly 60,000 souls, belonging to the Eastern Church.

d) Slavonians. These are the inhabitants of the Austrian kingdom of Slavonia and the duchy of Syrmia, between Hungary on the north and Bosnia in the south, about half a million in number. A small majority belongs to the Romish Church; the rest to the Greek Church.

e) Dalmatians. The country along the Adriatic, between Croatia and Albania, together with the adjacent islands, is called the kingdom of Dalmatia, and belongs likewise to the Austrian empire. It has, together with the Istrian shore north of it, towards 600,000 inhabitants; of whom 500,000 belong to the Slavo-Servian race. They are all Roman Catholics; with the exception of about 80,000 who belong to the Greek Church.

2. The Austrian kingdom of Croatia in our time, between Styria, Hungary, Slavonia, Bosnia, Dalmatia, and the Adriatic, is not the ancient Croatia of Constantine Porphyrogenitus. Together with the Croatian colonists in Hungary, and the inhabitants of the Turkish Sandshak Banialouka, it contains about 800,000 souls. Of these less than 200,000 belong to the Greek Church; the great majority are Catholics. We shall see further

on that the Croats are divided in respect to their language into two parts; one of them having affinity with the Servians and Dalmatians, the other with the Slovenzi of Carniola and Carinthia.

3. Slovenzi or Vindes. These names comprise the Slavic inhabitants of the duchies of Styria, Carinthia, and Carniola, (the two latter forming the kingdom of Illyria,) and also those of the banks of the rivers Raab and Muhr in Hungary. Their number is over one million. With the exception of a few Protestants, they are all Catholics. They call themselves *Slovenzi;* but are known by foreign writers under the name of *Vindes.*

III. BULGARIAN BRANCH.

The Bulgarians occupy the Turkish province Sofia Vilayeti, between the Danube, the Euxine, the Balkan, and Servia; they are about three and a half millions in number, the remnant of a great nation. About 80,000 more are scattered through Bessarabia and the other provinces of South Russia. Schaffarik enumerates seven thousand as Austrian subjects, living in that great receptacle of nations, Hungary. Most of them belong to the Greek Church.

B. WESTERN STEM.

I. CZEKHO-SLOVAKIAN BRANCH.

1. Bohemians and Moravians (Czekhes). These are the Slavic inhabitants of the kingdom of Bohemia and the Margravate of Moravia, both belonging to the Austrian empire. They are

about four and a half millions in number; of whom 100,000 are Protestants, the rest Catholics. Schaffarik includes also 44,000 of the Slavic inhabitants of Prussian Silesia in this race.

2. SLOVAKS. Almost all the northern part of Hungary is inhabited by Slovaks; besides this they are scattered through the whole of that country, and speak different dialects. They are reckoned at between two and three millions.

II. POLISH OR LECKIAN BRANCH.

This comprises the inhabitants of the present kingdom of Poland; of a part of what are called since 1772 the Russian-Polish provinces; of the duchy of Posen; and of Galicia and Ludomeria. The bulk of the people in this latter country are Russniaks or Ruthenians. In the Russian provinces, which were formerly called White Russia, Black Russia, and Red Russia, and were conquered by the Poles in former times, the peasantry are Russians and Russniaks; in Lithuania, they are Lithuanians or Lettones, a race of a different family of nations. In all these countries, only the nobility and inhabitants of the cities are really Poles, or Slavi of the Leckian race. To the same race belongs also the Polish population of Silesia, and an isolated tribe in the Prussian province of Pomerania, called the Kassubes. The Slavi of the Leckian race hardly amount to the number of ten millions; all Catholics, with the exception of about half a million of Protestants.

III. SORABIAN-VENDISH BRANCH.

There are remnants of the old Sorabæ and several other Slavic races in Lusatia and some parts of Brandenburg. Their number is less than 2,000,000; divided between Protestants and Catholics.

There is no doubt, that besides the races here enumerated, there are Slavic tribes scattered through Germany, Transylvania, Moldavia, and Walachia, nay, through the whole of Turkey. Thus, for instance, the Tchaconic dialect, spoken in the eastern part of ancient Sparta and unintelligible to the other Greeks, has been proved by one of the most distinguished philologists to have been of Slavic origin.[12] But to ascertain their number, at any rate very small, would be a matter of impossibility, and in every respect of little consequence.

We thus distinguish among the nations of the Slavic race two great families, the connection of whose members among each other is entirely independent of their present geographical situation; and this division rests upon a marked distinction in the Slavic language. To specify the marks, by which the philologist recognizes to which of these families each nation belongs, seems to be here out of place. The reader, without knowing the language itself, would hardly be able to comprehend them sufficiently; and he who understands it, will find better sources of information in philological works. All that concerns us here, is the general character, the genius of the language. For this purpose we will try to give in a few words a general outline of its grammar; exhibiting principally those features, which, as being common to all or most of its different dialects, seem to be the best adapted to express its general character.

The analogy between the Slavic and the Sanscrit languages consists indeed only in the similar sound of a great many words;

---

[12] By Kopitar; see the *Wiener Jahrbücher*, 1822, Vol. XVII. Kastanica, Sitina, Gorica, and Prasto, are Slavic names. There is even a place called Σκλαβοχωρί, *Slavic village*. Leake in his Researches observes that Slavic names of places occur throughout all Greece.

the construction of the former is purely European, and it has in this respect a nearer relation to the Greek, Latin, and German; with which idioms it has evidently been derived from the same source.[13] The Slavic has three genders. Like the Latin, it knows no article; at least not the genuine Slavic; for those dialects which have lost their national character, like the Bulgarian, or those which have been corrupted by the influence of the German,[14] employ the demonstrative pronoun as an article; and the Bulgarian has borrowed the Albanian mode of suffixing one to

---

[13] The affinity of the Slavic and Greek languages it has recently been attempted to prove in several works. Dankovsky in his work, *Die Griechen als Sprachverwandte der Slaven,* Presburg 1828, contends that a knowledge of the Slavic language is of the highest importance for the Greek scholar, as the only means by which he may be enabled to clear up obscure passages and to ascertain the signification of doubtful words. Among the historical proofs, he furnishes a vocabulary containing 306 Slavic and Greek words of striking analogy. "Of three sisters," he observes, "*one* kept faithful to her mother tongue—the Slavic language; the *second* gave to that common heritage the highest cultivation—the Greek language; and the *third* mixed the mother tongue with a foreign idiom—the Latin language." A work of the same tendency has been published in the Greek language, by the Greek priest Constantine, Vienna 1828. It contains a vocabulary of 800 pages of *Russian* and Greek words, corresponding in sound and meaning.—That these views are not new, is generally known; although they hardly ever have been carried so far, except perhaps by the author of the History of Russia, Levesque, who considers the Latins as a Slavic colony; or by Solarich, who derived all modern languages from the Slavic. Gelenius in his *Lexicon Symphonum,* 1557, made the first etymological attempt in respect to the Slavic languages. In modern times, great attention has been paid to Slavic etymology by Dobrovsky, Linde, Adelung, Bantkje, Fritsch, and others. An *Etymologicon Universale* was published in 1811, at Cambridge in England, by W. Whiter.—Galiffee, in his *Italy and its Inhabitants,* 1816 and 1817, started the opinion, that the *Russian* was the original language, and that the Old Slavonic and all the rest were only dialects.

[14] Or rather some writers in Lusatia and the Austrian provinces comprised in the kingdom of Illyria.

the noun. For this very reason the declensions are more perfect in Slavic than in German and Greek; for the different cases, as in Latin, are distinguished by suffixed syllables or endings. The Singular has seven cases; the Plural only six, the vocative having always the form of the nominative. As for the Dual, a form which the Slavic languages do not all possess, the nominative and accusative, the genitive and local, the dative and instrumental cases, are always alike.

For the declensions of adjectives the Slavic has two principal forms, according as they are *definite* or *indefinite*. The Old or Church Slavonic knows only two degrees of comparison, the positive and comparative; it has no superlative, or rather it has the same form for the comparative and superlative. This is regularly made by the suffix *ii*, mostly united with one of those numerous sibilants, for which the English language has hardly letters or signs, *sh*, *tsh*, *sht*, *shtsh*, etc. In the more modern dialects this deficiency has been supplied; in most of them a superlative form is made by prefixing the particle *naï;* e. g. in Servian, *mudar*, wise, *mudrii*, wiser, *naïmudrii*, the wisest. The Russian, besides this and several other superlative forms, has one that is more perfect, as proceeding from the adjective itself: *doroghii*, dear, *doroshe*, dearer, *doroshaïshii*, dearest. Equally rich is this language in augmentative and diminutive forms not only of the substantive but also of the adjective, a perfection in which even the Italian can hardly be compared to it; of which however all the Slavic dialects possess more or less. Almost all the Russian substantives have two augmentatives and three diminutives; some have even more. We abstain with some difficulty from adducing examples; but we are afraid of going beyond our limits. It deserves to be mentioned as a peculiarity, that the Slavi consider only the first four ordinal numbers as adjectives, and all the following ones as substantives. For this reason, the governed word must stand in the genitive instead of the accusative: *osm sot* (nom. *sto*), eight hundred. In all negative phrases they employ likewise the genitive instead of the accusative. A double negation occurs in Slavic frequently, without indicating an affirmation; for even if another negation has already taken place, they are accustomed to prefix to the verb the negative particle *ne* or *nje*.

In respect to the verb, it is difficult to give a general idea of its character; for it is in the forms of this part of speech, that there reigns the greatest variety in the numerous dialects of the Slavic language. The same termination which in Old Slavonic and in Russian indicates invariably the first person of the present, *u* or *gu*, is in Servian that of the third person Plural of the present and imperfect; and the general termination of the Servian and the Polish for the first person of the present, *am*, *em* or *im*, is in Old Slavonic and Russian used for the Plural, *em* and *im*. There is however one fundamental form through all the Slavic dialects for the second person of the present, a termination in *ash*, *esh* or *ish;* and this is consequently the person, by which it is to be recognized to what conjugation a verb belongs.

The division of the verbs adopted in all other European languages into *Active* and *Passive*, seems to be useless in Slavic; for their being active or passive has no influence upon their flexion; and the forms of the Latin Passive and Deponent must in Slavic be expressed by a circumlocution. A division of more importance and springing from the peculiarity of the language itself, is that into verbs *Perfect* and *Imperfect*. Neither the Greek, nor the Latin, nor the German, nor any of the languages derived from them, admits of a similar distinction. It seems therefore difficult for persons not perfectly acquainted with any Slavic dialect, to form to themselves a clear idea of it. It is however one of their most striking features, which adds very considerably to their general richness and power. The relation in which the perfect and imperfect verbs stand to each other, is about the same as that of the perfect and imperfect tenses in the conjugation of the Latin verb. Perfect verbs express that an action takes place a single time, and therefore is entirely completed and past; from their very nature it results, that they have no imperfect tense, and their conjugation must be in general incomplete. Imperfect verbs express that the same action continues. Both have in most cases the same radical syllable, and may be formed with a certain degree of freedom; thus in Servian, *viknuti*, to cry once, *vikati*, to be crying; *umriyeti*, to die, *umirati*, to be dying. There are however others, which stand in the same relation to each other without issuing from the same verbal stock; e. g. in Servian, *tchuti* and *slushati*, to hear; *retji* and *govoriti*, to speak, etc.

The Polish language, which is remarkably rich in every kind of flexion, has a still simpler and more regular way of forming also a frequentative out of almost every verb; e. g. *czytam*, I read, *czytivam*, I read often; *biore*, I take, *bieram*, I take often, etc. In Bohemian, which in respect to grammar is by far the most cultivated of the Slavic languages, there is a refinement in the tenses, of which even the most perfect knowledge of the classical languages gives hardly any idea, and the right use of which is seldom, if ever, acquired by foreigners. Duration, decision, repetition, all the different shades of time and purpose, which other languages have to circumscribe in long phrases, the Bohemian expresses by a slight alteration of one or two syllables.

Not less rich in these variations of the verb is the Russian. Besides a vast treasure of original, genuine *indefinite* verbs, as they call all those, which have the general character of the verb of other languages, without any allusion to the duration or continuance of the action, they have verbs *simple*, *frequentative*, and *perfect*. A single example will illustrate the fact:

Verb indefinite, *dvigat'*,[15] to move.
Verb simple, *dvinut'*, to move a single time.
Verb frequentative, *dvigivat'*, to move repeatedly.[16]
Verb perfect, *sdvigat'*, to move completely.

The reader may judge for himself, of what precision, compactness, and energy, a language is capable, which has so little need of circumlocution. It must be mentioned, however, that not all these verbs are complete; as indeed it is obvious from their very nature, that in many of them, various tenses must be wanting. It is probably for this reason, that some of the most distinguished grammarians do not acknowledge this division of the verb itself; but put all its variations under the conjugation of a single verb, as different tenses,—a proceeding which contributes much to make the Slavic grammar a horror to all foreigners.

If this short and meagre sketch is hardly sufficient to give the reader an idea of the richness, precision, and general perfectibility of the Slavic languages, it will be still more difficult to reconcile his mind to their *sound;* against which the most decided prejudices exist among all foreigners. The old Slavic alphabet has forty-six letters; and from this variety it can justly be concluded, that the language had originally at least nearly as many different sounds, although a great part of them are no longer to be found in the modern Slavic languages. It is true, that all the dialects are comparatively poor in vowels, and, like

---

[15] The t' signifies the *Yehr*, or *soft sign* of the Russians in addition to the *t*. This letter not existing in the English language, we have endeavoured to supply it in the best possible way by the aspirate of the Greek language, which when it follows *τ*, is not very unlike it; e. g. *νυκτ' ἥμερον*, written *νυχθήμερον*. The real sound, however, is more like the German soft *ch* after *t*, as in *Städtchen*, *Hütchen*.

[16] They are to be compared with the Latin verbs frequentative, as *factitare* instead of *facere*, *cursitare* instead of *currere*, etc.

the oriental languages, utterly deficient in diphthongs.[17] They have neither the *oe* nor *ue*, which the Germans consider as the best sounds of their idiom; nor the Greek *ει*, *υι*, *αυ*, *ευ*, and the like; still less the variety of pronunciation of one and the same vowel, peculiar to the English. The Poles, Russians, and Bohemians, possess however a twofold *i*,[18] a finer and a coarser one; the latter of which is not to be found in any other European language, and is unpleasant to the ear of foreigners. The Poles, besides this, have *nasal vowels*, as other languages have nasal consonants.[19]

It is a striking peculiarity, that Slavic words very seldom *begin* with a pure *a*,[20] hardly ever with *e*.[21] There are in the whole Russian language, only two words of Slavic origin, which have an initial *e*, and about twenty foreign ones in which this letter has been preserved in its purity; in all the rest the *e* is introduced by *y;* e. g. *Yelisaveta*, Elizabeth; *yest'*, Lat. *est*, it is; *Yepiscop*, *episcopus*, bishop; *yeress*, heresy, etc. The initial *a* is more frequent, and is especially preserved in most foreign proper names, e. g. Alexander, Anna; or in other foreign words, where they omit the *H*, as *Ad*, Hades, Hell, *Alleluya*, Hallelujah. But the natural tendency of the language is to introduce it likewise by *y;* thus they say *yagnya*, in preference to *agnya*, Lat. *agnus*, although this last also is to be found in the old church books; *yasti*, to eat, *yakor*, anchor, *yavor*, maple, German *ahorn*.[22] The *o* in the beginning of words is pure in

---

[17] With the exception of the Slovakish dialect.

[18] Pronounce the *i* as in the word *machine*.

[19] To make, in writing, the different shades in the pronunciation of the same letters in Polish, is absolutely impossible. They must be caught with the ear; and, even then, cannot be imitated by the tongue of a foreigner.

[20] The English *a* in *father*.

[21] Like the English *e* in *they*.

[22] Compare the smooth breathing of the Greeks, and the Shemitish *Aleph* or *Elif*.

most Slavic dialects, i. e. without a preceding consonant. In Russian it sounds frequently more like an *a* than an *o;* e. g. *adin*, one, instead of *odin ; atiotz*, father, instead of *otetz*. But the Vendes of Lusatia pronounce it *vo;* as also the Bohemians in the language of common life; although in higher style they have a pure initial *o*. The Croats, on the other hand, have no pure initial *u ;* they say *vuho*, ear, instead of *uho* or *ucho*.

As to consonants, there is a great variety in the Slavic languages. There is however no *f* to be found in any genuine Slavic word ; and even in words adopted from foreign languages, this letter has frequently changed its sound. So the Bohemian has made *barwa* from the German *farbe*, color. In respect to the connection of the Slavic with the Latin, it is interesting to compare *bob* with *faba*, *bodu* with *fodio*, *vru* with *ferveo*, *peru* with *ferio*, *plameñ* with *flamma*, *pishczala* with *fistula*, etc.

The greatest variety among the Slavic letters exists in the sibilants. Of these there are seven, perfectly distinct from each other ; some of which it would be difficult to denote by English characters.[23] They are the favourite sounds of the language. Not only the guttural sounds, *g*, *ch*, and *k*, but also *d* and *t*, are changed in many cases into analogous sibilants, according to fixed and very simple rules. On the other hand, the Slavic nations have a way of softening the harshness of the consonants, peculiar in that extent to them alone. The Frenchman has his *l mouillé*, the Spaniard his *elle doblado* and *ñ*, the Portuguese his *lh* and *nh ;* the Slavic nations possess the same softening sound for almost all their consonants. Such is the usual termination of the Russian verb in *at'* or *it'*, etc. where other Slavic nations say *ati* or *iti*, or those of the western branch *acz* or *ecz*. In the same

---

[23] There is e. g. a single letter in Old Slavonic and Russian for *shtsh*. The Pole writes *szcz*.

manner it occurs after initial consonants; thus *mjaso*, meat; *bjel*, white; *ljubov*, love, etc.

The letters *l* and *r* have in all Slavic languages the value of vowels; words like *twrdy*, *wjtr*, which judging from their appearance a foreigner would despair of ever being able to pronounce, are always in metre used as words of two syllables. Thus *Wlk*, *Srp*, are not harsher than *Wolk* and *Sorp*. We feel however that these examples cannot serve to refute the existing prejudices against the euphony of the Slavic languages. Instead of ourselves, let one of their most eloquent and warmest advocates defend them against the reproach of roughness and harshness.[24] "Euphony and feminine softness of a language are two very different things. It is true that in most of the Slavic dialects, with the exception of the Servian, the consonants are predominant; but if we consider a language in a philosophical point of view, the consonants, as being the signs of ideas, and the vowels, as being mere bearers in the service of the consonants, appear in a quite different light. The more consonants, the richer is a language in ideas. *Exempla sunt in promtu.* The euphony of single syllables is only partial and relative; but the harmony of a whole language depends on the euphonic sound of periods, words, syllables, and single letters. What language possesses these four elements of harmony in equal measure? Too many vowels sound just as unpleasantly as too many consonants; a suitable number and interchange of both is requisite to produce true harmony. Even harsh syllables belong to the necessary qualities of a language; for nature herself has harsh sounds, which the poet would be unable to paint without harsh sounding tones. The roughness of the Slavic idioms, of which foreigners have complained so frequently, is therefore exclusively to be ascribed to the awkwardness of inexperienced or tasteless wri-

[24] Schaffarik in his *Geschichte*, p. 40 sq.

ters; or they are ridiculous mistakes of the reader, who, unacquainted with the language, receives the sounds with his eyes instead of his ears."—" The pure and distinct vocalization, which does not leave it to the arbitrary choice of the speaker to pronounce certain vowels or to pass them over, as is the case in German, French, and English, gives at the same time to the Slavic languages the advantage of a regular quantity of their syllables, as in Greek; which makes them better adapted than any other for imitating the old classic metres. We must confess, however, that this matter has been hitherto neglected in most of them, or has been treated with little intelligence. We mean to say: Each Slavic syllable is by its very nature either short or long; since each Slavic vowel has a twofold duration, both short and long. This natural shortening and lengthening of a syllable is, as with the Greeks, entirely independent of the grammatical stress or falling of the voice upon them, or in other words, of the *prosodic tone;* the *quantity* being founded on the nature of the pronunciation, on the longer or shorter duration of the vowel itself, and not on the grammatical accent. This latter may lie just as well on syllables prosodically short, as on those which are long."

From these introductory remarks, we turn again to the historical part of our essay, referring the reader back to our division of the whole Slavic race into Eastern and Western Stems. We have, first of all, that most remarkable Old or Church Slavonic, the language of their Bible, now no longer a living tongue, but still the inexhaustible source of the sublimest and holiest expressions for its younger sisters. Then follow the *four* languages, perfectly distinct from each other, spoken by the Eastern Slavic nations, viz. the Russian, Illyrico-Servian, Vindish, and Bulgarian. Three of them possess a literature of their own; and one of them, the Illyrico-Servian, even a double literature; for political circumstances and the influence of the early division of the oriental and occidental churches, having unfortunately split the nation into two parts, caused them also to adopt two different methods of writing one and the same language, as we shall show in the sequel. And lastly, among the Slavic nations of the Western stem, we find either *three* or *four* different languages, according as we regard the Czekhish and Slovakian idioms as essentially the same or distinct, viz. the Bohemian, [Slovakian,] Polish, and Sorabic in Lusatia. Of these, the first and third have each an extensive literature of its own.[25]

---

[25] We abstain here from giving any historical references, as it would swell the volume beyond all due proportion; and historical notices, with the exception of those circumstances in immediate connection with the *language*, cannot properly be expected. All philological sources have been faithfully mentioned.

PART I.

HISTORY OF THE OLD OR CHURCH SLAVIC (COMMONLY CALLED SLAVONIC) LANGUAGE AND LITERATURE.

It can hardly be doubted that in very ancient times the whole Slavic race spoke only one language. This seems however very early to have been broken up into several dialects; and such indeed must have been the natural result of the wide extension of the people. Eginhard, the secretary and historian of Charlemagne, (ob. 839,) calls the Slavic nations, whom his hero subjugated, Veletabæ, Sorabæ, Obotrites, and Bohemians; and mentions expressly that they did not all speak the same, but a very similar language. It would be difficult to decide what portion of the still existing Slavic tongue has kept itself the purest; the Old Slavic has its Græcisms, the Servian its Turcisms, the Polish and Bohemian their Germanisms, the Russian its Tartarisms, Germanisms, and Gallicisms. No language in the world will ever resist the influence of the languages of its neighbours; and even the lofty Chinese wall cannot protect the inhabitants of that vast empire from corruptions in their language. It was formerly the general view, that the ecclesiastical Slavonic was to be considered as the *mother* of all the living Slavic dialects; and there are indeed even now a few philologians and historians who still adhere to that opinion. The deeper investigations of modern times, wherever an equal share of profound erudition and love of truth has happened to be united in the same persons, have sufficiently proved, that the church Slavonic is to be considered, not as the mother of all the other Slavic languages, but as standing to them only in the relation of an elder sister,—a *dialect* like them, but earlier developed and cultivated. The original mother-tongue, from which they were all derived, must have perished many centuries ago. But *where* the Old Slavic was once spoken, and which of the still living dialects has been developed *immediately* out of it,—an honour to which all the nations of the eastern stem, and one of the western, aspire,—is a question which all the investigations and conclusions of able historians and philologians have not hitherto been able to answer in a satisfactory manner. The highest authorities in Slavic matters are divided on this point. The disputes relating to it have been conducted with a degree of zeal, little proportioned to its intrinsic importance; nay, recently, with a passion bordering upon fierceness; and what is still more to be regretted, without that regard to truth and candour, which ought to be the foundation of all historical researches. The great political questions which in the East of Europe have already disturbed the peace of nations—the idea of Panslavism, the disputed preponderance of Austria or Russia, the jealousy of the Slavic races against the Germans and among each other—have been allowed to exert a decided influence even on this purely historical question.

The claims of the Russians in this matter have long since been given up as easily refuted; being indeed destitute of any historical foundation. The circumstance, however, that the language of the Slavic Bible was, in Russia, until the reign of Peter the Great, exclusively the language of books, confirmed the natives for a long time in the belief, that the old Russian and the church Slavic were one and the same language; and that the modern Russian was the immediate descendant of the latter; until modern criticism has better illustrated the whole subject.[1]

The great similarity of the *Slovakish* language with the Old Slavic, especially of the national dialect spoken by those Slovaks who live scattered through Hungary; and the correspondence of their grammatical forms and flexion, to a degree not found in any other Slavic language; seemed to decide for the Slovaks. An historical basis is likewise not wanting to this hypothesis; for the Slovaks belonged formerly to the great kingdom of Moravia; where, according to all the ancient historians, Cyril and Methodius lived and taught the longest.[2]

On the other side, the venerable Bohemian Abbot Dobrovsky, who has examined the opinions of his predecessors with more exactness and erudition, and investigated the nature of the different Slavic dialects more deeply than any philologist before him, decides for the *Servians*. According to him, the Old Slavic was, in the time of Cyril and Methodius, the Servian-Bulgarian-Macedonian dialect, the language of the Slavi in Thessalonica, the birthplace of these two Slavic apostles.[3]

His grounds seemed indeed incontestable, until Kopitar, a name of equally high authority and importance in Slavic matters, who formerly agreed with him,[4] proved in a later work,[5] by

---

[1] See below in the History of the Russian Language, and the so called *Improvement* of the Bible and church books.

[2] In modern times this view has been defended principally by Russian philologists, the Metropolitan Eugene, Kalajdovitch, etc.

[3] See his *Kyrill und Method*, Prague, 1823. Schlözer considers likewise the Old Slavic as a Bulgarian dialect of the ninth century. See his Northern History, p. 330. In another place he calls it the mother of the other Slavic languages; see his Nestor, I. p. 46.

[4] In his Grammar of the Slavic Language in Carniola, Carinthia, and Stiria.

[5] *Jahrbücher der Literatur*, Vienna, 1822, Vol. XVII. Grimm is of the

arguments of no less weight, that the true home of the language of the Slavic Bible was to be sought among the *Pannonic* or *Carantano-Slavi*, the *Slovenzi* or *Vindes* of the present times.[6] The adoption of a number of *German* (not *Greek*) words for Christian ideas, as *tzerkwa* Kirch, *post* fast, *chrestiti* christening, etc., can only be explained, he asserts, by German neighbourhood and German influence. These Pannonian Slavi were Methodius' own diocesans; for their instruction the Scriptures were first translated, and only carried by the two brethren, at a later period, to the Bulgarians and Moravians, who easily understood the kindred dialect.

Kopitar's arguments have hitherto failed to convince other eminent Slavic scholars, especially those of the Bohemian school; who still accept it as a fact, that the language of the Slavic Bible was, in the ninth century, the Servian-Bulgarian dialect; and Bulgaria its home. Schaffarik, another great name in Slavic philological researches, seemed in an earlier work to adopt the opinion of Kopitar; but, after continuing his investigations further, he too came to the result, that Bulgaria was the home of the Old Slavic; and that the language still spoken in that province, corrupted indeed by foreign influences more than any other Slavic dialect, is its direct descendant.[7]

Be this as it may, the Old Slavic has long since become

---

same opinion; see the Preface to his translation of Vuk Stephanovitch's Servian Grammar.

[6] See above, p. 11.

[7] This view Schaffarik takes in his work on *Slavic Antiquities*, and in his *Slavic Ethnography*. Palacky, a distinguished Bohemian scholar, adopted the same opinion in his *History of Bohemia*, Prague 1836. Both were combatted in a furious review by Kopitar, in Chmel's *Oestr. Geschichtsforscher*, III. 1838; printed separately under the title: *Der Pannonische Ursprung der Slavischen Liturgie*, etc.

the common property of all the Slavic nations, and its treasures are for all of them an inexhaustible mine. Dobrovsky counted in it 1605 radical syllables.[8] Hence, it is not only rich in its present state, but has in itself the inestimable power of augmenting its richness, the faculty of creating new forms of expression for new ideas. But its great perfection does not consist alone in this multiplicity of words. Schlözer, the great historian and linguist, justly observes: "Among all modern languages the Slavonic (Old Slavic) is one of those which are most fully developed. With its richness and other perfections I have here no concern. How it became so, the history of its cultivation sufficiently explains. Its model was the Greek language, in those days the most cultivated in the world; although Cedrenus no longer wrote like Xenophon. No idiom was more capable than the Slavonic of adopting the beauties of the Greek. The translators, intending a literal version, and not like Cædmon the Anglo-Saxon, or Otfried the German, a mere *poetic metaphrase*, were in a certain measure compelled to *subdue* their own language, to make it flexible, to invent new turns, in order faithfully to imitate the original."[9]

After having ceased for centuries to be a language of common life, the Old Slavic has of course lost that kind of pliancy and facility, which only a living language, employed to express all the daily wants of men, can possibly acquire. But for this same reason it has gained infinitely in solemnity and dignity. Imposing by its very sound, exciting in the minds of millions sanctifying religious associations, it seems to have grown almost unfit for any vulgar use, and to have become exclusively devoted to holy, or at least to serious and dignified subjects.

---

[8] Dobrovsky's *Entwurf zu einer allgemeinen Slavischen Etymologie*, Prague 1812. See also the *Slovanka* of this celebrated scholar.

[9] Schlözer's Nestor, III. p. 224.

There are, as we have mentioned above, many circumstances, which seem to justify the opinion, that the Slavi were very early in possession of a degree of cultivation, which would make it indeed difficult to believe, that they should not have known how to read and write before the ninth century. Ditmar of Merseburg, the German, speaks of the inscriptions with which the pagan Obotrites, the Slavic inhabitants of Mecklenburg, used to cover their idols. The southern Slavi had much greater advantages. Neighbours of the Greeks, and in constant intercourse with them; both as a nation, by war and traffic, and through individuals who lived at the court of Constantinople; it can hardly be supposed, that no earlier attempt should have been made to adapt the Greek alphabet to the Slavic language, or to invent a new one founded on that basis. There was however not a single *satisfactory* proof, that this was ever done with any degree of success before that time; notwithstanding all the grounds by which some modern writers, zealous and eloquent advocates of this opinion, endeavoured to support it.[10] It is only since Kopitar's discovery of some Glagolitic manuscripts *at least* cotemporary with the most ancient Cyrillic documents known, that this question has taken another aspect. But whether there existed already a Slavic alphabet or not, it is very doubtful whether Cyril knew it; since the Slavic tribes among whom he and Methodius lived, were not acquainted with it; for all the legends and early historical annals agree in calling Cyril the inventor of the Slavic alphabet.

---

[10] Rakoviecky, in his edition of the *Pravda Russka*, Warsaw 1820–22. Katancsich, *Specimen Philologiæ et Geographiæ*, etc. 1795. See also Frähn's publication, "Ueber die älteste Schrift der Russen," St. Petersb. 1835; where a specimen is given of the form of writing which the Arabian author Ibn Abi Jakub el Nedim ascribes to the Russians. This writer lived at the close of the tenth century. He quotes as his authority an envoy sent from some Caucasian prince to the king of the Russians.

This alphabet, as arranged by Cyril, is founded on the Greek. In adjusting it, Cyril employed all the Greek characters; although a few of them have so much altered their shape in the course of time, as hardly to be recognized in their present form, e. g. the *Z* and the *H* of the Greeks. The first has the English, not the Greek pronunciation of that letter; the latter in its altered shape is the common *I* of the Slavic language, and thus corresponds with the pronunciation of the modern Greeks. The *H* or *Eta* in an unaltered form, on the other hand, is the *N* of the Slavic alphabet. The Greek *B*, *β*, went over into the still softer sound of *V*, *v*;[11] and another sign was selected for Buki or *B*. This and all the characters to denote Slavic sounds, which he did not find in the Greek alphabet, Cyril took from other oriental languages, wherever he could find similar sounds; and thus very judiciously avoided that accumulation of letters to mark a single sound, which occur so often in all the systems of writing derived from the Latin. In this manner he extended his alphabet to forty-six characters or signs; some of them indeed merely signs for expressing shades of pronunciation, which in other languages are denoted by marks and points. Some others are not pronounced at all, and seem, at least according to the present state of the Slavic languages, utterly superfluous. Hence the Russians and Servians have diminished the number of their letters considerably; although the Russian has still some which could be amalgamated with others, or entirely omitted. Whether the Old Slavic actually had, at the time of Cyril's invention, so many different shades of sound, it would be difficult to decide at present, after that language has existed for so many centuries as a mere language of books.

Cyril, or, according to his baptismal name, Constantine, and Methodius his brother, must be reckoned among the benefactors

---

[11] As in modern Greek; see also Buttmann's Gram. § 3. 2.

of mankind; for it was they who procured for the Slavic nations, so early as the ninth century, the inestimable privilege of reading the Holy Scriptures in a language familiar to their ears and minds; whilst the sacred volume yet remained, for centuries after, inaccessible to all the other European Christians, the exclusive property of the priesthood. They were born in Thessalonica, in the early part of the ninth century, of a noble family; it does not appear whether of Greek or of Slavic extraction. Macedonia, of which province Thessalonica was in the times of the Romans the capital, was inhabited by many Slavi at a very early period. Constantine, who obtained by his learning and abilities the surname of the Philosopher, could have learned Slavic here, even without belonging to the Slavic nation. As a flourishing commercial city, this place was peculiarly favourable for learning languages; and it was probably here too, that Constantine learned Armenian; for the introduction of several Armenian letters into the Slavic alphabet seems to prove, that this language was not unknown to him. When grown up, his parents sent him to Byzantium, where he entered the clerical profession.

It is reported that there came ambassadors from the Khazares, a Hunnic-Tartaric tribe, to the emperor Michael, to ask for a teacher in Christianity. On the recommendation of Ignatius, Constantine was chosen for this mission, as being particularly qualified by his eloquence and piety. On the road he stopped for some time in Cherson on the Dnieper, where he learned the Khazaric language. The empire of the Khazares extended from the Volga and the Caspian Sea, across the Caucasian isthmus and the peninsula of Taurida, as far as to Moldavia and Walachia. Several Slavic tribes were tributary to them; but about the middle of the ninth century, at the time of Cyril's mission, their power began to decline; their vassals became their enemies, and gradually their conquerors; until towards the end of the tenth and at the beginning of the eleventh century, their empire became entirely extinct.[12] Constantine converted and baptized their Khan, whose example was followed by a great part of the nation. It was probably after he had returned from this mission, that Cyril went to convert the Bulgarians. At this time, or just before, according to Dobrovsky's opinion, he invented the Slavic letters, and translated the Gospels, during his stay in Byzantium. This however is nothing more than an hypothesis, against which other hypotheses have been started by other scholars. Between A. D. 861 and 863, there came another embassy to the emperor from the Moravian prince Rostislav, who asked for a teacher, not only to instruct his subjects in Christianity more perfectly than it had been done before, but also to teach them *to read.* Most of the Moravians were already baptized. Constantine, accompanied by his brother Methodius, was sent to Moravia, where the people received them with expressions of joy. They introduced here the Slavic liturgy, and preached in the Slavic language.

One peculiar circumstance served to give to their persons a more than common sanctity. Constantine had been so fortunate as to discover in Cherson the bones of the holy Clement, relics which he every where carried with him. After three or four years, the pope invited the two brethren to Rome, where the possession of these relics procured them great honour and distinction. The pope Adrian, followed by the clergy and people, met them and their treasure before the gates of the city. Both the brothers were consecrated as bishops; those of their Moravian disciples who had accompanied them to Rome, were made priests and deacons. Constantine received the consecration, but did not accept the diocese allotted to him. With the permission of the pope, he adopted the name of Cyril, and died forty days after-

[12] See Rees' Cyclopedia, art. *Khazares;* where however it is incorrectly said, that they were a Turkish tribe.

wards, Feb. 13, A. D. 868. His remembrance is cherished as holy by the Slavic nations; and even as early as A. D. 1056, we find, in the calendar of the *Evangelium of Ostromir*, the fourteenth of February set down for the celebration of his memory.

Methodius returned to Moravia the same year, A. D. 868. He was what was called an *episcopus regionarius*, and had therefore no fixed residence. In the letters of pope John VIII, he is called bishop of Moravia and Pannonia. The first of these countries was at this period the theatre of bloody wars; the Slavic inhabitants of the other had been already converted to Christianity by German priests, as early as A. D. 798. In consequence of this, Methodius found the Latin worship established here, and the Latin language in use. The innovation made by him, however, was of course greatly favoured by the people; who for the first time heard the gospel read to them in a language they understood. But he met with the more opposition from the priests. The whole jealousy of the Romish church seems to have been awakened by Methodius' proceedings. He found however a protector in the pope himself; who feared perhaps an entire alienation of the Slavic population, and their transition to the Oriental church; but was at the same time desirous to preserve the whole authority of the Latin language. In a letter to the Moravian prince Svatopluk, he enjoins expressly, "that in all the Moravian churches the gospel, for the sake of the greater dignity, should be read first in Latin, and afterwards translated into Slavic for the people ignorant of the Latin."

The question, what part of the Scriptures was translated by Cyril himself, what by his brother, and what supplements were made by their immediate successors, can now hardly be answered in a satisfactory manner. The honour of the invention of the alphabet appears to belong exclusively to Cyril; but in the sacred work of translation, Methodius was not less active;

and his merits in respect to the conversion and instruction of the Slavi, were more favoured by a longer life. According to John, exarch of Bulgaria, Cyril translated only *selections* from the Gospels and the *Apostle*, as the book of Acts and the apostolic epistles are together called in Slavic; i. e. a *Lectionarium*, or extracts from those parts of the Scriptures, arranged in such a way as to serve as a lesson for every sacred day through the whole year. The Russians call such a collection *Aprakoss*, the Greeks *εὐαγγελία, ἐκλογαδία*. A work of this description is the above mentioned Evangelium of Ostromir, of the year 1056, written out expressly for the domestic use of Ostromir, *posadnik*[13] of Novogorod, a near relation of the grand-duke of Izjaslav. It is however held to be more probable, that Cyril translated at first the whole of the Gospels, as still contained in a Codex of A. D. 1144, in the library of the Synod of Moscow. The Presbyter of Dioclea, who wrote about A. D. 1161, ascribes to Cyril not only the translation of the Gospels, but also of the Psalter;[14] and at a later period that of the whole Old and New Testaments, as well as of the *Massa*, i. e. the Greek liturgy of Basilius and Chrysostom. This opinion has since been generally received. In respect to the Old Testament, however, it is much to be doubted; since no ancient Codex of it exists, or has ever been proved to have existed. As to the New Testament, the Apocalypse must at any rate be excepted.

What part of the translation was performed by Methodius does not appear. John, exarch of Bulgaria, who lived in the same century, translated the books of Johannes Damascenus into Slavic. In the course of the tenth and eleventh centuries, the Russian and Servian princes called into their empires many learned Greeks, versed in the Slavic language, that they might

---

[13] *Posadnik* is about the same as *mayor*.

[14] In the Slavic version of the Chronicle of Dalmatia, the Epistles instead of the Psalter are named.

continue the holy work of translation. From the historian Nestor it appears, that the Proverbs of Solomon existed in the twelfth century in Slavic. The book of Wisdom, Ecclesiastes, the Prophets, and Job, were translated in Servia in the thirteenth or fourteenth century; the Pentateuch in Russia or Poland A. D. 1400, or about that time. It is certain, that towards the close of the fifteenth century, the whole Bible was already translated into Old Slavic. According to Dobrovsky, the different parts of it were not collected until after A. D. 1488, when the Bohemian Bible of Prague was printed. This latter served as a model for the arrangement of the Slavonic Bible; what was wanting was at that time supplied, and those books of the Old Testament which had been translated from the Greek, were reviewed and corrected according to the Vulgate. The Codex of Moscow of A. D. 1499, the most ancient *existing* copy of the whole Bible in the Old Slavic, is probably at the same time the first which was ever wholly completed.

The domains of the Old Slavic language, which seemed at first to be of very great extent, were soon, by the well known jealousy of the Romish church, limited to Russia and Servia. In Bohemia, which owed its conversion to German priests, the Slavic liturgy seems never to have been generally introduced; and the old Slavic church language has therefore exerted only an inconsiderable influence on the Bohemian. In Poland too, the Slavic liturgy was only *tolerated*, although the first books with Cyrillic types were printed there. In Moravia, Pannonia, and Illyria, the Slavonic worship was, after some struggle, supplanted by the Latin; in the two latter countries, however, the language was retained, and the occidental church service conducted in the Slavic language; i. e. in a language which at that time was perfectly intelligible to the Illyrians.

It appears that the priests of this part of the country had never adopted the alphabet, which Cyril invented for the benefit of their brethren in Pannonia or Bulgaria;[15] who, less advanced in civilization than the tribes bordering on Italy, could as yet neither write nor read; while the latter were already in possession of an alphabet of an ancient and mysterious origin. For the first appearance of the Glagolitic letters, (*glagol* signifies in Slavic *word*, or rather *verb.*) is still buried in perfect darkness. An almost fabulous antiquity has been ascribed to this alphabet by various old writers. According to some it was derived from the Goths or Getæ; according to others, from the Phrygians and Thracians; and a very common tradition made St. Jerome, who was a native of Dalmatia, the inventor of it. The sounder criticism of our age seems at last to have proved that all these opinions were untenable. The oldest Glagolitic manuscript known before 1830 was a Psalter of A. D. 1220; i. e. more than three and a half centuries younger than the Cyrillic alphabet, and evidently copied from a known manuscript written in this latter. This, in connection with some other circumstances, induced the learned Dobrovsky to declare the whole alphabet to be the result of a pious fraud. It seems surprising that this view should have been generally adopted,—at least for a certain time. It was explained by Dobrovsky in the following way.

At a Synod held at Spalatro in Dalmatia, in A. D. 1060, Methodius, notwithstanding he had been patronized by several popes, was declared a heretic, nearly two hundred years after his death; and it was resolved that henceforth no mass should be read except in the Latin or Greek language. From the decrees of that Synod, it appears that they took the Gothic and Slavonic

---

[15] That the Glagolitic alphabet, as has been affirmed, was the one invented by Cyril, and was gradually changed into that afterwards known as the Cyrillic, is an untenable position; partly, because no form of writing could change in such a degree in one or two centuries; and partly, because in some early manuscripts both alphabets appear *mixed*, or rather are used alternately.

for the same idiom. A great part of the inhabitants of Illyria remained nevertheless faithful to their language, and to a worship familiar to their minds through that language. A singular means, Dobrovsky asserts, was found by some of the shrewder priests, to reconcile their inclinations with the jealous despotism of Rome. A new alphabet was invented, or rather the Cyrillic letters were altered and transformed in such a way, as to approach in a certain measure to the Coptic characters. To give some authority to the new invention, it was ascribed to St. Jerome. This, it was maintained, is the Glagolitic alphabet, so called, used by the Slavic priests of Dalmatia and Croatia until the present time. Cyril's translation of the Bible and the liturgic books were copied in these characters, with a very few deviations in the language; which probably had their foundation in the difference of the Dalmatian dialect, or were the result of the progress of time; for this event took place at least 360 years after the invention of the Cyrillic alphabet. With this modification, the priests succeeded in satisfying both the people and the chair of Rome. It *sounded* the same to the people, and *looked* different to the pope. The people submitted easily to the ceremonies of the Romish worship, if only their beloved language was preserved; and the pope, fearing justly the transition of the whole Slavic population of those provinces to the Greek church, permitted the mass to be read in Slavonic, in order to preserve his influence in general.

This hypothesis had come to be pretty generally received; when in the year 1830, some Glagolitic manuscripts, which bore very decided evidence of being at least as old as the middle of the eleventh century, were discovered by Kopitar in the library of Count Clotz in Tyrol. The existence of the calumniated alphabet at a period cotemporary with the oldest Cyrillic manuscript known (the Evangelium of Ostromir), was a death-blow to the above singular narrative. Kopitar published the newly discovered Codex, accompanied by a thundering philippic against the defenders of the former theory, and in favour of the antiquity of the Glagolitic alphabet, and of the Pannonian origin of the Slavic liturgy.[16] But here the matter rested. Nothing has since been discovered, (so far as we are informed,) to throw light on the first invention or introduction of this alphabet; no connecting link to explain its relation to the Cyrillic forms of writing.

According to Vostokof, a Russian scholar of great learning, and one of the principal names in Old Slavic literature,[17] the history of the Old Slavic or Church language and its literary cultivation, may be divided into three periods:

1. From Cyril, or from the ninth century, to the thirteenth century. This is the *ancient* genuine Slavonic; as appears from the manuscripts of that period.

2. From the thirteenth to the sixteenth century. This is the *middle* age of the Slavonic, as altered gradually by Russian copyists, and full of Russisms.

3. From the sixteenth century to the present time. This comprises the *modern* Slavonic of the church books printed in Russia and Poland; especially after the *Improvement* of those writings, so called.

The most ancient documents of the Old Slavic language, are not older than the middle of the eleventh century. There has been indeed recently discovered a manuscript of the translation of John of Damascus, written by John, exarch of Bulgaria, in the ninth century. Vostokof however proves on philological grounds, that it cannot be the original, but is a later copy. The above-mentioned Evangelium of Ostromir (1056) is the earliest monument of the language, as to the age of which no doubt

---

[16] *Glagolita Clozianus,* Vindeb. 1836.

[17] In his essay *On the Old Slavic Language.* See the Russian periodical: *Treatises of a Society of Friends of Russian Literature,* No. XVII. Mosc. 1820.

exists. It is preserved in the imperial library at St. Petersburg.[18] According to Vostokof, this is the third, or perhaps the fourth, copy of Cyril's own translation. This latter is irretrievably lost, as well as the copy which was made for Vladimir the Great, a hundred years afterwards.

Only a few years younger is a *Sbornik*, A. D. 1073, or a collection of ecclesiastical writings, discovered in the year 1817, and a similar *Sbornik* of 1076; the former in a convent near Moscow, the other now in the library of the imperial Hermitage of St. Petersburg. Further, the *Evangelium of Mistislav*, written before the year 1225, for the prince Mistislav Vladimirowitch; and another *Evangelium* of the year 1143, both at present in ecclesiastical libraries at Moscow.

Besides these venerable documents, there are several inscriptions on stones, crosses, and monuments, of equal antiquity; and a whole series of political documents, contracts, ordinances, and similar writings; among which one of the most remarkable is the oldest manuscript of the *Pravda Russkaya*,[19] a collection of the laws of Jaroslav, A. D. 1280. The libraries of the Russian convents possess a large number of manuscripts; some of which proved to be of great value, when examined about twenty years since by a Commission of scholars, appointed expressly for that purpose by the Academy of Sciences.[20] The spirit of critical-

[18] Extracts from it may be seen in the valuable collection of Documents prepared by P. von Köppen: *Sobranie Slovenzki Pamjatnikov*, St. Petersburg 1827. See also Hanka's Edition of Dobrovsky's *Slavin*, Prague 1834.

[19] This remarkable manuscript was not known until 1738, when it was discovered in the chronicles of Novogorod. It has since been published in six different editions, the first prepared by Schlözer, 1767; the last by the Polish scholar Rakowiecky, enriched with remarks and illustrations. See note 10, above.

[20] *Aktu Sobrannyje etc.* i. e. Collection of Acts and Documents found in the Libraries and Archives of the Russian Empire, by the Archæographical Commission of the Academy, etc. 4 vols. St. Petersburg, 1836, 1837. The oldest of these documents does not go farther back than A. D. 1294.

historical investigation, which took its rise in Germany within our own century, has penetrated also the Russian scholars; and their zeal is favoured by their government in a manner at once honourable and liberal. The task was not small. The Synodal library of Moscow alone has a treasure of 700 Old Slavic Codices; the Academy of Sciences in St. Petersburg possesses likewise numerous Slavic manuscripts. Among the libraries of other countries, there is hardly one of any importance, which has not like Codices of more or less value to exhibit. Those of Vienna and the Vatican are in this department especially rich. These two were thoroughly searched by a like Commission.[21] Of the great activity, and the critical spirit which the Russian historians of our day have shown in respect to their own past, more will be said in our sketch of the Russian literature.

The number of the monuments of the Old Slavic increases considerably in the *second* period; and we find ourselves the more obliged to be satisfied with mentioning only the most important among them. At the head of these, stands the *Laurentian Codex*, the oldest existing copy of Nestor's Annals, A. D. 1377, now in the imperial library at St. Petersburg. Nestor, a monk in a convent near Kief, born A. D. 1096, was the father of Russian history. He wrote Annals in the Old Slavic language, which form the basis of Slavic history, and are not without importance for the whole history of the middle ages. They were first printed in A. D. 1767, and subsequently in four editions, the last in 1796. Schlözer, the great German historian, who published them anew in 1802–9, with a translation, added considerably to their intrinsic value by a critical and historical commentary upon them. But even his edition could not satisfy

---

[21] On the remarkable Slavic manuscript called "Texte du Sacre," which was first re-discovered on this expedition, see *Glagolitic Literature*, in Part II. Chap. II.

the more critical spirit of our days. A new one has been published in the course of the last seven years; for which, not less than fifty-three manuscripts were carefully compared. The merit of it belongs to the Archæographical Commission of the Academy.

The *third* period begins with the sixteenth century. In the course of time, and after passing through the hands of so many ignorant copyists, the holy books had of course undergone a change; nay, were in some parts grown unintelligible. The necessity of a revision was therefore very strongly felt. In A. D. 1512, the Patriarch of Constantinople, at the request of the Tzar Basilius Ivanovitch, sent a learned Greek (a monk of Mount Athos) to Moscow, to revise the church books, and to correct them according to the Greek originals. As this person some years afterwards fell into disgrace and could not accomplish the work, it was taken up repeatedly in the course of the same and the following century, until the revision of the liturgical books was pronounced to be finished in A. D. 1667; but that of the Bible not before A. D. 1751. The principles on which this revision, or, as it was called, *Improvement*, was made, were in direct conflict with the reverence due to the genius of the Slavic language. The revisers, in their unphilosophical mode of proceeding, tried only to imitate the Greek original, and to assimilate the grammatical part of the language, as much as possible, to the Russian of their own times. They all acted in the conviction, that the language of the Bible and liturgical books was merely *obsolete Russian*. Even the latest revisers of the Bible, in 1751, knew nothing of Cyril or Methodius; and had no doubt, that the first translation was made in Russia under Vladimir the Great, A. D. 988, in the language which was then spoken.

Such other works in Old Slavic, as were the productions of this period, seem rather to belong to the history of the Russian and Servian literature. We have seen from the preceding, that the Old Slavic had altered considerably; nay, was in a certain measure amalgamated with those dialects. We shall see in the sequel, how it was gradually supplanted by them.[22]

The printing of works in the Old Slavic, at the present day, is almost exclusively limited to the Bible and to what is in immediate connection with it. The first printed Slavonic work was not in Glagolitic letters. This was a missal of A. D. 1483.[23] The earliest Cyrillic printing office was founded about A. D. 1490, at Kracow, by Svaipold Feol. Nearly at the same time, 1492, they began in Servia and Herzegovina to print with Cyrillic types. In A. D. 1518, a Cyrillic-Slavonic printing office was established at Venice; and about the same time, a part of the Old Testament in the White-Russian dialect, printed with Cyrillic letters, was published at Prague in Bohemia.

In Russia, now the principal seat of the eastern Slavic literature, printing was not introduced until after the middle of the sixteenth century. The first work was published in Moscow A. D. 1564, an edition of the *Apostle*, executed by the united skill of two printers. It would seem, however, that they did not succeed in Russia; for a few years after we find one of them in

---

[22] According to Vostokof, the dialects of all the Slavic nations deviated not only much less from each other at the time of Cyril's translation than they now do; but were even in the middle of the eleventh century still so similar, that the different nations were able to understand each other, about as well as the present inhabitants of the different provinces of Russia understand each other. The difference of the Slavic dialects was then almost exclusively limited to the lexical part of the language; the grammatical varieties, which exist among them at the present day, had not then arisen. The principal features which distinguish the Russian of the present day from the Old Slavic, are exhibited in an article *on Russian Literature* in the Foreign Quarterly Review, Vol. I. p. 602.

[23] We learn that P. von Köppen several years ago discovered a Slavic work printed in 1475; but being unacquainted with the details, we are unable to give a particular notice of it.

Lemberg, occupied in printing the same book; and the other at Wilna, in printing the Gospels. In Russia, the Gospels were printed for the first time in A. D. 1606. The first complete Slavonic Bible was published at Ostrog in Volhynia (Poland) A. D. 1581, fol. printed after the manuscript of 1499, which also was the first that comprehended the whole Bible.[24] The second edition of the whole Slavonic Bible was printed eighty-two years later, at Moscow, A. D. 1663. An enumeration of all the subsequent editions, is given in the note below.[25]

The philological part of the church Slavonic language was not cultivated so early as would have been desirable. There exists however a grammar by Zizania, published A. D. 1596 in Warsaw. Twenty years afterwards another by M. Smotrisky appeared, Wilna 1618. This work, written like Zizania's grammar in the White-Russian dialect,[26] was for a long time considered as of good authority; it reappeared in several editions, and served as the basis of most of the grammars written during the 17th and 18th centuries. M. Stroyeff found in the Paris library the manuscript of an Old Slavic grammar, written in

---

[24] See above p. 36.

[25] The first two editions are described above. The *third* edition did not appear till nearly a century later, after the revision of the text had been completed, Moscow 1751, fol. Subsequent editions are as follows: Moscow 1756, fol. ib. 1757, fol. St. Petersb. 1756, fol. Kief 1758, fol. St. Petersb. 1759, fol. Moscow 1759, 3 vols. 8vo. ib. 1762, fol. ib. 1766, fol. ib. 1778, 5 vols. 8vo. Kief 1779, fol. Mosc. 1784, fol. Kief 1788, 5 vols. 8vo. Mosc. 1790, fol. ib. 1797, fol. ib. 1802, fol. Ofen (Buda) 1804, 5 vols. 8vo. Mosc. 1806, 4 vols. 8vo. ib. 1810, fol. ib. 1813, 5 vols. 8vo. ib. 1815, 8vo. St. Petersb. 1816, 8vo. stereotype edition, issued sixteen times up to 1824. Also in 4to, stereotype edition, issued five times from 1819 to 1821.

[26] In the work of J. Lewicky, *Grammatik der ruthenischen oder kleinrussischen Sprache in Galizien*, Przmysl 1836, to which is annexed a short history of the Ruthenian Literature, the Russinian and White-Russian dialects seem to be wholly confounded.

Latin by John Uzewicz, a Student of Theology at the University of Paris in 1643. In the year 1822, Dobrovsky published his *Institutiones Linguæ Slavicæ dialecti veteris*, a grammatical work which, like all the productions of this distinguished scholar, throws a new light upon the subject, and renders all former works of a similar character useless.

The lexical part of this literature is more defective. Most of the existing dictionaries are merely short and unsatisfactory vocabularies. The most ancient is the work of P. Berynda, *Lex. Slaveno-Russicum*, Kief 1627. More in use at present are the *Kratkoi Slowar Slavjanskoi*, or 'Short Slavic Dictionary,' by Eugenius, St. Petersb. 1784; and the larger 'Church Dictionary' by Alexejef, 4th ed. St. Pet. 1817–19. A dictionary of this dialect for the special use of foreigners, does not yet exist.[27]

In modern times considerable attention has been devoted to the examination of the Old Slavic language and its relation to its kindred dialects. Antiquarian and paleographical researches have been happily combined with philological investigations; and the eminent names which are found among these diligent and philosophical inquirers, insure the best prospects to their cause.[28]

---

[27] Schaffarik mentions that an Old Slavic Grammar and a Dictionary were prepared and ready in manuscript, by Vostokof, in 1826. Whether these works have been since printed we are not informed.

[28] Very valuable and detailed notices on all the subjects in immediate connection with the Old Slavic and modern Russian Bible, are to be found in Henderson's *Biblical Researches and Travels in Russia*, Lond. 1826. As this book is accessible in this country, and our limits are narrow, we abstain from giving more than a general reference to it, as containing the best information on Slavic matters ever written in the English language. The reader will find there too a table of the Cyrillic and Glagolitic alphabet, taken from Dobrovsky's *Institutiones*.

PART II.

EASTERN SLAVI.

CHAPTER I.

HISTORY OF THE RUSSIAN LANGUAGE AND LITERATURE.

The name of *Russia* and the *Russians* is not older than the ninth or tenth century. The northern part of that vast empire, however, was long before inhabited by Slavic nations, who seem to have been divided into small states under chiefs chosen by themselves; to have been peaceable in their character, and most of them tributary to more powerful neighbours. About the middle of the ninth century, civil dissensions arose among the Slavi of Novogorod, at the election of a new head or *posadnik*. Troubled at the same time from without, by the conquering and enterprising spirit of the Varegians, a Scandinavian tribe, they no longer felt able to make resistance against them; and therefore, A. D. 862, they chose Rurik, the chief of the Varegians, for their own head. These Scandinavians were by the Finns called *Ruotzi*, an appellation which in their language signifies *strangers*. This name, in a somewhat altered form, passed over to the inhabitants of the acquired territory, with whom the conquerors soon amalgamated. Rurik founded thus the first Slavo-Russian state; and his followers, long accustomed to a warlike nomadic mode of life, settled down among the Slavic inhabitants of the country. The nationality of the *strangers*, comparatively few in number, was merged in that of the natives; but still, in one respect, it exercised a strong influence upon the latter, by infusing into them the warlike spirit of the former. It is only since that time, that we find the Slavi as conquerors. Their empire rapidly extended in the course of the following hundred and fifty years, and their power and external influence also rose; while at the same time the ancient civil institutions of the native Slavi were respected and improved.

In the beginning of the eleventh century, Jaroslav, the son of Vladimir the Great, imitating his father's example, divided on his death-bed his empire among his sons, and thus sowed the seeds of dissension, anarchy, and bloody wars; a case repeated so often in ancient history, that it seems to be one of the few from which modern princes have derived a serious lesson. The Mongols broke into the country; easily subdued the Russians thus torn by internal dissensions; succeeded, A. D. 1237, in making them tributary; and kept them for two hundred years in the most dishonourable bondage. During this long period, every germ of literary cultivation perished. In the middle of the fifteenth century, Ivan Vasilievitch III,[1] delivered his country from the Asiatic barbarians, then weakened by domestic dissensions; conquered his Russian rivals; and united Novogorod with his own princedom of Moscow. From that period the power and physical welfare of Russia have increased without interruption to the present time. The literary cultivation of its inhabitants has likewise advanced; at first indeed with steps hardly proportioned to the

[1] Also called Ivan I.

external progress of the empire; but now for more than a century, in consequence of the despotic activity of their sovereigns, with a wonderful rapidity.

The history of Russian literature has five distinct periods. The *first* period comprises an interval of more than nine centuries, from the date of our first knowledge of the Russian Slavi, to the coming of age of Peter the Great, A. D. 1689. This period would easily admit of several subdivisions; and did we pretend in these pages to give the reader more than a *sketch* of literary history, we should perhaps find it advisable to adopt them. This long period, however, both in a comparative and an absolute sense, is so very poor, that, limited as we are, a few words will suffice to give a general survey of it; and so much the more, because the productions of this period are closely connected with the history of the Old Slavic language, and have mostly been already mentioned under that head.

The *second* period extends from the coming of age of Peter the Great to the accession of Elizabeth his daughter, A. D. 1741, which was the commencement of Lomonosof's influence.

The *third* period extends from Lomonosof, the creator of Russian prose, to Karamzin, the reformer of it, who was born in 1765.

The *fourth* period covers the interval from Karamzin to the accession of the emperor Nicholas in 1825.

The *fifth* period begins with the accession of Nicholas in 1825, and continues to the present time.

Before however we begin our historical notices, a few words relating to the characteristic features of the Russian language, may find a place here. Three principal dialects are to be distinguished, viz.

1. The *Russian proper*, the true literary language of the whole Russian nation, and *spoken* in Moscow and all the central and northern part of the European Russian empire. And here

we will mention the remarkable fact, that the peasant on the Wolga, on the Oka, and on the Moskwa, speaks the same pure Russian which is heard in the parlour and from the pulpit. Vulgar and corrupted branches of this dialect, are those of Suzdal and Olonetzk, the last of which is mixed with Finnish words.

2. The *Malo-Russian*, the language of the south of Russia, especially towards the east. The principal difference between this dialect and the Russian proper, consists partly in the pronunciation of several letters; e. g. in that of the consonant Г, which sounds in the latter like *g* hard, but in the former like *h*, as *hospodin* instead of *gospodin*, master, lord; partly in many obsolete forms of expression, which seem to give to the Malo-Russian a nearer relationship to the Old Slavic, in which similar idioms are to be found. The influence of the Poles, who for nearly two centuries were rulers of this part of the country, is also still perceptible in the language. This dialect is especially rich in national songs. Many of them are of peculiar beauty, touching *naiveté*, and a poetical truth which far outshines all artificial decorations. The greater part of these songs have an elegiac character; as is the case indeed with most productions of the common people.[2] The dialect itself, however, is far from being less adapted to the expression of the comic. There exists in it a travesty of the Æneid, written by J. Kotliarevski, a Kozak, which has found great favour throughout all Russia, although a foreigner is less able to appreciate its peculiarities and beauties; since indeed all poetic excellence of a comic description can be felt only by those who are familiar not only with the poetic language, but also with all those minute local and historical circumstances, the allusions to which contribute so frequently to augment the ludicrous.

---

[2] See more on this subject in Part IV.

Essentially the same with the Malo-Russian is the idiom of the *Russniaks* in Red Russia, in the eastern part of Galicia, and the north-eastern districts of Hungary; and the few variations which occur in it have not yet been sufficiently investigated. Comparatively little attention has been paid to this branch of the Slavic race; and their beautiful national songs, scattered among a widely extended people, have only recently become the object of curiosity and examination.

3. The *White-Russian* is the dialect spoken in Lithuania and a portion of White Russia, especially Volhynia. The situation of these provinces sufficiently accounts for its being full of Polisms. All the historical documents of Lithuania are written in this dialect; and several Russian writers in the sixteenth and seventeenth centuries employed it in preference to the Old Slavonic. The first Russian translation of the Bible was written in it. It is the youngest of the Russian dialects.

What first strikes us in considering the Russian language as a whole, is its immense copiousness. The *early* influence of foreign nations appears here as a decided advantage. The German, in the highest degree susceptible for foreign *ideas* and forms of *thought*, repels nevertheless all foreign *words* and forms of *expression* as unnatural excrescences. It is evidently disfigured by the adoption of foreign words, and can preserve its beauty only by adhering to its own national and inexhaustible sources. The Russian, having been in early times successively subjected to the influence of the Scandinavian, Mongolian, Tartar, and Polish languages, is in this respect to be compared, in a certain measure, with the English, in which the ancient British, the Latin, the Saxon, the Danish, and the French, amalgamated in the same proportion as the ideas of these different nations were adopted. Hence nothing that ever contributed to the singular composition of this rich language, appears to be borrowed; but all belongs to it as its lawful property. But the great pre-eminence of the Russian appears in the *use* which it made of these adopted treasures. Its greater flexibility made it capable of employing foreign words merely as *roots*, from which it raised stems and branches by means of its own native resources. It is this copiousness and variety of *radical* syllables, which gives to the Russian in certain respects a claim over all other Slavic languages.

Another excellence is the great freedom of construction which it allows, without any danger of becoming unintelligible or even ambiguous. It resembles in this point the classic languages; from which however its small number of conjunctions decidedly distinguishes it. This want of conjunctions has been objected to the language as a defect; it seems however to be one of the causes, why it is so remarkably clear and distinct; since it can only admit of comparatively short phrases. In spite of this clearness, its adaptedness for poetry is undeniable; and in this branch the incomparable national songs extant in it would afford a most noble foundation even in respect to forms, if nature could ever obtain a complete victory over the perverted taste of fashion. Whether this language is really capable of entirely imitating the classic metres, is still a matter of dispute among distinguished Slavic philologians.[3] As to its euphony, what has been said above in respect to the Slavic languages in general, may be applied particularly to the Russian. Here however the ear of the unprejudiced listener alone can decide.

FIRST PERIOD.

To the coming of age of Peter the Great, 1689.

The influence of the Varegians in respect to the language, appears to have been inconsiderable; their own idiom on the

[3] See Schaffarik, *Geschichte* p. 178, note 4.

contrary being soon absorbed by that of the natives. Rurik's grandsons had already Slavic names.[4] The principal event in those ancient times, and one which manifested its beneficent consequences in respect to civilization here, as every where, was the introduction of Christianity, towards the end of the tenth century. Vladimir the Great, the first Christian monarch, founded the first schools; Greek artists were called from Constantinople to embellish the newly erected churches at Kief; and poetry found a patron and at the same time her hero in Vladimir. Vladimir and his knights are the Russian Charlemagne and his peers, king Arthur and his Round table. Their deeds and exploits have proved a rich source for the popular tales and songs of posterity; and serve even now to give to the earlier age of Russian history a tinge of that romantic charm, of which the history of the middle ages is in general so utterly void. The establishment of Christianity was followed by the introduction of Cyril's translation of the Scriptures and the liturgical books. The kindred language of these writings was intelligible to them; but was still distinct enough from the old Russian to permit them to exist side by side as two different languages; the one fixed and immovable, the voice of the Scriptures, the priests, and the laws; the other varying, advancing, extending, adapting itself to the progress of time.

That this latter, the genuine old Russian, had its poets, was, until the close of the last century, only known by historical tradition; no monument of them seemed to be left. But at that time, A. D. 1794, a Russian nobleman, Count Mussin-Pushkin, discovered the manuscript of an epic poem, 'Igor's Expedition against the Polovtzi,' apparently not older than the twelfth century. It is a piece of national poetry of no common beauty, united with an equal share of power and gracefulness. But what strikes us even more than this, is, that we find in it no trace

---

[4] Sviatoslav, Jaropulk, Jaroslav, etc.

of that rudeness, which would naturally be expected in the production of a period when darkness still covered all eastern Europe, and of a poet belonging to a nation, which we have hardly longer than a century ceased to consider as barbarians! There hovers a spirit of meekness over the whole, which sometimes even seems to endanger the energy of the representation.

The genuineness of this poem has, so far as we know, never been questioned; but it is indeed a very surprising feature, that during the recent diligent search through all the libraries in the country after old manuscripts, not a single production has been discovered, which could in any way be compared with it. This remarkable poem stands in the history of ancient Russian literature perfectly isolated; and hence exhibits one of the most inexplicable riddles in literary history.[5]

On the whole, the Russians enjoyed at this early period as much mental cultivation as any other part of Northern Europe. There were several writers even among their princes. Jaroslav, the son of Vladimir the Great, was not less active than his father had been in advancing the cause of Christianity, and all that stands in connection with religion. He sent priests throughout the whole country to instruct the people, and founded in Novogorod a theological seminary for three hundred students. He took care that the translation of the church books was continued; but the most remarkable monument of his reign, as well in an historical as in a philological respect, is the *Pravda Russka*, a collection of laws.[6] Another grand duke of Russia, Vladimir

---

[5] The chronographic manuscript in which the above poem was found, entitled *Slowo o polku Igora,* literally *Speech on Igor's Expedition,* is said to have also contained several other pieces of poetry. By an unpardonable carelessness, the manuscript, after Igor was copied, was lost again. We hear too of an old poetical tale, *History of the wicked Tzar Mamai;* but have no means of ascertaining its age or value, nor even its existence.

[6] *Pravda Russka,* Jus Russorum. See above, p. 40, n. 19.

Vsevolodovitch Monomach, who died in 1125, wrote 'Instructions for his Children;' one of his successors, Constantine Vsevolodovitch, a hundred years later, produced a history of the Russian princes, which is now lost. The clergy, safe in their cells from the tempests of war, were busy in translating from the Greek; Nestor wrote his valuable annals;[7] another priest, Basilius, described the cotemporary events in the south of Russia; Sylvester, bishop of Perejaslavl, ob. 1124, and several others of the clergy, continued Nestor's annals;[8] while Hegumen Daniel wrote his travels to Palestine in the beginning of the twelfth century.

The theological productions of the early portion of this period, are of less value than the historical. It was however this field, that was cultivated most diligently. There are several sermons, or rather synodal *oraisons*, still extant; some of which, by another Cyril, metropolitan of Kief, A. D. 1281, are said to be not without real eloquence. Most of the productions of this early period, which belong indeed more to the history of the Slavonic than of the Russian literature, perished in the devastations and conflagrations of the Mongols.

From A. D. 1238 to 1462, the Russian princes, as we have seen, were vassals of the Mongol Tartars, or the *Golden Horde.*[9] In the course of these two centuries, nearly every

---

[7] See above, p. 41.

[8] These valuable chronicles were continued under different titles, but without interruption, until the reign of Alexis, father of Peter I.

[9] The Mongols and Tartars have been frequently confounded by historical writers; they are however two races perfectly distinct from each other, the first a North-Eastern, the second a South-Western Asiatic nation. The Mongols, however, between the thirteenth and fifteenth centuries, conquerors of the Tartars as well as of half Asia, and of Europe as far as Silesia, and comparatively not numerous, amalgamated gradually with the subjugated Tartars among whom they settled. The present Mongols are partly under the sovereignty of China in the ancient Mongolia, the country whence Jenghis

trace of cultivation perished. No school existed during this whole time throughout all Russia. The Mongols set fire to the cities; sought out and destroyed what written documents they could find; and purposely demolished all monuments of national culture. The convents alone found in their policy a sort of protection. Science therefore became more than ever the exclusive possession of the monks. Among these, however, no trace of classical learning, and hardly a show of scholastic wisdom, was to be found. Fortunately they improved their time as well in respect to posterity by writing annals, as for their own personal benefit by accumulating wealth.

The re-establishment of Russian independence in the middle of the fifteenth century, had a reviving influence on national science and literature. The nation however had been too long kept back, ever to be able to overtake their western neighbours. From this point a new division of this period begins. Some of the Russian princes were men of powerful and active minds; they invited artists and physicians from Greece, Italy, and Germany, into their country, and rewarded them liberally. Ivan IV,[10] A. D. 1538–84, ordered schools to be founded in all the cities of his empire; under his reign the first printing-office was established in Moscow in 1564. Soon afterwards a theological academy was founded at Kief. Boris Godunof, 1598–1605, sent eighteen noble youths to study at foreign universities. The princes of the house of Romanof showed themselves not less active. Alexeï and Fedor, the father and brother of Peter the Great, opened the way for that bold reformer, and appear as his worthy predecessors; indeed the merit of several improvements, which have been generally ascribed to Peter, belongs to them. During

---

Khan came; partly Russian subjects, scattered through the government of Irkutzk, and mixed with Kalmucks and other Asiatic tribes.

[10] Also called Ivan II, and Ivan the Cruel; by modern historians the Russian Nero.

this whole later period, the Polish language and literature exerted a decided influence on the Russian; and some writers began to use the dialect of White Russia, an impure mixture of the two,[11] while the pure Russian was despised as merely fit for vulgar use. The Malo-Russian also, or Ruthenian dialect, was, by the influence of the Polish language, cultivated before the pure Russian, which last began, only in the latter half of the seventeenth century, to shake off these chains and acquire for itself an independent form.

The first germs of dramatic art were likewise carried from Poland to Russia. In Kief, the theological students performed ecclesiastical dramas; and travelled about during the holidays, to exhibit their skill in other cities. The scenes which they had to repeat most frequently. were the three Children in the fiery furnace, and Haman's execution. The tragedies of Simeon of Polotzk, in the Old Slavic language, had great success in the middle of the seventeenth century. Their renown penetrated from the convents to the court; where they were performed before Tzar Fedor, the predecessor of Peter.[12] His minister, Matveyef, the Slavic Mecænas of his time, and himself a writer, invited the first stage-players to Russia; and at his instigation, the first secular drama, a translation of Molière's "Médecin malgré lui," was played before the gratified princesses and their enraptured maids of honour. The sister of the two Tzars, the Tzarevna Sophia, was a great patroness of the dramatic art; and was herself the author of several tragedies and comedies, which were acted before her by her ladies.

This latter portion of the first period, poor as it is, has never-

[11] See above, p. 51.

[12] Most of these dramas are extant in manuscript in the synodal library at Moscow. A selection has been printed in the *Drewn. Rossisk. Bibliotheka*, i. e. Old Russian Library, Moscow 1818.

theless several books of travels to exhibit. A merchant of Tver, Athanasius Nikitin, travelled in the year 1470 to India, visited the Dekkan and Golconda, and gave on his return a description of those countries. Two other merchants of Moscow, Korobeïnikof and Grekof, described a century later their travels through Syria, Palestine and Egypt. Fedor Baïkof, Russian envoy to China, published likewise a book of travels in that remarkable country.

In the department of history, this portion of the first period was surprisingly productive. Not only were the Annals of the venerable Nestor, the basis of all Slavic history, continued by the monks with fidelity and zeal; but a whole series of other annals, biographies of single princes, and chronographies, were produced; and even some foreign nations received their share of attention.[13] The reader however must not expect to find a vestige of philosophical genius, nor a philosophical representation of the events. Entirely unacquainted with classical literature, the Greek writers of the Byzantine age were their only models. The best that can be expected is a dry and faithful narrative of facts.[14]

The weakest part of the literature of this later portion of the period, is the theological branch; a sketch of which however may not be inappropriate here. It is true, that the *Improvement* of

---

[13] The above mentioned chronicles, and another series of annals of a genealogical character, known under the title *Stepennaja Knigi,* mutually supply each other. Simon of Suzdal, the metropolitan Cyprian a Servian by birth, and Macarius metropolitan of Moscow a clergyman of great merits, are to be named here. Another old chronicle called *Sofiiskii Wremenik* was first published in 1820 by Stroyef. A chronicle of Novogorod referring to the sixteenth century was found by the same scholar in the library at Paris.

[14] There is, however, in the style of Nestor and his immediate successors, a certain effort towards animation. Speeches and dialogues are introduced, and pious reflections and biblical sentences are scattered through the whole.

the old church books was executed with much zeal; but in what spirit this was done, in a philological respect, we have mentioned above in the history of the Old Slavonic literature, to which the labours of the translators properly belong. Nikon, patriarch of Russia, ob. 1681, carried on this work with the greatest activity; and besides this set on foot a collection of historical annals.[15] The light of the Reformation, which at that time spread its beneficent beams over all Europe, and exerted particularly such a strong influence on Poland, did not penetrate into the night of the Russian church; the gloom of which, however, had always been mitigated by a spirit of meekness and Christian charity. Still, we notice among the pulpit productions of this time somewhat of the polemic genius of the age. It was not, however, against the bold innovations of Lutherans or Calvinists, that the clergy found occasion to turn their weapons, but against the *Jewish* heresy![16] A translation of the Psalms of David, Moscow 1680, deserves to be distinguished among similar productions. The writer was the monk Simeon of Polotzk, author of the above-mentioned spiritual dramas, and instructor of the Tzar Fedor. Still more remarkable is the first attempt to translate the Bible into the Russian dialect. Francis Skorina, the translator, likewise a native of Polotzk, where the Polish influence was stronger

---

[15] Known under the title *Nikonov spisok*, published St. Petersburg 1767–92, 8 vols. For the *Improvement* of the Slavonic Bible, Nikon alone, by applying to the Patriarch of Constantinople and other Greek dignitaries, obtained 500 Greek MSS. of the whole or portions of the N. Test. Some of them contained also the Septuagint. These were mostly from Mount Athos, and are now the celebrated Moscow MSS. collated by Matthæi. See Henderson, p. 52, 53.

[16] Joseph Sanin, a monk, wrote a history of the Jewish heresy, so called, in the fifteenth century, and a series of sermons against it. This last was also done by the bishop of Novogorod, Gennadius. The Russian church had a zealous advocate in the archbishop Lazar Baranovitch, ob. 1693.

than in any other quarter, was a doctor of medicine; but the time had now come when it began to be felt over all Europe, that the holy volume did not belong exclusively to the clergy. Some parts only of his translation have been printed.[17]

In the course of the sixteenth century, several printing offices had been established in Russia, almost exclusively for the benefit of theological works. Nearly all the historical writings were preserved in manuscript; and have been first printed in modern times. The awkward appearance of Cyril's alphabet seemed to add an unnecessary difficulty to the diffusion of the knowledge of reading. Towards the end of the seventeenth century Elias Kopiovitch made some improvement in the appearance of the Slavic letters; it was however reserved to Peter's reforming hand, to give to them a fixed and permanent shape.

SECOND PERIOD.

From the majority of Peter the Great, A. D. 1689, *to Lomonosof, A. D.* 1741.

The history of the genuine Russian literature begins only with the adoption of the language of the people for all civil writings. It was Peter the Great, who raised this language to be the language of public business, in which all transactions of the courts of justice henceforth were to be held, and all ordinances to be issued. Ere this energetical man was able to establish a Russian printing office in his own empire, in order not to lose

[17] A part of the O. T. Prague 1517–19; the Acts and Epistles, Vilna 1525. Skorina, in one of his prefaces, found it necessary to excuse his meddling with holy things by the example of St. Luke, who, he says, was of the same profession. The dialect of this translation is the White Russian; and the book of Job contains the first specimen of Russian *rhymed* poetry.

time, he gave a privilege for fifteen years to the Dutch printer Tessing for Russian works. It was in Amsterdam, in 1699, that the first Russian book was printed. About the year 1704, Peter himself invented some alterations in the Slavic letters, principally so as to make them more similar to the Latin. He caused a fount of these new types to be cast by Dutch artists; and the first Russian newspaper was printed with them at St. Petersburg in 1705. These letters, with some additional alterations during the course of the following ten years, were generally adopted for the Russian language, and are in use at the present time. The same letters, with a few slight variations, are also used by that portion of the Servians who belong to the eastern church; the other portion making use of the Latin alphabet. In all theological writings, however, the ancient forms of the letters are preserved. This is the difference between the *grashdanskii* and *tzerkvennii*, or the civil and church alphabet.[18]

The energy with which this emperor, *a real autocrat*, proceeded, caused his people to overleap a whole century. If there is something revolting to a liberal mind, in the despotic haste with which he deprived a great nation at once of a part of their nationality, through his arbitrary decision in all that he deemed best for them; still it serves greatly to allay this feeling, to observe that the resistance which he experienced did not proceed from the people, but almost exclusively from the obstinate pride of a spoiled nobility, and the narrow-minded policy of an ignorant and jealous priesthood. The Russian nation itself is indeed, more than any other people, susceptible of deep impressions. Hence they are in general not averse to innovations; and were in Peter's time, as now, willing to be conducted by a hand

[18] The Russians, however, out of the forty-six characters of the Slavonic alphabet, could make use only of thirty-five; the Servians, according to Vuk Stephnanovitch, only of twenty-eight.

acknowledged as that of a superior. In consequence of these very national qualities, good or bad, they are capable of being readily moulded into any new form.

Whether the rapidity, nay, vehemence of the Tzar's improvements were a real benefit to the nation, this is not the place to examine; but for the free development of the language and literature, it is evident, that his proceedings were injurious, notwithstanding their apparently wonderful effect. Although the language possesses all the elements of completeness, and notwithstanding the not inconsiderable mass of talent which has developed itself in the course of time, the Russian literature has perhaps not yet produced a single work of great and decided *original* value. The best works which they have, are imitations; and he is the most distinguished writer whose discernment leads him to choose the best model. No doubt, the present standing of the Russian literature *in general* would have been much lower, and its extent especially would have been much smaller, than it now is, had the Russian genius been permitted to break its own way through the darkness; but there is still less doubt, that in this case it would have preserved its original peculiarity, that wonderful blending of the East and the West, of Asiatic suppleness and European energy, of which their popular songs give such affecting, and in some cases powerful specimens.

Peter, without delay, caused many books to be translated into Russian, from the German, French, English, and Dutch languages. The haste however with which this was performed, and the greater attention of the Tzar to the *matter* than to the *form*, had the natural consequence, that most of these translations were miserable productions, executed without the least regard for the language itself. Peter's only object was to enable his subjects to become a *reading* people, and to communicate to them useful knowledge through the medium of books. Beauties of style, and even mere purity of language, belong in a certain measure to the luxuries of literature; the Tzar thought only of utility.

These innovations in literature found of course a great many opponents among the clergy; but there were some enlightened priests, among those who held the highest standing in the church, who favoured in general the Tzar's plan. The field of theology became somewhat more cultivated during this period. Theophan Prokovitch, archbishop of Novogorod, ob. 1736, alone wrote sixty works, of which however only about half were printed. He was Peter's faithful assistant; and not only his learning and mental gifts, but his high moral character, gained him a decided influence. He was styled the Russian Chrysostom.

The metropolitan of Rostof, called the holy Demetrius, ob. 1709, was likewise a very productive theological writer. He was considered by his cotemporaries as a true pattern of Christianity; and was equally distinguished for his learning. The metropolitan Stephen Javorsky, ob. 1722, was celebrated for his eloquence in the pulpit. Gabriel Bushinsky, bishop of Rjazan and Murom, ob. 1731, was not only a theological writer, but translated also works on history. A remarkable example in this period, is Elias Kopiyevsky,[19] ob. 1701, who studied theology in Holland, and became a protestant, and afterwards a pastor at Amsterdam. He aided zealously in Peter's great work of translations. Several historical and philological works translated by him, were published by Tessing. Luther's Catechism was translated about the same time by the pastor Glück of Livonia, who had been made a prisoner by the Russians and carried to Moscow. It was in his house that Catharine, the future empress of Russia, was brought up.[20]

---

[19] Or *Kopiyevitch*, the same whom we have mentioned as having improved the appearance of the alphabet.

[20] The same Glück had translated the Gospels into Lettonian, and made

Among the secular writers of this period, prince Antiochus Kantemir, ob. 1745, must above all be mentioned. Of Greek extraction and born in Constantinople, with all the advantages of an accomplished education, and in full possession of several highly cultivated languages, he nevertheless chose the Russian idiom for his poetical productions. These are mostly satires, and evidently bear the stamp of a thorough knowledge of the classics. Besides these he wrote on different subjects of natural philosophy; and translated a selection from the Epistles of Horace, and Fontenelle's work on the plurality of worlds. About the same time, Leont. Magnitzky wrote the first Russian Arithmetic with Arabic numerals.

Among the lyric poets two Kozaks, Cyril Danilof and Semen Klimofsky, are named with some distinction. The first of the two, better known under the diminutive of his name, *Kirsha* Danilof, deserves particular attention. The Russians have their cyclus of heroic legends, as well as the occidental nations. Vladimir and his Boyars are to them what Arthur and his Round table, Charlemagne and his twelve peers, are to Britons, Franks, and Germans. These traditions lived still among the people in Kirsha Danilof's time; and yet live to some extent as nursery tales. Kirsha versified them; and, we fear, changed them according to the spirit of his time. They have only been printed and published in the present century, at least seventy-five years after they were written; for Kirsha was a cotemporary of Peter I. It is no doubt to him, that we owe their preservation through an age of a false and pedantic taste, which could only have despised these relics of barbarism, and during which they were forgotten by the Frenchified literati.[21]

---

also an attempt to furnish the Russians with a version of the Scriptures in their vulgar tongue. The detail may be read in Henderson's Researches, p. 111.

[21] Kirsha Danilof's work was first published at Moscow, 1804, with the

In historical contributions this period is not wholly poor; but as the writers paid not the slightest attention to style, or did not know from what principles to begin, the language remained entirely uncultivated. There was as yet no thought of a Russian *Grammar*. In poetry the system of rhymed verses, in which the syllables were not measured, but counted, in imitation of the Poles, reigned exclusively. Meanwhile the popular songs held faithfully to the old Russian irregular but highly musical numbers, consulting only the ear. Trediakofsky, born 1703, was the first who examined more closely the nature of the language, and advised the adoption of the classical metres founded on quantity. He applied on this point merely the principles which Zizania and Smotrisky, nearly a century before, had established for the Old Slavic idiom, and with equal propriety. But, as the talent for illustrating his rules by good examples was wanting in him, he made very little impression; and his name and endeavours were soon forgotten.[22]

THIRD PERIOD.

From Lomonosof to Karamzin, A. D. 1741—1796.

We have now reached the epoch from which the temple of Russian literature, as it appears at present, must be dated. It

title *Drevniya Ruskiya Stichotvoreniya*, Old Russian Poems. A more complete edition, by Kaloidovitch, appeared in 1818.—A valuable little work in German by C. v. Busse, *Fürst Vladimir und seine Tafelrunde*, Leipzig 1819, was probably founded on that of Danilof.

[22] As a characteristic of this poet, we mention only that the empress Catharine, in her social parties, used to inflict as a punishment for the little sins against propriety committed there, e. g. ill humour, passionate disputing, etc. the task of learning by heart and reciting a number of Trediakofsky's verses.

was Peter's hand that laid the corner-stone; it was Lomonosof who raised it above the ground; whilst the fortunate turns of Elizabeth's and Catharine's vanity caused it to be filled with more worshippers than would otherwise ever have sought the way thither. Academies were founded for the sciences and arts; numerous institutions for the education of all classes and ages were created and endowed with true imperial magnificence. In the year 1758 the university of Moscow was founded; while other scientific institutions of all descriptions were established by Catharine's unbounded liberality. In the year 1783 the free establishment of printing offices was permitted; of course not without reserving to the government the privilege of a strict censorship. A seminary for educating teachers for popular schools was erected, with the intention of founding Gymnasia all over the country. These measures, no doubt, had an essential and beneficial influence on the general civilization of the nation. But the common people, the peasantry, remained entirely neglected.

It was however in a family of the lowest standing, that Michael Lomonosof was born, A. D. 1711. His father was a fisherman in the government of Archangel. During the long winters, when his father's trade was interrupted, Lomonosof learned to read of one of the church servants. The beauties of the Bible, and the singing of the Psalms during the church service, in the rhymed translation of Simeon of Polotzk, first awakened his own poetical faculties. An ardent desire for an education caused him to leave home privately and seek his way to Moscow, where, he was told, was an institution, in which foreign languages were taught. Circumstances proved fortunate; he found liberal patrons; was educated afterwards in Kief and St. Petersburg, and obtained means to go to Germany. Here he connected philosophy with the mathematical studies which he had hitherto chiefly pursued; devoted a part of his time to the science of mining, at the celebrated school in Freiburg; and sat in Marburg at the feet of the philosopher Wolf. In passing through Brunswick, he escaped with difficulty the horrors of the Prussian military system. He succeeded in reaching Holland, and thence returned to his own country; where he was well received and honourably employed by the government. He died A. D. 1765, in the enjoyment of high general esteem, but not that degree of reputation which has been allotted to him by a more judicious posterity. He first ventured to draw a distinct boundary line between the Old Slavic and the Russian languages; which hitherto had been confounded in a most intolerable manner. In his Russian Grammar, he first laid down principles and fixed rules for the general compass of the language; without however checking the influence of the Church Slavonic more than was necessary, in order to preserve the identity of the former. He wrote a sketch of Russian History, a long and tedious epic poem called the *Petreide*, speeches, odes, tragedies, and several works on chemistry and mineralogy. None of his productions are without merit; but he was more a man of sagacity and strong talent, than of poetical genius. His poems are all cold and artificial; excepting perhaps his version of a few chapters of the book of Job, where the beauties of the original appear to have inspired him. His speeches and odes are written in the same style of panegyric, which then reigned, and which reigns still, in all the creations of Russian poetry or prose having the least reference to the imperial family; and which, in connection with the boastful style of all productions purporting to describe national deeds, is a real blemish upon the Russian literature, fitted to render it disgusting to all foreigners.[23]

The two most celebrated writers among Lomonosof's cotem-

---

[23] Lomonosof's works were first collected and published by the Academy of Sciences of St. Petersburg, 1803, 6 vols. in several editions.

poraries, though somewhat younger than he, were Alexander Sumarokof, ob. 1777, and Michael Kheraskof, born 1733, ob. 1807. Both were very productive writers in prose and poetry, overwhelming the reading public with tragedies and comedies, odes and epistles; and the latter also with two long epic poems, one in twelve, and the other in eighteen cantos! Both were highly admired, and the overflowings of their pens were devoured with avidity. Kheraskof was called the Russian Homer. The childhood, in which Russian literature then was, is not the age of criticism; sounder judges of later times have allotted to those productions a place hardly above mediocrity.

The first Russian theatre was instituted in Jaroslav, A. D. 1746. The permisson, which the actors obtained A. D. 1754, to establish themselves in St. Petersburg, and still more the foundation of a national stage in Moscow in 1759, served much to awaken the decided dramatic talent of the Russians; a faculty in which they are perhaps incomparable, and certainly are not surpassed by any other nation. Several gifted literary men employed themselves in writing for the stage. Such were J. Knjashnin, ob. 1791, an imitator of the French, but not without talent of his own; Von Wisin, ob. 1792, the author of two comedies, full of genuine comic power; Maïkof, Nicolef, Klushin, etc. The distinguished productions of Von Wisin alone have continued to hold possession of the stage.[24]

As the most prominent poets of a miscellaneous character the following may be mentioned: Hippolit Bagdanovitch, born 1743,

---

[24] His masterpiece, *Nedorosl*, ‘ Mama's Darling," literally *the Minor*, published 1787, presents an incomparable picture of the manners, habits, etc. of the Russian country gentry. Potemkin, who was Von Wisin's patron, felt so enchanted once after a theatrical representation of this comedy, that he advised the author to die now. " Die, Denis!" he cried, " thou canst not write any thing better! do not survive thy glory." A posthumous drama by the same author has recently been found and printed.

ob. 1805, author of a tale in verse, *Dushenka*, Psyche, not without gracefulness and *naiveté;* Chemnitzer, ob. 1784, the writer of the best Russian fables; Gabriel Dershavin, born 1743, ob. 1816, the most celebrated Russian poet of his time. The glory of Catharine II, and of the Russian army, was his favourite theme; but even the panegyrical style of his odes, the most dangerous enemy not only of moral, but likewise of poetical truth, cannot destroy the power of his truly poetical genius. His ode *To God* has obtained the distinction of being translated not only into several European languages, but also into Chinese, and hung up in the emperor's palace, printed with golden letters on white satin.[25] Further, Vasilii Kapnist, born 1756, ob. 1823, who as a lyrical poet stands next to Dershavin; Bobrof, familiarly acquainted with English literature, which he endeavoured to imitate, full of imagination, but bombastic and obscure; Prince Dolgoruky, distinguished by a philosophical vein; Neledinsky-Meletzky, whose songs are known even by the lower classes.

During this period also the field of translation was not less cultivated. Kostrof translated the Iliad in rhymed verses, A. D. 1787, and also Macpherson's Ossian from the French. Petrof gave a version of the Æneid in 1793. Bulgakof first made the Russian public acquainted with Ariosto; Popovsky with Pope and Locke, etc.—As a writer of general and favourable influence on literature, we must not forget to name N. Novikof, editor of several periodical journals, author of the first Russian bibliographical work, and a man of that general literary activity, which, even without productiveness of its own, induces others to exercise theirs.

---

[25] Also into Japanese, according to Golovnin's account, and suspended in like manner in the temple of Jeddo. See Bowring's Russian Anthol. I. p. 3.

The patriotism which caused the Russians ever to pay a certain degree of attention to their national history, deserves the highest praise. During all periods of their literature, this branch has been attended to with diligence. It is however especially the laborious collection and faithful preservation of materials, for which posterity is indebted to them; since there is little of a philosophical spirit to be found in their arrangement of these materials; and in regard to the language in which they are presented, it is striking to observe how the Russian prose was always far behind the Russian poetry. G. F. Müller, ob. 1783, a German by birth, but who devoted all his life to Russian literature, published the first Russian periodical, dedicated chiefly to historical objects.[26] He also caused several old manuscripts to be printed; and added greatly to their value by his investigations and commentaries. Prince Shtsherbatof wrote fifteen volumes of Russian history, besides several smaller works,—a mere collection of facts, but rendered more important by a review and criticism upon them by Boltin, ob. 1792, a distinguished historian. Tchulkof wrote a history of commerce; Jemin, Rytchkof, Golikof, and others, wrote on particular portions of Russian history.

For the philological studies of the language, the foundation of the Russian Academy, A. D. 1783, was of great importance. A standard grammar and etymological dictionary were published by it in 1787–90, founded on a plan perfectly new, and in the merit of which the empress Catharine had no small personal

---

[26] This was a monthly periodical, first published 1755. The list of Germans whose labours have proved of the highest importance to Russia is very long; among them are those of Pallas, Schlözer, Frähn, Krug, etc. The department of statistics has been exclusively cultivated by Germans, Livonians, etc. and all that the Russians have done in the philological and historical departments, rests on the preceding solid and profound labours of German scholars.

share. Her example awakened not a few Mecænases among the *magnates* of the country; and it became a point of high ambition to favour literature and literary men.[27]

As for theological and biblical science, scarcely any thing interesting, certainly nothing gratifying, meets our eye in this vast deserted field. Except a few didactic works on dogmatics and rhetoric, several catechisms and similar productions, this department is limited exclusively to sermons, or rather synodal discourses. There is not always a want of talent, and sometimes even a rich share of natural power; but the language, though first developed in similar productions, is here so full of bombastic, tasteless, and mere rhetorical ornaments, that the *thought* seems to be entirely drowned in them.

Demetrius Sjetchinof, metropolitan of Novogorod, ob. 1767, and the archbishop of White Russia, Konissky, ob. 1795, are considered as not being without eloquence. Platon Levshin, metropolitan of Moscow, was the most productive of the ecclesiastical writers. He died in 1812, and continued to write until the end of his life; his productions consequently, in respect to time, belong partly to the next period of Russian literature.[28] Anastasius Bratanofski, archbishop of Astrachan, ob. 1806, takes the first place among Russian ecclesiastical orators, in respect to style and command of language; though higher powers and profounder feelings are ascribed to an arch-priest of Kief, Ivan Levanda, ob. 1814. Here our catalogue terminates. All the remaining ecclesiastical writers of any distinction, although only

---

[27] To the honour of the Russians it must be said, that it is still so. Dershavin and Dmitrief were ministers of state; Griboyedof was an ambassador; Karamzin occupied, and Shishkof and Shukovski still occupy, high offices of the empire.

[28] His *Summary of Christian Divinity* has been translated by Dr. Pinkerton, and published in his "Present state of the Greek Church in Russia."

a few years younger than those here mentioned, seem in respect to language to belong to the following period.

FOURTH PERIOD.

From Karamzin, A. D. 1796, *to the commencement of the reign of the emperor Nicholas in* 1825.

The number of Russian writers increases during this period so considerably, that we feel more than ever obliged to limit ourselves to the most distinguished; thus, no doubt, passing over in silence many a name more deserving to be mentioned than others of the preceding periods, which borrowed a comparative lustre only from the poverty of the times.

The emperor Alexander, during the first years of his reign, showed a zeal for the mental cultivation and enlightenment of his subjects, which presented him to the eyes of admiring Europe in the light of one of the great benefactors of mankind. Whoever will take the trouble to follow the career of this prince closely, and contrast the shouts of acclamation with which the world hailed him at first, with the disesteem into which the same individual a few years afterwards shrunk, as a weak and insignificant being,—and then again compare the enthusiasm with which during the time of his better fortunes he was received anew as the deliverer of Europe, with the part which was afterwards assigned him in the system of *obscurantismus* supposed to be adopted by the united sovereigns of Europe,—whoever considers all this, cannot but be struck with the small portion of discernment and discrimination which is manifested in the world. A sober and keen-sighted observer might have seen even in the beginning, glorious as it was, that not all is gold that glitters. All that was done, was accompanied with a noise and boasting which strangely imposed upon foreigners. Universities, on the plan of the venerable institutions of learning in Germany, were founded, where all the preparation necessary in order to profit by them was wanting; and the profoundest sciences were professedly taught to pupils, who were still deficient even in elementary knowledge. We do not however mean to say, that much real good was not done; and even if some of the new institutions were not propitious in their immediate results, still the time has come, or will come, when all of them are or will be at least in a measure useful. The establishment of numerous common schools of a less elevated character throughout the whole empire, deserves unqualified praise. More than fifty higher schools, called gymnasia or governmental schools, and twice as many lower or provincial schools, were established under Alexander's reign alone.[29]

Besides the universities, eight in all, of which Alexander founded five, there are a considerable number of professional schools; among which are four theological academies. In the year 1823, an Institution for the study of oriental languages was founded at St. Petersburg; and in 1829 a similar one at Odessa, a city which has by its location more natural advantages for the learning of Asiatic languages than any other, and where for most of them native teachers may be readily obtained. On the other hand, the Asiatic Museum, attached to the school at St. Petersburg, contains all the means and aids for those studies to be met with at a more remote place. Richly endowed by the munificence of the emperor Alexander, who caused scientific treasures of every kind to be liberally purchased, it was also greatly augmented during the late war with Persia; where by order of the

[29] A survey of the number and general classification of the universities and schools in Russia at this period, is to be found in the American Quarterly Observer for Jan. 1834, Vol. II. No. 1.

emperor all conquered cities were deprived of their libraries, whether public or private; while, by a stipulation in the treaty of peace, the Persian government was compelled to deliver to Russia towards four hundred manuscripts, a list of which was drawn up by the orientalists Frähn and Senkofsky. Among these were the geography of Ptolemy, and several Arabic translations of Greek and Latin works, lost in the original languages. Although the object of the oriental schools in Russia was originally to educate translators for diplomatic missions, they have proved themselves very useful to oriental philology in general; especially through the many gifted Germans in the Russian service, who avail themselves gladly of opportunities for those studies which their own country cannot give. It will however be seen in the sequel, that several learned Russians also have paid an honourable attention to this branch, especially within the last twenty years.

The Russian Bible Society, founded A. D. 1813, was at first patronized by the emperor. Under its auspices, and at the instigation of the emperor himself, there was prepared a version of the Scriptures in the Russian dialect. In the year 1820, not less than 50,000 copies of the Gospels and the Acts were issued from the press; in 1823 the whole New Testament was finished, and in the course of eight months 20,000 copies were distributed. For this translation the peasantry, to whom the Old Slavic church Bible was only half intelligible, showed such an eagerness, as soon to excite trouble among the clergy. In some of the governments, remote from the capital, the readers of this version of the Bible had to encounter serious persecution. In respect to translations into foreign languages, a kind of rivalship arose between the parent society in England and the daughter in St. Petersburg. Besides the preparation by the latter of translations into *thirty-one* different languages and dialects within the limits of the Russian empire, she likewise took care of several

Asiatic nations, and founded auxiliaries in the deserts of Siberia, and also in the midst of the Kozaks of the Don and the Circassian provinces. In A. D. 1820, this society had fifty-three sections and 145 auxiliaries; and the number of copies of whole Bibles and of New Testaments distributed, exceeded 430,000. But in 1822, the society held its last aniversary; and three years later, some of the more important Russian clergy succeeded in closing the series of annual reports. In April 1826, the activity of the society was ultimately terminated, or, as it was expressed, *was suspended*, by the Ukase of the emperor Nicholas, at the instigation of the metropolitans Eugene and Seraphim. Since that time, only the sale of the copies already printed has been permitted.[30]

The Russian Bible Society stood of course in connection with societies for Foreign Missions; but was active in this respect chiefly through the agency of the United or Moravian Brethren. In 1823 the Moravians of Sarepta sent, with the express consent of the minister of Ecclesiastical Affairs, two missionaries to the Kalmuks; into whose language the Gospels had been translated at St. Petersburg by Schmidt. In the same degree that they found the people susceptible for divine truth, did they meet with opposition from the priesthood. The Khans, yielding to the influence of the priests, threatened to emigrate; and the Russian government found it advisable to withdraw the mission. An interesting report of this mission was published in 1824, in the Journal of St. Petersburg. In the year 1824, a mission of the Greek church, at the instigation of the bishop of Archangel, was sent to the Samoyedes. This was the first attempt ever made to

---

30 On all that relates to the Russian Bible Society, Henderson's Biblical Researches contain most interesting details. The active part, however, which he ascribes to the Jesuits in effecting the suppression of the Society, is far from being historically ascertained.

convert that savage people to Christianity; of the results we are not informed.

The compass of Russian literature extended itself during the course of Alexander's reign, or rather from A. D. 1800 to 1822, with a most remarkable rapidity. In the year 1787 the number of books written in the Old Slavonic and Russian dialects, did not exceed 4000;[31] before 1820 twice that number was counted; the year 1820 alone produced 3400 works, 800 of them translations from the French, 483 from the German, and more than 100 from the English. Sopikof, in his bibliographical essay, enumerates the titles of 13,249 Russian and Slavonic books, printed in Russia from A. D. 1552 to 1823. But at this time literature seems to have reached its height in respect to productiveness; and sunk again with a still greater rapidity, probably in consequence of the political measures of the government. The year 1824 produced only 264 Russian works. The yearly average of literary productions, original and translated, from 1800 to that time, is about 300 to 400. This number perhaps will not strike the reader as so very small, if he is informed that in the whole eighteenth century only 1000 works were printed. Three hundred and fifty living authors were enumerated in the year 1822; mostly belonging to the nobility, and only one eighth part to the clergy. Their literary activity towards the end of this period. and at the commencement of the next, was in a great measure confined to works of fiction; especially novels end lyrical poetry. But at this time a deeper interest in their national history began to be awakened. This department indeed had never been entirely neglected; and more than 10,000 manuscripts, unopened and unexamined, lay scattered throughout the imperial and monastic libraries.

Nicholas Karamzin, from the commencement of whose influ-

[31] See Backmeister's *Russische Bibliothek*, Riga 1772–87.

ence this period of Russian literature is in general dated, was born A. D. 1765. He was educated in the house of a German professor at Moscow. In spite of the early development of his literary propensities, he entered the military service, which was then considered as the most honourable in Russia. After two years spent in travelling through Europe, he opened his literary career with the publication of a periodical work called the Moscow Journal, which exercised a decidedly favourable influence on Russian literature; although those productions of Karamzin himself, which first appeared in this journal, evidently bear the stamp of the author's youth. Both in his prose writings and in his scattered lyrical poems, at this period, there is a certain dulcet sentimentality, behind which we look in vain for energetic or true poetic thoughts. He showed more maturity in his second periodical, called the European Messenger; where political and moral subjects occupied his pen. But his principal reputation rests upon his History of the Russian Empire. In composing this work, he was greatly favoured by the government; all the archives were opened to him; all documents delivered into his hands; and when it was completed, rewards and gratuities of every description were heaped upon the author with imperial munificence, and continued to his widow and children after his decease in 1826.[32]

The beauties of Karamzin's style are so entirely *idiomatic*, that no one, who is not perfectly and thoroughly acquainted with the language, is able to appreciate in what the charm of his

---

[32] Of Karamzin's *Istorija Gosudarstva Rossissavo*, History of the Russian Empire, (extending only to the reign of the house of Romanof, A. D. 1613,) in eleven volumes, a second edition was published in 1818. His other works have been collected in nine volumes, of which a third edition was published in 1820. This great historical work has been translated twice into German, first by Hauenschild and Oertel, and later by Tappe; and twice into French, St. Pet. 1818, and by St. Thomas and Jauffort, Paris 1820.

writings consists. To foreigners of sound critical taste, on the contrary, the productions of his early life exhibit an affectation, a pretension to feeling, and an emptiness of original thought, sometimes quite intolerable. And as to the more condensed and exact style of his great historical work, even the highest beauties of diction, and the acknowledged diligence and accuracy of the writer's examination of facts, could never reconcile us to that *want of truth*, which, without wresting the fact itself, impresses upon it a false character by the whole colouring and mode of representation. Over the characteristic barbarism of ancient times his dexterous hand throws a veil of embellishment, and lends a spirit of chivalry and romantic charm to historical persons and deeds, where all the circumstances of place and time stand in absolute contradiction to it. Not seldom do we seem to be perusing a novel.

By this mode of proceeding he of course flattered the national feelings of his countrymen; and thus gained their approbation and applause, in the same measure that he disgusted all other nations. His History of Russia will nevertheless remain a standard work in Slavic literature, partly on account of the copiousness of its sources, partly because of the great learning and research displayed by its author.

In respect to Karamzin's innovations on the language, his influence was early counterbalanced. He considered the French or English mode of construction as better adapted to the present state of the Russian language, than that imitation of the classical structure, which had hitherto given to the Russian prose writings so stiff and awkward an air. He himself adopted with ease and gracefulness the peculiarities of these modern languages; but a portion of his followers thought to reach the same object by introducing Gallicisms. Just at the proper time an opposition was formed; the head of which, Admiral Shishkof, insisted upon preserving the influence of the Church Slavonic upon the Russian language; and reproached Karamzin with having injured the purity of the latter by the introduction of foreign forms. These two parties, which still divide the Russian literature in some measure, are called the *Russian* and *Slavonic*, or also the Moscow and St. Petersburg parties.

Not much less influence than Karamzin on the Russian prose, has Ivan Dmitrief, born 1760, exercised on poetry. He had more taste and purity than any of his predecessors; and was the first to prove by a great many poetical tales, fables, odes, etc. that imagination and correctness of language are not incompatible. The most successful of his followers are the following:

Vassilii Shukofsky, born 1784, a poet of true and deep feeling, without affectation, possessing more of what the Germans call *subjectivity*, than any other Russian writer. He took the Germans for his models, and partly imitated and partly translated them with success. Ivan Koslof, interesting by his personal character and trying misfortunes, must be mentioned as one of the most happy translators from the English and German. His literary talents were awakened only when he had lost the power of enjoying the world. Early in life he was deprived by sickness of the use of his limbs; and of his eyes, some years after. He bore this great affliction with the most amiable philosophy; devoted himself entirely to literature; and studied and imitated the English poets, chiefly Byron. Another successful translator of this great poet, who excited as much interest in Russia as in any other country, was Baron Rosen. Further, as lyrical poets, are also esteemed: Prince Vjazemsky, Vostokof distinguished as an Old Slavic philologist, Chwostof, Batjushkof,[33] Rileyef,[34] Baron Delwig, Glinka, etc.

[33] The Foreign Quarterly Review contains under the head *Critical Sketches*, a review of Batjushkof's works and a specimen of his poetry. Vol. IX. p. 218.

[34] Executed as involved in the conspiracy of 1825.

At the head of the Russian poets stands, almost without a rival, Alexander Pushkin, born 1798, ob. 1835; but as his principal productions belong to the next period, and his influence is chiefly perceptible among the more recent poets, we defer for the present a fuller notice of his writings and his fortunes.

The Russians are particularly fond of fables. Besides Chemnitzer, mentioned above, who is flat and prosy, Ivan Krylof, born 1768, is celebrated in this department. He may be truly called the favourite of the nation. His fables, equally popular among all classes and conditions of life, are the first book that a Russian child reads. A considerable portion of them has been translated into French and Italian; partly by Count Orlof at Paris, and partly by friends of the latter, ladies and gentlemen of the most fashionable society in that capital, among whom that nobleman distributed the labour of translation. He then published them, with the original, in the year 1825. The perfect harmlessness and *naiveté* of this author has made him also a favourite of the government; and when, twelve years ago, he celebrated his seventieth birthday, honours and distinctions of all kinds were accumulated on his head.

As dramatic poets, Shakhofskoi, Chmelnitzky, Gribojedof,[35] and Ozerof, must be mentioned; the first three chiefly as writers of comedies; the last as the author of a very popular drama entitled *Gore ot Uma*, Miseries of Intellect. While it cannot be doubted that the Russians have a decided talent for the comic, both as writers and as actors, it is still a fact that they have never produced a single tragedy of great power. Ozerof, who wrote quite a number of them, belongs more in spirit to the preceding period; during which the French was the

---

[35] He was sent as Russian ambassador to Persia; and was there slaughtered by a mob in 1829.

only acknowledged model. The success he met with can be explained only by the want of competitors.

No form of poetry has found more favour in Russia than the historical novel. It was cultivated to some extent at this time; but the flower of this branch falls more properly within the following period. A voluminous novel, entitled *Bursak*, by B. Nareshnoi, belonged to another species. It was written with a good deal of harmless humour, somewhat in the style of Le Sage's Gil Blas. It narrated the history of a *Bursarian*, or scholar of one of the monastic seminaries in Malo-Russia; and is full of adventures, lively descriptions of manners, and amusing incidents.[36]

The literature of translations continued to occupy very many pens. Here must be mentioned: Gnjeditch's version of the Iliad; Merzljakof's translation of Tasso's Jerusalem; Wojeikof's Æneid; Martynof's translation of several ancient classics, etc.

To foreigners, the travels of the Russians by sea and land offer the most interesting and instructive part of their literature. The most distinguished of their well known expeditions have indeed been conducted by Germans, as Krusenstern, Kotzebue, Bellinghausen, Wrangel; some however by Russians, as Golovnin, Lazaref, and others; and the results of all of them contribute to the honour of Russia, and are laid up in the temple of her literature. The regions of Malo-Russia, the Caucasus, and Taurida, of which comparatively little was known, were explored by Muraviev-Apostol, Glinka, Bronefsky, and others; and described by them in valuable volumes. An account of China by Timkofsky, was translated in 1827 into the English language. The works of the monk Hyacinth Bitchourin, head of the Russian ecclesiasti-

[36] *Bursak, Malorossiiskaja powiest*, Mosk. 1824.

cal mission at Pekin, published in 1828–32, are of great importance for the knowledge of China, Thibet, and the country of the Mongols.[37] The great patriot and protector of science, Romyanzof, whose name is known throughout the civilized world, caused Abulghasi's *Historia Mongolorum et Tartarorum* to be printed in 1825, under the special care of the distinguished German oriental scholar Frähn. The publication of the Mongol work, *History of the Eastern Mongols and their Princes*, written by Ssanang Ssetzen, with a German translation and illustrations and remarks by J. J. Schmidt, although no Russian work, may be mentioned here; as it was only made possible by Russian means, and the support of the emperor. The same author, known to the literary world by his learned Researches in Eastern Asia, translated also the Gospels into the Mongol and Kalmuk

---

[37] This venerable missionary, who resided at Pekin from 1807 to 1821, published after his return to his own country a series of valuable and instructive works, a catalogue of which, as they have met with general acknowledgment in foreign countries, will not be unacceptable to the American reader.—1. *Sapiski o Mongolii,* Account of Mongolia, St. Pet. 1828, 2 vols. It contains a part of his travels, a description of the country and people, and a translation of the Mongol code of laws.—2. *Opisanie Tibeta,* i. e. Description of Thibet in its present state, translated from the Chinese, with remarks and illustrations, St. Pet. 1828. This work has been translated into French and published by Klaproth under the title: *Description du Tubet partiellement du Chinois en Russe, par le P. Hyacinth Bitchourin, et du Russe en Français par M . . . . etc. Accompagnée de Notes par M. Klaproth,* Paris 1831.—3. Description of Dshongary and Eastern Turkestan, in 2 vols. under the title: *Opisanie Dshongarii i vostotchnavo Turkestana,* etc. St. Pet. 1829.—4. *Istorija pervych tchetyrech Chanov,* i. e. History of the first four Khans of the House of Jenghis, St. Pet. 1829. This and the preceding work are not properly translations, but original works drawn from *Chinese* sources, all o which are specified. Besides these works, Hyacinth has published some of less importance, translations from the Chinese, etc. etc.

languages for the Russian Bible Society. A Mongol Grammar was prepared by him in 1828, and the Mongol-German-Russian Dictionary was announced in 1834. A Mongol-Russian Dictionary had been previously published by Igumnof of Irkutzk. Volkof composed a Tartar Dictionary, an earlier one having been written by Giganof in 1804. For the study of the Armenian, numerous opportunities are presented; the Armenian archimandrite Seraphim published in 1819 an Armenian elementary Encyclopedia, and in 1822 a Russian Armenian Dictionary. But the oriental studies of the Russians are not limited to the languages of the Russian empire. A Hebrew Grammar has been published by Pavsky, the learned author of the Russian version of the Old Testament; and in the year 1821 there were, according to Henderson, not less than forty of his pupils employed as teachers in the different academies and seminaries throughout the country. An Arabic Grammar has been published by Boldryef, and also a Persian Chrestomathy in 1826. Senkofsky translated the *Derbent-Nahmeh;* and also edited with considerable additions the French-Arabic dictionary, originally written by the Swede Berggren, a work of great utility to the Arabic scholar; not a mere vocabulary, but full of geographical notices and general information; in short a work which, according to the prospectus written by the learned Frähn, "contains every thing that can be useful to the traveller, diplomatic agent, missionary, physician or merchant." The editor among other things has added in Roman characters the vulgar pronunciation of the Arabic, which differs materially from that given by the grammarians.

Among the ecclesiastical writers of this period, Ambrosius Protasof archbishop of Kazan and Simbirsk, and Philaret Drozdof archbishop of Moscow, are considered as the most eloquent. The last is the author of several works on church history. Other theological writers are the following: Eugene

Bolchovitinof metropolitan of Kief,[38] Ambrosius Podobjedof metropolitan of Novogorod, and Michael Desnitzky metropolitan of St. Petersburg. Stanislas Bogush, a Roman Catholic priest, published a history of Taurida and several other historical works in the Russian language. The branch of *Memoires*, in the French sense of the word, has recently been much cultivated. The publications of Count Munich, in 1818; of Prince Shakhofsky, 1821; of General Danilevsky, 1830; and of Admiral Shishkof, 1832; are valuable contributions to the history of our time. The two latter, although belonging to the next period in respect to the years of publication, are nevertheless productions of the period now under review, and refer chiefly to it.

The national feeling of the Russians has led them, during the period of their literary history, to examine the nature of their language; and all philosophical investigations, or antiquarian researches, which could throw additional light upon the past, have been favoured by persons of distinction and influence; as for example, by Admiral Shishkof, himself a writer on various subjects. With this view he caused a new edition of the Dictionary of the Russian Academy to be published; and set on foot the preparation of another more perfect work of that kind, founded on an improved plan.[39] To this class of philological antiquarians belong the names of Vostokof already cited in these pages, Sokolof, Kalaïdovitch, and Stroyef; the two latter learned and judicious commentators on old manuscripts which they first published, and which but for them would still lie mouldering in dust

---

[38] The reputation of this clergyman rests however more on his publications in the department of bibliographical and literary history, than on his own theological works.

[39] The etymological tables, published since 1819 by Shishkof, as a specimen of the labours of the Academy, are highly interesting. We see here the words reduced to the first elements of the language; and in some cases more than 2000 words springing from a single root.

and oblivion. In the department of literary history and bibliography, we find as writers of merit, P. Köppen, author of the well-written article "Kunst und Alterthum in Russland" in the Vienna *Jahrbücher*, and of various valuable paleographic and other essays in the Russian language; also Gretsch, Sopikof, Anastasevitch, the metropolitan Eugene above mentioned, Pletuef, Mussin-Pushkin, Korshavin, Katchenofsky, etc. etc. The principal activity and success of this school falls within the next period.

FIFTH PERIOD.

From A. D. 1825 *to the present time.*

The reign of the emperor Nicholas opened with a bloody tragedy, which concerns us here only so far, as the dissatisfied, effervescing, unhealthy spirit of the literary youth of Russia was in a very striking manner exhibited in it.

Several poets and men of some literary fame were among the conspirators. Rileyef, Bestushef, and others, became the victims of their imprudence. An analogous spirit had some years before banished young Pushkin from the capital. It was evident, that the Russian muse was no longer the good old gossiping lady in French court-dress and hoops, who was ready to drop a humble courtesy to every person of rank and influence; she was no longer the shepherdess who had inspired Dmitrief with his sweet yet tame verses; she had been by the example and the pernicious influence of the modern philosophical schools gradually metamarphosed into a wild romantic girl, burning with desire to drink freely, and without being watched by police agents, from the true source of poetry open to all nations; to rove about in the world of imagination free from fetters and restraint. The means which the emperor chose to cure her from these eccentricities; to chain her at home by endearing it to her; in short, to *Russify* her again; were certainly very *judicious.*

We have seen that the spirit of historical and archæological researches, as well as the interest for the study of the Slavic languages, was already awakened in the preceding period. The government did every thing to favour it, and to nurse that truly patriotic zeal which tries to penetrate the past in order to search for those links which connect it with the present. All influence from without was as much as possible checked; the professorships of philosophy were abolished at all the universities (1827); the scissors of censorship were directed to cut sharper; the catalogue of forbidden books was made longer; the permission to travel was often denied, and the term of lawful absence for a Russian subject confined to five years. But in the interior, within the safe inclosure of the Chinese walls of protection against the epidemic fever of the age, the most energetic measures were taken to promote national education, and to cultivate those fields of science where no political tares could be sown among the grain.

Of all political ideas, one at least was favoured; and this was the great idea of *Panslavism*, that is, of the close connection or union of all the Slavic races among themselves. Of this great family, some of whose members after a short period of flourishing life are withering fast away, if not supported by the whole, Russia is the natural head, the great animating soul, into which the other parts all must naturally be absorbed at last. This idea, first scientifically wrought out by Bohemian scholars, and cherished by their pride, which was justly offended by the oppressions and undisguised contempt experienced from the Germans, was well received by the Russian literati; and even by many of those who naturally loved the Poles, and did not approve of the harsh measures of the Russian government. There was even in Poland itself a school which adopted this view; nay, some distinguished Polish scholars claim it as their own original idea. According to them, the Austrians and Prussians alone were the real usurpers; in being absorbed by Russia as a member of the great Slavic empire, Poland yielded only to its fate, and could hope for a more glorious *Panslavic* resurrection, i. e. a resurrection as a member of the great whole.[40]

In reference to the critical researches, which were made through all branches of history, the period now under review may be appropriately called the *historical* period. The investigations of the Archæological Commission, have been mentioned above. It was first appointed in 1834; and considerably enlarged in 1837. The examination of manuscripts was not confined to the libraries of the empire; Stroyef was sent to Paris, Newerof to Germany, Solovyef to Denmark and Sweden, Wenelin to Bulgaria; and Nadeshdin travelled among the despised Russian tribes of Northern Hungary. In 1844, five volumes of Russian annals were printed; besides a series of historical and juridical documents which had preceded them. The Moscow Historical and Geographical Society, an older institution, and also the St. Petersburg Historical Society founded in 1846, have contributed their share of information; and a general interest has been awakened among the higher classes of society.

The new critical spirit of the times was first perceptible in the bold attitude assumed by the editor of a periodical work, called the *Telegraph*. Polevoi was a self-made man, a merchant without classical education, without deep learning, and indeed without depth in any thing. He had however by an uncommon share of sagacity, by a rare energy of thought, and a restless activity,

[40] This view seems to have been taken by Count Adam Gurowski, now in this country, the author of the *European Pentarchy*, Leipzig 1839; a work in which a great deal of mental power and an admirable acuteness is employed to defend the despotic claims of Russia, and to shake the independence of Germany.

gained more influence over his countrymen than any previous writer; and succeeded in giving to his very popular periodical an important voice in all matters of literature. In the year 1829 he announced a new History of Russia, in twelve volumes; and at the same time expressed the opinion, that Karamzin's work was to be called neither practical nor philosophical, and was no longer worthy of the present standing of Russian literature. His own publication, which followed soon afterwards, and was executed with the rapidity which was characteristic of the man, proved that it is easier to point out the deficiencies of others, than to avoid them ourselves.

The young historical school found another champion in Sergei Skromnenko, who attacked the authority of Nestor, or at least the age ascribed to this first Russian annalist; essaying to prove that he did not write before the beginning of the fourteenth, or perhaps towards the end of the thirteenth century.[41] Another young historian, J. Bodianski, defended this opinion. W. Perewostschikof examined it in a separate work.[42] Pogodin, a name of more weight, refuted it in his *Studies on Nestor;* and it seems since to have been given up.

Another production of some importance was an "Essay towards a Geography of the Old Russian World," by Nadeshdin; in which the author attempted with ability and success to trace the old seats of the Slavic nations. Several monographs and histories of particular regions or periods appeared in the interval between 1830 and 1842. Such were the histories, e. g. of the unfortunate Prince Ivan and his relatives, by Polenof; of Catharine II, by Lefort; of Tzar Boris Godunof, by Krayefski;

---

[41] *O mnimoi drewnosti etc.* i. e. On the pretended age, the original form, and the sources of our History; first printed in the periodical, "The Library," in 1835.

[42] *O Russkich Letopisiach, etc.* i. e. On the Russian Chronicles and their writers, Petersb. 1836.

of Peter II, by Arsenief. Also a History of the time of troubles (as the period between Boris Godunof and the reign of the house of Romanof is called) by Buturlin; the biographies of the first three Tzars of the house of Romanof, by Berg; the histories of Kief by Samailof, of Pskow by Pogodin, of Siberia by Slowzof; of the fair of Nishni Novogorod, which goes back to the fourteenth century, by Zubof; of the Zaporoguean Kozaks by Sreznefski. This latter valuable work is especially rich in historical popular songs, never before printed. Further, the History of the insurrection of Pugatschef, by the poet Pushkin; the Historical and statistical survey of Russia, by T. Bulgarin; and the Memoirs for Russian History by Svinyin (ob. 1839); must be here mentioned. The two latter had hitherto been more known as writers of novels than as historians; and the rosy light which the first of the two tries to throw over his subject, seems still to testify more to his talent for romance than to his historical truthfulness.

This was however the spirit in which the government wished its historians to write. A work of decided importance appeared in 1839, a History of Russia, in which the principles of *Panslavism* were developed in a striking manner. The author, Professor Oustrialof, who had made himself favourably known by several monographs relating to Russian History, has displayed in the above-mentioned work not only considerable acuteness, but also a great deal of research, consistency, and thoroughness.[45] His principal tendency is to represent Russia as the natural central point of the Slavic race. The immediate result of the appearance of this work was, that Oustrialof was commissioned by the government to write a compendium or guide for historical instruction in all the schools of the empire.

Although this view may be called the most popular in

---

[45] It appeared in a German translation as early as 1840.

Russia, it appears from the decided predilection with which Russian writers of history devote their pens to subjects anterior to the reign of Peter I, that they consider the comparatively greater liberty which is allowed them in their researches into the history of this earlier period as a decided advantage. Karamzin had proved by the picture he drew of Ivan the Terrible, that, at this remote period at least, justice was free. It may thus be explained, why Boris Godunof, the friend of the people, the promoter of liberal ideas and modern improvements, is a favourite subject of the young historical school.

The treatment of modern history has in Russia its own difficulties, which may easily be comprehended; and nothing is permitted to appear without the approval of the government. General Michailovski-Danilevski, who wrote a history of the war of 1812–14, may be considered as its true representative. He ascribes all the merits of the final victory of the Allies to the Russians alone. Among several works of that time written in an analogous spirit, the "Description of the campaigns of 1812 and 1814" must be noticed; because the author is a lady by the name of Dorof, who served in the army as a common soldier, and describes only what she saw. An anonymous work, written by an eye-witness, gives an account of the Turkish war in 1828–29. The work entitled "Biographies of the Russian Admirals" (1834), gives a history of the Russian navy.

In no department has Russian Literature remained more behind its age, than in the treatment of foreign history, and especially European history. The series of publications which have appeared relating to it, consist almost exclusively of defective translations, or weak imitations. For the Russian scholar this defect was less essential than for the public in general, as all of them read foreign languages. Pogodin has recently begun to give more attention to this subject.

In respect to several Asiatic nations we are almost entirely dependent on Russian writers. The priest Hyacinth, honourably mentioned in connection with this branch, continues his useful activity. Chopin on the provinces of the Caucasus (1840); Nefedyef on the Wolga-Kalmuks (1835); several articles in the Siberian Mercury, a periodical; a History of the Mongols, from the Persian, by Grigoryef; the Kirgises of the inner Horde, by Khanlkof; and several publications of the Geographical Society of St. Petersburg; deserve to be noticed here. The works of two foreigners, one by Haguemaster on the Commerce with Persia and Turkey, the other by Chaudoir on the Numismatics of China, Japan, and Korea, may also be included; as they appeared simultaneously in the Russian and French languages, and were both of them occasioned by the Russian government.

The interest of the Russians for Law as a science has only recently been excited. Prince Peter of Oldenburg, a cousin of the emperor, founded a Law School in 1832. Since that time the nobility have endowed several professorships of law in the universities; and the names of N. Krylof and Manoshkin have become favourably known in this department.

In Statistics the name of Arsenyef is an authority. Many valuable contributions are to be found in Stepanof's Description of the Government of Yennissei, and in various Russian periodicals; especially in the annals of several Bureaus, which are from time to time published by the government, and the Statistical Annuals edited by the Academy.

The literature of Travels cannot well be very rich at the present day, in a country where travelling to foreign lands meets with so many difficulties; and where even travels in the interior are at least not made very easy. To the most valuable productions in the first department belong: Norof's Journey to the Holy Land, St. Pet. 1838; Davidof's to Greece and Italy; Demidof's to Moldavia and Wallachia; Korf's to Persia; Wcewolodski to the East and through Europe; Gretsch to the Western countries of Europe, etc. Two collections of *old* travels, viz. one containing those made by Russians to foreign countries, among which is the description of a journey to the Holy Land in the twelfth century; another comprising the accounts of foreigners who travelled in Russia in olden times; have also recently been published.

Modern works of travels in Russia have been written by A. Demidof, Baer, Böthlingk, Glagolyef, Kavelin, and others. Most of these journeys were made for certain scientific purposes. Mouravyef's Pilgrimage to the holy places of Russia must be classified rather as a work of religion.

And here a short survey of this latter branch of Russian literature may naturally be subjoined. To it belong the other works of the writer just mentioned; who is attached to his own church with an almost fanatical enthusiasm. They are, first, a History of the Greek Church; secondly, Letters on the Greek Church Service. An elaborate History of the Russian Patriarchate, published a few years ago, is ascribed to the bishop Philarete, a clergyman who is said to have shown an immoderate zeal in making proselytes in the Baltic provinces. A biographical History of the Russian Saints, by Yeristof, belongs also here. Of theological *science* there can hardly be a trace, in a country where all free investigation in exegetical matters is cut off. Theological literature is entirely confined to synodal orations and some ascetic writings. The spirit of the present age in Russia is strictly orthodox; and the monocracy of the Greek Church is the great object for which clergy and laity exert themselves; especially in the Baltic provinces. Among sermons, those of Innocenz, vicar of the metropolitan of Kief, are much admired.

Literary history has recently been a favourite branch. Polevoi, Gretsch, Schevyrof, Maximovitch, Nadeshdin, Nikitenko;

and, in respect to languages and antiquities, Kalaidovitch, Vostokof and Köppen, the latter of German extraction, and mentioned in the preceding period; are the names which have most weight in these matters.

We have at last come back to *belles lettres*, the department of literature by which the genius of a nation is most distinctly characterized. The tendencies which in Russia prevail in the other branches, viz. a revival of interest for all that is native, Slavic, or relating to the past; the reaction from a period of fondness for all that was foreign and outlandish; is very clearly perceptible also in this portion of literature. Yet the Russians, once forcibly thrust into the way of *imitation* by their great Tzar, appear here even now only as imitators; and are still far from having found the path back to their simple popular poetry.

After this remark it cannot surprise us, that towards the close of the last, and especially at the beginning of the present period, the historical novel was cultivated with particular fondness; and was almost exclusively devoted to *Russian* history. T. Bulgarin, P. Svinyin, Sagoskin, Massalski, wrote the most approved works of that kind. More recently the novelists have rather returned to the description of morals and manners, as their more appropriate province. Pawlof, Prince Odoyeski, Lermontof, Gogol, Laschetnikof, Weltmann, Dahl, who writes under the name of Kozak Luganski, are the most popular writers of tales. Karamzin and Shukofski are still considered as models in this department.

We must not forget to mention here the unhappy youth Alexander Bestushef; who, as lieutenant in one of the Petersburg regiments, was, like his friend Rileyef, implicated in the conspiracy of 1825. He was deprived of his nobility and illustrious name, and sent to the mines of Siberia; afterwards, as a species of pardon, he was placed as a common soldier in the army of the Caucasus, where he rose to the rank of an officer and fell soon after by the balls of the Therkesses. He had been well known to his countrymen as the editor of a favourite Annual, entitled the *Polar Star;* and as the author of a very spirited and clear survey of Russian literature, distinguished by characteristic sketches of some of their principal poets. The name of Bestushef was buried; but its bearer succeeded a second time in acquiring a literary reputation under the name of Alexander Marlinski. His Sketches of the Caucasus and of Siberia, his tales entitled Amulat Beg and Mullah Nur, are animated and spirited pictures of scenes quite novel and fresh. He has been compared to the German novelist Spindler; but, although this latter has the advantage in respect to invention, we think Marlinsky *far* superior to him in a poetical respect. There is a vigour, a freshness, an originality, in some of his descriptions, which would class him among true poets, even when stripped of the novelty of the scenery among which they are laid, and which gives them indeed a peculiar attraction. Nothing was more natural nor even more honourable to the Russian public, than that, as an unavoidable effect of the pity and interest felt for this young writer, his real talent should have been for a short time overrated. But even after his death, it seems that the government regarded this enthusiasm with suspicion; for in a literary collection in which the unprinted works of one hundred writers are promised,[44] accompanied by their portraits, Marlinsky's portrait was not permitted to appear.

The attention of the Russian literati has been for some time directed mainly by the Germans to their own treasures of popular poetry. They are particularly rich in nursery tales, for which the nation indeed has always had a great fondness; but which, during an age of a false pedantic taste, were after all not

[44] *Sto Literaturow, etc.*, edited by Smirdin, Petersb. 1840, etc.

thought worthy of literary preservation until of late. In close connection with this subject is the cultivation of popular dialects. Grebenko and Kwitka, the latter under the name of Osnovianenko, wrote their charming novels in the Malo-Russian or Ruthenian dialect. Several writers of talent, natives of Malo-Russia, endeavoured to establish their language as a literary language in opposition to the Great Russian. The judiciousness of these proceedings, especially as the Russian literature has hardly passed from childhood to youth, would seem very questionable, even if their practicability was settled.

As to poetry, the reader will be surprised to hear, that Russian critics themselves think the short-lived flower of the Russian soil already in danger of fading; the productiveness of their poets being already apparently on the decline. No genius has risen as a rival to Pushkin. Alexander Pushkin, born 1799, showed his uncommon talents early; he was educated at one of the imperial Institutes, and was in the service of the government; when an Ode to Liberty, written in too bold a spirit, induced the emperor Alexander to banish him from St. Petersburg. He obtained however employment in the southern provinces of Russia; and life in these wild and poetical regions was more favourable to the development of his genius, than that of the capital ever could have been. All his poetry bears strong testimony to Byron's influence; but he would be wrongly judged if taken as a mere imitator of that great poet. His poetical tales, *Ruslan and Ludmilla*, from the heroic times of Russia; *The Prisoner of the Mountains*, a Caucasian scene (1823); and the *Fountain of Baktshiserai*, a Tartar Story (1824); have each great beauties. The emperor Nicholas, when at Moscow on the occasion of his coronation, recalled him, and showed himself his patron. He made him one of the historiographers of the empire; and the archives were opened to him. The effect on the whole was not favourable to the poet's genius. The first production after his return to fashionable life was 'Eugene Onegin,' a novel in verse, the life of *un homme blasé*. Of this Byronic tendency, his Prisoner, and a great many of his small poems likewise, bear strong evidence. And it is this feature chiefly, which, in turn, Pushkin's followers and imitators have seized upon; for instance, Lermontof. It it is painful to see, how, instead of the freshness, the vigour, the joyfulness, which we ought to meet in the representatives of a young and rising literature, resting on the foundation of a rich, uncorrrupted, original language, we find in them the ennui, the dissatisfaction, and the indifference of a set of *roués* disgusted with life. It seems as if after having emptied the cup of the vanities of the world to the very dregs, this world, which has nothing left for their enjoyment, is despised by them; unfortunately, however, without having educated their minds for a better one. In his later productions, especially in his *Boris Godunof*, a drama, which may be rather called a tragical historical picture than a regular tragedy, Pushkin showed a more elevated mind, and a more objective way of viewing things. His last work, we believe, was his *Istorija Bunta*, History of the Insurrection of Pugatshef; no noble struggle for liberty, but a mere mutiny. He died in St. Petersburg in 1835, a short time after a marriage of choice and inclination; in a duel occasioned by a fit of jealousy, maliciously provoked by some of the courtiers.

Other successful lyrical poets of this period are, Chomiakof, Baratinski, N. Jazikof, A. Timofeyef, Benedictof, Sokolovski, A. Podolinski, Lucian Jakubovitch, A. Ilitshevski, etc. Several ladies also have recently mounted the Pegasus. A Princess Volkonski, a Countess Rostoptshin, a Miss Teplef, are favourably mentioned; as are also Anna Bunin and a Mrs. Pawlof, the latter as a happy translator. A Mrs. Helene Han, who writes under the name of Zeneide B., is compared to George Sand. Nor must we forget two natural poets so called, that is, men from the people, who write verses; one named Alipanof, born a serf, and the other Kolzof. The lyric poets enumerated in the last period are all mostly still alive and continue to write.

The very limited productiveness of the Russian poets is however a very striking and discouraging feature. While in the animated forest of German poetry, even during the most trying struggles of the times, a full chorus of songs and ballads resounds from every branch, we hear from Russian groves only solitary voices, and these voices seem to be exhausted almost as soon as they are heard. A volume of twenty sheets is in general considered in Russia as quite a respectable collection. Pushkin is almost the only one of their poets, whose very thoughts were verses.

The more exuberant, however, do we find the productiveness of some of their dramatic writers. Polevoi, whom we have mentioned as the editor of the "Telegraph," and as a keen critic who exerted great influence, poured out a whole flood of tragedies and comedies. To judge from the applause with which they were received on the stage, the writer was more successful in this branch, than in his historical enterprises. Besides him, Lenski, Koni, Feodorof, and others, as well as numerous translators, furnished provision for the stage. The most respectable talent was shown by Kukolnik; of whom his countrymen have a very high idea, but to whom foreign critics assign rather a lyric than a dramatic genius. The reverential attachment of Russians to their monarch is exhibited in the very titles chosen by several dramatic poets. One of Kukolnik's dramas bears the rather prolix name, "The hand of the Almighty shelters the Tzar." A piece of Glinka is called, "Our Life for the Tzar," etc.

The popular poetry which is scattered over all Slavic countries, has at last received the attention due to it. That of Russia is not so early as that of some other branches of the same family; with the exception however of certain songs for harvest, weddings, festivals, funerals, and some other like verses, sung or recited on certain stated occasions. There are among them some, which in their most essential portions are derived from pagan times. The Ukraine, and indeed Malo-Russia in general, and all the regions where Ruthenian tribes have settled, are particularly rich in popular poetry. Valuable miscellaneous collections have been made by Prince Tzertelef, Maximovitch, Sacharof, by the Polish literati Bielowski and Siemienski, Bodianski, etc.[45]

To the philological works enumerated on page 84, we may add the following productions of the present period: Brosset, on the Literature and Language of Armenia and Georgia;[46] also the Dictionaries of these languages by Chodubashef and Tschubinof, the latter (Georgian or Grusinian) the first which was ever published; a Chinese grammar by the priest Hyacinth, who prepared likewise a history of China some years ago, which we must suppose has been published. A new Turkish dictionary was published in 1830 by Rhasis. Prince Alexander Handsheri prepared another of French, Arabic, Turkish, and Persian; in aid of which the Sultan subscribed for 200 copies. Sjogren, an academician, known by his Studies on the Finnish Language and Literature, devoted himself in connection with the latter to the Caucasian idioms, and published the results in the Transactions of the Academy. A Turco-Tartar grammar was written by Kasembeg, a Tartar by birth, but educated in European Russia, and professor of those languages at the university of Kazan.

In the different departments of natural science, although the Russians may be still called beginners, their progress has recently been immense. This has resulted in a great measure from the judicious plan of the government, in sending out annually a cer-

---

[45] See in Part IV.

[46] In connection with this work stands the Grammar by the same writer, written in French: *Elémens de la Langue Georgienne*, 1838.

tain number of young men to study at German universities. Philosophy as a science was formerly despised, and considered as the exclusive property of German pedants and bookworms;[47] but since German philosophy has seemed to take a more practical turn, it has begun to excite more interest. The government, which in the first affright after the conspiracy of 1825, had abolished all the professorships of philosophy, began to relax; and went even so far as to send young men to Germany for these studies, and to re-establish the chairs in several of the Russian universities. It was, however, still regarded as a *dangerous* science; and the learning which some young clergymen acquired in it—Golubinski, Gabriel, and above all Sidonski—was carefully watched, and proved of little value to the public.

In regard to periodical literature, the number of *political* journals is of course very small. That which most highly extols the merits and exploits of the Russians is always considered as the best, and is most patronized by the government and the nation. In Russia the *praise* of one's country and *love* for it are regarded as synonymous ideas. The literary journals, most of which are of a miscellaneous character, are more in number, and are generally conducted with some critical talent. Those of a purely scientific character are rarely sustained longer than a few years; for instance, the very valuable Bibliographical Journal, edited by P. Köppen in 1825–26. The ephemeral race of *Annuals*, those vehicles of superficial taste and knowledge, early took broad possession of the Russian Parnassus. In the year 1839, eight hundred and eighty different works were published in Russia; of which seventy-three only were translations. The

---

[47] There are a few honourable exceptions. The work *Essais philosophiques sur l'homme, publiés par De Jakob,* Halle 1818, although written in French, was the production of a Russian, the late writer Poletika, brother of the former Russian ambassador of that name in this country.

number of journals and periodicals, which in general are quite thick pamphlets, amounted only to fifty-three. In 1842 these latter had increased to one hundred and thirty-nine; nearly three times as many as in the former year. Of these 98 were in the Russian language, 22 in German, 8 in French, 1 in Italian, 3 in Polish, and 3 in Lettonian.[48]

In a recent work on Russian literature, by F. Otto,[49] the Lexicon of authors subjoined comprises about 250 names; and the English translator speaks of having seen a list of nearly *twelve hundred* more in the author's hands. We are compelled to regard this last statement with some distrust; especially when we perceive, that among the names printed in the Lexicon, at least *thirty* are Germans and Poles who wrote *on* Russian matters, but not *in* Russian. It is also singular to find among Russian *authors*, not only the Grand-duke Constantine of Kief, because he was a *patron* of science, and first caused the Old Slavonic Bible to be printed; but also even the old traditional bard Bojan, mentioned in the ancient epic of Igor![50]

The recent movements in Europe have of course built up still higher the Chinese wall which surrounds the Russian empire. Even in anticipation of them, the government had been seized with a new shock of fear; and attempted to shut out the intrusive new lights. This was indicated by several strong and very unpopular measures; among which we may here mention, that travellers in foreign countries were called home, and the

---

[48] According to official reports, more than seven millions of volumes of Russian books were printed in the ten years from 1833 to 1843; and four and a half millions of foreign books were imported. During the same ten years 784 new schools were established. In 1842, there were in the Russian empire 2166 schools of all kinds; among them *six* universities.

[49] F. Otto, *History of Russian Literature, with a Lexicon of Russian Authors. Translated from the German by the late G. Cox.* Oxford 1839.

[50] See above, p. 51.

number of students at each university was suddenly limited to *three hundred.*

This is not the place to enlarge on the distinguished merits which foreigners, and especially Germans, have acquired in relation to Russian history, statistics, etc. But their labours in relation to the language, form a part of the literature to which they were devoted; and cannot of course be separated from the works of native writers. The most distinguished names in this department are again Germans, viz. Heym, Vater, Tappe, Puchmayer, etc. The catalogue of elementary works upon the Russian language, is too long to be inserted here; we limit ourselves therefore to those only which are written in English, and the best in German and French. The English grammars and dictionaries of the Russian, are indeed so few, that an American or Englishman would hardly succeed in acquiring a full knowledge of the language, except through the medium of the German and French. The first Russian Grammar, however, that was ever printed, was published at Oxford. We give the titles of this and of the other principal grammars and lexicons of the Russian language, in the note below.[51]

---

[51] This was Ludolf's *Grammatica Russica et manuductio ad linguam Slavonicam,* Oxon. 1696.—English Russian Grammars are, *Novaya ross. Gram. dlja Anglitshani,* 'Russian Grammar for Englishmen,' St. Petersburg, 1822. Heard's *Practical Grammar of the Russian Language,* St. Pet. 1827. 2 vols. 8vo.—German Russian Grammars are: Heym's *Russ. Sprachlehre für Deutsche,* Riga, 1789, 1794, 1804. Vater's *Prakt. Gramm. der russ. Sprache,* Leipz. 1808, 1814. Tappe's *Neue russ. Sprachlehre für Deutsche,* St. Pet. 1810, 1814, 1820. Schmidt's *Prakt. russ. Grammatik,* Leipz. 1813. Puchmayer's *Lehrgebäude der russ. Sprache,* last edit. Prague 1843. Gretsch, *Grundregeln der russ. Sprache,* from the Russian by Oldekop, 1828. The newest German Russian Grammars are: J. E. Schmidt's *Russische Sprachlehre, und Leitfaden zur Erlernung, etc.* Leipz. 1831. *Noakovski Grammatica Rossiiskaya,* Lipsk. 1836. A Malo-Russian Grammar, *Malo-Ross. Grammatica,* was

published by Pawlofski, St. Pet. 1818.—FRENCH Russian Grammars are: Maudru's *Elémens raisonnés de la langue Russe*, Paris 1802. Langan's *Manual de la langue Russe*, St. Pet. 1825. Charpentier's *Elémens de la langue Russe*, St. Pet. 1768 to 1805, five editions. Gretsch, *Grammaîre raisonnée de la langue Russe*, par Reiff, St. Pet. 1828.

DICTIONARIES.—ENGLISH. Parenoga's *Lex. Anglinsko-ross.* and *Russian-English Lexicon*, 4 vols. 1808–17. Zdanof's *Angl.-ross.* and *Russian-Engl. Dict.* St. Pet. 1784. Constantinon's *Russian Grammar and Dict.* 3 vols. 8vo. Lond. *A Russian-Engl.* and *Engl.-Russ. Dict.* 18mo. Leipz. Tauchn. 1846. — GERMAN. Heyne's *Russisch-Deutsch und Deutsch-Russ. Wörterb.* Riga 1795–98. The same writer's *Russ. Deutsch and Frauz. Wörterb.* in several forms and editions, Riga 1796 to 1812; also Moscow 1826; last improved edit. Leipz. Tauchn. 1844. Oldekop's *Russ.-Deutsch und Deutsch-Russ. Wörterb.* St. Pet. 1825. J. A. E. Schmidt's *Russ.-Deutsch und Deutsch-Russ. Wörterb.* Leipz. Tauchn, 1841. The same writer's *Poln. Russ. Deutsch. Wörterb.* 2 vols. 8vo. Breslau 1834–6. — FRENCH. Tatishtchef's *Nouveau Dict. Franc.-Russe*, etc. 2 vols. 8vo. Moscow 1832.

CHAPTER II.

HISTORY OF THE ILLYRICO-SERVIAN LANGUAGE.

SECTION I.

LANGUAGE AND LITERATURE OF THE ILLYRICO-SERVIANS PROPER.

THE literature of the western Slavo-Servians has hitherto been altogether separated from that of their brethren of the oriental church, and treated as a distinct branch.[1] Their language,

---

[1] This portion of the Slavic race was formerly more commonly known under the general appellation of *Illyrians*. With the exception of the Bulgarians, who never have been comprehended under it, this name has alternately been applied to the Southern Slavic nations; sometimes only to the Dalmatians and Slavonians; sometimes to them together with the Croatians and Vindes; by others again to the Turkish Servians and Bosnians, etc. The old Illyrians, i. e. the inhabitants of the Roman province Illyricum, were not Slavi, but a people related to the old Thracians, the forefathers of the present Albanians; see Schaffarik *Gesch.* p. 23, n. 2. *Illyricum Magnum* comprised in the fourth century nearly all the Roman provinces of eastern Europe. Napoleon affected to renew the names and titles of the ancient Roman empire, and called the territory ceded to him by Austria in 1809, viz. Carniola and all the country between the Adriatic, the Save, and the Turkish empire, his Illyrian provinces, and their inhabitants Illyrians. In the year 1815 a new kingdom of Illyria was founded as an Austrian province, comprehending Carniola, Carinthia, and Trieste with its territory. It was partly on account of this indefiniteness, that the name of *Illyrians* had been entirely relinquished by modern

however, being essentially the same, we do not see why the rather accidental circumstance, that the former use the Roman letters, while the latter adhere to the Cyrillic alphabet, should be a sufficient reason for such a separation. The literature of neither of them has as yet treasures enough, to renounce willingly the claims which their mutual and naturally rich though uncultivated language gives to the one upon the productions of the other. We now proceed, in a short historical introduction, to show the origin of this separation; after making a few preliminary remarks on the character of the language as a whole, unaffected by its division into different dialects, not more distinct indeed from each other than is the case in almost every other living idiom.

The Servian language is spoken by about five millions of people. It extends, with some slight variations of dialect, over the Turkish and Austrian provinces of Servia, Bosnia, Herzegovina, Montenegro, and Dalmatia; over Slavonia and the eastern part of Croatia. It is further the property of several thousands, who emigrated from their own country on account of the Turkish oppression, and are now settled as colonists along the southwestern bank of the Danube, from Semlin to St. André near Buda. The southern sky, and the beauties of natural scenery existing throughout nearly all these regions, so favourable in general to the development of poetical genius, appear also to have exerted a happy influence on the language. While it yields to none of

---

philologists; until it was quite recently again taken up by some Croatian and Dalmatian writers. In its stead the name of *Servians*, or more properly *Serbians, Serbs*, has been adopted as a general appellation by the best authorities. See below in § 1, on the Literature of the Servians of the Greek Church. The word *Srb, Serb, Sorab*, has been alternately derived from *Srp*, scythe; from *Siberi, Sever*, north; from *Sarmat;* from *Serbulja*, a kind of shoe or sock; from *servus*, servant, etc. The true derivation has not yet been settled. See Dobrovsky's History of the Bohemian Language, 1818; and also his *Inst. Ling. Slav.* 1822.

the other Slavic dialects in richness, clearness, and precision, it far surpasses all of them in euphony. The Servian has often been called the *Italian* among the other Slavic idioms. Comparisons of this sort are always superficial, and tend to give a false view of the character of an object. Be this as it may, the Servian is decidedly the most melodious of the Slavic languages, rich in vowels, and abounding alike in soft and powerful accents. The accumulation of consonants, with which the other dialects are so often reproached, is rarely, if ever, to be met with in Servian. The reader may compare the Servian *wetar* with *wjtr*, *krilo* with *krzydlo* or *skrzydlo*, *pao* with *padl*, etc. Those who ascribe this mildness of the Servian language to the Italian neighbourhood of Dalmatia, forget that the eastern Servians are remote from Italy. It is true that the dialects of these latter are at the same time full of Turcisms; but these are mere excrescences, which may easily be removed without touching the essential structure of the language. The Turkish words adopted into the Servian, are mostly nouns, and verbs derived from them; and may naturally be explained by their political relation to the Turks during so many centuries. If we may confide in a remark of the profound philologist J. Grimm, *some* foreign ingredients are useful and even necessary to languages. They act as a cement, and fill up gaps; nay, they not seldom serve to give to the expression colouring and pliancy. The attention of the civilized world, although directed at the beginning of the present century to the Servians and their heroic struggles, has only recently been excited in respect to their language; and this through the efforts of a single individual. We shall have more to say on this point in the section devoted to the literature of the Servians of the eastern church.

The ancient Illyricum comprised all the countries situated between the Adriatic and the Black Sea, and along the Danube and Save.[2] Towards the middle of the seventh century, we find this vast country mostly occupied by a Slavic people of one and the same race, alternately called Bulgarians, Croatians, and Servians. We find also six kingdoms gradually established by them: Bulgaria, Servia, Bosnia (Rama), Croatia, Slavonia, and Dalmatia; some of them powerful and of great influence in their time, but now and long since sunk into ruin, and existing only as Turkish or Austrian provinces. An impenetrable night rests on the early history of these regions; and if the judicious criticism of modern philologists has thrown comparatively some light on this general topic, still, their investigations have been of little consequence for the history of the language. All that it concerns us to note here, is, that as early as the seventh century a part of these nations were already Christians, converted by Romish priests. Among the remainder, Christianity as taught by Greek missionaries found a welcome reception in the eighth and ninth centuries, and soon was fully established. The oriental Servians had the chief seat of their power in the present Turkish province of Serf-Vilayeti; and governed by princes called *Shupans*, we see them in a constant war of resistance against the Greek emperors, and during several centuries also against the powerful Khans of Bulgaria; now conquered, subjugated, destroyed almost to annihilation, but recovering with effort and rising again in power, with such energy as to enable them under the great Tzar, Stephan Dushan, not only to hold all their neighbours in awe, but to take a menacing position towards Byzantium itself, and dictate conditions of peace to the imploring envoys of that proud imperial court. But this brilliant point of Servian glory, which even now after five hundred years still lives in the hearts of the people, and is the subject of a thousand legends and songs, was only a meteor. It vanished in almost

---

[2] See above, p. 9 sq. and the preceding note.

the same moment that it appeared. Stephan's immediate successors, enfeebled by their domestic dissensions, sunk under the superior forces of the Turks, who had broken into Europe thirty-four years earlier. They soon became the conquerors of the Servians, though not without fierce and bloody struggles; and they still remain their masters and oppressors.[3]

The western Servians were early divided into small states, some of which adopted an aristocratic republican form of constitution. Among these, only the republic of Ragusa requires to be mentioned here, as the cradle of the Dalmatian branch of Servian literature. The local situation of these western states made them dependent on Hungary; and thus Croatia, Slavonia, Dalmatia, sometimes under the title of kingdoms, and now as dukedoms, became at length mere provinces of that larger kingdom, and ultimately of the Austrian empire. Bosnia and Herzegovina, which form the boundary between the Servians of the East and West, were subject to the influence of both; and are to the present day divided in religion and in language.

1. *Literature of the Servians of the Oriental or Greek Church.*

However small the circuit of country, properly called Servia, is in proportion to the whole extent over which the southern Slavi are spread, the name of Servians nevertheless appears to

---

[3] The Servians, however, under the government of their own energetic countryman, Prince Milosh, for some years enjoyed a certain degree of freedom, which no doubt has had good results for the mental life of the nation. A good view of their country, constitution, and literature, is given in a modern German work: *Reise nach Serbien im Spätherbst* 1829, by Otto von Birch, Berlin 1830. See also *Servia und Belgrade in* 1843–44, by A. A. Paton, Lond. 1845.

modern philologists as the best adapted for being employed as the common name of them all. Dobrovsky thinks it even appropriate to become the general appellation for all Slavic nations. Although of obscure derivation, it is at least sufficiently ascertained that it is of pure Slavic origin; glorious associations are attached to it; it is moreover still a living name, while the learned appellation of *Illyrians*, formerly more in use, is dead; and that of *Bosnians*, preferred by some Dalmatian writers, rests upon no satisfactory grounds. The name of Servians, however, was never, till recently, applied to the Dalmatians. It is indeed still rejected by themselves; and they continue to call themselves *Illyrians*.

Under the present head, besides the Servians proper, of whom great numbers have emigrated in early times to Hungary, are also strictly comprised the Bosnians, the greater portion of the inhabitants of Herzegovina, the Montenegrins or Czernogortzi, and the Slavonians of the Greek Church. These all use the same language and alphabet; but the four latter have no distinct literature, except some collections of popular poetry.

The literature of the eastern Servians, the result of their intellectual life as a nation, does not yet date back a hundred years; nay, if regarded from another point of view, it is not yet forty years old. Up to that time, all the Servians belonging to the Greek Church, notwithstanding the honourable example of Russia to the contrary, had written in the Old or Church Slavonic; or, in more modern times, in a language mixed up from this latter and several other dialects. Schaffarik remarks, that out of about 400 Servian books printed between the years 1742, or more properly 1761, and 1826, about one eighth part are written in Old Slavic; another eighth in the common dialect of the people; while all the rest vary between these two in innumerable shades and degrees.[4] This eighth part written in ordinary Servian,

[4] See Schaffarik *Gesch.* p. 217.

and essentially the same language which the Dalmatians and the greater part of the Croats speak, are all of very recent date. Indeed, with the exception of a single writer, Obradovitch, who found no immediate followers, the dialect of the people was in general despised by the clergy and those who laid claim to education, as being wholly unfit for books, and (as Vuk Stephanovitch strongly expresses himself) only proper for "cowherds and swineherds." How the once flourishing literature of Ragusa could ever have sunk into oblivion to such a degree, is hardly to be conceived; as indeed, in general, the division so sharply drawn in respect to literature between those two branches of the same people, while they were still bound together by the strong ties of one and the same language of common life and in part also of the same government, belongs among the most remarkable facts in literary history.

The most ancient document of the Servian Old Slavic language, is out of the middle of the thirteenth century, viz. the Hexaemeron of Basilius, with a preface by John, exarch of Bulgaria. Then follow the "Acts of the Apostles," written by the hieromonach Damian, A. D. 1324. Of higher historical importance are some secular writings from the end of the thirteenth to the middle of the fourteenth century, viz. a genealogical register of the Servian princes and the events of their reigns, called *Radoslov*, written by archbishop Daniel; a similar work called the *Tzarostavnick;* and above all the statutes of Tzar Dushan the Powerful, A. D. 1336–56. These statutes, dated from the year 6837, or A. D. 1349, not only afford us a good survey of the constitution of the Servian kingdom, but are a remarkable contribution to the history of its moral state at that early period. The philanthropist cannot but perceive, with satisfaction, the rare union that reigns in these laws of stern justice and true Christian benevolence, attempting to alleviate those evils which it was not in the power of an individual to abolish,—

the hardships of slavery, the insecurity of property peculiar to those barbarous times, and those rash and bloody acts of self-protection, which are preferred by the powerful all over the world to the slower steps of avenging justice. It is indeed remarkable to observe, how these statutes not only counteracted the grosser vices and crimes, (which for the most part is the only object of laws,) but also favoured the characteristic virtues of the times, for instance hospitality. One statute ordains, that when a traveller asked for night-quarters at the dwelling of a landed proprietor and was not admitted, he had the right to take lodgings in his village wherever he pleased; and did he lose any thing, not his host, but the proprietor who had refused to harbour him, was bound to remunerate the loss.[6]

The monks of this and the following centuries must have written a great deal; as is proved by the many manuscripts that still lie accumulated in the numerous Servian and Macedonian monasteries,—the mere remnant of those which perished in the long tempests of bloody wars and desolating conflagrations. About fifty years after the invention of printing, some of the church books from time to time were published in Servia and Syrmia. The earliest Servian print extant is from the year 1493, viz. an Octateuch, published at Zenta in Herzegovina. In Russia they did not begin to print until sixty years later. In 1552 the Gospels were printed in Belgrade; in 1562 another edition in Negromont. But these faint signs of life soon became extinct; and we hear no longer of the least trace of literature among the Servians of the Turkish empire. Among the Austrian Servians also, literature seems to have been equally dead; with the exception of a History of Servia, written and left in manu-

---

[6] These statutes were first printed by Raitch, in his great work on Slavic history (see Note 8); and translated by Engel in his History of Hungary and the adjacent Territories, Vol. 2, p. 293.

script by George Brankovitch, the last despot of that country, towards the close of the seventeenth century. A genealogical work published by Dshefarovitch at Vienna in 1742, had to be engraved, for the want of proper types. In the year 1755, under the reign of Maria Theresa, when some attention began to be paid to the schools of her Illyrian provinces, the archbishop of Carlovitz was compelled to have Smotrisky's Grammar[6] printed in Walachia, because no Slavic types were to be found in the whole Austrian empire. Some years afterwards, A. D. 1758, a private Slavic press was founded at Venice. In Austria, Cyrillic-Slavonic books could not be printed earlier than A. D. 1771, when a printing office was established at Vienna; the monopoly of which for all Slavo-Servian scientific works throughout the empire, was given to the university of Buda. From this one point, therefore, the whole literary cultivation of the Servians of the oriental church in the Austrian empire, could alone proceed.[7]

After the partial revival of Servian literature in 1758, a considerable number of works were composed; and there are among them not a few, which, notwithstanding the mixed and unsettled idiom in which they are written, attest the general capacity of the nation, and may serve as imperfect specimens of the mass of talent buried there. Among the historical writers, we must name above all J. Raitch. He wrote on many different subjects; and also left behind him a whole library of theological manuscripts. His 'History of the Slavic Nations'[8] has given

---

[6] See above, in the History of the Old Slavic Language, p. 44.

[7] There is however still another Cyrillic printing office attached to an Armenian convent in Vienna. Since the printing of Vuk's second edition of the Servian popular songs at Leipsic, several other Servian books have also been printed there. The Vladika of Montenegro has also established a printing office at his residence of Tzetinja. Vuk's "Proverbs" have been printed there.

[8] The complete title of this valuable work is: *Istorja raznich Slaven-*

him a lasting reputation. Other historical writers of some merit, are, Kengelatz, Magarashevitch, Julinatz, Solaritch.[9] Writers on different subjects of natural philosophy and medicine, are, Orphelin, Stoïkovitch, Beritch, Jankovitch, P. Hadshitch, etc. On statistics and geography the above-mentioned Solaritch, Vuitch, Bulitch, Popovitch, and others. In the department of theology, we hardly meet with a single book of a doctrinal character; but there are quite a number on ethics. The principal writers of the language, therefore, may perhaps be more properly arranged under the heads of philosophy (comprehending logic), rhetoric, ethics, etc. as Obradovitch, Raitch, Terlaitch, Lazarevitch, Vuitch, Davidovitch, Masovitch, etc.[10]

Poetry and belles-lettres being more dependent on the state of the language than purely scientific works, we can proceed no further, without first making our readers acquainted with the recent innovations of a few patriotic individuals.

It was Dositheï Obradovitch, born A. D. 1739 in the Banat of Temeswar, who first among the eastern Servians ventured to write books in the despised language of the country. The fortunes of this person are, in several respects, of uncommon interest. Brought up in a monastic school, he became monk when he was only fourteen years old. After several years of severe struggles, he fled. For twenty-five years he travelled over all

---

skich narodov nairatchvedshe Chorvatov, Bolgarov, i Srbov, Vienna 1792–95, 4 vols.

[9] The writings of this very productive philologist and historian are however more remarkable for boldness and singularity of assertion, than for depth. In his *Rimljani slavenstvovavshii,* Buda 1818, he undertakes to derive the entire Latin language from the Slavic. In an earlier work, written 1809, he contends that the German language was a corruption of the Slavic dialects spoken on the Elbe.

[10] The reader will find a more complete catalogue of the Servian writers and their works, in O. v. Birch's Travels; see above, p. 107, n. 3.

Europe; and then returned to his comparatively barbarous native land, where he died in 1811, as inspector of the schools, and the instructor of the children of the celebrated Kara George. He left several works.

A far greater influence, however, has been exerted on Servian literature by Dem. Davidovitch and Vuk Stephanovitch Karadshitch, who have not only followed the same literary course, but were the first to defend both theoretically and practically the principle, that the Servians ought to *write* as they *speak*. Their boldness met with strong and decided opposition from the old school; and the contest and rivalry which have been the consequence, although tending for a time to prevent the progress of the good cause, cannot but have, ere long, beneficial results, by exciting the minds of the people to a higher activity than they have had until then occasion to exert.

Davidovitch published from 1814 to 1822 a Servian newspaper in Vienna, not exclusively of a political character, by which he intended to diffuse information on various subjects; the first undertaking of the kind in his language. His influence however is not confined to the language alone; as secretary of Prince Milosh, then at the head of the Servians, his influence on the general cultivation of his countrymen was very decided.

Vuk Stephanovitch Karadshitch, born 1786 in Turkish Servia, is the author of the first Oriental-Servian grammar and dictionary; and in the arrangement of the former has manifested the true spirit of a genuine grammarian. Besides these he has written several works of value, a biography of Prince Milosh, a series of annuals, a volume on the Proverbs, and idiomatic phrases of the Servians, etc.[11] But the best proof which he could give of the beauty, richness, and perfectibility of the

[11] *Narodne Serpske Poslovitze*, Zetinya 1836.

vulgar Servian dialect, is his Collection of the Servian popular Songs, in four volumes, comprising nevertheless only about the fourth or fifth part of the similar treasures hidden among the mountains of his country. In making this collection, he very judiciously wrote down only those songs which he had himself caught from the lips of the Servian peasantry. There had already been a rumour among the literati of Europe, for more than fifty years, of the beauty and singularity of the Illyrian national songs, founded mostly on the communications of Italian travellers and the citations of Dalmatian dictionaries. Herder, in his valuable Collection of popular Poetry, gave two historical fragments from the work of a Dalmatian clergyman, A. Cacich.[12] Goethe also has a beautiful tale, taken from Abbate Fortis' Travels among the Morlachians. Both translated by means of the French; and although this double translation could not possibly do justice to the originals, they were sufficiently admired. But when Vuk's collection appeared, and a part of its contents was made intelligible to the civilized world by a translation attempted by the author of this work, imperfect and deficient as any translation of popular poetry must necessarily ever be, the public and the critics were nevertheless alike struck with the strong expression of the high and incomparable beauties of nature. All that the other Slavic nations, or the Germans, the Scotch, and the Spaniards, possess of popular poetry, can at the utmost be compared with the lyrical part of the Servian songs, called by them *female* songs, because they are sung only by females and youths; but the long epic extemporized compositions, by which a peasant bard, sitting in a large circle of other peasants, in unpremeditated but perfectly regular and harmonious verse, celebrates the heroic deeds of their ances-

---

[12] See below in § 2. b, Dalmatian Literature.

tors or cotemporaries, has no parallel in the whole history of literature since the days of Homer.[13]

Vuk Stephanovitch Karadshitch,[14] in his successful attempts

---

[13] See more on Servian popular poetry in Part IV. The title of Vuk's collection, a part of which appeared 1814–15 at Vienna, in two small volumes, is *Narodne Srpske pjesme*, Lpzg. 1823–24, three volumes. A fourth volume was published at Vienna 1833, with a very instructive preface. Some of these remarkable songs have been made known to the English public in Bowring's Servian Popular Poetry, London 1827. This little collection contains also an able and spirited introduction, which serves to give a clear view not only of the state of the Servians in particular, but also of the relation of the Slavic nations to each other in general; with the exception of some mistakes in respect to classification.—In Germany a general interest for Servian national poetry was excited by Goethe; see his ***Kunst und Alterthum***, Vol. V. Nos. I and II. German translations are: *Volkslieder der Serben*, by Talvj, 2 vols. Halle 1825–26; from which work Bowring seems chiefly to have translated. *Die Wila*, by Gerhardt, 2 vols. Lpzg. 1828. These two works contain nearly all the songs published by Vuk, in his first three volumes; but only half of those he has collected. *Serbische Volkslieder*, by v. Götze, St. Pet. and Lpzg. 1827. *Serbische Hochzeitlieder*, by Eugen Wesely, 1826. A French translation of these songs does not yet exist, although they have excited a deep interest among the literati of France. The work *la Guzla*, published at Paris in 1827 and purporting to contain translations of Dalmatian national songs, is not genuine; it was written by the French poet Mérimée, with much talent indeed, but without any knowledge of the Servian language.

[14] That is: Wolf, son of Stephan, belonging to the family of the Karadshians, inhabitants of a certain district or village. The Servians in Servia proper and Bosnia have not yet any family names. Those who emigrated in early years to other countries mostly adopted their fathers' names with the suffix of *vitch* as a family name; for instance Markovitch, Gregorovitch, i. q. Markson, Gregorson, etc. The Servian subjects of Turkey, who settle in other parts of the country, still mostly follow this rule. Vuk neglected this; and acquired therefore his literary fame under his Christian name of *Vuk*. But, as a father of a family and an Austrian citizen, he is called *Karadshitch* after his tribe; which for reasons we do not know he seems to have preferred to the name of Stephanovitch.

to reduce a language, which hitherto had been merely an unwritten dialect of the common people, to certain general rules and principles, had, besides the more philosophical part of the work, also to adapt the Slavonic alphabet to his purpose. The mixed and unregulated language, which up to his time had been employed, had been written alternately with the Old Slavonic and the Russian letters. To the Russian language, with its multitude of sounds, the latter is perfectly suitable; in Servian, however, several letters could be easily spared; while others had to be added. Some change of the alphabet seemed therefore necessary. As those Servians among whom Vuk was born, and among whom chiefly he had gathered the treasures of remarkable poetry, which serve as so beautiful a base to their young literature, all belonged to the Greek or Oriental Church, he seems never to have thought of the possibility of adopting the Latin alphabet, which had already served for several centuries for the once flourishing literature of their Catholic brethren, who spoke essentially the same language.

We are ready to acknowledge that the Slavic alphabet, as arranged by Vuk, is better adapted to express the sounds of the Slavic languages, than the Latin; it is at once simpler and richer. But we nevertheless cannot help regretting, that he did not yield to the various reasons, which on the other side spoke in favour of the Latin alphabet. It was already used by some millions for the same language, and had been so for centuries. It would have given a *history* to the young Servian Literature built on the solid foundation of that of Ragusa. It had been, with the exception of the Russians, adopted by all the other Slavic nations. It would have indeed estranged him, seemingly, from his nearer countrymen, who made the most passionate objections against his innovations, even as they were; but as they, at any rate, had to go to Austria for a literary education, this opposition would probably not have lasted longer than it will last now. There was some fear, that, with the Roman alphabet, the Roman chair would try to get possession of their church; but those were not the times of Rome's power; and the Turkish patronage seemed to secure them against such arrogance. One thing is certain. Instead of strengthening for ever the artificial wall of separation between the two classes of Illyrico-Servians, it would have undermined that which already existed; and Vuk, by his strong philosophical-grammatical talent, would soon have gained influence enough on the Illyrico-Dalmatian literature to mend the imperfections of their orthography, and to induce the Croats and Servians to give up their capricious varieties. The many detached parts of the products of Illyrico-Servian intellect would have grown into one great whole; and would have become at least accessible to foreigners; who, puzzled by all these varieties of letters and forms of writing, lose the courage to penetrate into a structure where they meet so much confusion at the very door. Indeed, whether they turn to the eastern or to the western branch of the Southern Slavi, they find equal individual and provincial anarchy; a state of things which the latter at least have taken great pains to amend.

Vuk published at Vienna, in 1824, the Gospel of St. Luke, as a 'Specimen of a translation of the New Testament into Servian.' What part he had in the version printed at Leipsic by the British and Foreign Bible Society, and now circulated among the Servians, we are unable to say.[15]

[15] We must correct here a mistake made by Dr. Henderson in his Biblical Researches, in respect to the Servian New Testament. He says, p. 263, "A version of the (Servian) New Testament was indeed executed some years ago, but its merits were not of such a description as to warrant the committee of the Russian Bible Society to carry it through the press; yet, as they were deeply convinced of the importance of the object, they were induced to engage a native Servian, of the name of Athanasius Stoïkovitch to make a new translation, the printing of which was completed in the year 1825, but owing to the cessation of the Society's operations, the distribution of the copies has hitherto been retarded." Dr. Henderson probably received his information at St.

Modern educated Servian poets, upon whose writings the very general interest which the national popular poetry has excited, and no doubt also their own consciousness of its power, have had

---

Petersburg, and felt himself of course entitled to depend on it, being very likely not acquainted with the great schism in modern Servian literature above mentioned. If we may confide in our own recollections, the translation, the merits of which the committee of the Russian Bible Society was so little disposed to acknowledge, was made by Vuk Stephanovitch, who knew better than any one else the wants of the Servian people, and who presented in the above mentioned Gospel of St. Luke a specimen to the learned world, which received the approbation of all those Slavic scholars entitled to judge of the subject. The committee of St. Petersburg, however, was probably composed of gentlemen of the opposite party; as indeed the Russian Servians are, in general, advocates of the mixed Slavo-Servian language, in which for about fifty years all books for the Servians were written, and which we have described above in Schaffarik's words; see p. 108. According to their ideas of the Servian language, the mere use of the common dialect of the people was sufficient to inspire doubts of the competency of the translator; although it was for the people, the unlearned, that the translation was professedly made. They engaged in consequence Professor Stoïkovitch, the author of several Russian and Slavo-Servian books (see above p. 112), and who had been for more than twenty years in the Russian service, to make a new translation. This person, who, to judge from our personal acquaintance with him, probably on this occasion read the Gospels for the first time in his life with any attention, took the rejected version for his basis; altered it, according to his views of the dignity of the Servian language, into the customary mixed Slavo-Servian Russian idiom; and received the reward from the Society. Whether this is the version afterwards printed at Leipsic and distributed in Servia by the English Bible Society, we are not informed. From private letters we know, that in the year 1827, that Society proposed to Vuk Stephanovitch to allow him £500, if after obtaining appropriate testimonies for the correctness of his version, he would print oue thousand copies in Servia; and also authorized its correspondent in Constantinople, Mr. Leeves, to arrange the matter finally with Vuk. From M. Kopitar's remark however, that the translation for the Dalmatian Roman Catholics needed only to be transcribed with Cyrillic letters to come into use among the eastern Servians, we are entitled to conclude that the version now

a favourable influence, are the following: Lucian Mushitzky, bishop of Karlstadt, a writer in many departments, and the author of odes and other lyrical pieces, all of them highly esteemed by his countrymen; Milovan Vidakovitch, Mich. Vitkovitch, J. Popovitch, G. Kovatzevitch, etc.

More generally known is Simeo Milutinovitch, the author of several small volumes of poetry, and of a larger epic poem entitled *Serbianka*, which describes the Servian war of 1812. In 1837 he published an historical work on Servia during the years 1813–15. Both these latter narratives are valuable, as he himself had been an eye-witness of many of the events described; had acted as secretary to Czerny George, who could neither write nor read; and was afterwards also employed by Prince Milosh.[16]

Two interesting collections of the popular poetry extant among the inhabitants of Montenegro and Herzegovina were published in the course of a few years by Tshubar Tshoikovitch; one of them edited by J. Milowuk, himself a modern Servian writer of praiseworthy activity; the other by the collector himself.[17]

Last, although not least, the present Vladika or bishop of Montenegro, must be named among the modern Servian poets. The constitution of this little mountain state, half warlike, half patriarchal, is an anomaly in the system of European state governments in general. They form a community of about 20,000

---

circulated, is not such as it ought to be; and a correct one, for that part of the nation, is still a desideratum. It would seem therefore that Vuk Stephanovitch cannot have accepted the offer in question. See Kopitar's Letter to the Editor of the Bibl. Repos. Vol. III. 1833, p. 186.

[16] The *Serbianka* of Milutinovitch was published at Leipsic, 1826; his History at the same place, 1837.

[17] *Pjevanija Tzernogorska i Herzegovatshka etc. izdana Josifom Milowukom,* Ofen 1833.—*Pjevanija Tzernogorska i Herzegovatshka sabrana i izdana Tshubrom Tshoikovitchom, etc.* Leipz. 1839.

families, pressed into the valleys and scattered along the slopes of the dark mountain ranges between Cattaro, Herzegovina, Bosnia, and Albania; covering a surface of 80 or 90 geographical square leagues. Hitherto they have been permitted to enjoy a perfect independence in respect to both their great neighbours, Austria and Turkey. They look up only to the emperor of Russia as a kind of liege lord; but more in his quality of Head of the Slavic-Greek Church, than in that of a powerful sovereign. They stand under the rule of a Vladika or bishop; who, besides being their spiritual guide, is their chief judge and their leader in war; as also, since 1832, exclusively their executive magistrate. Up to that time they were accustomed to elect a *governor;* but he assumed too much power; and the post had become hereditary in the family of Radonich. They therefore dismissed him; and his functions were likewise intrusted to the bishop.

Although the office of the Vladika had been formerly purely elective; yet towards the close of the seventeenth century, through the influence of Vladika Daniel Petrovitch of Niegosh, it became hereditary in his own family; a member of which since that time has always been appointed by the Russian emperor. As the Greek bishops belong to the monastic clergy, who of course are not permitted to marry,—while the secular clergy are *required* to do so,—the succession goes in a collateral line. The present Vladika, Peter Petrovitch Niegosh, a man of uncommon size, handsome features, considerable talent, and a highly respected character, was partly educated in Russia. When his predecessor died,—a powerful man who had ruled for fifty-three years, during which time he had led his flock to many a bloody battle, and who was canonized as a saint by the present bishop,—this latter was appointed by the emperor Nicholas. But as he was then only fifteen years old, Montenegro was governed by a sort of guardian; and the Vladika did not enter upon his office until he had completed his eighteenth year. The wisdom, the energy, the consistency in his improvements, which he has displayed since that time, constitute him, in connection with his youth, one of the most remarkable personages of our time. His chief aim seems to be to make Montenegro a member of the great civilized family of Europe, without depriving her of her freedom and independence; and the firmness with which he proceeds further and further in a course, where he meets with difficulties at every step, deserves praise and admiration.

The first circumstance which directed the attention of literary Europe to this remote corner, was a visit of the present king of Saxony, who in 1838 made a botanical excursion into those "black mountains."[16] Since then, the celebrated Egyptian scholar, Wilkinson, has visited it; and this country is no longer closed against travelling artists. The Vladika has naturally the manners of a gentleman; he is said to speak French, and to understand German, Italian, and of course Russian. That he is considered as one of the best riflemen and horsemen in his country, we cannot esteem as of much importance in a bishop; but he studies also the classics and translates the Iliad for his own pleasure. His Servian poems seem mostly to have been written on particular occasions. He addressed an ode to the king of Saxony after his return to Dresden, which unfortunately not a person of the whole court could understand; and the author of this volume, who happened then to be at the "German Athens," was applied to for a translation.[17]

---

[16] *Montenegro,* properly *Montenero,* is the Italian translation of *Tzernagora,* Black Mountain, a name which is applied to these ranges on account of the dark colour of the rocks and woods.

[17] More on the Vladika and on Montenegro in general, see in the recent work of Sir J. G. Wilkinson, *Dalmatia and Montenegro,* 2 vols. Lond. 1848. Also an article in the *British and Foreign Review,* July 1840, by Count Krasinski. A full and very interesting account of the country and people, is found in the little work of Vuk Stephanovitch Karadshich, *Montenegro und die Mon-*

In their own productions, all these educated writers imitate the modern literature of other nations further advanced in civilization, especially the Germans. Milutinovitch has even a tinge of their philosophy. There is no want of talent; but there is no nationality in them. Nothing of that wonderful amalgamation of the East and the West; of mountaineer wildness and Christian principles; of barbarism and civilization; nothing of that interesting blending of Asia and Europe, which we feel entitled to expect from the poetry of *Servians*, who stand on the border between Muhammedanism and Christendom. Nothing which these educated writers have hitherto produced, can be compared with the effusions of their old blind men, and of their peasant lads and girls, that is, their popular poetry.

Vuk's grammar, printed at Vienna 1818, before his dictionary, has since been rendered accessible to other European nations by Grimm's translation. Another Servian grammar has been published in German, by Schaffarik. Vuk's judicious alphabetical arrangement and orthography, we are sorry to say, have not been generally adopted; and the Russian alphabet is still partly in use, with a number of letters superfluous for the Servian language, which has not the shades of sound they are meant to denote.

The political movements in Servia, during the last twelve years, have of course been exceedingly injurious to the development of its infant literature. While it seemed, under the energetic administration of prince Milosh, in a fair way of progress, the confused cries of war and insurrection since his abdication have drowned the modest voice of the young muse. Of late, indeed, intelligence from that country has been so rare, that we are unable to give a picture of the present state of things.

---

tenegriner, 8vo. Stuttg. u. Tüb. 1837; published in Cotta's "Reisen u. Länderbeschreibungen der ältern u. neuern Zeit."

2. *Literature of the Dalmatians or Illyrico-Servians of the Romish Church.*

a) GLAGOLITIC LITERATURE.

It is not without some hesitation that we approach a region, into which we cannot penetrate without stepping through a border of perfect darkness. We allude to the introduction of the Glagolitic alphabet; the great antiquity of which, supported by numerous traditions and legends, as well as by its venerable and almost hieroglyphic look, Kopitar's recent investigations and discoveries have again made probable; without, however, throwing any more light upon its origin.

As Christianity was first introduced into Dalmatia by Romish priests, the Latin language was of course adopted for religious purposes. But so soon as the people became acquainted with the liturgy of Methodius in a language intelligible to them, this innovation met with such a general and heartfelt welcome, that all the severe decrees of synods, nay, of the holy chair of Rome itself, were unable to stop its progress.

Even more than a hundred and fifty years afterwards, when Methodius was solemnly declared by pope Nicolas II. a heretic, and the Romish mass again introduced, the attachment to their own language was too deeply rooted to be taken away at once. Hence the Old Slavic idiom, with the pope's reluctant permission, continued to be the language of the Church service. It appears, however, that the alphabet which their priests employed for writing their ecclesiastic documents, was not the same with that used by other Slavi of the oriental church; but was of a different character, and evidently *not* derived from the Greek, with the exception of a few letters. It was called the *Glagolitic.*

Glagol signifies in Old Slavic *the word* or rather *the verb;*

but the reason of the application of this term to the Illyrico-Servians of the catholic communion (*Glagolitæ*), and to the language of their sacred writings (*Glagolic* or *Glagolitic*), has not yet been ascertained; all that has as yet been asserted by Slavic philologians being mere hypothesis. The oldest monument known up to 1830, in which these letters were extant, was a Psalter of A. D. 1220. This Psalter was by tradition ascribed to St. Jerome himself, who was in general called the inventor of the Slavic, that is the *Glagolitic* alphabet. According to a popular legend of the Dalmatians, this father, who was a native of Illyria, also translated the whole Bible into the Slavic; but it has been since clearly proved, that while (as is well known) he corrected the old Latin version of the Bible, he yet never wrote a single line of Slavic.

The mystery, in which the origin of the Glagolitic was and still is buried, gave birth to the singular hypothesis already above mentioned.[18] The discovery however of several very ancient Glagolitic manuscripts, and especially of one which could be proved to be older than the Council of Spalatro,[19] destroyed it at once; but unfortunately, without clearing up the mystery either of its invention or of its introduction.

Another Glagolitic manuscript of some interest may be mentioned here. It was generally known, that the kings of France were accustomed, at their coronation at Rheims, to take the oath on a large book, called *Texte du Sacre*, bound in gold or gilding, and covered with unwrought precious stones, which contained the Gospels written in some unknown hieroglyphic language. When in 1717 Tzar Peter I. visited Rheims, this book was shown to him among other curiosities, and he exclaimed at once: "This is my own Slavonic!" This view was soon spread

[18] See above, p. 37 sq.

[19] Kopitar, *Glagolita Clozianus*, Vindob. 1836.

among Slavic scholars. But the precious parchment was written in two columns, and in two languages. What idiom could the other be? The French, it is said, took it for Greek; more probably for Coptic. In 1789, a learned English traveller, Thomas Ford Hill, was shown some Glagolitic manuscripts in the imperial library at Vienna; whereupon he declared without hesitation, that this was the mysterious writing of the Rheims manuscript. Before the Vienna scholars, Dobner and Alter, then at the head of Slavic matters, had time to investigate the matter further, the revolution broke out, and the precious document disappeard. No trace was left of it; and for half a century the patriotic Slavic scholars supposed they had cause to lament the loss of a document of the very highest antiquity. It was conjectured that the book had originally been brought to France by some Slavic princess; for instance, by a princess of Kief, who is said to have been sent for by Henry I., son of Hugh Capet and king of France in the beginning of the eleventh century. Application was made on the subject to Sylvestre de Sacy; whose report gave some hope, that the precious relic might still be preserved. Search was made by Kopitar in Italy and at Paris, but all in vain. At last it was again found at Rheims by the Russian scholar Stroyef;[20] who, however, seems not to have been acquainted with the Glagolitic writing, and therefore laid little stress on it. The volume was stripped of its costly ornaments, and had therefore been the more easily recovered during the reign of Napoleon; who endeavoured, as much as was in his power, to restore the spoils of the revolution, while he himself filled Paris with the spoils of all other nations.

The librarian at Rheims, in order best to meet the numerous inquiries of Slavic scholars, caused a *fac simile* of it to be taken; and it was finally committed to the learned Kopitar's care. It was now discovered, that this long deplored document contained two

---

[20] See above, p. 41.

unconnected portions of the Gospels; one in Cyrillic letters, the other, considerably longer, in Glagolitic; and both executed with remarkable calligraphic skill. The Glagolitic portion was marked with the date 1395. It was written at Prague, and presented by the emperor Charles IV. to the Abbot of Emaus; with the injunction, that these *Evangelia* should be chanted at mass; and the remark was added, that the accompanying Cyrillic portion was written by St. Procopius with his own hand. Procopius was one of the patron saints of Bohemia, who died in 1053. How this valuable manuscript was finally removed to France, is still unexplained. At Rheims nothing further was known, than that it had been presented by the Cardinal of Lorraine in A. D. 1554. A rumour ascribed to the Cyrillic portion a Greek origin; the Glagolitic part was generally considered as a relic from St. Jerome's own library. This supposed immediate connection with two saints, may well account for the reverence with which the book was treated in France.[21] A splendid edition of this work, under the patronage of the emperor of Russia, was prepared by Kopitar, and appeared in 1843 at Paris.[22]

Although the use of the Slavic language was in a certain measure authorized by the pope, yet the clergy of Dalmatia preferred unanimously the Latin for their theological and ecclesiastical writings. The Glagolitic literature was therefore almost exclusively limited to copies of the productions of their Cyrillic brethren. The Glagolitic letters had, however, the precedence of the Cyrillic alphabet, in respect to printing. The first printed Glagolitic missal, is of the year 1483; whilst the earliest work

---

[21] On the still earlier Glagolitic manuscript discovered at Trent, there was also found a note written by one of its former noble owners, that "dises puech hat Sant Jeronimuss mit aigner hant geschriben in krabatischer sprach."

[22] A fine copy of the above splendid work is now on sale by the publisher of this volume.

printed in the Cyrillic letters is not older than A. D. 1491. In the sixteenth century books were printed at Zengh (Segna), at Fiume, at Venice, and at Tübingen, with Glagolitic letters. In the year 1621, the emperor Ferdinand II. presented the Propaganda with a font of Glagolitic types, which he obtained from Venice. Several improved breviaries and missals have since been printed at Rome. In our day, this city possesses the only Glagolitic printing office in existence. On the Dalmatian islands, books are still copied in manuscript, just as before the invention of printing.

Among the Dalmatian clergy, there were a few who united a real interest for the preservation of their language and for science in general. Raph. Levakovitch improved the breviary in 1648, in respect to language; the archbishop Vincenz Zmajevitch, ob. 1771, a great patron of the literature of his country, founded a hundred years later a theological seminary in Zara. Matthias Caraman, on occasion of a new edition of the missal by the Propaganda in 1741, undertook a fundamental revision and correction of it. The Propaganda also founded a Slavic professorship in the *Collegio Urbano;* and for the benefit of this Society a new translation of the whole Bible was resolved upon, which however has never been published. A notice of the exertions of the priest Rosa belongs rather to the history of Dalmatian secular literature.

b) Secular Literature.

It is not certain at what time, nor by whom, the Latin letters were first adopted for the Servian language. The earliest teachers of the occidental portion of that people having been Romish priests, they of course used their own letters for writing such Slavic words or names as occasion required. The Latin alphabet probably came into use without any particular pains, long before the introduction of the Glagolitic letters. These, in their awkward hieroglyphic form, were little adapted to supersede the Latin forms. The example of the Poles and Bohemians could only encourage the first Dalmatian writers to continue in the same course; although each of these nations follows a different system of pronouncing the same letters. The orthography of the Dalmatians remained, however, for a long time entirely unsettled; and is so still in some measure. A greater difficulty arose from the absurd practice of the Slavonians and Croatians, who, although speaking and writing the same language, yet write and print it each according to a different system of combination; thus limiting the perusal of their own scanty productions almost exclusively to the few readers of their small provinces respectively, whilst the remainder of their countrymen are hardly able to understand them. This division, however, compels us likewise to separate in our sketch the literature of the Dalmatians proper, and that of the catholic Slavonians.

Literature of Dalmatia Proper.

The neighbourhood of the Italians exercised in very early times a happy influence on the literature of the Dalmatians. The small republic of Ragusa, during the fourteenth and fifteenth centuries, was at the zenith of its splendour and welfare. Celebrated Italians were teachers in her schools; and the persecuted Greeks, Lascaris, Demetrius Chalcondylas, Emanuel Marulus, and several others, celebrated over all Europe for their learning, found an asylum within her walls. Thus the treasures of the classics and of the Italian middle ages became familiar to the noble youths of Ragusa, until, in the beginning of the sixteenth century, poetry began to appear in a national dress. The Italian influence remained strikingly visible. Blasius Darxich, Sigismund Menze, Mauro Vetranich, and Stephen Gozze (ob.

1576), are mentioned as the first Dalmatian poets. The latter wrote a comic epic, the *Dervishiade*, which met with great success. A poem of the same kind is *Jegyupka*, the Gipsy, by Andreas Giubronavich, printed at Venice 1559. Dominic Zlatarich (ob. 1608) translated Tasso and the Electra of Sophocles, and was himself a lyric poet.

The annals of this period, towards the end of the sixteenth century, report likewise the name of a lady, Svietana Zuzerich, as an Illyrian poetess; called also Floria Zuzzeri, as an Italian poetess; for she wrote with success in both languages. Several other ladies followed the example, as Lucrezia Bogashinovich, Katharina Pozzo di Sorgo, etc.

During the sixteenth and seventeenth centuries, Ragusa enjoyed peace, and a degree of wealth and prosperity most favourable to high attainments in science and literature. The first Slavic theatre was founded here, and the dramatic art seems to have been considered so honourable, that even noblemen acted publicly; as is related of Junius Palmota, who died in 1657. The noble names of Palmota or Palmotich, Gondola or Gondolich, for they appear alternately both in the Slavic and Italian form, are very frequent in Ragusian literature. Junius Palmota wrote tragedies; selecting his subjects principally from Slavic history. But his most esteemed production is a Slavic version of a great Latin epic on Christ, by M. H. Vita, which may be considered as a kind of precursor to Klopstock's Messiah. John Gondola, a dramatic writer before him, translated Tasso's Jerusalem Delivered; and left many lyrical poems.

In the year 1667, a horrible earthquake in a few moments destroyed the prosperity of the state for whole centuries. It was as if the genius of the Ragusian literature had been crushed under the ruins. From that period we find all that relates to literature in a rapid decline. The catastrophe itself, however, furnished the poets with a new subject. In the same year, N.

Bonus published a poem entitled, The city of Ragusa to her Rulers; and Jacob Palmota (ob. 1680) wrote an elegiac poem, The renovated Ragusa. But the most interesting production of this period is a collection of national songs, published by the Franciscan monk, And. Cacich Miossich.[23] This work, although executed with little critical taste or judgment, and disfigured by many interpolations, might have given to the literary world a foretaste of the treasures, which fifty years afterwards were to be discovered here.

Whilst Slavic poetry found so many votaries among the Dalmatians, it is a remarkable fact, that all their historians wrote in Latin or Italian. They possess indeed a very old chronicle, of the date of A. D. 1161, written in the Slavic language by an anonymous Presbyter of Dioclea, and translated by himself into Latin; but in the more flourishing period of the Dalmatian literature, the love of their own language was overcome by the stronger desire of a more universal reputation than any works written in Slavic could procure for them. The names of N. Ragnini, Francisco Gondola, Razzi, and Caboga, must here be mentioned. The dialect of the country, however, found some advocates even among the clergy. For some theological works it was preferred to the Old Slavic; or at least the Latin letters were chosen for this language instead of the Glagolitic types. An Old Slavic translation of the Gospels and Epistles by Bernardin de Spalatro was printed with Latin letters, Venice 1495. At the same place appeared, in 1613, Bandulovich's translation of the same holy books in the common language. A Jesuit, Barth. Cassio, A. D. 1640, had translated both the Old and New Testaments; but the printing of it was prevented by the bishops. Anton Cacich wrote a work on moral theology, in

[23] *Razgovor ugodni naroda slavinskoga,* Venice 1759. A new edition appeared in the year 1811.

the common dialect of the country; and several ecclesiastics of high standing published works for religious instruction in the same language. The period following the catastrophe of Ragusa was fertile in theological, or rather religious, productions. The works of the archidiaconus Albertus, as also of Gucetich and others, contain treatises for spiritual edification, devotional exercises, etc. Diankovitch, bishop of Makarska, wrote a treatise of Christian doctrine, Venice 1708, in the common Dalmatian dialect. But this dialect found its most ardent champion in a priest, Stephan Rosa, who exerted himself greatly to have the old church Slavonic entirely superseded by the Dalmatian-Servian language. He made a complete translation of the whole Bible, and sent it to the pope, requesting that it might be printed and introduced under his high authority instead of the Cyrillic Bible. At the same time, he proposed that the mass should be read in the Dalmatian dialect; dwelling especially on the circumstance, that the Cyrillic language was an ingredient of the Greek church, and consequently the use of it in sacred things a species of Greek heresy. The pope appointed a committee to examine the new translation; the result of which was, as may easily be supposed, the rejection of a measure which savoured so strongly of Protestantism. From the time of this decision in A. D. 1754, nothing was done to provide the catholic inhabitants of Dalmatia, Bosnia and Slavonia with a version of the Bible, until at last a new translation, the first satisfactory one in the language, made by the Franciscan monk and professor Katancsich, was accepted and introduced in 1832 The merit of having procured it to be printed and published, belongs to the late primate of Hungary, cardinal Rudnay.[24]

The inconvenience of such an anarchical state of orthography, and likewise in part of the grammar itself, must of course have been felt very early; but it would seem that in this department

[24] Letter of Kopitar to the Editor, Bibl. Repos. 1833, p. 136.

also, the Dalmatian writers acted with more zeal and diligence, than success. The above-mentioned Barth. Cassio, and after him another Jesuit, J. Micalia, endeavoured in the first half of the seventeenth century to settle the orthography and subject it to fixed rules. Ardelio della Bella, a member of the same order, published in 1728 a dictionary and grammar, in which he abandoned the way opened by his predecessors, without however finding a better one. Jos. Voltiggi endeavoured to establish a third system of pronunciation and orthography; his dictionary and grammar appeared in the year 1803. A few years later a useful grammar was published by Appendini; also the great dictionary of J. Stulli, a work of considerable merit, and far excelling all previous works of the same kind.[25]

All the different systems and rules of orthography, exhibited and laid down in these works, had unfortunately no permanent result. The Dalmatians, the Slavonians, the Croats, and the Servians in Hungary, whenever they used Latin letters, all continued to write each in their own way. This continued until about twelve years ago; when new efforts began to be made to unite all the different branches of the Illyrico-Servians, and if possible also the Servians of the Greek Church, in the use of one general system of orthography. We have seen above the anarchy in respect to their literary language, which some years before the two Servians Davidovitch and Vuk Stephanovitch

---

[25] F. Verantii *Dictionarium quinque nobiliss. Eur. Ling. Lat. Ital. Germ. Dalm. et Ung.* Venice 1595. Micalia *Thesaurus linguae Illyricae,* etc. Ancona 1651. Della Bella *Dizionario It. Lat. Illyr.* Venice 1728; later edit. Ragusa 1785. Voltiggi *Ricsoslovnik illyricsiskoga, ital. i nimacsk,* Vienna 1803. Stulli *Lexicon Lat. Ital. Illyr.* etc. Buda and Ragusa 1801–10, 6 vols. Prefixed to the four last works, are also grammars. Other Dalmatian grammars are: Cassii *Institutiones linguae Illyricae,* Rome, 1604. Appendini *Grammatik der illyrischen Sprache,* Ragusa 1808. Starchsevich *Nuova Gramm. Illyrica,* Trieste 1012. Babukich *Illyrische Grammatik,* Wien 1839.

had found prevailing among their Cyrillic brethren; and what pains they took to introduce the pure dialect of the people (essentially the language of the Dalmatians) as the literary language of the whole race; as also the efforts made by Vuk to establish a new alphabetical system. It can hardly be doubted that these efforts; the interest they excited; and, above all, the claims preferred by some eminent scholars connected with them; roused the jealousy and just ambition of the Illyrico-Servians. They were far from being willing to give up the name of *Illyrians* for that of *Servians;* they felt themselves a part of a great whole, but they wanted to be acknowledged as the *principal* part. In order to become strong, they had above all to unite. A gentleman of uncommon energy and intelligence at Agram, Dr. Ludovic Gaj, the editor of a Croatian periodical, took the matter in hand. He prepared a new system of orthography for all the Illyrico-Servian dialects, founded on the Bohemian model, and greatly approved by the Bohemian scholars. He himself established a printing office in order to carry out his plan. At the same time he enlarged his paper, which now became "The Illyrian National Gazette;" and contrived to secure patrons of name and influence. Schaffarik declared himself decidedly in his favour. How far he has succeeded, and how far in general the few Illyrico-Servian literati have been able to keep up their budding literature during the recent tempests of the times, we are unable to say. We may say truly that we have wished for Dr. Gaj's system of union the very best success; and have expressed above, how desirable we deem it in every respect.[26]

Literature of the Catholic Slavonians.

The Slavonians of the Greek Church make use of the Cyrillic letters; and their productions belong therefore to that

[26] See above, p. 116, 117.

division of Servian literature.[27] We have seen above, that the catholic Slavonians also neither speak nor write a different dialect; but that only their mode of writing, the strange combination according to which they express the sounds of the same language, separates them from the Dalmatian Servians.[28] To enter into the details of these varieties would be of little interest for our readers.

The light of the Reformation penetrated at an early day into Slavonia, and gave birth to a kind of limited theological or ecclesiastical national literature. But the catholic clergy soon succeeded in extinguishing it; and in the same proportion, the Latin language continued to supersede the dialect of the people. In more modern days, the Latin has been preferred by nearly all catholic Slavonic writers; and their own literature is now almost exclusively limited to works for religious instruction, catechisms, prayer-books, etc.

But although their language was thus relinquished in a practical point of view, it remained nevertheless the object of investigation to some of their profoundest scholars. Thus the Latin works of Prof. Katancsich, are almost all of them devoted to Slavic philological inquiries, etc. The translation of the Bible mentioned above, was made by the same learned individual.[29]

---

[27] See above in § 1. p. 108.

[28] See p. 128 above.

[29] See p. 131.—As dictionaries and grammars of this dialect are to be mentioned: Relcovich *Deutsch illyrisches and illyr. deutsches Wörterb.* Vienna 1796. By the same: *Neue Slawonisch-deutche Grammatik,* Agram 1767. Vienna 1774. Buda 1789. Lanossovich *Einleitung zur Slav. Sprache,* several editions from 1778–1795.

SECTION II.

LANGUAGE AND LITERATURE OF THE CROATIANS.

Schaffarik in his history of the Slavic Language and Literature enumerates, on Dobrovsky's authority, the Croatians or Croats as a distinct branch of the great Eastern Slavic stem. Later researches however have identified them, to a certain extent, with the other Southern Slavi or Illyrico-Servians, with whose language theirs is essentially the same. The recent political events, and their struggles against the Hungarians, have made the Croats in our days again the subject of some interest and curiosity. There is however such a confusion in the early history of this race; such a change of names, boundaries, and constitutions; such a contradiction between the accounts of ancient writers and the experience of modern times; that it would require a long historical exposition to give to the reader a clear view of their relation to each other and to their Slavic brethren. For such an exposition there is no room in these pages.[30]

The subject becomes far simpler if we consider the Croats only in respect to their language, as it prevails among them at the present time. Here they do *not* appear as a distinct race; but still are divided into two portions. One, in Military Croatia, comprising the military districts of Carlstadt and Varasdin, and also the Banal Border, speak the Dalmatian-Servian dialect with very trifling variations; the other, in Provincial Croatia, i. e. the provincial counties of Agram, Kreutz, and Varasdin, approach nearer to the Slovenzi or Vindes, whose language will be the sub-

---

[30] See the second volume of Engel's *History of Hungary* etc. Katancsich *Specimen phil. et geogr. Pannon.* etc. 1795. Schaffarik's *Geschichte*, etc. p. 226–31, 235, 265.

ject of our next section.[31] The dialect of this latter division of the Croatians forms indeed, in a certain measure, the transition and connecting link between the Dalmatian-Servian and the Vindish languages.

We have mentioned above,[32] that the Croatians adopted a system of writing different from that of the Dalmatians. The earliest docments of their literature are of the sixteenth century, and all belong to the history of the Reformation. Here also the new doctrines found minds willing to receive them; and as several of the *magnates*, among whom is the illustrious name of Zriny, were also their supporters, there was no difficulty in establishing a press, in order to diffuse the new light with greater speed and certainty. In the course of the last half of the sixteenth and the beginning of the seventeenth centuries, a large number of Croatian books, catechisms, postillae, etc. were printed. One of the warmest champions of the Reformation was Michael Buchich, curate of the island Murakoz, who publicly adopted the Calvinistic confession, and endeavoured to spread abroad his own convictions by sermons and writings. Persecuted by the bishops, condemned by synods, he and his followers found some protection in the Christian tolerance of the emperor Maximilian II. But the successors of this prince thought otherwise; and the most powerful of the Hungarian noblemen took arms for the defence of the Romish religion. At the diets held in 1607 and 1610, destruction was sworn to the new doctrines and to their adherents; and all steps were taken for the fulfilment of the oath.

In the middle of the seventeenth century, all Croatia had

---

[31] These two divisions of Military and Provincial Croatia constitute the modern Austrian kingdom of Croatia, which is united with that of Hungary. See For. Quart. Review, Vol. VII. p. 423 sq.

[32] See p. 128 above.

reverted to Romanism. From that time onward, for more than fifty years, there was not a thought of cultivating the language of the people; all books were again written in Latin, and are so mostly even to the present day. The first who interested himself anew for the foundation of a national literature, was Paul Ritter, of Vitezovich, ob. 1713, who procured a printing office to be established by the estates, and himself wrote several books in the Croatian language. A few writers followed his example; but the activity of the press was, and is now, almost exclusively devoted to the printing of the ordinary catholic books for spiritual edification and religious instruction. The Gospels are extant in the Croatian dialect; but not the whole Bible. Most of the Croats, however, are able to read and understand the books of their Dalmatian neighbours.[38]

The idea of a union among the Illyrico-Servians in respect to orthography and literature, was principally favoured by the Croatians, and indeed originated among them. Here Dr. Gaj and Count Janko Draskovich, who endeavoured to interest the Illyrian *ladies* in the subject, by a patriotic address, had their residence. The events of our own days have taught us, how in general the feeling of *Slavic nationality*, in opposition to the Magyar nationality, was roused among the Croatians; for although all the different Slavic tribes scattered throughout Hungary—Slovaks, Ruthenians, and Servians—participated in them, yet that feeling was strongest among the South-western Slavi; who united, as is generally known, to elect Jellachich as their Bann.

---

[38] Croatian philological works are: *Einleitung zur croat. Sprachlehre*, Varasdin 1783. Kornig's *Croat. Sprachlehre*, Agram 1795. Gyurkovshky's *Croat. Grammatik*, 1825. Rukovina v. Liebstadt *Kroatische Sprachformen*, etc. Triesto 1813. Habdelich *Dictionarium croat. lat.* Grätz 1670. Bellosztenecz *Gazophylacium s. Latino-Illyricor.* etc. Agram 1740. Jambressich's *Lex. Lat. interpr. illyrica, germ.* etc. Agram 1742.

SECTION III.

LANGUAGE AND LITERATURE OF THE VINDES OR SLOVENZI.

The Slavic inhabitants of the Austrian provinces Carinthia, Carniola, and Stiria, extending from thence in scattered villages into Udine once the territory of Venice, and of the Hungarian counties Eisenburg and Szala, about a million in number, call themselves *Slovenzi.* By foreign writers they have generally been called *Windes* or *Vindes;* a name, however, less definite and less correct; inasmuch as the term Vindes or Vendes served in ancient times among the Germans as a general name for *all* Slavic nations. The Slavic settlements in Carniola took place at a very early period, certainly not later than the fifth century. In the course of the following centuries their number was increased by new emigrations from the southeast; and they extended themselves into the lower parts of Stiria and Carinthia, and the western counties of Hungary.[34]

In regard to the language of this people, it was formerly considered a matter of certainty, that it had never been a written language before the time of the Reformation. But the investigations of modern philologians have proved, on the contrary, that this portion of the Slavic race was earlier acquainted with the art of writing than were any of the other branches; probably even before the time of Cyril; and since the discovery of several very old manuscripts in the library of Munich, every doubt of this fact has been silenced. According to Kopitar,[35] the true home of the Old Slavic Church language is to be found among

---

[34] See Engel, etc. III p. 469.

[35] See the *Wiener Jahrbücher,* 1822, Vol. XVII. See too the *Glagolita Clozianus,* and the article "On the Pannonian Origin of the Slavic Liturgy." See above, pp. 28, 39.

the Pannonian and Carinthian Slavi; and it was for them that the Old Slavonic Bible was translated. The liturgy of Methodius was, however, soon supplanted by the Latin worship; which at any rate must have been earlier established in this part of the country; since Christianity appears to have been introduced about the middle of the eighth century, by German priests.

Be this as it may, the definite history of the language begins only with the Reformation; and it is principally to the exertions of one distinguished individual, that it owes its introduction into the circle of literature. There is nothing more pleasing in the moral world, than to behold the whole life of a man devoted to one great cause, his thoughts all bent on one great object, his exertions all aiming at one great purpose; and so much the more, if that object has respect to the holiest interests of mankind. Such was the case with the *primus* Truber, who may be called the apostle of the Vindes and Croatians. The direct results of his labours long ago perished in the lapse of time; but this does not render them less deserving, although it diminishes his fame. Truber, born A. D. 1508, canon and curate at several places in Carniola and Carinthia, seems to have been early in life impressed with the truth of the new doctrines of the Reformation. His sound judgment taught him, that the surest way of enabling his flock, and the common people in general, to receive the new light in a proper spirit, would be the diffusion of useful knowledge among them. And as the German, which at the present day is almost exclusively the language of the cities of Stiria, Carniola, and Carinthia, was at that time far less generally understood, he ventured to commit to paper a dialect apparently never before written. In the second edition of his New Testament, A. D. 1582, he states expressly: "Thirty-four years ago, there was not a letter, not a register, still less a book, to be found in our language; people regarded the Vindish and Hungarian idioms as too coarse and barbarous to be written or read."

Truber and his assistants in this great work of reformation and instruction, among whom we mention only Ungnad von Sonnegg and Dalmatin, met every where with opposition and persecution; but their activity and zeal conquered all obstacles, and succeeded in at least partially performing that at which they aimed. Meantime, Christopher duke of Würtemburg, a truly evangelical prince, had opened in his dominions an asylum for all those who had to suffer elsewhere on account of their faith. The translation of the Scriptures every where into the language of the common people, was regarded by this prince as a holy duty; and this led him to cause even Slavic printing-offices to be established in his dominions. Thither Truber went; and after printing several books for religious instruction, he published the Gospel of Matthew in a Vindish translation, Tübingen 1555; and two years later the whole New Testament. As Truber did not understand the Greek original, his translation was made from the Latin, German, and Italian versions. At the same time a translation for the Dalmatic-Croatians was planned; and several works for their instruction printed and distributed. Truber, thus an exile from his own country, died in 1586 as curate in the duchy of Würtemburg, engaged in a translation of Luther's House-postillæ.

Two different systems of orthography had been adopted by Truber and Dalmatin. For this reason, when in 1580 the whole Vindish Bible was to be printed at Wittemberg, it seemed necessary to fix the orthography according to acknowledged rules. This led also to grammatical investigations. In the year 1584, a Vindish grammar was printed at Wittemberg, the author of which, A. Bohorizh of Laibach, was a pupil of Melancthon, and a scholar of that true philosophical spirit, without which no one should undertake to write a grammar, even where he has only to follow a beaten path; much less when he has to open for himself a new one. Thus the Vindish written language, almost in its birth, acquired a correctness and consistency, to which other languages hardly attain after centuries of experiments, innovations, and literary contests. According to the judgment of those who are best acquainted with it, the Vindish language has undergone no change since the time of Bohorizh,—a fact indeed scarcely credible; and the less so, because during that whole interval it has been maintained almost exclusively as a spoken language. About thirty years after the publication of this grammar, the Roman Catholics, sheltered by the despotic measures of the archduke Ferdinand, afterwards the emperor Ferdinand II, gained a complete victory. All evangelical preachers, and all Protestants who faithfully adhered to their religion, were exiled; their goods confiscated; and, more than all, their books *burned*, and their printing-office in Laibach destroyed.[36] Fragments of the Gospels and of the Epistles were however printed at Grätz, in 1612, for the Slavic Catholics, in their own language.

A whole century passed, and the Vindish language seemed to be entirely lost for literature and science. Towards the close of the seventeenth century, an academy was founded by some learned men of Carniola, on the plan of the Italian Academy; and some attention was again paid to the language of their forefathers. In A. D. 1715 a new edition of Bohorizh's work, with several alterations and without mentioning the true author, was printed by a capuchin, P. Hippolitus; who left also in manuscript a Vindish dictionary, the first in that language. Fifty-

[36] Schaffarik observes, *Geschichte*, p. 283, "The public library in the statehouse was delivered to the Jesuits, who had just been introduced. The books which these did not commit to the flames on the spot, perished in the great conflagration in 1774, together with the edifice of their college. In all Carniola only two copies of Bohorizh's grammar are known to exist."

three years later, another grammar was published by the monk Marcus Pochlin; a work in itself, according to the best authorities, utterly devoid of merit, but which from the necessity of the case, and for the want of a better, met with success, was reprinted in 1783, and remained in common use until the appearance of Kopitar's grammar. This last work,[37] written by one of the most eminent Slavists of the age, made a decided epoch; not only in the history of the Vindish language, but also, by its learned preface and comments, in the Slavic literature at large. Several grammatical works, not without merit, and for the most part founded on Kopitar's grammar, have since been published;[38] and since scholars like these are now occupied with the cultivation of the Vindish language, there exist for it and for its kindred dialects the happiest prospects.

That this Slavic branch, a mountain people, had its treasures of popular poetry, has always been supposed; and many single pieces, not without beauty, have been communicated to the public in German translations. A *collection* of these flowers, which fade rapidly away in this German neighbourhood, was ten years ago made by Achazel and Korytko.[39]

The literature of a people, among whom every individual of any education may call another highly cultivated language in the fullest sense his own,—as is the case with the Bohemians and Slovenzi in respect to the German,—cannot be very extensive. There have, however, in modern times, been published several works of poetry and prose in the Vindish language; among the

---

[37] *Grammatik der Slavischen Sprache in Krain, Kärnthen, und Steyermark,* Laibach 1808.

[38] These are: V. Vodnik's *Pismenost ali gramm. saperve shole,* Laib. 1811. Metelko's *Lehrgebäude der Slovenischen Sprache,* 1825. Schmigoz *Theor. pract. wind. Sprachlehre,* Grätz 1812. P. Dainko *Lehrbuch der wind. Sprache,* Grätz 1825. Mali *Bezedniak Slovenskich,* Laibach 1834.

[39] *Slovenske pjesmi Krajnskiga Naroda,* Laibach 1839.

writers of which we can mention only the most distinguished. Such are, V. Vodnik, author of some collections of poems; Ravnikar, author of a biblical history of the Old and New Testament, and several works for religious edification; Farnik, Kumerdey, Popovich, etc.

But the most important work, both in a philological and moral point of view, is the translation of the whole Bible, set on foot by G. Japel, and executed by a society of learned men. This version being intended for Catholics, was made from the Vulgate, and was published at Laibach 1800, in five volumes; the New Testament appeared also separately, in two volumes, Laib. 1804. A Slavic pulpit, which was established ten years ago at the same place, has also been of great service to the language.

The inhabitants of the provincial counties Agram, Kreutz, Varasdin, and the neighbouring districts, called Provincial Croatia, who speak a somewhat different dialect of the Vindish language, but are able to read that version of the Bible, have nevertheless several translations in their own dialect, lying in manuscript, and only waiting for some Mæcenas, or for some favourable conjuncture, in order to make their appearance.

The only portion of the Vindish race among whom the Protestant religion has been kept alive, are about 15,000 Slovenzi in Hungary. Their dialect approaches in a like measure to that of the Slovaks; and hence serves as the connecting link between the languages of the Eastern and Western Slavic stems. For them the New Testament exists in a translation by Stephen Kuznico, Halle 1771; reprinted at St. Petersburg, 1818.

CHAPTER III.

LANGUAGE OF THE BULGARIANS.

ACCORDING to the opinion of the Russian, and especially of the Bohemian philologians, Bulgaria and the adjacent regions of Macedonia, are the real home of the Old Slavic language; which was here, as they suppose, the language of the people in the time of Cyril, who was born in Thessalonica.[1] No other Slavic dialect however, as Kopitar remarks, has been so much affected as the Bulgarian by the course of time and foreign influence, both in its grammatical structure and its whole character.[2] It has an article, which, as if in order to show whence it was borrowed, is put *after* the word it qualifies, like that of the Walachians and Albanians. Of the seven Slavic cases, only the nominative and vocative remain to it; all the rest being supplied by means of prepositions. As Bulgaria has been for centuries the great thoroughfare of other nations, the Slavic natives have become mixed with Rumenians, Turco-Tartars, and perhaps Greeks. It is in this way, that the state of their language may be accounted for.

Up to 1392, when Bulgaria was an independent kingdom,—tributary to the Greek empire, until the decline of the latter en-

---

[1] See above, pp. 27, 28.

[2] *Wiener Jahrbücher der Literatur*, 1822, Vol. XVII.

couraged them to break the weak tie of vassalage,—their writings were in the Old Slavic language; and many documents in it are still extant in monastic libraries. Venelin, a young Russian scholar, who by his researches on the Bulgarian, or, as he would fain call it, the *Bolgarian* language, had excited great hopes in the learned Slavic world, was sent in 1835 to Bulgaria, by the Russian Archæographical Commission, to search after historical documents and to examine the language. The publication of a "Bolgarian Grammar," and two volumes of a "History of the Bolgarians," were the result. While engaged in preparing a third volume, he died; less regretted by the literary world, it is said, than would have been anticipated some years before; since his productions had not justified the expectations raised by his zeal. He seems to have been one of those visionary etymologists, who found their conclusions on the analogy of sound and similar accidental features; a class of scholars, which, in our age of philosophical research, has no longer much chance of success.

The history of the Bulgarians is a series of continued warfare with the Servians, Greeks, and Hungarians, on the one hand; and on the other, with the Turks, who subdued them, and put an end to the existence of a Bulgarian kingdom in A. D. 1392. The people, first converted to Christianity by Cyril and Methodius, had hitherto adhered to the Greek church; except for a short interval in the last half of the twelfth century, when the Roman chair succeeded in bringing them under its dominion. Since the establishment of the Turkish government, apostasy to Muhammedanism has been more frequent in Bulgaria, than in any other of the Christian provinces of the Porte. Still, the bulk of the population has remained faithful to the Slavic Greek worship. The scanty germs of cultivation sown among them by two or three of their princes, who caused several Byzantine works to be translated into the Bulgarian dialect, perished during the Turkish invasion. The few books used by the priesthood in our days, are obtained from Russia. They have no trace of a literature, and the only point of view from which their language, uncultivated as it is, can excite a general interest, is in respect to their popular songs. In these this dialect likewise is said to be exceedingly rich.

The Russian Bible Society had prepared a Bulgarian translation of the New Testament, intended more especially for the benefit of the Bulgarian inhabitants of the Russian province of Bessarabia. But the specimen printed in 1823 excited some doubt as to the competency of the translator in respect to his knowledge of the Bulgarian language ; and it was deemed advisable to put a stop to its further progress. Among the Albanian portion of its inhabitants, the New Testament has been distributed by the British and Foreign Bible Society.

In the dearth of all philological helps in respect to the Bulgarian language, it is matter of grateful acknowledgment to Slavic scholars, that an American missionary, the Rev. E. Riggs, stationed at Smyrna, should recently have taken up the subject, and furnished us with a brief sketch of the principal features of the Bulgarian grammar. It seems that the Bulgarians have availed themselves of the printing establishment founded by the American missionaries at Smyrna ; and some books in this language have been there printed. Mr. Riggs says of the language, that "its literature is very slender, consisting almost entirely of a few elementary books, printed in Bucharest, Belgrad, Buda, Cracow, Constantinople, and Smyrna." A Bulgarian translation of Gallaudet's "Child's Book on the Soul," was sent by the same gentleman to New York. From the same source we learn that a Bulgarian version of the New Testament was printed at Smyrna in 1840, for the British and Foreign Bible Society ; and that in 1844 the first number of a monthly magazine, entitled "Philology," was issued from the same press.

PART III.

WESTERN SLAVI.

CHAPTER I.

CZEKHO-SLOVAKIAN BRANCH.

SECTION I.

HISTORY OF THE CZEKHISH OR BOHEMIAN LANGUAGE AND LITERATURE.

Of all the Slavic languages, the Bohemian dialect with its literature is the only one, which, in the mind of the protestant reader, can excite a more than general interest. Not so much indeed by its own nature, in which it differs little from the other Slavic languages; but from those remarkable circumstances, which, in the night of a degenerate Romanism, made the Bohemian tongue, with the exception of the voice of Wickliffe, the first organ of truth. Wickliffe's influence, however great and decided it may have been, was nevertheless limited to the theologians and literati of the age; his voice did not find that responding echo among the common people, which alone is able to give life to abstract doctrines. It was in Bohemia, that the spark first blazed up into a lively flame, which a century later spread an enlightening fire over all Europe. The names of Huss and Jerome of Prague can never perish; although less success has made them less current than those of Luther and Melancthon. In no language of the world has the Bible been studied with more zeal and devotion; no nation has ever been more willing to seal their claims upon the Word of God with their blood. The long contests of the Bohemians for liberty of conscience, and their final destruction, present one of the most heart-rending tragedies to be found in human history. Not less ready to maintain their convictions with the pen than with the sword, the theological literature of the fifteenth, sixteenth, and the first twenty years of the seventeenth centuries, is of an extent with which that of no other Slavic language can be compared. It is true, however, that most of these productions bear decidedly the stamp of the period in which they were written. Dictated by the polemical spirit of the age, and for the most part directed by one protestant party against another, there is very little to be found in them to gratify the Christian, or from which the theological student of the present day could derive any other than historical instruction. On the other hand, while the theological literature of all the other Slavic nations is almost exclusively limited to sermons, catechisms, prayer-books, and other devotional exercises, among the Bohemians alone do we meet with exegetical researches and interpretations, founded on a scientific examination of the original text of the Scriptures.

There are few branches of science or art in which the Bohemians have not to boast of some eminent name. But the talent for which this nation is the most distinguished is that of music A fondness for music and a natural gift to execute it is indeed common to all Slavic nations; but whilst their talent is mostly confined to a susceptible ear, and a skill in imitating,—for the Russians and Poles possess some celebrated musical *performers* though very few distinguished *composers*,—the talent of the Bo hemian is of a far higher order. He unites the spirit of harmony which characterizes the Germans, with the sweet gift of melody belonging to the Italians, and thus seems to be the true *ideal* of a complete musician. A great part of the most eminent names among German composers are Bohemians by birth; and there is hardly any thing which strikes the American and English traveller in that beautiful region more, than the general prevalence of a gift so seldom met with in their own countries.

Bohemia, until the sixth century was inhabited by a Celtic race, the Boii. After them the country was called *Boiohemum*, i. e. home of the Boii; in German still Böheim.[1] The Boii were driven to the south-west by the Markomanns; the Markomanns were conquered by the Lombards. After the downfall of the great kingdom of Thuringia in the middle of the sixth century, Slavic nations pushed forward into Germany, and the *Czekhes* settled in Bohemia, where an almost deserted country offered them little or no resistance. The Czekhes, a Slavic race, came from Belo-Chrobatia, as the region north of the Carpathian range was then called.[2] Their name has been usually explained from that of their chief, Czekh; but Dobrovsky more satisfactorily derives it from *czeti*, *czjti*, to begin, to be the first; according to him Czekhes signifies much the same as Front-Slavi.[3] The person of Czekh has rather a mythological than an historical

---

[1] More generally contracted into *Böhmen.*

[2] The country along the banks of the Upper Vistula. According to other writers, Belo-Chrobatia was the name of the country on both sides of the Carpathian chain. In some old chronicles the Czekhes are said to have come from *Croatia*, which induced more modern historians to suppose them to have emigrated from the present Croatia; others conclude that under this name Chrobatia was understood, as these names were frequently confounded.

[3] In his essay *Ueber den Ursprung des Namen Czech*, Prague and Vienna, 1782. In his later works he confirms this opinion; see *Geschichte der böhmischen Sprache und alten Literatur*, Prague, 1818, p. 65.

foundation. The whole history of that period, indeed, is so intimately interwoven with poetical legends and mythological traditions, that it seems impossible at the present time to distinguish real facts from poetical ornaments. The hero of the ancient chronicles Samo, the just Krok, Libussa the wise and beautiful, and the husband of her choice, the peasant Perzmislas, all move in a circle of poetical fiction. There is, however, no doubt that there is an historical foundation for all these persons; for tradition only expands and embellishes; but rarely, if ever, invents.

What we have said in our introduction, in regard to the vestiges of an early cultivation of the Slavic nations in general, must be applied to the Czekhes particularly.[4] The courts of justice in which the just Krok and his daughter presided, and which the chronicles describe to us, present indeed a wonderful mixture of the sacred forms of a well organized society, and of that patriarchal relation, which induced the dissenting parties to yield with childlike submission to the arbitrary decisions of the prince's wisdom. According to the chronicle, so early as A. D. 722, Libussa kept a *pisak* or clerk, literally, *a writer;* and her prophecies were written down in Slavic characters. The same princess is said to have founded Prague. A considerable number of Bohemian poems, some of which have been only recently discovered, are evidently derived from the pagan period. Libussa's choice of the country yeoman Perzmislas for her husband, in preference to her noble suitors, indicates the early existence of a free and independent peasantry. All these scattered features are however insufficient to give us a distinct picture of this early period; and here, as among all other Slavic nations, *history* commences only with the introduction of Christianity. The small states originally founded by the Czekhes, were first united into one dukedom during the last years of Perz-

---

[4] See above, pp. 6, 30.

mislas; while under his son Nezamysl, in the year 752, they are said to have first distributed the lands in fee, and to have given to the whole community a constitutional form.

The name of Boii, Bohemians, was transferred to the Czekhes by the neighbouring nations. They continued to call themselves Czekhes, as they do even now. The Moravians, a nearly related Slavic race, who probably came to these regions at the same time with the Czekhes, called themselves *Morawczik*,[5] from *Morawa*, morass, a name frequently repeated in Slavic countries. Until A. D. 1029, they were as a people entirely separated from the Bohemians. They had formed different petty states; their chiefs were called *Kniazi*, like those of their eastern brethren. The ancient Moravia, however, spread far beyond the limits of the present country of this name, and extended deep into Hungary. Hence this portion of the Slavic race was also generally comprised under the name of the Pannonic Slavi. We have shown above, in the history of the Old Slavonic language, that Moravia, then for a short period a powerful kingdom, was the principal theatre of Methodius' exertions.[6] As at this

---

[5] In writing Russian and Servian names, we have adapted our orthography to the English rules of pronunciation, so far namely as English letters are able to express sounds partly unknown to all but Slavic nations. The Poles and Bohemians however, who use the same characters as the English, have a right to expect that in writing their national names in the English language, their orthography should be preserved; just as it is in the case of the French, Spaniards, Italians, etc. No English writer would change French or Spanish nnmes according to the English principles of pronunciation. We consequently alter letters only in cases where otherwise a foreigner, unacquainted with the Bohemian language, would find an absolute impossibility of pronouncing them correctly.—In both Polish and Bohemian *c* is in every case pronounced like *ts*; hence Janocky must be pronounced *Janotsky*; Rokycana, *Rokytsana*; Ctibor, *Tstibor*, etc. The Bohemian *cz* is equivalent to the English *ch* in *check*; so in their national name, *Czekhes*. The vowels *a*, *e*, *i*, *y*, are every where to be pronounced as in *father*, *they*, *machine*, *frisky*.

[6] See above, pp. 33, 34.

time Christianity had been already introduced into these regions, and the kings Rostislav and Svatopluk, as well as most of their subjects, were already baptized, it is very probable that they were induced by motives of policy to send to Constantinople for a Christian teacher. Oppressed by the Germans, the usurpations of whose emperors were in a certain measure sanctioned by the chair of Rome, they desired to secure for themselves in the Byzantine court a powerful ally. After the dissolution of the Moravian kingdom in A. D. 1029, the present Moravia fell to Bohemia; was separated from it repeatedly in the course of the following centuries; and at length, in the beginning of the seventeenth century, became together with this kingdom an ingredient part of the Austrian states.

The Moravians were among the earliest Slavic tribes converted to Christianity. As early as the seventeenth century a considerable portion of them were baptized by German priests. It was however not before the first half of the ninth century, that the first Christian missionaries entered Bohemia. In the year 845, fourteen Bohemian princes were baptized at Ratisbon. In the year 894 the duke Borzivog, the head of the nation, received baptism; but his successors went back to idolatry, and with them the greatest part of the people. Christianity was not firmly established in these regions until the second half of the tenth century. At this time the Slavic liturgy introduced by Methodius into Moravia was already, in some measure, by the indefatigable exertions of the Romish German priesthood, superseded by the Latin worship. Thus it never was fully established in Bohemia; with the exception of a few churches, attached to convents founded expressly in memory of the Slavic saints, Jerome, Cyril, and Methodius. Their inmates however were expelled in favour of German-Bohemian monks, or they died; and with them disappeared every vestige of the innovations of Cyril and Methodius. Hence the Old Slavic language, and the noble translation of the

Bible extant in it, have exercised only an inconsiderable influence on the Bohemian idiom.[7]

Bohemia, under the sovereignty of her dukes, and from A. D. 1198, under that of kings, was independent of the German empire, or at least did not belong to its circles; it recognized however a kind of sovereignty in that powerful neighbour, and the kings of Bohemia deemed it an honour to belong to the seven Electors, who chose the worldly head of Christianity. In the year 1306, the last male descendant of Perzmislas was murdered. His house had reigned in Bohemia in uninterrupted succession; although the kingdom was properly not hereditary, but elective, like Germany, Hungary, and Poland. After a short interval, the crown of Bohemia fell by succession to the house of Luxemburg, and thus became several times united with the Roman imperial crown. Under the emperor Charles IV, Bohemia rose to the summit of its lustre. It was he who founded, A. D. 1348, the university of Prague, the first Slavic institution of that description.[8] Under his successor, Wenceslaus, the war of the Hussites began. In the year 1457, the Bohemians maintained their right of election by placing George Podiebrad, a Bohemian, on the throne. The wisdom and equity of this individual justified their choice. In A. D. 1527, Ferdinand I, archduke of Austria, was elected king; and from that time the Bohemians have never again been able to detach themselves from Austria;

---

7 On the fate of the Old Slavic liturgy and language in Bohemia, see Dobrovsky's *Geschichte der böhm. Sprache*, etc. pp. 46–64.

8 According to the Pole Soltykowicz, Casimir the Great laid the foundation of the high school of Cracow as early as A. D. 1347; but it is certain, that this institution was not organized before 1400; whilst the papal privilege granted for the University of Prague is dated A. D. 1347, and the imperial charter in A. D. 1348. Jerome of Prague, one of its most celebrated professors, was invited to Cracow in 1409, to assist in the organization of that institution.

with the exception of a short interval, during which the unfortunate palatine Frederic, known in the history of the thirty years' war, was placed on their throne. During the fifteenth, sixteenth, and the first half of the seventeenth, centuries, Bohemia was almost without interruption the theatre of bloody wars and contests in behalf of their religious liberties. Then came the awful stillness of death, which reigned for more than a hundred years over this exhausted and agonized country. For its revival and its present comparatively flourishing condition, it is indebted to its own rich natural resources, and to the wiser policy and milder dispositions of the more recent Austrian sovereigns.

The Bohemian language is the common property not only of the Bohemians and the Moravians, constituting together about three and a half millions in number, but also of nearly two millions of Slovaks, those venerable remains of the ancient Slavic settlements between the Carpathian mountains and the rivers Theiss and Danube. This people, so nearly related to the Czekhes, occupy the whole north-western part of Hungary; and are, besides this, scattered over that whole kingdom. They *speak* indeed a dialect or rather several dialects essentially different from the language spoken in Bohemia and Moravia; but the circumstance of their having, since the Reformation, chosen the Bohemian for their literary language, amalgamates their contributions to literature with those of the Bohemians, and gives them an equal right to the productions of these latter.

Of all the modern Slavic languages, the Bohemian was the first cultivated. Two bishops of Merseburg, Boso towards the middle of the tenth century, and Werner at the close of the eleventh, as also fifty years later another German priest, Bruno, were above all active in promoting the holy cause of Christianity by religious instruction. The application of Latin characters to Slavic words had long been familiar to the German priesthood; inasmuch as very early attempts had been made to convert the subjugated Slavic tribes, scattered through the north of Germany.

They now were applied to the Bohemian, so far as writing was requisite for religious instruction. According to the old chronicles, there were even some regular schools erected in those early times, one at Budecz, near Prague, and another somewhat later in Prague itself, where Latin was taught. Be this as it may, the Latin and German languages had an early influence on the formation of the Bohemian. Many foreign words were adopted and amalgamated with the language; still more were formed from native roots, after the model of those two idioms. In later times this capacity of the Bohemian has been greatly improved; it being one of the few languages, which, in philosophy, theology, and jurisprudence, have not borrowed their terminology from the Latins and Greeks, but formed their own technical expressions for ideas received only in part from other nations. The extraordinary refinement of the Bohemian verb we have mentioned in our remarks upon the Slavic languages in general.[9] In respect to free and independent construction, the Bohemian approaches the Latin; by its richness in conjunctions it differs essentially from the Russian, and is able to imitate the Greek in all its lighter shades. Thus it yields neither in copiousness nor in pliability, neither in clearness nor in precision, to any other Slavic language; while in respect to lexical and grammatical cultivation it is superior to all of them. The Bohemian alone, of all the Slavic languages, has hitherto succeeded in imitating perfectly the classic metres; although the same degree of capacity for them is acknowledged in the Southern-Slavic dialects.

After so much well deserved praise, we must also mention, that in respect to sound, the reproach of harshness and want of euphony has been made with more justice against none of the

[9] See above, p. 17.

Slavic tongues. It is true that all the reasons, by which we have above seen the Slavic languages in general defended,[10] apply with equal weight to the Bohemian in particular. It appears also, that this apparent harshness is more a production of modern times, than a necessary ingredient of the original language; for the ancient Bohemian of legends and popular songs sounds by far more melodious; and the dialects spoken by the Slovaks, which are kindred to the Old Bohemian, are full of vowels, and are even distinguished from the other Slavic tongues by diphthongs. On the other hand, it cannot be denied, that the accumulation of consonants, in which the Bohemian surpasses by far, not the Polish, but the southern and eastern languages, and its peculiar preference of the vowels *e* and *i* over the fuller sounding *a*, *o*, *u*, do not add to the euphony of the language; although it seems singular to bring forward such a reproach against a people so distinguished for their musical talent.

The history of the Bohemian literature may be divided into five periods.

The *first* comprises the whole interval from our first knowledge of the Czekhes to the influence of Huss; or from A. D. 550 to A. D. 1400.

The *second* period comprises a full century, from Huss to the general diffusion of the art of printing.

The *third* period, the golden age of the Bohemian literature, comprises about the same interval, and extends to the battle at the White Mountain, A. D. 1620.

The *fourth* period, extends from the battle at the White Mountain to the revival of literature in 1774–1780.

The *fifth* period, covers the interval from 1780 to the present time.

---

[10] See p. 21.

FIRST PERIOD.

From the first settlement of the Czekhes, A. D. 550, *to John Huss, A. D.* 1400.

Of the language of the Czekhes as it existed when they first settled in Bohemia, nothing is left, except the names they gave to the rivers, mountains, and towns, and those of their first chiefs. All these names entitle us to conclude, that their language was then essentially the same as at the present time, though more nearly approaching the Old Slavic. The first *certain* written documents of the language are not older than the introduction of Christianity. There were indeed discovered, about thirty years ago, some fragments of poetry, which appear to be derived from the pagan period.[11] The manuscript has been deposited in the Museum of Prague, and the high beauties and evident antiquity of these poems have secured them warm advocates and admiring commentators. But the circumstance that Dobrovsky doubted their genuineness, induces us to regard this point at least as not incontestable in respect to the language; in respect to the manners they describe, and the institutions they allude to, they bear very strong evidence of a later origin.[12] Another highly valuable fragment is the celebrated manuscript of Königinhof, discovered in the year 1817 by the librarian Hanka, half buried

---

[11] First communicated in the periodical *Krok*, Vol. I. Pt. III. p. 48–61. Rokawiecki, Hanka, Czelakowsky, and Schaffarik, maintain their authenticity.

[12] This manuscript, which was sent in anonymously at the founding of the Museum in 1818, and which Dobrovsky was at first very much inclined to think a forgery, has since been published (1840) in the first volume of a collection of the most ancient documents of the Bohemian Language, edited by Palacki and Schaffarik.

among rubbish and worthless papers.[13] This collection, the genuineness of which is subject to no doubt, contains likewise several poems, the original composition of which belongs evidently to the eighth or ninth century. But the manuscript itself is not older than the end of the thirteenth century, and cannot therefore be considered as a sure monument of the language in an earlier age. All these national songs have an historical foundation; they celebrate battles and victories; and their evident tendency is to exalt the national feelings. They have not that plastic and *objective* character which makes Homer and the Servian popular epics so remarkable; and from which it appears that the poet, during the time of his inspiration, is rather *above* his subject; but like the Russian tale of Igor's Expedition, the epic beauties are merged in the lyric effusions of the poet's own feelings, who thus never attempts to conceal that his whole soul is engaged in his subject.

The oldest monuments of the Christian age are the names of the days, which are of pure Slavic origin. Of the Lord's Prayer in Bohemian, on comparing the oldest copy he could find among the ancient manuscripts, Dobrovsky presumes that the form must have been about the same in the ninth or tenth century; although the manuscript itself is somewhat later. A translation of the

---

[12] In a chamber attached to the church of Königinhof or Kralodwor. It was published by Hanka in 1819, with a translation in modern Bohemian and in German, under the title *Rukopis Kralodworsky*, Manuscript of Königinhof. According to Dobrovsky, who formed his judgment from the writing, this remarkable manuscript belongs to the interval from about A. D. 1290 to A. D. 1310. By the numbering of the chapters and books into which it is divided, it appears that the collection comprised three volumes; and that the manuscript thus accidentally rescued from oblivion, is only a small part of the third volume. Goethe honoured it with his peculiar attention and applause. Bowring has given some pleasing specimens of it, in his essay on Bohemian literature in the Foreign Quarterly Review, Vol. II. p. 151–153

Kyrie eleison, ascribed to Adalbert second bishop of Prague, dates from the same time. During the eleventh and twelfth centuries many convents were founded and schools attached to them; German artists and mechanics and even agriculturists settled in Bohemia. The influence of German customs and habits showed itself more and more, and the nobility began to use in preference the German language. In the course of the thirteenth and fourteenth centuries, this influence increased considerably, and exhibited itself most favourably in the lyric poetry of the time, an echo of the German Minnesingers; many of the poets belonging like them to the highest nobility. Of all the Slavic nations, the Bohemian is the only one in which the flower of chivalry has ever unfolded itself; and the cause of its developement here is doubtless to be sought in their occidental feudal system, and in their constant intercourse with the Germans. The natural tendency of the Polish nobility to heroic deeds and chivalrous adventures was counterbalanced, partly by the oriental character of their relation to the peasantry, which impressed on them at least as much of the character of the Asiatic satrap, as of the occidental knight; and partly by the want of a free middle class in Poland, as also in Russia. True chivalry indeed does not require simply the contrast of a low, helpless, and submissive class; its lustre never appears brighter than when placed side by side with an independent yeomanry.

In calling the Bohemian lyric poetry of this age the echo of the German, we do not mean to say it was wanting in originality; but wish rather to convey the idea, that the same spirit inspired at the time the Bohemians and the Germans, proceeding however from the latter, who themselves received it from the more romantic Provence. Of these heroic love-songs very few are left. There are, however, several productions of this period, in which the German influence is not to be recognized at all, but which exhibit purely Slavic national features. We will here enumerate the monuments of the Bohemian language from the twelfth and thirteenth centuries, which have been preserved, before we pass to the fourteenth, which was more productive and exhibited in some measure a new character.

The most remarkable is the above-mentioned manuscript of Königinhof. It contains, besides several epic songs partly complete and partly fragmentary, seven or eight charming lyric pieces. The near relationship of the Slavic nations among each other, is exhibited in no feature more strikingly than in their national popular poetry, especially in the little lyric songs, the immediate effusion of their feelings, wishes, and cares; whilst epic poetry, which draws her materials from the external world, must hence, in every nation, be in some measure modified by their different fortunes and situations. With the exception of this manuscript and a few scattered love-songs and tales, all we have from this early period is of a religious character, viz. a fragment of a history of Christ's passion in rhymes, another of a legend of the twelve apostles, and a hymn on the merits of the Bohemian patron saint, Wenceslaus. There is also a complete Psalter in Bohemian, with a whole series of hymns, or rather rhymed formularies, corresponding to those sung in the catholic church, viz. a *Te Deum*, an office for the dead, a prayer for the intercession of all saints, etc. A piece in prose, entitled "The complaint of a lover on the banks of the Moldau," a very rare appearance in those early times, was formerly considered as genuine, on the authority of Linde and Dobrovsky; but has since been proved to be spurious. The first historians of Bohemia, Cosmas and Vincentius, born towards the middle of the eleventh century, wrote both of them in Latin. The chronicle of the first is still extant.

During the fourteenth century the German influence increased so much, that the jealousy and impatience of a great part of the nation was powerfully excited. The king kept a German body guard; German fashions in dress and manners prevailed at the court; and even in the year 1341, when the privileges of the city of Prague were first solemnly committed to writing, it was done in the German language. Under the reign of Charles I, or the emperor Charles IV, for he united the two crowns on his head, Bohemia, as we have said, reached the highest point of its splendour. He wisely limited the privileges of the Germans in his own kingdom; and reconciled the minds of the Bohemians by granting to them similar privileges in the German empire. He honoured the Bohemian language so much as to recommend expressly, in the golden bull, to the sons of the Electors to learn it. His capital, Prague, was like the apple of his eye; and he did all he could to add to its embellishments and magnificence. Here he founded in the year 1348 the first Slavic university, on the plan of those of Paris and Bologna. The influence of this institution, not merely on Bohemia, but on Germany and indeed all Europe, was decided. From the time of its foundation until 1410, it was the general resort for students from among the Poles, Hungarians, Swedes, and Germans. It was doubtless the wish to give it this very kind of universality, which induced Charles IV, in the statutes of the institution, to allow to the Bohemians only one suffrage in the senate, and the three others to foreigners. We shall show in the sequel, with what jealousy this apparent preference was received by the natives, and what a violent reaction it caused in the Bohemian national feelings.

Experience every where teaches, that schools and academies never enkindle the spark of genuine poetry; nay, that the erection of formal scientific institutions is even not favourable to the free developement of that high gift. In Bohemia, too, the fourteenth century was indeed very productive in rhymed works; but most of them were utterly deficient in real poetry. On the other hand, as the natural result of a more strictly logical and clearer mode of thinking, by reason of a scientific education, the style of the prose writings became more cultivated, concise, and distinct; and the direction of mind more general and universal. We find in this period several historical works, viz. (1) A chronicle in Bohemian rhymes, extending as far as to 1313, and finished about the year 1318, written under king John the father of Charles IV, when the influence of the German had reached its highest point. A glowing hatred against that nation dictated this work, and made it for more than two hundred years the favourite book of the Bohemian people. The name of the author is not ascertained, although it has been usually ascribed to the canon Dalimil Mezericky.[14] (2) Another Bohemian chronicle, written by order of Charles IV in Latin, but translated into Bohemian by Przibik Pulkawa. It was first published by Prochazka in the year 1786; the Latin original in 1794. (3) Martimiani or the Roman chronicle, translated A. D. 1400 from the German, by Benesh of Horowic. (4) Another chronicle of the Roman emperors, translated from the Latin by Laurentius of Brezow, the writer of several other works, some of which were printed in the course of the following centuries.—There were also several collections of laws; among others the oldest Bohemian statutes, by A. of Duba, a valuable manuscript, preserved in the imperial library of Vienna; the common and the feudal law, translated from the Latin and kept in the library of Prague; the celebrated *Sachsenspiegel* or laws of Magdeburg, etc. The constant intercourse with foreigners directed the attention of the

[14] It was first published by Jeshin, A. D. 1620; later by Prochazka, Prague 1786. The author spurned no means to reach his patriotic object, viz. to inspire his nation with hatred against the Germans. The most absurd fables came through him into the early history of Bohemia. During the late rule of prince Metternich, this work was considered by the censors as too ultra-national, and was put on the list of the forbidden books. It is only quite recently (1849), that Hanka has been allowed to publish a new edition, carefully prepared by himself after the collation of several manuscripts.

Bohemians early to the utility of acquiring other languages, and made the possession of their own valuable to foreigners. We find, consequently, not less than seven dictionaries, or vocabularies as they were called, compiled in the course of this century; one of which, the *Bohemarius* so called of A. D. 1309, is even written in hexameters. As all these vocabularies are incomplete, and better ones, founded partly upon them, have been since compiled, they have never, so far as we know, been printed; but are extant in several copies, and are preserved in the libraries of Prague, Brünn, and several churches.

Poetry, during this century, took also in Bohemia the same course as in Germany, and degenerated into loose works of fiction between prose and verse, mostly allegorical compositions, and the basis of the modern novel. Such are Tristram, in 9000 verses, a translation from the German; the life of Alexander and the History of Troy from the Latin, both of them more novel than history; and a great number of similar works.[15] Some fragments of an heroic epic, entitled "The Bohemian Alexander," have been recently found in the archives of Budweis by Professor Kaubek, and published in the Journal of the Museum. All the other poetical productions of this century may be divided into fables, satires, and legends, or other allegorical pieces of an ecclesiastico-didactic tendency, as may be seen even from their

---

[15] The History of Troy was one of the first works which isssued from the Bohemian press, about A. D. 1476 according to Dobrovsky; and again A. D. 1488, and 1603. It was published for the fourth and last time by Kramerius in 1790. Even before it was printed, it appears to have been multiplied in a great many copies, as being a favourite book among the Bohemian knights and damsels. Its author was Guido di Colonna. See Dobrovsky's *Geschichte der böhm. Sprache*, p. 155. Another remarkable production of the fourteenth century is *Tkadleczek*, the Little Weaver, the manuscript of which is extant in several copies; but it has been printed only in an ancient German translation; see Dobrovsky, ibid. p. 157.

titles ; e. g. the Nine Joys of Mary, the Ten Commandments, the Five Sources of Sin, etc. All are equally deficient in poetical merit.

With what thoughts the minds of reflecting men and of the reading class were at this time chiefly occupied, and how well they were prepared to receive, in the beginning of the following century, the doctrines of Huss, Jerome, and Jacobellus, those teachers of a purer system of divinity, is manifested in some measure in the theological literature of the day. A treatise upon the great distress of the church, written by a clergyman called John Milicz, before 1370 ;[16] several others on the principal Christian virtues ; a book of Christian instruction written by Shtitny, a Bohemian nobleman, for his own children ; a translation of the Jewish Rabbi Samuel's book on the coming of the Messiah ; and several similar works,—all these seem to indicate that the religious system of the day was no longer able to satisfy reflecting minds. We find also that a great part of the Bible was already extant in the Bohemian language in the second half of the fourteenth century ;[17] although not yet collected together. Several translations of the Psalter from this period ; also of the prophets Isaiah, Jeremiah, and Daniel ; and the Sunday lessons from the Gospels ; are preserved in manuscript in the

---

[16] This work was printed in 1542 ; it was put into the renowned *Index librorum prohibitorum* first printed in 1629, and the Bohemian part last in 1767 ; the original author of which was the famous Jesuit Koniash, one of the most violent book-destroyers who ever lived. Not only all books written by the Hussites or their immediate predecessors, but even many catholic writers also of that period were put upon this list ; e. g. the historian Hagek, translations of Æneas Sylvius, etc.

[17] Ann, queen of England, sister to king Wenceslaus of Bohemia, possessed a Bible in Latin, German and Bohemian ; to which circumstance Wickliffe alluded in one of his writings, quoted by Huss in his reply to Stockes, Tom. I. p. 108. See Dobrovsky's *Gesch. der böhm. Sprache*, p. 142.

libraries of Prague, Vienna, and Oels in Silesia. Many others have doubtless perished in the lapse of time.

SECOND PERIOD.

From John Huss, A. D. 1400, *to the general diffusion of the art of printing, about A. D.* 1500.

At the commencement of the fifteenth century, the university of Prague was in the zenith of its splendour. Several celebrated German scholars occupied the professors' chairs, and the average number of students was twenty thousand. No department of science was neglected ; each faculty had its distinguished teachers; but it was theology which excited decidedly the warmest national interest among the Bohemians themselves; it was theology in which the Bohemians maintained the first rank as teachers. The interest in spiritual things was no longer confined, as in former times, to those who intended to devote themselves to the clerical profession; it pervaded all classes, high and low. Immediately after Wickliffe's death, an intercourse had been opened between England and Bohemia by the marriage of a Bohemian princess, Ann, sister of king Wenceslaus, to Richard II of England. A young Bohemian nobleman, who had finished his studies in Prague, repaired to Oxford, imbibed the sentiments and opinions of Wickliffe, and on his return put a copy of all Wickliffe's writings into the hands of John Huss, at that time one of the professors of theology at Prague; whose mind was probably already prepared for them, and who began to study them with great zeal and devotion. Indeed, the pretensions of the chair of Rome, and the corruption of the clergy, had been for some time since looked upon in Bohemia with private disgust and open disapprobation; and when the professors Huss,

Jerome, and Jacobellus, began to declaim against monks, auricular confession, and the infallibility of the pope, they found a responding echo in the breasts of their hearers; and all that was novel in their doctrines, was the boldness with which they were pronounced, and the logical consistency with which they were justified.

Another difference of opinion, which tended greatly to augment the excitement then reigning at the university, was the contest between the two philosophical schools, viz. that of the Realists, who were defended by Huss, and the Nominalists, to which nearly all the Germans adhered. This contest became very soon a national affair; or, more probably, had its principal origin in the unjust privileges of the Germans and the jealousy of the Bohemians. The preference given to the former at the foundation of the university, viz. the possession of three out of the four suffrages in all matters determined by vote, became anew the subject of debate, and was more especially assailed by Huss, then rector of the university. After a whole year of resistance, the king at length yielded. A decree of A. D. 1409 ordained that in future the proportion should be reversed, so that the Germans should possess only one suffrage, and the Bohemians three. For this victory of their national pride, the university, the city, nay the whole country, had to suffer severely. Immediately after this decision, the famous literary emigration took place. All the German professors and students left Prague at once. The immediate consequences of this step were, the foundation of the universities of Leipzig, Rostock, and Ingolstadt; and the building up of those of Heidelberg, Erfurt, and Cracow. Prague never again became what it had been; although it obtained a transient lustre through the victory itself, and the eminence and martyrdom of some of its national teachers. Before we proceed, we must devote a few words to the personal merits and fortunes of these latter.

John Huss was born A. D. 1373, at Hussinecz, a village in the southern part of Bohemia; from which he sometimes took the name of Huss of Hussinecz, or John of Hussinecz. Although without property himself, he was enabled, at the age of sixteen years, by the pecuniary assistance of the proprietor of his native village and some other patrons, to prosecute his studies at the university of Prague, where he distinguished himself by his abilities and diligence. In the year 1396 he was made Master of Arts, and two years later began to lecture on philosophical and theological subjects. In A. D. 1402 he was appointed curate and preacher to the chapel of Bethlehem at Prague, the duties of which office he united with his professorship. In the same year the queen Sophia chose him for her confessor. He thus at once acquired an influence over the people, the students, and at court. It was about this time that he became acquainted with the writings of Wickliffe. In the year 1407 he began publicly to oppose and preach against the errors in doctrine and the corruption then reigning in the church. The archbishop of Prague, Zbyniek, an illiterate and violent man, whose ignorance had made him the laughing-stock of the students, by whom he was called the *Alphabetarius*, or A B C doctor, collected two hundred manuscripts of Wickliffe's writings; and, without any further authority from the pope than his previous condemnation of them, committed them to the flames in the archiepiscopal palace. Huss, both in his lectures and sermons, not only blamed this act in strong terms; but translated the *Trilogus* and several other of Wickliffe's works into Bohemian, distributed them among laymen and females, and caused new Latin copies to be made. When the archbishop interdicted his preaching in the Bohemian language, Huss not only refused to obey, but continued to spread, by all legal means, those doctrines of Wickliffe which he approved. At the same time the first translation of the whole Bible—whether a collection of the parts already extant, or a new version, we are not informed—appeared, and was distributed in multiplied copies among the public. It is not known whether this translation was prepared by Huss; but it is certain that he did what he could to promote its circulation. On such proceedings the Romish clergy could not look with tranquillity. Twice he was called to Rome; twice he disobeyed; and at length appealed to a general council. In consequence of his doctrines, and of some tumultuous scenes among his followers, the excess of which he himself highly disapproved, he was by a decree of pope John XXIII solemnly expelled from the communion of the church. Deeming himself no longer safe at Prague under the weak king, he retired to the territory of his friend and patron, Nicholas of Hussinecz, where he prepared new works, some of which are among his most powerful ones, and preached repeatedly in the open fields before an innumerable audience. Those of his works which caused the greatest sensation, were his treatise 'On the Church,' and a pamphlet entitled 'The Six Errors;' both of which he caused to be fixed on the walls and gates of the chapel of Bethlehem. Both were directed against indulgences, against the abuse of excommunication, simony, transubstantiation, and the like; and, above all, against the unlimited obedience required by the see of Rome; maintaining that the Scriptures presented the only rule of faith and conduct for the Christian.

In consequence of this conviction, the correction and distribution of the Bohemian Bible was his constant care. In all his Bohemian writings he paid an uncommon attention to the language, and exerted a decided and lasting influence on it. The old Bohemian alphabet, which consisted of forty-two letters, he arranged anew; and first settled the Bohemian orthography according to fixed principles.[18] In order to render it more

---

[18] The Bohemians, like the Germans, adopted the Latin alphabet; but the former, receiving it from the Germans, adopted it in the corrupted form of these latter, viz. they imitated the Gothic letters, so called, in which also all ancient

interesting and impressive to learners, he imitated Cyril's ingenious mode of giving to each letter the name of some well-known Bohemian word, which had the same initial letter, e. g. H, *hospodin*, lord; K, *kral*, king, etc. Thus he devoted his whole life to the different means of enlightening his countrymen; and justly considered a general cultivation of the mind as the best preparation for receiving the truth.

Among the coadjutors of Huss, the most distinguished was Hieronymus von Faulfisch, more generally known under the name of Jerome of Prague; who was, like Huss, professor in the university. In erudition and eloquence he surpassed his friend; he accorded with him in his doctrinal views; but did not possess the mild disposition, the moderation of conduct, for which Huss was distinguished. His hatred against the abuses of the Romish church was so violent, that he used to trample under his feet the relics regarded as holy by that church. He is even said to have once ordered a monk who resisted him, to be thrown into the river. He was so great an admirer of Wickliffe, several of whose writings he translated into Bohemian, that even when preaching before the emperor at Buda, he could not but interweave that reformer's doctrines in his sermons; an imprudence which caused him to be arrested immediately afterwards at Vienna. He obtained his liberty in consequence of the solicitation of the university of Prague. He wrote several works in the Bohemian language, for the instruction of the people,

---

Bohemian books are printed. In modern times the genuine Roman letters have nearly supplanted them; to which several different signs are added to adapt them to the Slavic sounds. The Bohemian alphabet can only be said to have forty-two letters, in so far as the same letter with or without a sign can be considered as two different letters. The English alphabet would be almost without number, if all the three or four modes of pronunciation connected with one and the same letter in that language, were indicated by certain signs, and these signs made three or four letters out of one.

hymns, pamphlets, etc. His reputation for erudition and extraordinary powers rests, however, more on the testimony of his cotemporaries, than on his works, of which very few remain.

Another active assistant of Huss, especially in his improvement and distribution of the Bohemian Bible, was Jacobellus of Mies, known under the name Jacobellus of the [sacramental] Cup, on account of his zeal for the general introduction of the communion in both forms. He wrote commentaries on some of the epistles, sermons, religious hymns, etc. He too was a professor in the university of Prague.

In the year 1414 Huss was summoned to appear before the Council of Constance, to exculpate himself before the united theologians of all the Christian nations of Europe. Without the least reluctance, and rather with rejoicing at the opportunity of justifying himself from the extravagant charges brought against him by his enemies, and of demonstrating publicly the truth of his doctrines, he obeyed this call. Provided with a safe conduct from the emperor Sigismund, and accompanied moreover by several Bohemian noblemen at the express order of king Wenceslaus, he undertook the journey without fear for his personal safety, and arrived on the fourth of November at Constance. Here, before he was permitted to appear in the presence of the general Council, he had to undergo several private audiences before a few cardinals; at one of which, about three weeks after his arrival, he was arrested, cast into prison, and without being tried or even heard, kept more than *six months.* When the news of this treachery reached Bohemia, it was felt by the whole people as a national insult. Three petitions, signed by nearly the whole body of the nobility, were in the course of time successively tendered to the Council; and as the two first were without avail, the third was accompanied by one to the emperor, in which he was reminded of his broken word, in terms so strong,—he having pledged his imperial honour for the safety of Huss,—

that at length the 5th of June was fixed for a public hearing. Here however every attempt of Huss, not merely to justify himself, but even to speak, was frustrated by the most indecent and tumultuous clamour of the assembled clergy, who loaded him with invectives and reproaches. In the two following audiences he was indeed allowed a hearing, at the special demand of the emperor, who had been disgusted and offended by the indecent behaviour of the Council. Huss was now permitted to justify himself at large upon all the forty articles brought against him, most of them founded on his writings by the frequent aid of the most unfair deduction; but although he exculpated himself completely from some of the charges, yet he himself acknowledged so many others, that the Council could only be confirmed in its previous determination to condemn him as an obstinate heretic. A month wass allowed him, to give in his final answer. During this time cardinals and bishops tried their eloquence to persuade him to recant; especially at the instigation of the emperor, who wished to save his life on account of his own pledged honour. But all these efforts could not move the faith nor firmness of this pious and heroic man; and on the 6th of July, A. D. 1415, he was unanimously condemned, ignominiously degraded from the office of a priest, and burned alive the same day. His ashes were thrown into the Rhine.[19]

[19] The Bohemian writings of Huss are extant partly in manuscript, partly in single printed pamphlets, but have never been collected. They consist of sermons, hymns, letters to his friends, postillae, and other interpretations of the Scriptures, etc. His complete Latin works were first printed in Wittenberg 1558, and repeatedly afterwards. They contain many pieces which were originally written in Bohemian; as were also the letters which Luther caused to be printed with a preface of his own, Wittenberg 1536. Luther translated several of his hymns. The letters written by Huss from the prison at Constance are the expressions of a pure and elevated mind, and present the best evidence of his spotless Christian character. Some of them might serve as beautiful specimens of the sublime.

His friend Jerome of Prague, on hearing of his dangerous situation, hurried to Constance, to assist and support him, without even waiting for a safe conduct from the emperor or Council. In the vicinity of Constance he stopped, and tried all possible means to obtain some assurance for his personal safety. Not succeeding in this, he felt himself compelled by prudence to return, although slowly and reluctantly, to Bohemia. But on the road, in consequence of a dispute in which he became engaged with some bigoted priets, he was arrested by the duke of Salzbach and sent to Constance, where the same scenes were repeated before the Council, as in the case of Huss. At his first appearance, a thousand voices exclaimed: Away with him! burn him, burn him! It is most melancholy to read in the reports of the time, that even this strong and pious man could have been terrified into temporary submission; not by the prospect of death, which he met gladly, but by the horrors of a lonely and protracted imprisonment in a noxious dungeon. But his fortitude did not long abandon him; tortured by his own conscience, he solemnly announced at the next audience his recantation; and declared, that of all the sins he had committed, he repented of none more than his apostasy from the doctrines he had maintained. In consequence of this he was subjected to the same condemnation as his illustrious friend; and met his painful death with the same magnanimity and resignation. He was burnt the 30th of May, 1416.

The behaviour of both these eminent men; the Christian mildness with which they bore the infamous treatment of their enemies; the generosity with which they forgave their persecutors; the patience, nay cheerfulness of Huss, when during his imprisonment severe bodily sufferings united with the persecutions of his adversaries to make his life a heavy burden; the magnanimity and fortitude with which both of them submitted to their final fate, and maintained the truth of their religious opinions until the very moment of an excruciating death, praising the Lord with soul and voice; all this presents one of the most affecting and at the same time elevating pictures which the history of martyrs has to exhibit. The eloquence of Jerome made a powerful impression on his enemies; and there were some moments during his trial, when even his judges wished to save his life. The celebrated Poggio Bracciolini, one of the revivers of Italian literature, happened to be present at the trial and execution of Jerome; and although not agreeing with him, or rather being indifferent in point of religion, the eloquence, magnanimity and amiable deportment of the unfortunate martyr, excited his sympathy and admiration in an uncommon degree. This is manifested in his letters to Leonardo Aretius; who in his reply found it advisable to warn his friend, not to show too much warmth in this matter.[20]

The instigators of these cruel acts, when they kindled the faggots by which these two martyrs died, did not anticipate that the fire they had lighted would spread over a whole country, and carry horror and devastation through the half of Germany. The war by which the disciples of Huss avenged him, was one of the most bloody and destructive known in history. The news of his death, when it reached Bohemia, touched the heart of every individual like an electric spark. But this is not our province. Keeping only our own object, the fate of the language and literature in view, we must refer the reader to the historical accounts of this distressing period, and limit ourselves to the mention of those events only, which had an immediate influence on these two topics.

---

[20] These interesting letters, containing all the circumstances of Jerome's last days and death, his eloquent speeches before the Council, and a full account of the despicable conduct of his accusers, may be found at large in Shepherd's Life of Poggio Bracciolini.

Under the guidance of Nicholas of Hussinecz, the friend and patron of Huss, in whom even his enemies acknowledged more a defender of the Reformers, than a persecutor of the Catholics; of Zhizhka of Trocznow, a Bohemian knight of great valour, but disgraced by cruelty; and, after the death of these two, under Procopius, formerly a clergyman; the Hussites carried their victorious arms throughout all Bohemia, into Silesia, Franconia, Austria, and Saxony; and made these unhappy countries the theatre of the most cruel devastations. If, divided into several parties, as they were, they were thus powerful, they would have been twice as strong, had they been united in the true spirit of Huss. But even as early as A. D. 1421 dissensions arose among them; and they finally split into several sects and parties, who mutually hated each other even more than they did the Romanists. Among these the Calixtins or Utraquists, whose principal object was to obtain the sacrament in both forms; and the Taborites, who insisted on a complete reform of the church; were the two principal. The Calixtins comprehended the more moderate of the nobility and the wealthy citizens of Prague; between them and the Romanists a compact was concluded at Basle, in A. D. 1434, by which a conditional religious liberty was granted to them, and they acknowledged the emperor Sigismund as their sovereign; the weak king Wenceslaus having died in 1419. The Taborites were unable to resist any longer the united power of both parties. They partly dispersed; the rest united in the year 1457, in separate communities, and called themselves United Brethren. Under the severest trials of oppression and persecution, the number of these congregations, the form of which was modelled after the primitive apostolic churches, rose in less than fifty years to two hundred. In the middle of the sixteenth century, numerous emigrations to Prussia and Poland took place, where a free toleration was secured to them. In the beginning of the seventeenth century, their communities in Bohemia were finally dissolved. From the remnant of these persecuted Christians, who were called by the Germans, Bohemian or Moravian Brethren, has sprung the present community of United Brethren, often called in English, Moravians, which was founded at Hernhut in 1722, at first under the protection and ultimately under the patronage and direction of count Zinzendorf.

The consequences of the barbarous measures of the Council of Constance became immediately visible. Even the common people began to show an intense interest in the numberless theological pamphlets, which were published in Bohemia and Moravia for or against Huss. Among the former, one written by a female deserves to be distinguished. The copies of the Bohemian Bible became greatly multiplied; many of them were made by females; and Æneas Sylvius takes occasion to praise the biblical erudition of the women of the Taborites, whilst the abbot Stephen of Dolan in Moravia complains of their meddling in ecclesiastical affairs. In the revision of the text of the Bohemian Scriptures, the clergy were indefatigable. From 1410 to 1488, when the Bible was first printed, at least four recensions of the whole Bible can be distinguished, and several more of the New Testament. The different parties of the Hussites were united in a warm partiality for their own language; the Taborites began as early as 1423 to hold their service in Bohemian. After the compact of 1434, the Calixtins also attempted to introduce the mass in their own language, an innovation which caused new disturbances and contests. Meanwhile the language of the country assumed gradually even among the Romanists its natural rights; the privileges of the city of Prague, the laws of the painters' guild, the statutes of the miners, were translated into Bohemian. At the session of the Estates in Moravia in 1480, the Latin was exchanged for the Bohemian; in Bohemia itself not before 1495. The knowledge of the Bohemian language, which Albert duke of Bavaria had acquired at the court of king Wenceslaus, where he was educated, had a decided influence on the Bohemian Estates, when in 1441 they offered him their crown. Under George Podiebrad, a Bohemian by birth, this language even became that of the court. After the death of George, one of the reasons which led to the election of Vladislaus, king of Poland, was, that the Bohemians "could hope to see elevated through him the glory of the Bohemian nation and of the Slavic language."[21] Under this king all ordinances and decrees were issued in the Bohemian language, which gained prodigiously in pliancy and extent by the application of it to different uses. The most favourable influence on its formation, however, was effected towards the close of the fifteenth century, by the custom which began to prevail of studying the classics, and of translating them with all the fidelity of which the idiom was capable. Thus fostered by judicious application and patriotic feeling, the Bohemian language approached, with rapid steps, the period of its *golden age*,—a time, indeed, in a political respect, of oppression, war, and devastation; but affording a gratifying proof, how powerfully moral means may counteract physical causes.

At the head of the theological literature of this period may be named the Life of Huss, written by P. Mladienowicz. Although, strictly speaking, not a theological book, yet this character was in some measure impressed upon it by the custom which prevailed for a time, of causing it to be read aloud in the churches, in order to communicate to the people all the circumstances of the martyr's death. Mladienowicz, acting as a notary at Constance, had been an eye-witness of the whole transaction. Among the Romish theological writers of the day, Hilarius Litomierzicky, ob. 1467, Rosenberg bishop of Breslau, Simon of Tishnow, and others, wrote against the practice of communion in both forms. But they were inferior to their adversaries in talent, and still

---

21 See Dobrovsky's *Geschichte der böhm. Sprache*, p. 201.

more in productiveness. Rokycana, archbishop of the Calixtins, ob. 1471, Koranda, Mirosh, and others, defended their right to the sacramental cup; and exerted their pens in doctrinal controversies with the other sects. The Bohemian Brethren, Paleczek, Procopius, Simon, Mirzinsky, and others, wrote interpretations of portions of the Scriptures, polemical pamphlets, religious hymns, apologies, and the like, partly printed, and partly preserved in manuscript. In the contests of the different parties, the use of weapons of every description was regarded as lawful; and among them, satire and irony were employed with much skill and dexterity by the Hussites.[22] Uricz of Kalenicz wrote a satirical letter from Lucifer to Lew of Rozhmital. Bohuslav of Czechticz partly wrote and partly compiled the work, "Mirror of all Christendom," with many remarkable illustrations.[23] The Bohemian brother, Chelcicky, ob. 1484, called also the Bohemian doctor, because he did not understand Latin, and of course neither Greek nor Hebrew, undertook, nevertheless, besides several other works, to write an interpretation of the Sunday Lessons of the Gospels. His most popular book, called *Kopyta*, i. e. "The Shoe-last," (being himself a shoemaker by trade,) which was much read by the common people, is no longer extant. A pamphlet of Martin Lupacz, ob. 1468, called "The Sprinkling-brush," was likewise in the hands of every body. This cler-

---

[22] In a polemic satirical pamphlet the question was started: "Master, tell me what birds are the best, those which eat and drink, or those which eat and do not drink? and why are those which eat but do not drink, enemies to those which eat and drink?" A Latin pamphlet which decided for those which do not drink, was followed by a Bohemian refutation.

[23] This manuscript, one of the most remarkable of the age, is in the library of Jena. It has not less than eighty-eight pictures, partly on paper, partly on parchment; and besides this forty-one smaller figures, scattered through the text itself. See Dobrovsky's *Reise nach Schweden*, p. 7; also his *Geschichte der böhm. Sprache*, p. 235.

gyman, however, acquired better claims on the gratitude of his cotemporaries, by a careful revision of the New Testament, which he undertook with the aid of several learned friends. Indeed, both among clergymen and laymen, there was an ardent desire for the right understanding of the Scriptures; which induced many individuals, who were not satisfied with the existing Bohemian translations, to undertake the task themselves anew.

Out of this period alone the manuscripts of thirty-three copies of the whole Bible, and twenty-two of the New Testament, are still extant; partly copied from each other, partly translated anew; all, however, having been made from the Vulgate.[24] The Bohemian versions made from the original languages belong to the following period.

Although religion filled the minds of the learned during this period more than in any other, it did not absorb their interest so entirely as to occupy them exclusively. It could not, however, be expected, that in the midst of such struggles, both political and religious, the minds of men could elevate themselves so far above their circumstances, as to look at any science or art in the light of its independent value. Poetry, at least, with a few exceptions, was only regarded as the handmaid of religion. We find many books of legends, biographies of the fathers and saints, both prose and rhyme, written partly by Romish, partly by Hussite writers. The doctrines of Huss did not, like those of Luther a century later, shake the belief in saints. Dobrovsky mentions a very ancient printed work of 1480, in which the letters of Huss,

---

[24] By whole Bibles are here intended also those manuscripts, of which, although in their present state incomplete, it is presumed that the missing parts were lost accidentally. The New Testaments also are not all of them perfect. Of single biblical books, manuscripts of the Psalms are found the most frequently. See Dobrovsky's *Lit. Magazin für Böhmen. Reise nach Schweden*, p. 57. *Geschichte der böhm. Sprache*, p. 211.

his life by Mladienowicz, and the letter of Poggio on the execution of Jerome, are annexed to a *Passional*, as such collections of the lives and sufferings of the saints are called. There is also an abundance of Taboritic war-songs; many of them replete with life and fire. These appear to have been partly founded on ancient Bohemian popular songs; for there are passages in them which are also to be found in the old chronicles. Altered to suit the existing circumstances, their effect must have been the more powerful by association. This period was also rich in religious hymns; most of them translated from the Bible as literally as the rhyme would permit. But no form of poetry was more used, and none operated more strongly on the minds of the people, than the satirical ballads, with which the streets and alleys every where resounded. All these productions are only remarkable, as characteristic memorials of the age. Hynek of Podiebrad, fourth son of king George, who was born A. D. 1452, a highly accomplished and amiable man, is named as one of the most distinguished among the Bohemian poets of the age.

Politics, too, united with religion. Stibor of Cimburg, a patriotic and distinguished nobleman, wrote in 1467 an ingenious work in the form of a novel, "On the goods of the Clergy;" Waleczowsky wrote on the vices and hypocrisy of the clergy; and Zidek, in 1471, instructions on government. All these books were dedicated to king George, and the latter work was even written at his instigation. Hagek of Hodielin, and Wlczek, between 1413 and 1457, wrote strategetical works. Marco Polo's description of the East, and Mandeville's Travels, were translated from the Latin. Kabatnik, J. Lobkowicz, and Bakalarz, wrote descriptions of Palestine between 1490 and 1500; the two first in books of travels. Mezyhor wrote a journal of the travels of Lew of Rozhmital, whom he accompanied as jester through Europe and a part of Asia. Collections of statutes, of the decrees of diets, of judicial decisions, and of other documents, were made by patriotic and sometimes eminent men; and those merely extant in Latin were carefully translated into Bohemian.[25] Thus they gathered materials for future historians, although in their own day the field of history was but poorly cultivated, or at least with no more than common ability; for, as to quantity, there is no want. Procopius, following out the example of Dalimil, wrote a new rhymed chronicle; Bartosh of Drahenicz wrote a chronicle extending from 1419 to 1443, in barbarous Latin, to which he added some notes in Bohemian. Several other chronicles, the authors of which are not known, serve as continuations of those of the preceding century, which were devoted to the affairs of their own country. The above-mentioned Zidek, on the other hand, undertook to write a universal history, after the division of time then customary, into six ages. This book forms the third part of his great work, "Instructions on Government," to which we have above alluded. In this work the author seizes every opportunity to lecture the king, to give him advice, and to rebuke him. According to Dobrovsky, his boldness not unfrequently degenerates into coarseness and insolence. It is an amusing reproach, which among others he brings against the king, that he had not one camel, whilst Job had six thousand. The same individual wrote also a large work in Latin, a kind of Cyclopædia, the manuscript of which is in the library of the university of Cracow.

We finish the history of this period with a short account of the state of medicine and natural sciences in Bohemia. It is true, that the greater part of the learned men who wrote on these subjects, preferred the use of the Latin language. But many of

---

[25] Vict. Cornelius of Wshehrd composed in 1495 a work in nine books, "On the Statutes, Courts of justice, and Legislature (Landtafel) of Bohemia," which is the most celebrated among several similar works of this period, and was in its time indispensable to the Bohemian lawyer. It has since been published, 1841. The same learned individual translated Cyprian, Chrysostom, etc. See Dobrovsky's *Geschicte der böhm. Sprache.*

them were in the habit of making at least Bohemian extracts or abridgments of their most popular works, or sometimes had the whole of them translated by their pupils. Among the medical writers of this time, Christian Prachatitzky a clergyman, John Czerny and Claudian Bohemian brethren, Albik, and Gallus, must be mentioned; the two latter wrote only in Latin.

This section of the Bohemian literature is particularly rich in herbals. Several works of instruction in botany were also written. A manuscript of 1447, "On the inoculation of Trees," may be mentioned here, although belonging rather to the department of agriculture.

The Bohemian language, although improving and evidently rising in esteem with every lustrum of the fifteenth century, had however not yet supplanted the Latin. Many of the most eminent among the learned of this period preferred still to write in Latin; as Hieronymus Balbus, Bohuslav, Hassenstein of Lobkowic, Shlechta, Olomucius, and a number of others; who all contributed nevertheless to elevate the glory of the Bohemian name, and could not but exert a powerful influence on the nation.

In respect to the date of the introduction of printing into Bohemia, the first regular printing establishment at Prague is not older than A. D. 1487. Several Bohemian books, however, were printed before this time by travelling workmen. In regard to the first work printed in the Bohemian language historians are not entirely agreed. According to Jungmann,[26] a letter from Huss to Jakaubek, of 1459, was the first specimen of Bohemian printing; the above-mentioned chronicle of Troy of 1468 the second; and the New Testament of 1475 the third. According to Dobrovsky, the New Testament of 1475 is the earliest printed

[26] See his *Historie literatury Czeske*, Prague 1825, p. 49, 68. Schaffarik agrees with him. Pelzel presumed that the letter of Huss, of 1459, was printed in some foreign country by a travelling Bohemian.

work in Bohemian. From that year to 1488, only seven Bohemian works appear to have been issued from the press; among which was a Psalter and another New Testament. In 1488, after the foundation of a regular printing office, the whole Bohemian Bible was printed for the first time; in the same year the History of Troy again, and the Roman chronicle; and in the following year the first Bohemian almanac, and the Bible of Kuttenberg. The subsequent editions belong, as to time, to the following period; but are given in the note below.[27]

THIRD PERIOD.

Golden age of the Bohemian Literature. From the diffusion of printing, about A. D. 1500, *to the battle at the White Mountain, A. D.* 1620.

It is chiefly for the sake of clearness and convenience, that writers on the literary history of Bohemia separate this period from the former; in its character and its genius it was entirely the same. What the Bohemians had *acquired* in the one, they

[27] Other Bohemian Bibles are: Venice 1506, fol. Prague 1527, fol. ib. 1537, fol. Nürnberg 1540, fol. Prague 1549, fol. ib. 1556–57. ib. 1561. fol. the same edition with a new title. ib. 1570, fol. Kralicz 1579–98, 6 vols. sm. fol. prepared by the United Brethren, the first from the original languages. Without place 1596, 8vo. by the same. Without place 1613, fol. by the same. Prague 1613, fol. for the Utraquists. Prague N. Test. 1677. Old Test. 1712–15, 3 vols. fol. for Roman Catholics. Halle 1722, 8vo. for Protestants. Halle 1745, 8vo. for the same. Halle 1766, 8vo. for the same. Prague 1769–71, 3 vols. fol. for Roman Catholics. Prague 1778–80, 2 vols. 8vo. for the same. Pressburg 1786–87, 8vo for Protestants. Prague 1804, 8vo. for Roman Catholics. Berlin 1807, 8vo. by the Bible Society. Pressburg 1808, 8vo. for Protestants. Berlin 1813, by the Bible Society.

possessed in the other; what they had only aimed at in the former, they reached in the latter; what had been the property of a few, was now augmented by an abundant harvest in their diligent hands, and enriched a multitude. But the objects, the stamp, the character, of both centuries were essentially the same. Literary cultivation, which during the sixteenth century was every where else monopolized by the clergy and a few distinguished individuals, was now in Bohemia the common property of the people; who for the most part embraced the evangelical doctrines in their manifold, though but little differing shades. But although religion was to them the object of chief interest, it was yet far from occupying their minds exclusively. And this is the point, in which the history of the Bohemian Reformation materially differs from that of some other countries. Luther's elevated mind did not indeed give room to narrow prejudices against those flowers of life, with which a kind Creator has adorned this earth. But almost all the other Reformers were led, either by a one-sided zeal or by circumstances, to show themselves decidedly opposed to the cultivation of elegant literature and the fine arts; they destroyed or banished pictures, music, statuary, and every thing which they could in any way regard as worldly temptations to allure men from the only source of truth and knowledge; nay, they sometimes went so far as to look at science and art in themselves only in the light of handmaids to religion; and to deem a devotion to them without such reference, as sinful worldliness. Of such narrowness we do not find a trace in the fathers of the Bohemian Reformation, who were themselves men of high intellectual cultivation; and even their most zealous followers kept themselves nearly free from it. If, as we have seen in the preceding period, political, poetical, and religious subjects were merged in each other, it was only the necessary result of the confusion occasioned by the struggles of the time. Where one object is predominant, all others must naturally become subordinate; but wherever that which appears amiable only as the free tendency of the whole soul, is exacted as a duty, a spiritual despotism is to be feared; of which we find very little in the history of Bohemian literature. The classics never were studied with more attention and devotion, were never imitated with more taste. Italy, the cradle of fine arts, and then the seat of general cultivation, was never visited more frequently by the Bohemian nobility, than when three-fourths of the nation adhered to the Protestant Church. At the very time, too, when the Bohemian Protestants had to watch most closely their religious liberties, and to defend them against the encroachments of a treacherous court, they did not deem it a desertion of the cause of religion to unite with the same Romanists, whose theological doctrines they contested, in their labours in the fields of philology, astronomy, and natural philosophy.

The extent of the Bohemian national literature increased during the sixteenth century so rapidly; the number of writers augmented so prodigiously; and the opportunities for literary cultivation presented to the reading public, by the multiplication of books through the press, became so frequent; that the difficulty of giving a condensed yet distinct picture of the time is greatly augmented. A sketch of the political situation of the country may serve as a back-ground, in order by its gloomy shades to render still brighter the light of a free mental development.

After the death of George Podiebrad in 1471, the Bohemians —or rather the catholic party, after the pope had excommunicated this prince—elected Vladislaus, a Polish prince, for their king; who, like his son and successor Louis, united on his head the crowns of Hungary and Bohemia. The different evangelical denominations were during these reigns in some measure tolerated; except that from time to time a persecution of one or another sect broke out, and again after a year or two was dropped, when the minds of the community had become somewhat pacified. It is a melancholy truth for the evangelical Christian, that at this time the most violent persecutors were to be found among the Calixtins or Utraquists. During the first years of the sixteenth century, persecution was mostly directed against the United Brethren and their writings. The latter were burned; the former banished; until, driven from place to place, they found an asylum in the territory of some high-minded nobleman, where they established themselves anew; and then after some years perhaps a new persecution began. Of a more revolting and bloody description were the measures directed principally against the Lutherans in the years 1522–26; in which the most shocking tortures were employed, and several faithful Lutherans and Picardites were burned alive. During all this time the Romanists and Calixtins exercised a severe censorship; and it was ordained, that every individual who brought a newly printed book into the city of Prague, must submit it to the revision of the consistory. These laws, however, were no better observed than all similar ordinances, when directly in opposition to the spirit of the age. Meanwhile the Calixtins and Romanists, although writing against all others, had their own mutual contests. When, however, the former caused a new edition of the Bible to be printed in the year 1506,[28] it was unanimously adopted by the Roman Catholics also; who, as is amusing to observe, did not notice that a wood cut is appended to the sixth chapter of the Apocalypse, in which the pope is represented in the flames of hell.

In the year 1526 king Louis died in the battle of Mohacz.

---

[28] At Venice; see the preceding note. Dobrovsky calls it a splendid edition, and thinks the reason why the Bohemians had it printed at Venice was, that it could not have been executed so well in Bohemia. *Gesch. der böhm. Sprache*, p. 343.

According to a matrimonial treaty, he was succeeded by his brother-in-law Ferdinand, archduke of Austria and brother of the emperor Charles V. This prince was received by the Bohemians with reluctance as their king, and only on the condition, insisted on by the Estates, that he should subscribe the compact of Basle, by which their religious liberties were secured to them. So long as Ferdinand was occupied in Hungary against the Turks, all went well in Bohemia; but when, in the war which followed the league of Smalkalde (1547), the Protestants of this country refused to fight against their brethren, a new and unremitted persecution began against all, who could in any way be comprised under the name of *sectarians*. The compact of Basle was strictly only in favour of the Utraquists or Calixtins; the Lutherans and Taborites, or, as they were then called, United Brethren, as also the Picardites and Grubenheimer, were considered as *sects*, and did not belong to the indulged.[29] Their

[29] The Picardites, or Picards, who are also called Adamites, existed as early as 1421, when Zhizhka crushed them, without annihilating them entirely; the Utraquists detested them because they denied the doctrine of transubstantiation, although they agreed with them in their general principles. They were frequently confounded with the Taborites, among whom at last the remnants of them became lost. The Grubenheimer were the remnants of the Waldenses, who fled to Bohemia in the middle of the 14th century; where, under persecution and ridicule, they used to hide themselves in caves and pits, *Gruben;* hence their name. Under the shield of the Reformation they thought themselves safe; but met only with new oppressors and persecutors. There were numerous other sects, and still more different names of one and the same sect. A sect of the Taborites, for instance, founded by Nicholas Wlasenicky, were alternately called *Miculassenci* (i. e. Nicolaites, the Bohemian form for Nicholas being Miculass), or *Wlasenitzi,* from his name; *Pecynowshi,* from the place of their meetings; and *Plachtiwi,* i. e. the crying, from their manner. See Dobrovsky's *Gesch. der böhm. Sprache,* p. 234. It may be the place here to remark, that the Calixtins or Utraquists, although at first decidedly against the infallibility of the pope, nevertheless in forming the

churches were shut up; their preachers arrested; and all who did not prefer to exchange their religion for the Roman Catholic, were compelled to emigrate. The scene altered under Maximilian II, Ferdinand's successor, a friend of the Reformation, and in every respect one of the most excellent princes who ever took upon himself the responsibility of directing the destinies of a nation; to use Schaffarik's happy metaphor, the benefits of his administration fell on the field, which Ferdinand's strength had ploughed, like a mild and fertilizing rain. During his life, and the first ten years of his son Rudolph's reign, Bohemia was in peace; the different denominations were indulged; literature flourished, and the Bohemian language was at the summit of its glory. But we regret to add, that the Protestants, instead of improving this fortunate period by uniting to acquire a legal foundation for their church, instead of a mere indulgence depending on the will of the sovereign, lived in constant mutual warfare, and attempted only to supplant each other. An ordinance in 1586 against the Picardites, a name under which the Bohemian Brethren were then comprehended; and still more the strict censorship introduced in 1605; first aroused them to unite their strength against oppression; and in 1609 they compelled the emperor to subscribe the celebrated *Literæ Imperatoriæ*, or edict, by which full liberty in matters of religion was secured to them. During the rest of this period, the Protestants remained the ruling party. The university of Prague, by the side of which from A. D. 1556 another of the Jesuits existed, was by that treaty given entirely into their hands. This institution, although in consequence of the foundation of so many similar

---

compact of Basle, submitted in the main to the doctrine of Rome, with these four conditions; viz. the free distribution of the Bible to the people; the administration of the sacrament in both kinds; reform of the clergy after the pattern of the Apostles; and punishment for "mortal sins" in proportion to their enormity.

schools it never recovered completely from the shock it received in 1410, and though for more than a hundred years it had been decidedly on the decline, yet rose in reputation towards the middle of the sixteenth century; and among the professors who filled its chairs, there were always celebrated names. Among the schools of a less elevated rank, those of the Bohemian Brethren at Bunzlau, Prerow, and other places, were distinguished.

Rudolph was a great patron of literature and science; and was quite favourably disposed towards the Bohemian language. Nearly two hundred writers were numbered under his reign; and among these many ladies and gentlemen of his court, of which Tycho Brahe, Kepler, and other scientific foreigners were the chief ornaments. Zeal for the cultivation of their mother tongue, seemed to be the point in which all religious denominations in Bohemia united. But during this century, as in the preceding one, the language of the country existed only side by side with the Latin; which was still preferred by many, for the sake of a more general reputation. It became the chief object of other eminent men, to make their countrymen acquainted with the classics in a Bohemian dress; and to improve the language by a strict imitation of Latin and Greek forms. Among these a rich and noble citizen of Prague named George Hruby must be first named;[30] also Pisecky, ob. 1511, who translated Isocrates' Epistle to Demonicus; Nicholas Konacz and Ulric of Welensky, the translators of Lucian; Krupsky, of Plutarch; Ginterod, of Xenophon's Cyropædia. Kocyn, celebrated for his eloquence and

---

[30] His full name was George Hruby Gelenshky. This patriotic and active individual translated and published a whole series of valuable books; among which we mention only Petrarch's Letters, Cicero's Lælius and Paradoxa, several works of Jovian, etc. Nicholas Konacz followed in the same path. He translated the Bohemian History of Æneas Sylvius, two dialogues of Lucian, and wrote, edited, and printed other meritorious and elaborate works.

other gifts, translated the ecclesiastical history of Eusebius and Cassiodorus; Orliczny, the Jewish wars of Josephus, several of the Latin classics, etc.

When we consider this general zeal for the cultivation of the language, it is a matter of surprise that the first Bohemian grammar should not be older than A. D. 1533. Its author was Benesh Optat, who also translated Erasmus' Paraphrase of the New Testament. Another grammar was published by Beneshowsky in 1577, a third by the Slovak Benedicti in 1603. But the individual to whom is justly assigned the chief merit in regard to the language, is Weleslawin, ob. 1599, professor of history in the university of Prague, and the proprietor of the greatest printing establishment in Bohemia. Partly by his own works, original and translated, and among these three dictionaries for different purposes; partly by the encouragement he gave to other writers, and the activity with which he caused works whether old or new deserving of a greater circulation, to be printed; he acquired a most powerful influence among his cotemporaries.

The field however which was cultivated with the most diligence, was that of theology; and fortunately, during this whole period, with an equal measure of talent and zeal. The writings of the Bohemian Brethren, Thomas Prelavsky, Laurentius Krasonicky, and more especially of Lucas, belong partly to the former, partly to the present period. The latter was a most productive writer; and as being one of their best scholars, he was generally chosen to answer the charges made against the United Brethren, in learned and elaborate pamphlets.[31] Several of the productions of the

[31] This venerable man was ten years president or bishop (Zprawce) of the United Brethren; and his whole life appears to have been devoted to religious purposes. He prepared the hymn-book in use among all the congregations of the Brethren; wrote an interpretation of the Apocalypse, 1501; of the Psalms, 1505; a treatise on Hope, 1503; on Oaths, etc. His writings, most of which are replete with erudition, are enumerated in Dobrovsky's *Gesch. der böhm. Sprache*, pp. 238, 239, 372, 378, 379.

Brethren, mentioned in the former period, were written and printed in the beginning of this. Among these in 1508, Procopius' question, "Whether it is right for a Christian to compel infidels or heretics to embrace the true faith?" is remarkable, as one of the earliest instances in which this position of intolerance was made the subject of public debate, or at least answered in the negative. In 1563 the New Testament was first translated directly from the Greek, by J. Blahoslav, another president of the Bohemian Brethren, a man of profound erudition. The first translation of the whole Bible from the original languages, did not take place until several years later. The first edition of this latter splendid work, for which the patriotic and pious baron John of Zherotin expressly founded a printing office in his castle of Kralicz in Moravia, and advanced money for all the necessary expenses, was printed in 1579. This version is still considered, in respect to language, as a model; and in respect to typography, as unsurpassed. On the fidelity of the translation and the value of the commentary, Schaffarik remarks, that "they contain a great deal of that which, two hundred years later, the learned *coryphaei* of exegesis in our day have exhibited to the world as their own profound discoveries." The translators were Albert Nicolai, Lucas Helic, Joh. Æneas, George Stryc, E. Coepolla, J. Ephraim, P. Jessenius, and J. Capito.—G. Stryc wrote also a good translation of the Psalms in rhyme, and several theological works. J. Wartowsky likewise translated the Old Testament from the Hebrew and left it in manuscript; but his version has never been published. Of his translation of Erasmus' Paraphrase of the Gospels, only that of the Gospel of Matthew has been printed. Among the Bohemian Brethren, Augusta surnamed Pileator, ob. 1572, Stranensky, the above-mentioned Blahoslav, Zamrsky, ob. 1592, were distinguished by great erudition. They and many others wrote voluminous works on theological subjects, e. g. biblical researches, systematic divinity, sermons, etc. Several of these writers, and also many others, were authors of numerous religious hymns; among which not a few are still considered as unsurpassed in any language. Nicholas Klaudian, who was at the same time physician, printer, and theologian, wrote an apology in favour of the Brethren. This individual, who, besides being the printer and editor of several medical works written by himself and others, was in part the translator of Seneca and Lactantius, has further the merit of having published in 1518 the first map of Bohemia. Luther's sermons and other writings were translated into Bohemian; and the religious affairs of Germany began to excite an intense interest among all classes.

The theological productions of this period written by Roman Catholics—among which we distinguish the names of Pishek surnamed Scribonius, Makawsky, and the Jesuits Sturm and Hostowin—are mostly of a polemical character; while some also are translations of the fathers, especially of Augustine's writings; or original ascetic productions in the form of allegorical novels. Among the Utraquists several individuals were celebrated as preachers; above all Ctibor Kotwa, who was called the Bohemian Cicero, and Dicastus Mirkowsky. Others wrote theological treatises and interpretations of portions of the Scriptures. Such were Beransky, author of an interpretation of Daniel, of the gospels, and the epistles; Orliczny, or, as he is called in Latin, Aquilinas, known chiefly as a translator of the classics;[32] Turnowsky, a Slovak by birth; Bydzhowsky, Bilegowsky the writer of a Bohemian church history and of a history of the Hussites and Picardites; Rwaczowsky, Zeletawsky, Tesak author of many popular religious hymns; Palma, who published towards twenty theological works; Peshina, Maurenin, and Borowsky, who wrote interpretations of the epistles and gospels; Wrbensky, author of a biblical Synopsis, a Harmony, etc.; Rosacius Sushichky, distin-

[32] See page 189.

guished as a Latin poet; Martin of Drazow, Jacobides Stribrsky, Jakesius Prerowsky, and others.[33]

There are few among the theological writers of this century,—of whom we have named perhaps the twentieth part,—who have not left at least ten volumes of their own writings; while many have reached twice, and some thrice the number. More than one third of the printed works in this department contain sermons. The eloquence of the pulpit acquired a high degree of cultivation; and besides the two Utraquist preachers mentioned above, many other names were celebrated among them. In respect to erudition, however, the Brethren occupied decidedly the first rank. In religious hymns all sects were equally productive; and there are, as we have mentioned already, not a few among them of a high excellence. To the names of spiritual poets alluded to in the preceding paragraphs, we may here add the following: T. Sobeslawsky Reshatko, Gryllus, Herstein of Radowesic, Horsky, Mart. Pisecky, Taborsky, Sylvanus a Slovak by birth and called by way of eminence *Poeta Bohemicus*, Chmelowecz, Mart. Philomusa, Karlsberg, Hanush; and more especially Lomnicky, *poeta laureatus*, who is regarded as the first Bohemian poet of that age.

These names comprise also nearly all we have to say of the state of Bohemian poetry in general. Not that some of them did not occasionally desert the sacred muse, and compose specimens of secular poetry; for some of Lomnicky's larger and most celebrated works belong to this class, as may be seen by the titles; e. g. 'The arrows of Cupid,' 'The golden Bag,' etc.[34]

---

[33] The five last named were banished in 1621.

[34] Simon Lomnicky of Budecz, was court poet; and in addition to the poetical crown, his talents procured him a patent of nobility. He wrote twenty-eight volumes, most of which are printed. For more general information respecting his works, and those of the other writers here mentioned, we must refer our readers to Jungmann's *Historie Literatury Czeske*, Prague, 1825, and Schaffarik's often cited work.

But every thing of real poetical value is of a religious character; and bears too much the stamp of its age, to be relished at the present day. The secular poets of the time wrote, with a few exceptions, in Latin.

Among the historians of merit we may name the following writers of Bohemian history: Hagek of Liboczan, Kuthen, Procopius Lupacz, Paprocky a Pole who however wrote some of his works in the Bohemian language, Racownicky, and the above-mentioned Weleslawin and Bilegowsky. In respect to universal history, or that of other lands, we find the names of Placel, Sixt von Ottersdorf, Konstantinovicz, Kocin, and others. This period is equally rich in valuable books of travels. Count Wratislaw of Mitrowicz, ob. 1635, described his interesting embassy from Vienna to Constantinople; C. Harant, a courtier and statesman, published his travels in Egypt and Palestine; Prefat of Wlkanow likewise gave a description of his journey from Prague to Palestine; Charles of Zherotin, the son of the munificent patron of the United Brethren, and like him their protector and friend, left letters and a description of his travels.

As lawyers, orators, and political writers, the following names may be adduced: Baron Kocin of Kocinet, whom we have had occasion to mention repeatedly; the counts Sternberg, Wratislaw of Mitrowicz, and Slawata; the latter known as one of the persons thrown from a lofty window of the castle by the violence of count Thurn—one of the introductory scenes of the thirty years' war; Baron Budowecz of Budow, equally excellent as a Christian and a statesman, the protector and public defender of the Bohemian Brethren, and faithful to his religious conviction until his last breath; Christopher Harant, another nobleman of great merit, whom we have mentioned above as a traveller in the East. Both these last were executed in 1621. Writers of merit in the department of jurisprudence, were also the counsellors Ulric of Prostiborz under Ferdinand I, Wolf of Wresowicz, the chancellor Koldin, and others. But on topics like these, by far the greater number wrote only in Latin; and these of course we do not mention here.

Writers on the medical and natural sciences we cannot well separate; since, in most cases, the same individuals distinguished themselves in the departments of medicine, astronomy, and mathematics. The following, along with many others, are named with distinction: Th. Hagek, body physician of the emperors Maximilian and Rudolph, and a celebrated astronomer; Zhelotyn, author of medical and mathematical works; Zaluzhansky, physician and naturalist, who anticipated Linnæus in his doctrine of the sexual distinction and impregnation of plants; P. Codicillus, historian, philosopher, theologian, and astronomer, who wrote on all these different subjects; Huber von Reisenbach, a physician and rector of the university of Prague; Shud, a celebrated astronomer; and many more.[35]

The number of books printed during this period cannot well be ascertained; since by far the greater number were burned, or otherwise destroyed, in the dreadful catastrophe which signalized its close. Prague alone had eighteen printing offices; and fourteen more existed in other places in Bohemia and Moravia. Besides these, many Bohemian books were printed at Venice, Nürnberg, Wittenberg, and some in Holland and Poland.

In 1617, the emperor Matthias succeeded in obtaining the crown of Bohemia for his nephew Ferdinand, archduke of Austria. This was the signal for the Romanists, in spite of the *Literæ Imperatoriæ* of the emperor Rudolph, to make new attempts for the suppression of the Protestants. The Estates belonging to this denomination brought their complaint before the emperor, who gave them no redress; and thus the spark was kindled into flames, which for thirty years continued to rage throughout all

---

[35] See the two works named in the preceding note.

Germany. At the death of Matthias in 1619, the Bohemians refused to receive Ferdinand II as their king; and elected the Protestant palatine Frederic V, a generous prince, but incapable of affording them support. The battle at the White Mountain, near Prague, in 1620, decided the destiny of Bohemia. Twenty-seven of the leaders of the insurrection were publicly executed; sixteen were exiled or condemned to prison for life; their property, as also the possessions of seven hundred and twenty-eight noblemen and knights, who had voluntarily acknowledged themselves to have taken part in the insurrection, and of twenty-nine others who had fled, was wholly confiscated; and thus the amount of fifty-three millions of rix dollars transferred from Protestant to Romish hands. The *Literæ Imperatoriæ* were annulled; the Protestant religion in Bohemia abolished; and that kingdom declared a purely catholic hereditary monarchy. All non-catholic preachers were banished; thirty thousand families, who preferred exile to a change of their religion, emigrated. Among them 185 were noble families; the others artists, mechanics, merchants, and labourers. Yet in the villages, among the woods and mountains, where neither soldier nor Jesuit had penetrated, and there alone, many Protestants remained, buried in a fortunate obscurity. From the time of this catastrophe, the Bohemian language has never again been used in public business. The thirty years' war completed the devastation of this unfortunate country. In 1617, Bohemia had 732 cities and 34,700 villages; when Ferdinand II died in 1637, there remained 130 cities and 6000 villages; and its three millions of inhabitants were reduced to 780,000.

FOURTH PERIOD.

From the battle at the White Mountain, A. D. 1620, *to the Revival of Literature in A. D.* 1774–80.

Of this melancholy period we have but little to say. A dull pressure lay upon the nation ; it was as if the heavy strokes inflicted on them had paralyzed their very limbs. Innumerable monks came to Bohemia from Italy, Spain, and the south of Germany, who condemned and sacrificed to the flames every Bohemian book as necessarily heretical. There were individuals who boasted having burned with their own hands 60,000 literary works. They broke into private houses, and took away whatever Bohemian books they could find. Those which they did not burn, were deposited in separate chambers in the convents, provided with iron grates, bolts, and chains, drawn before the door, on which was written, *The Hell.* They distributed pamphlets respecting hell and purgatory, the reading of which produced derangement of mind in many weak persons ; until, at last, the government was wise enough to lay a severe prohibition upon these measures. The Bohemian emigrants indeed continued to have their religious books printed in their foreign homes ; but they wrote comparatively few new works. These however they contrived to introduce into Bohemia, where they were answered by the Jesuits and Capuchins in thick folio volumes, written in a language hardly intelligible. There were however some honourable exceptions among these fathers ; some persons, who, independent of religious prejudices, continued to labour for the benefit of a beloved mother tongue. The Jesuits Konstanz, Steyer, and Drachovsky, wrote grammatical works, and the two first attempted to translate the Bible anew. Plachy, ob. 1650, Libertin, and

Taborsky, were distinguished preachers; Peshina, ob. 1680, Hammerschmidt, ob. 1731, and Beckowsky, ob. 1725, wrote meritorious historical works; Rosa, ob. 1689, composed another grammar and a dictionary. Others wrote in Latin; and among these must be named the Jesuit Balbin, ob. 1688, who prepared several historical and bibliographical works of importance, part of which, however, were not published until long after his death.[36]

We turn once more to the unfortunate emigrants, and in the midst of the distress, privations, and sacrifices, which were the natural accompaniments of their exiled condition, we rejoice to meet with a name, which owes its splendour not alone to the general poverty of the period; but which outshines even the most distinguished of the former age, and is indeed the only one in the literary history of Bohemia, which has acquired a *European* fame. This is Comenius, the last bishop of the Bohemian Brethren. Although he belongs partly to the former period, and, in respect to his style, decidedly to the golden age of the Bohemian literature, the time of his principal activity falls within this melancholy interval. A few words may be devoted to the life of this remarkable individual. He was born A. D. 1592, in the village of Komna in Moravia. His baptismal names were John Amos; his father had probably no family name, as was frequently the case at that time among the lower classes throughout all Europe. According to the custom of the time, he was called Komnensky from his native place, the Latin form of which is Comnenius, or more commonly Comenius. His parents, who belonged to the community of the Brethren, sent him to school at Herborn. He

[36] Balbin was professor of rhetoric at Prague. His works are of importance for the literary history of Bohemia: *Epitome rer. Bohem.* Prague 1677. *Miscellanea hist. rer. Bohem.* Prague 1680–88. After his death Unger edited in 1777–80 his *Bohemia docta*, and Pelzel in 1775 his *Dissertatio apologetica pro lingua Slavonica, præcipue Bohemica.* See below under the fifth period of Bohemian literature, near the beginning.

distinguished himself so much as to be made rector at Prerow, when only twenty-two years old; and two years later was transferred to Fulnek. In 1618 this latter city was plundered by the Spaniards, and Comenius lost all his books and other property. When the great persecution of the Protestants broke out, he fled to Poland. Here he found many of his countrymen, of the sect of the Brethren, whom the persecutions of the former century had already driven hither, and who had here gathered themselves into communities essentially of the same constitution; although in some measure they were amalgamated with the dissenters in Poland. In 1632 they elected him their bishop. In 1631 he published his *Janua linguarum reserrata*, a work which spread his fame over all the world, and which was translated into twelve European languages, and also into Persian, Arabic, and Mongolian. His object in this work was to point out a new method of teaching languages, by which they were to be used as keys for acquiring other useful knowledge. In 1641 he was invited to England to prepare a new arrangement of the schools; but the civil war having prevented the execution of this project, he went from England to Sweden, whither the chancellor Oxenstiern had invited him for a similar purpose. After protracted journeys through half Europe, he returned to Lissa, the principal seat of his activity. In 1659 he published his *Orbis pictus*, the first picture-book for children which ever appeared, and which acquired the same reputation as the work above-mentioned. The war and the destruction of Lissa compelled him some years later to leave Poland; he sought another asylum in Germany, and settled at length at Amsterdam, where he died in 1671, occupied with literary pursuits until his last hour. According to Adelung, he wrote not less than ninety-two works, of which only fifty-four have come down to us; and among these, twenty are in the Bohemian language. His style has a classical perfection; the contents of his works are manifold, and have mostly lost their interest for the present age.[37] In the last years of his life Comenius is said to have devoted himself to a mystical interpretation of the prophetic Scriptures; he discovered in the Revelation of St. John the state of Europe, as it then was; awaited the millennium in the year 1672; and believed in the far-famed Bourignon, as an inspired prophetess.

A few names only among the emigrants require to be mentioned as writers, after Comenius. They may find their place here: Paul Stransky, who was exiled in 1626 and found an asylum as professor at Thorn, wrote a history of Bohemia in Latin in 1643, which was translated and accompanied with supplements and corrections by Cornova, in 1792. Elsner, pastor of the Bohemian Brethren at Berlin, and Kleich at Zittau, printed works for religious instruction and devotional exercises for Protestants.

The greater part of what was written during this period proceeded from the Slovaks in Hungary, a nation related to the Bohemians in race and language, who after the Reformation had adopted the Bohemian dialect as their literary language.[38] Although also constantly struggling against oppression and persecution, the Protestants in Hungary were not formally annihilated, as in Bohemia; but belonged rather to the tolerated sects, so called. A certain degree of activity in behalf of their brethren in faith was consequently allowed to them; especially later under Maria Theresa. We meet among them with hardly any other than theological productions, or works for religious edifica-

---

[37] One of Comenius's works: *Labirynt swieta a rag srdce*, i. e. the World's Labyrinth and the Heart's Paradise, reminds us strongly of Bunyan's celebrated Pilgrim's Progress. It was first published at Prague, 1631, in 4to; and after several editions in other places, it was last printed at the same city in 1809, 12mo. His Latin works were printed at Amsterdam in 1657, under the title *Opera didactica*.

[38] See above p. 154.

tion. The two pastors Krman and Bel, who both died towards the middle of the eighteenth century, men of no inconsiderable merit as Christians and as scholars, prepared a new edition of the Bohemian Bible, and also translated several works of Luther, Arndt, etc. Ambrosius, their cotemporary, wrote a commentary on Luther's catechism, and several other useful religious works. G. Bahyl published an introduction to the Bible, a history of the symbolical books, and assisted Comenius in his *Orbus pictus.* Matthias Bahyl became the object of a cruel persecution, on account of a translation of Meissner's *Consultatio orthod. de fide Lutherana.* Numerous religious hymns were written in Bohemian by Hrushkowic, the two Blasius, Glosius, Augustini, and others. Michalides translated the *Summarium biblicum* of the theologians of Wittenberg; and another Protestant minister, Dolezhal, wrote in 1746 a Bohemian grammar. But their books, with a few exceptions, were little read beyond the frontiers of Hungary; and had consequently little or no influence on the Bohemians. The works written in the Slovakian dialect do not belong here.

FIFTH PERIOD.

Revival of Bohemian Literature, from A. D. 1774–80 *to the present time.*

In A. D. 1774, the marshal count Kinsky published a work on the advantages and necessity of a knowledge of the Bohemian language. At that time so great was the neglect of the mother tongue, that even for a work of so patriotic a nature, he had to employ a foreign language in order to be understood! One year later appeared an apology for the vernacular tongue of the country, written a hundred years before by the Jesuit Balbin in Latin,[39] and edited by Pelzel. These two writings created a deep sensation; and even the government would seem to have taken notice of them. We find, at least, that in the same year teachers of the Bohemian language were appointed in the university of Vienna and in two other institutions in that city. At the same time, the royal normal school at Prague began to print several Bohemian books for instruction. When the tolerant views and principles by which Joseph II was actuated, became known, more than a hundred thousand concealed Protestants immediately appeared; their hidden books were brought to light again; and many works, of which only single copies existed, were reprinted. In 1781 the severe edict of Ferdinand II was repealed, and a censorship established upon more reasonable principles. In 1786, the Bohemian language had gained friends enough to induce the government to institute a Bohemian theatre; which, with a short interruption during the present century, has ever since existed. The unfortunate system of general centralization adopted by Joseph II, was on the whole not favourable to the cultivation of any but the German language; but during the reign of his two successors, the Bohemian received more encouragement. In 1793 a professorship for the language and literature of the country was founded in the university of Prague; the use of that language in all the schools was ordained by several decrees of the government; and by a law of A. D. 1818, a knowledge of it was made a necessary qualification for holding any office.

In the very outset of this revival of Bohemian literature, there appeared so great a multitude of writers; such habits of diligence and productiveness were immediately manifested throughout the whole nation; and such a mass of respectable talent was brought to light; that the long interval of a dull and deathlike

[39] See above, p. 197.

silence, which preceded this period, presents indeed an enigma difficult to be solved. No small influence may be ascribed to Germany. The principles of the government were changed; the country, physically as well as morally exhausted, could recover but gradually; but all this could not create talents where there were none; nor could all external oppression and unfavourable conjunctures destroy the germs of real talent, if they had been there. The list of modern Bohemian writers of merit is very extensive; but we must be satisfied with bringing forward the most distinguished of them, and refer the reader to works less limited than these pages, where he may find more complete information.

Among those whose desert is the greatest in respect to the revival of Bohemian literature, Kramerius, born 1753, ob. 1808, must be named first. He was one of those indefatigable and creative minds, which never sleep, never lose a moment, and by a restless activity and happy ingenuity know how to render the difficult easy,—the apparently impossible, practicable. From the year 1785, he was editor of the first Bohemian newspaper; from 1788, of the annual called the *Toleranz Kalender*, or Almanac of Toleration; and published besides this more than fifty works, written by himself and others, but accompanied with notes or commentaries of his own. None of his productions surpassed mediocrity; but according to the best judges, they were well and perspicuously written; they became popular and exerted a very favourable influence.

As literary historians, Slavic philologians and antiquaries, Pelzel, Prochazka, Durich, Puchmayer, Negedly, Jungmann, Tomsa, Hanka, and above all Dobrovsky, must be distinguished. One of the principal merits of most of these scholars consists in their preparing for the press and editing valuable old manuscripts; or in the judicious commentaries which they added to new editions of ancient works already printed. Pelzel we have named above as the editor of the writings of the Jesuit Balbin. Most of his works are in German, but some also in Bohemian. In 1804 Prochazka and Durich translated the Bible for Roman Catholics; the former had already translated the New Testament in 1786. His principal labours besides this were in the department of history. Durich wrote in Latin; but his researches were nevertheless devoted to the Bohemian language and history. Tomsa and Negedly have written Bohemian grammars, and several other Slavic-philological works and essays.[40] Puchmayer published a large collection of poetry,[41] consisting partly of his own productions, a token of the reviving poetical genius of the nation, which had slept for centuries; while his elaborate Russian grammar is also a valuable contribution to Slavic literature in general.

Joseph Jungmann, besides a translation of Chauteaubriand's Atala and of Milton's Paradise Lost, which Bowring calls "the most admirable among the many admirable versions of that renowned and glorious heroic,"[42] has written many important essays scattered in periodicals; and also published in 1820 a Bohemian chrestomathy, in 1825 a history of Bohemian literature, and in 1830–31 a complete dictionary of that language.

W. Hanka, librarian at Prague, has made himself particularly known by critical editions of valuable writings out of the golden

---

[40] J. Negedly translated the Iliad, and also Young's Night Thoughts under the name of *Kwileni*, Lamentations. He and his brother Adalbert are also favourably known as lyric poets. A series of new translations of the Classics in their original measures has recently been prepared; in which a Bohemian version of the Iliad by J. Wlckowski (Prague 1842), forms the first volume.

[41] In the year 1795; the fifth and last volume appeared in 1804. Bowring has given several specimens of this collection in the For. Quart. Review, Vol. II. p. 145.

[42] For. Quart. Review, Vol. II. p. 167.

age of Bohemian literature. In 1817 he was so fortunate as to discover a manuscript of high importance, as well in a philological respect, as for its intrinsic poetical value; which he published in 1819 with a modern Bohemian translation, and also a German translation by Swoboda.[43] He has written several works, and also essays in periodicals, of a bibliographical and antiquarian character.

Joseph Dobrovsky, born 1753 in Hungary, but of Bohemian parents, ob. 1829, is called the patriarch of modern Slavic literature, and was one of the profoundest scholars of the age. His merits in regard to Slavic philology and history are so generally acknowledged, and we have so often had occasion to cite his name in these pages, and to refer the reader to his authority, that without attempting to present a critical view of one, or an analysis of another of his works, we are contented to give in a note the title of his principal works. We are the more willing to adopt this course, because the most of his works form in a certain measure one great whole, and mutually supply each other; and because too, the author having in part first explored unknown regions, and having of course sometimes found it necessary to retract hypotheses started in his earlier writings, his works cannot well be separated. He wrote mostly in German; sometimes in Latin; while comparatively very few of his numerous books are in the Bohemian language. In this way only could they gain that kind of universality, which the subject required; and which has so much contributed to promote the cause of Slavic literature in general.[44]

---

[43] The celebrated manuuscript of Königinhof; see above, pp. 157, 158.

[44] Dobrovsky's principal works are the following: *Script. rer. Bohem.* (with Pelzel) Prague 1784. *Böhm. und Mähr. Literatur,* Prague 1779–84. *Lit. Magazin für Böhmen und Mähren,* 1786–87. *Lit. Nachrichten von einer Reise nach Schweden und Russland,* Prague 1796. *Geschichte der böhm. Sprache und Lit.* Prague 1792; new edition much altered, ib. 1818. *Slavin,*

There were also some scholars among the Slovaks, who aided the same cause with diligence and talent. Leska, ob. 1818, published from 1785 onward the first Slovakian newspaper, and was a diligent and judicious compiler in respect to Slavic lexicography. Palkowicz published a Bohemian dictionary, and prepared in 1808 a more correct edition of the Bible. Plachy, besides many volumes of prose and poetry, published a valuable periodical; Schramko wrote some philological works; Schaffarik and Kollar, of whom more will be said in the sequel, were also Slovaks.

After the collection of poetry by Puchmayer above alluded to, several others of a miscellaneous kind appeared; poetry having been hitherto limited almost exclusively to religious purposes. Kamaryt, Palacky, Chmelensky, Zdirad Polak, Czelakowsky, Snaidr, Hnewkowsky, Turinsky, Stulcz,[45] Jablonsky, Tupi, Sabin, are favourably known as poets. A. Marek has translated several dramas of Shakspeare; Machaczek several from Goethe; Kliczpera, Stepanek, and Sychra, are esteemed dramatic writers. Among the Slovaks, Holli translated the Latin and Greek elegiac poets; Roshnay, Anacreon.

As historical writers Tomek and Jordan must be honourably mentioned. An excellent work on Bohemian Antiquities, written in German by J. E. Wocel, ought also to be noticed.[46]

Prague 1808; new improved edition by W. Hanka, Prague 1834. *Slovanka*, Prague 1814–15. *Lehrgebäude der böhm. Sprache*, Prague 1809, 1819. *Etymologicon*, Prague 1813. *Deutsch-böhm. Wörterb.* 1802–21. *Institutiones Linguæ Slav.* Vienna 1822. *Kyrill und Method*, Prague 1823. Also a great number of smaller treatises, essays, reviews, either printed separately or in periodicals.

[45] A collection of poems by this author recently appeared under the title *Pownenky no cestach Zivota, od Waclawa Stulce*, Prague 1845, which has been translated into German: *Errinnerungsblumen auf dem Lebenswege*, aus den Neuczechischen, von J. Wenzig, Prague 1846.

[46] *Grundzüge der Böhmischen Alterthumskunde*, Prague 1845. Jordan's History of Bohemia is also written in German.

In the department of natural science are to be mentioned, Presl, count Berchtold, Strnad, Sedlaczek, Wydra, Smetana, etc. Others, Bohemians by birth, have written in German, e. g. Hænke, Sieber, etc. etc. Count Buquoy also is of Bohemian origin.—Writers of merit on moral and religious subjects are, Rautenkranz, Zahradnik, Parizek, and others. The Slovak Bartholomæides, a distinguished scholar, has written several useful works on various topics.—Periodicals full of learned researches and variety of interest were edited, *Dobroslaw* by Hromadko and Ziegler, *Krok* by Presl, etc. Modern journals of a more general tendency are *Wlastimil* (the Patriot), *Dennica*, etc. Among the highest nobility the national language found powerful patrons; and in the establishment of a national Museum, a Bohemian Academy of Sciences, and similar patriotic institutions, the national literature received great encouragement. One of the principal objects of this institution was to publish old works and to patronize new ones. Its first publication was an old treatise on Bohemian law.[47] The names of the counts K. Sternberg and Kolowrath-Liebsteinsky must be mentioned here; to which, in our days, may be added those of the counts J. M. and Leo Thun.

The leading poet of the present day in the Bohemian language is J. Kollar, born 1793 at Thurocz in Hungary. In 1821 he published a volume of poems; and some years later a larger beautiful poem in two cantos, called *Slawy dzery*, the Daughter of Glory, by which he meant *Slavina*, or the Slavic nations personified; for *Slava* means glory. With talents of the first order, and at the same time purely national, he imitates Petrarch in some measure; making his nation his Laura, praising her beauty, and prophesying her ultimate triumph.[48]

---

[47] *Victorina Kornelia ze Wshehrd, Knitry dewatery prawiech o siediech i o dskoch zeme Cêkê*, Prague 1841, edited by W. Hanka. It is the work mentioned above, p.180, n. 25.

[48] For several beautiful specimens of this poet, see Bowring's Essay on Bohemian Literature, in the Foreign Quart. Rev. Vol. II.

The patriotic zeal which in our days has instigated the Slavic scholars to follow out the traces of their language and history into the remotest past, in order to clear up more satisfactorily the origin and primitive connection between the different members of the great Slavic family, and their relative position to the Germans, has nowhere been exhibited in a more energetic and disinterested way than in Bohemia. The idea of Panslavism was here first worked out systematically.[49] If we are not entirely mistaken, it was the same Kollar, the Czekho-Slovakian poet, who first conceived, or at least expressed, that idea. In a Slavic periodical, published in Hungary, entitled *Hronka*, he came out with an address to his Slavic brethren, which he himself translated into German. He urged the Slavi to drop their numerous intellectual family feuds; to consider themselves as *one* great nation; their mutual languages essentially as *one;* their respective interests as one. He prophesied power and predominance to the Slavi *united* as a whole. The idea was seized with eagerness; especially by the Bohemian scholars, in whom a certain irritation against the Germans, the oppressors of their nation for centuries, was far from being unnatural. At the head of this movement, so far as it respects philological investigations, was P. J. Schaffarik; in respect to historical researches, Fr. Palacky; the first a Slovak, the second a Moravian by birth; and both of them highly esteemed as scholars of great learning, uncommon acuteness, and indefatigable research; but both also, from a very laudable national partiality, inclined to favour those results of their researches, which should serve to support their own patriotic or Panslavic views. It will therefore not be found surprising, that they should have met with a strong, nay passionate opposition.

Schaffarik, whose valuable work on the Slavic languages and

---

[49] See p. 86 above.

their history we have chiefly consulted in our present sketch, (not however without due regard to his own altered and corrected views, as given to the public in his later works,) was born in 1795 at Kbeljarowo in Northern Hungary. He received a German education; and, following the example of other leading Slavic scholars, like Dobrovsky and Kopitar, notwithstanding his partiality for all that is Slavic, he wrote most of his earlier works in German. His "History of the Slavic Language and Literature," although a production of his youth, and written before the full maturity of the author's views, has perhaps contributed more than any other work to a knowledge of the Slavic literature in general, and of the classification and mutual relation of the Slavic languages. After further researches, he prepared a "History of the Southern Slavi;" which however, so far as we are informed, has never been printed. Instead of it he published a work on "Slavic Antiquities" in the Bohemian language. It was patriotism which induced him not only to choose this language in preference to the German, and thus give up a far greater field of influence; but he also declined a well endowed Slavic professorship in the university of Berlin, from the same generous and patriotic motive, and settled in Prague. Here he undertook the editorship of a periodical founded by Palacky; and operated in connection with him and other Slavic scholars for the promotion of Slavic, and principally Bohemian, literature. For this end a society was founded among the Bohemian and Slovakian scholars and gentry, called the *Stalci*, the Constant. They bound themselves to buy every respectable book, which should be printed in the Bohemian language. In 1842 Schaffarik published a "Slavic Ethnography," a small introductory work, but founded on extensive studies. Of this he himself prepared a German translation.[60]

[60] Schaffarik's principal works are: A Collection of Bohemian Poems, pub-

The faithful fellow-labourer of Schaffarik is Francis Palacky, a scholar of great diligence and research, a few years younger in age; who however seems to have adopted an opposite course, in so far as his early works were written in Bohemian, while his later and principal ones are in German. In 1829 he was appointed Historiographer of Bohemia by the Estates; but he was too warm a *Bohemian* to hope for the confirmation of the Austrian government under the emperor Francis, and it was not obtained until under his successor. By means of the "Journal of the Bohemian National Museum," of which he was the founder and editor, he had early gained a leading voice in all that concerned the revival of Bohemian literature; and, in that capacity, had to fight his way through a series of literary struggles and combats, sometimes conducted with personal vehemence and bitterness. He had the satisfaction, however, of finally coming off as victor in the more essential points. His most important work is his *History of Bohemia;* of which two volumes were published in the German language in 1836. A Bohemian edition, with additions and a historiographical introduction, appeared in 1848.

The spirit which pervades this great work makes the author to a certain extent the representative of his nation. One of the objects of the work is to point out the *primitive* relations of Slavism on the one hand, and of Germanism, the heir of Romanism,

---

lished at Leutschau 1814; also another of Slovakian Popular Poetry, printed at Pesth 1823. Along with Palacky he published: *Anfangsgründe der Böhmischen Dichtkunst,* Presburg 1818. His *Geschichte der Slav. Sprache und Literatur* appeared at Ofen 1826; and two years later at the same place a work *Ueber die Abkunft der Slaven,* 1828; also *Serbische Lesekörner,* 1833. The title of his great work on Slavic Antiquities is *Slovanske Starozitnosti,* Prague 1837. A German translation appeared under the title, *Schaffarik's Slavische Alterthümer,* aus dem Böhm. von Aehrenfeld, herausgeg. v. Wutke, Leipzig 1844. See a notice of this work in For. Quart. Rev. Vol. XXVI. No. 51.

on the other; their contrasts and necessary conflicts; the Germans, warlike, conquering, oppressing all their neighbours, and bearing the germs of privileged castes in their earliest institutions; the Slavi, peaceful, industrious, living in patriarchal communities, and in their fundamental elements purely democratic. Hence, the author says, the principal idea and fundamental feature of Bohemian history is the uninterrupted clashing and struggle of Slavism and Germanism; and in another place he remarks, that "the history of Bohemia consists chiefly in the combat with Germanism; or in the alternate reception and rejection by the Czekhes of German manners and institutions."[51]

Our own days have witnessed the enthusiasm with which the thought of a total separation between Slavism and Germanism was received, when the events of the month of March 1848 seemed to open an unexpected prospect of realizing a long cherished idea. A great congress of all the Slavic nations was convoked at Prague. But at that very moment, at the gathering together of so many members of that wide-spread family, it became strikingly apparent that they were a *family* of nations; but could never again become, what for thousands of years they had not been, *one* nation. In order to be understood, several of their deputies had to speak in German; and even for the journal founded as the great central organ of Slavism, the *German* language had to be employed.

The patriotic efforts made to prevent the Bohemian language from gradually yielding to the German, are honourable and

[51] Palacky's Bohemian works, besides the various productions of his youth, and many valuable articles in the Journal of the Museum both in German and Bohemian, are the following: *Aelteste Documente der Böhmischen Sprache*, Prague 1840. *Literärische Reise nach Italien in* 1837, with Schaffarik, Prague 1838. *Geschichte von Böhmen*, Th. I. Prague 1836; in Bohemian, *Dějing narodu Czeského*, I. Prague 1848.

laudable; but whether they will have any ultimate result seems to be quite doubtful. The times indeed are somewhat changed, since Jungmann called the present literature of Bohemia "the produce of a few enthusiasts, who, exposing themselves to the hatred of their enemies and the ingratitude of their countrymen, have devoted themselves to the resuscitation of a language, neither living nor dead." Twenty-five years have brought on a great revolution; and those enthusiasts are no longer "a few." But they have still a hard combat to fight. It may be doubtful whether their strength will hold out to struggle against the torrent of time; which, in its resistless course, overwhelms the nations, and only throws their vestiges in scattered fragments on the banks, as feeble memorials to show to an inquiring posterity that they once existed.[52]

---

[52] For more complete information in respect to Bohemian literature, a knowledge of one of the Slavic idioms or of the German language is absolutely required; we know of nothing written on this subject in the English language, except the article of Bowring already cited. This gives an able survey of the poetical part of the literature, but does not profess to cover the whole ground. —The grammatical and lexical part of the Bohemian literature is uncommonly rich, and exhibits no small mass of talent. We confine ourselves to citing the titles of those written in German or Latin. No helps in English or French for learning the Bohemian language, so far as we know, ever existed.—GRAMMARS. *Kurze Unterweisung beyder Sprachen, teutsch und böhmisch,* Pilsen 1531, and several later editions. Klatowsky *Böhmisch-deutche Gespräche,* Prague 1540, and several later editions. B. Optat *Anleitung zur böhm. Orthogr.* etc. 1533, Prague 1588 and 1643. Beneshowsky *Gram. Bohem.* Prague 1577. Benedict a Nudhozer *Gram. Bohem.* Prague 1603. Drachowsky *Gramm. Bohem.* Olmütz 1660. Constantin's *Lima linguae Bohem.* Prague 1667. *Principia linguae Bohem.* 1670–80; new edition 1783. Jandit *Gramm. ling. Bohem.* Prague 1704, seven new editions to 1753. Dolezal *Gramm. Slavico-bohem.* Pressburg 1746. Pohl *Böhmische Sprachkunst,* Vienna 1756, five editions to 1783. Tham *Böhm. Sprachlehre,* Prague 1785; also his *Böhm. Grammatik,* 1798–1804. Pelzel *Grandsätze der böhm.*

SECTION II.

LANGUAGE AND LITERATURE OF THE SLOVAKS.

The northwestern part of Hungary is inhabited by the Slovaks, a Slavic nation, who appear to be the direct descendants of the original Slavic settlers in Europe. Numerous colonists of the same race are scattered all over the other parts of that country. The Byzantine historians, and, somewhat later, the Russian annalist Nestor, speak of the region on the north of the Danube as being the primitive seat of the Slavi. In early times the *Sarmatae limigantes* or *Jazyges metanastae*, nomadic tribes between the Danube and the Theiss, whose name indicates incontestably their having been Slavi,[53] are mentioned as having troubled the Byzantine empire. But they soon disappeared entirely from his-

---

Sprache, Prague 1797–98. Negedly *Böhm. Grammatik*, Prague 1804, fourth edition 1830. Dobrovsky's *Lehrgebäude der böhm. Sprache*, Prague 1809, second edition 1819. Koneczny *Anleitung zur Erlernung der Böhm. Sprache*. Prague 1846.—Dictionaries. Of these we mention only such as would aid persons who wish to learn the language so far as to read Bohemian books; referring the reader for an enumeration of the others to Schaffarik's *Gesch.* p. 301. Weleslawin *Sylva quadrilinguis*, Prague 1598. *Gazophylacium bohem. lat. graec. germ.* Prague 1671. Rohn *Böhmisch-lat. deutscher Nomenclator*, Prague 1764–68. Tham *Böhmisch-deutsches National-lexicon* Prague 1805–7. Also his *Deutsch-böhmisches und Bohmisch-deutsches Taschenwörterbuch*, Prague 1818. Tomsa *Böhm. deutsch-lat. Wöiterbuch*, Prague 1791. Palkowicz *Böhmisch-deutsch-lateinisches Wörterbuch*, Pressburg 1821. Koneczny *Böhmish-Deutsches und Deutsch-Böhm. Taschenwörterbuch*, Prague 1846. The same, *Handbuch der Böhmischen Sprache*, Prague 1847.

[53] See Schlözer's edition of Nestor, Vol. II. p. 76, 97. *Jazyk* signifies in Slavic, *lingua*, tongue.

tory, and it is not before the ninth century, when they were already Christians, that we meet them again. At that time Slovakia, in Slavic *Slovansko*, viz. the regions adjacent to the two rivers Waag and Gran, reappears as an ingredient part of the ephemeral kingdom of great Moravia. The rest of Pannonia was inhabited by other Slavic tribes, by Bulgarians, Rumelians and Khazares. In A. D. 894, the Magyars conquered Pannonia, drove back the Slovaks into the mountains, and made them tributary; whilst they themselves settled on the plains. But although the Slovaks appear to have submitted to their fate, and to have thenceforth lived on good terms with their conquerors, it cannot unconditionally be said that the two nations were merged in each other; since, even after nearly a thousand years have passed, they still speak different languages. The Magyars learned the arts of peace from the Slavi; who, besides being already Christians, had built many cities, and were mechanics, traders, agriculturists. All words and terms relating to these occupations, the Magyars had to obtain from them. The Slovaks on their side lost their national existence in that of their Asiatic conquerors, entered into their ranks as soldiers, and participated thenceforward in all their fortunes; but the influence of the Magyars on their language could be only inconsiderable, since the circle of new ideas which the Slovaks had to receive in exchange from them, barbarians as they were, could be only very limited. The language however is the only remnant of their national existence which the Slovaks have preserved; in every other respect they belong to the Hungarian nation, of which they form an ingredient part, as the Magyars form another; and on the glory of whose valiant deeds they have an equal claim.

Hungary, traversed by two large rivers, the Danube and the Theiss, is divided into four great districts, usually called this side the Danube and beyond the Danube, this side the Theiss and beyond the Theiss. The district this side the Theiss is the principal seat of the Slovaks. The counties Trencsin, Thurocz, Arva, Liptau, and Sohl, are entirely inhabited by them, amounting to about 550,000 in number. In the other counties of the same district they live more mingled with Russniaks and Magyars; and, together with the numerous Slovakish settlements which are scattered over all Hungary, are computed in all at about 1,800,000. About 1,300,000 of them are Roman Catholics, and the remaining 500,000 Protestants.

The Slovakish language, exposed through the geographical situation of the nation, to the influence of various other Slavic idioms—as the Polish, Bohemian, Malo-Russian, Servian, and Vindish—is more broken up into different dialects than perhaps any living tongue. In its original elements it is very nearly related to the Old Slavic language;[54] a fact which is easy to be explained, when we consider that the development of this language must have been the result of the primitive cultivation of the Slavi; and that the region about the Carpathian mountains, the seat of the ancient as well as of the present Slovaks, was the cradle of all the Slavic nations which are now spread over the whole of eastern Europe. Of all living Slavic tongues, the Bohemian is the nearest related to the Slovakish, especially as it appears in the oldest Bohemian writers; a circumstance which induced Dobrovsky at first to consider both languages as essentially the same; or rather to maintain, that the Slovakish was nothing more than Old Bohemian. But after entering more deeply into the subject, he found reason to regard the Slovakish idiom as a separate dialect, which forms the link of connection between

---

[54] We have seen in the history of the Old Slavic language, that on account of the great similarity of the old Slavic and the Slovakish dialects, both in respect to form and grammatical structure and in the meaning of words, it has been maintained by several philologists, that the language of Cyril's translation of the Bible was in the translator's time the Moravian *Slovakian* dialect. See above, p. 27.

the Bohemian and Croatian-Vindish dialects, or between the two principal divisions, the Eastern and Western stems, of the great Slavic family.[55]

To enumerate the features by which the Slovakish dialects are distinguished from the other Slavic languages, would oblige us to enter more into detail than would be acceptable to persons not acquainted with any of them; as we may suppose to be the case with most of our readers. Besides, most of the peculiarities which could be alleged as *general* characteristics, are contradicted by so many single cases, that all general rules would be in danger of being rendered void by a plurality of exceptions. The only thing which belongs to the Slovaks alone, and is not common to any of the other Slavic tongues, is a variety of diphthongs where all the rest have simple vowels; e. g. *kuoñ*, horse, for *koñ; lieucz*, light, for *lucz*, etc. In the counties situated on the frontiers of Galicia, the Slovakish language participates in many of the peculiarities of the Polish tongue; on the frontier of Moravia, the dialect of the people approaches nearer to the vernacular idiom of that province, and consequently to the Bohemian; which has been adopted as their own literary language. On the Slovaks who live more in the interior of the country, the influence of the Magyars, or of the Transylvanian-Germans, or of the Russniaks, or of the Servians, is more or less prominent, according to their locality. The less exposed to the influence of other races, the purer of course has the proper Slovakian idiom been preserved. But even in its purest state, it has, as we mentioned above, a strong and decided resemblance to the Bohemian tongue; from which it is however distinguished by a more harmonious and pleasing sound; its vowels being fuller and occurring more frequently. But a peculiarity which distinguishes it more materially, is a treasure of words and phrases obsolete

[55] See above, p. 143.

or entirely unknown in the present Bohemian language; although they were to be found in the old Bohemian, and are so still, in part, in the Old Slavic, Russian, and Vindish dialects. Schaffarik mentions that G. Rybay, a minister in the county of Bacz, who possessed many valuable manuscripts, had collected 15,000 words for a Slovakish *Idioticon*, and that it would be easy to enlarge this number.[56]

The Slovakish language has never been a literary language; the first attempt to render it so, with a few trifling exceptions, was made about forty years ago; but the opposition which it met with from the literati who had already adopted the kindred Bohemian tongue for their literary language, together with the political obstacles which it had to encounter from the jealousy of the Magyars, seems to have been too strong to be conquered. Indeed, in consequence of this jealousy of the Magyars, the Slovakish language is so far oppressed, that even in the higher schools of the Slovaks themselves this language is not permitted to constitute a branch of instruction, like the Hungarian and Latin. Schaffarik thinks it probable, that in ancient times the vernacular tongue of the counties inhabited by Slovaks was used in public documents and similar writings; and that such historical monuments must be buried in the libraries and archives of the catholic archbishops, noblemen, and cities.[57] But this subject has never been sufficiently examined. The historical popular songs, which nearly a hundred years ago were familiar to the Slovakian peasants, and some of which appear to have been derived even from the pagan period, have perished, with the exception of a few initial verses.[58]

---

[56] *Geschichte der slavischen Sprache*, etc. p. 377. G. Palcowicz, who bought this manuscript, has inserted a large number of Slovakish provincialisms in his Bohemian dictionary.

[57] See the same work, p. 381.

[58] More modern Slovakish popular songs are to be found in Czelakowsky's

There is no trace known to be left of the mental existence of this nation of nearly two millions of souls, until the middle of the fifteenth century. At that time a great body of Hussites, who were exiled from Bohemia, broke into Upper Hungary, and, under the conduct of Giskra von Brandeis, were hired by the queen Elizabeth against the rival Polish-Hungarian monarch Vladislaus, afterwards king of Bohemia. The Bohemian soldiers were accompanied by their wives and children, and settled finally in different parts of Hungary. Other Taboritic colonists followed them, and amalgamated gradually with the Slovaks, among whom they principally established themselves. It is probable, that at this time the Slovaks became familiar with the Bohemian as a literary language; which from its kindred genius and its similarity of forms was perfectly intelligible, and must have been highly acceptable to them. When the doctrines of the German Reformers penetrated into Hungary, they found the Slovaks already so well prepared, that those doctrines were at once spread among the people by numerous books written by Slovakian clergymen in the Bohemian language. The Bible and the liturgical books were written and printed in Bohemian; and many Bohemians and Moravians came into Hungary as preachers and teachers. Thus the dominion of the Bohemian language over the pulpit, and, since *all* the Slovakian writers of this period were clergymen, in the republic of letters also, was established among the Slovaks without struggle. There is nothing known of any

---

collection, *Slowanske narodni pisne*, Prague 1822, 1827; also in ***Pisnie swietske lidu slowenskeho w Uhrich***, Pesth 1823, edited by Schaffarik. The little work *Slavische Volkslieder*, by Wenzig, Halle 1830, contains sixteen Slovakish songs, mostly taken from Czelakowsky's work, in a German translation A large collection of Slovakish popular poetry was made in 1834 by the distinguished poet J. Kollar. It is said to contain 2300 pieces.

catholic Slovakish writers at this period; if there were any, they probably followed the beaten track, and wrote also in Bohemian or in Latin. But the produce of the literary cultivation of the Slovaks during the sixteenth and seventeenth centuries, is at most but small; for the times appear to have been too heavy, and men's minds too much oppressed, for a free development of their powers. The civil wars, the devastations of the Turks, the religious controversies, and after the battle at the White Mountain, religious oppression and persecution, chased the peaceful muses from Pannonia, and put the genius of the people in chains. All the productions of these two centuries, with a few exceptions, are confined to theology, and are mostly sermons, catechisms, devotional exercises, or religious hymns. Schaffarik observes, that from these latter there speaks a melancholy gloomy spirit, crying for divine aid and deliverance.[59] Among the clergymen who during the first half of the eighteenth century exerted themselves for the diffusion of biblical knowledge, were Matth. Bel and D. Krman, who prepared a new edition of the Bible; G. Ambrosius and G. Bahyl, authors of theological commentaries, etc. Those Slovakian writers who in any measure distinguished themselves, have been enumerated under their proper heads in our sketch of the Bohemian literature.[60]

The Bohemian dialect, as we have mentioned repeatedly, is perfectly *intelligible* to the Slovaks. But as it is not to them the language of common conversation, it cannot be *familiar* to their minds. If, in listening to their preachers in the churches, the people succeed in straining up their minds sufficiently to enable them to follow the course of the sermons and devotional exercises, it still seems rather unnatural, that even their prayer books, destined for private use, should not be written in their vernacu-

---

[59] See *Geschichte der sl. Spr.* p. 383. [60] Pages 199, 205.

lar tongue; but that even their addresses to the Most High, which, more than any thing else, should be the free and natural effusions of their inmost feelings, should require such an intellectual exertion and an artificial transposition into a foreign clime. It is a singular fact, that, whilst every where else Protestantism and the friends of the Bible have advocated and attempted to raise the dialect of the people, in opposition to a privileged idiom of the priesthood, among the Slovaks the vindication of the vernacular tongue has been attempted by the Romanists, and has met with strong opposition from the Protestants. In the year 1718, Alex. Macsay, a catholic clergyman, published sermons at Tyrnau, written in the common Slovakian dialect. The Jesuits of Tyrnau followed his example, in publishing books of prayers and several other religious works, in a language which is rather a mixture of the dialect of the people and the literary Bohemian language. During the last ten years of the eighteenth century, a more successful attempt was made to elevate the Slovakian dialect spoken on the frontiers of Moravia, and which approaches the Bohemian language most, to the rank of a literary language. At the head of this undertaking were the Roman catholic curates Bajza, Fandli, and Bernolak, especially the last. A society was formed, the members of which bound themselves to buy the books written in Slovakish by Bernolak and his friends. The Romanists proceeded in the work with great zeal and activity, and were patronized by the cardinal Rudnay, primate of Hungary; who himself published some of his orations held in the Slovakian dialect, and caused a voluminous Slovakish dictionary, a posthumous work of Bernolak's, to be printed.[61] A version of the Bible in the same dialect, made by the canon G. Palkowicz, who is

---

[61] The same individual who caused the Dalmatian Bible to be printed; see p. 131 above.

also the author of the fourth volume of the above dictionary, was printed in the year 1831.

The Protestant Slovaks, who several centuries ago had already acquired by their own contributions the right of citizens in the Bohemian republic of letters,—especially during the course of the seventeenth century, when most of the native Bohemians had been banished from it,—feared to endanger the cause of literature itself by innovations of this kind. They too united themselves into a society, and founded a professorship of Bohemian-Slovakian literature at the Lyceum of Pressburg, which was occupied by another G. Palkowicz, honorably mentioned in our History of Bohemian literature.[62] The number of Protestant Slovaks being comparatively small, this institution was not sustained longer than ten years. To the names of the principal Slovakish-Bohemian writers during this and the last century, which have been given above,[63] we add here those of Bartholomæides, Tablicz, Lovich, and Moshotzy, themselves writers of merit, or promoters of literature and science.

Many among the Slovaks, like many of their brethren the Magyars, and among other Slavi the Bohemians and Illyrians, have received a German education, and have that language at command. For the sake of more fame, or a larger field of influence, these mostly prefer to write in German. Among them was

---

[62] These two individuals of the same baptismal and family names, George Palkowicz, both following the same pursuits, and both not without desert in respect to their countrymen, but nevertheless serving opposite interests according to their different views, must not be confounded. Professor Palkowicz prepared a new edition of the Bohemian Bible for the Slovaks; see p. 205 above. Canon Palkowicz translated the Scriptures into the Slovakian dialect. Professor P. published a Bohemian dictionary, see pp. 205, 212; Canon P. the fourth volume of Bernolak's Slovakian lexicon, as said in the text above.

[63] See pp. 199, 205.

Schaffarik; until, from a principle of patriotism, he adopted the Bohemian.[64]

---

[64] There does not yet exist a philological work, from which a complete knowledge of the Slovakian language, in its different dialects, could be obtained. The following works of Bernolak regard chiefly the Slovakish-Moravian dialect: *Grammatica Slavica*, Posonii 1790. *Dissertatio de literis Slavorum*, Posonii 1783. *Etymologia vocum Slavicarum*, Tyrnau 1791. *Lexicon Slav. Lat. Germ. Hung.* Buda 1825.

CHAPTER II.

HISTORY OF THE POLISH LANGUAGE AND LITERATURE.

THE regions of the Baltic and Lower Vistula, after the Goths and Vandals had finally left them, were occupied, towards the fourth century, by the Lettonians and Lithuanians, who are according to some historians Slavic, and according to others Finnic-Scythic tribes.[1] It appears, that the various nations which inhabited this country were by the ancients comprised under the name of Sarmatæ. In the sixth, or according to others, in the seventh century, the Lekhes, a people kindred to the Czekhes, and coming like them from the Carpathian regions, whence they were urged forwards by the Bulgarians, settled on the banks of the Vistula and Varta. Lekh (Ljakh) signified in old Bohemian a free and noble man, and had

---

[1] On the origin of these tribes, which seem to have been kindred nations with the ancient Livonians, Esthonians, and Borussians, many hypotheses have been started, but the truth has not yet been sufficiently ascertained. It seems evident to us, that they are not of Slavic origin; although this has been maintained by many historians, who were misled by local circumstances. Even Schaffarik in his Antiquities regards them as originally a Slavic race. See Parrot's *Versuch einer Entwickelung der Sprache, Abstammung, etc. der Liven, Letten, etc.* The Foreign Quarterly Review contains an interesting essay on Lettish popular poetry, Vol. VIII. p. 61.

this meaning still in the fourteenth century.[2] The Lekhes were divided into several tribes, of which, according to Nestor, at first only those who settled on the vast plains, *polie*, of the Ukraine, were called *Polyane*, Poles, i. e. inhabitants of the plain. The tribes which occupied Masovia were called *Masovshane;* the Lekhes who went to Pomerania, *Pomoriane*, etc. The specific name of *Poles*, as applied to all the Lekhish tribes together, does not appear until the close of the tenth century, when the generic appellation of Lekhes or Ljakhes had perished. In the year 840, the chiefs of the different tribes united themselves under one common head; at that time they are said to have chosen a husbandman by the name of Pjast for their duke, and the male descendants of this, their first prince, lived and reigned not less than six hundred and thirty years. From Germany and Bohemia Christianity was carried to Poland by Romish priests, probably as early as the ninth century. In the beginning of the tenth, some attempts were made to introduce the Slavic liturgy into Poland. Both species of worship existed for some time peacefully side by side; and even when, through the exertions of the Latin priesthood, the Slavic liturgy was gradually superseded by the occidental rites, the former was at least tolerated; and after the invention of printing, the Polish city of Cracow was the first place where books in the Old Slavic dialect, and portions of the Old Slavic Bible, were printed.[3]

In the year 965, the duke Miecislav married the Bohemian princess Dombrovka, and caused himself to be baptized. From

---

[2] Kopitar, in his review of Schaffarik's *Geschichte,* declares this etymological derivation to be a mistake; without however giving any other explanation of the name Lekh. *Wiener Jahrbücher,* Vol. XXXVII. 1827. According to Schaffarik in his Slav. Antiquities, *Lekh,* like *Czekh,* means a leader, a high officer.

[3] See pp. 36, 43.

that time onward, all the Polish princes and the greatest part of the nation became Christians. There is however not one among the Slavic nations, in which the influence Christianity must necessarily have exerted on its mental cultivation, is so little visible; while upon its language it exerted none at all. It has ever been and is still a favourite opinion of some Slavic philologists, that several of the Slavic nations must have possessed the art of writing long before their acquaintance with the Latin alphabet, or the invention of the Cyrillic system; and among the arguments by which they maintain this view, there are indeed some too striking to be wholly set aside. But neither from those early times, nor from the four or five centuries after the introduction of Christianity, does there remain any monument whatever of the Polish language; nay, with the exception of a few fragments without value, the most ancient document of that language extant is not older than the sixteenth century. Until that time the Latin idiom reigned exclusively in Poland. The teachers of Christianity in this country were for nearly five centuries foreigners, viz. Germans and Italians. Hence arose that unnatural neglect of the vernacular tongue, of which these were ignorant; the private influence of the German, still visible in the Polish language; and the unlimited dominion of the Latin. Slavic, Polish, and heathenish, were to them synonymous words. Thus, while the light of Christianity every where carried the first dawn of life into the night of Slavic antiquity, the early history of Poland affords more than any other part of the Christian world a melancholy proof, how the passions and blindness of men operated to counterbalance that holy influence. But although so unfavourably disposed towards the language, it cannot be said that the influence of the foreign clergy was in other respects injurious to the literary cultivation of the country. Benedictine monks founded in the beginning of the eleventh century the first

Polish schools; and numerous convents of their own and other orders presented to the scholar an asylum, both when in the year 1241 the Mongols broke into the country, and also during the civil wars which were caused by the family dissensions of Pjast's successors. Several chronicles in Latin were written by Poles long before the history of the Polish literature begins; and Polish noblemen went to Paris, Bologna, and Prague, to study sciences, for the very elements of which their own language afforded them no means.

Polish writers are in the habit of dividing the history of their language into five periods.[4]

The *first* period extends from the introduction of Christianity to Cassimir the Great, A. D. 1333.

The *second* period extends from A. D. 1333 to A. D. 1506, or the reign of Sigismund I.

The *third* period is the golden age of the Polish literature, and closes with the foundation of the schools of the Jesuits, A. D. 1622.

The *fourth* period comprises the time of the preponderance of the Jesuits, and ends with the revival of literature by Konarski, A. D. 1760.

The *fifth* period comprehends the interval from A. D. 1760 to the revolution in 1830.

As the Polish literature of our own day bears a different stamp from that of former times, we may add a *sixth* period, extending from 1830 to the present time.

Before we enter upon a regular historical account of these different periods, we will devote a few words to the history and character of the language itself.

The extent of country, in which the Polish language is predominant, is much smaller than would naturally be concluded

---

[4] See Bentkowski's *Hist. literatury Polsk.* Warsaw 1814.

from the great circuit of territory, which, at the time of its power and independence, was comprised under the kingdom of Poland. We do not allude to the sixteenth century, when Poland by the success of its arms became for a short time the most powerful state in the north; when the Teutonic knights, the conquerors of Prussia, were compelled to acknowledge its protection; and when not only were Livonia and Courland, the one a component part of the Polish kingdom, and the other a Polish fief, but even the ancient Smolensk and the venerable Kief, the royal seat of Vladimir, and the Russian provinces adjacent to Galicia, all were subjugated by Poland. We speak of this kingdom as it was at the time of its first partition between Russia, Austria, and Prussia. Of the four or five millions of inhabitants in the provinces united with Russia at the three successive partitions of 1772, 1793, and 1795, only one and a half million are strictly Poles, that is, Lekhes, who speak dialects of that language;[5] in White and Black Russia, the Russniaks are by far more numerous; and in Lithuania the Lithuanians. Besides the independent language of these latter, the Malo-Russian and White Russian dialects are spoken in these provinces; and all documents of the grand-duchy of Lithuania before it was united with Poland in A. D. 1569, were written in the latter.[6]

The Polish language is farther spoken: 1) By the inhabitants

---

[5] The statistical information respecting the Russian-Polish provinces is very imperfect, and contains the most striking contradictions. Benken gives the number of inhabitants at four millions; Wichmann in 1813, at 6,380,000; Arsenjef at seven millions. According to Brömsen's *Russland und das rüssische Reich*, Berl. 1819, there are not more than 850,000 Poles among them, nearly all noblemen; the lower classes are Russniaks and Lithuanians. In our statement of the number of Poles in these provinces, we have followed Schaffarik.

[6] See above, p. 51; also, pp. 59, 60, n. 17.

of the kingdom of Poland formed in 1815, three and a half millions in number, or reckoned together with the Poles of the Polish-Russian provinces, five millions; 2) By the inhabitants of the cities and the nobility of Galicia, belonging to Austria, and the Poles in the Austrian part of Silesia, about three millions; 3) By the inhabitants of the small republic of Cracow, about one hundred thousand; 4) By the inhabitants of the Prussian grand-duchy of Posen, and a part of the province called Western Prussia, together with the Poles in Silesia and the Kassubes in Pomerania; in all less than two millions.[7]

Thus the Polish language is spoken by a population of about ten millions.[8] Like all living languages, it has different dialects, and is in one place spoken with greater purity than in another. As these varieties, however, are neither very striking nor have ever had an influence on literature, they do not concern us here.

The ancient Polish language seems to have been very nearly related to the dialects of the Czekhes and the Sorabian Vendes. Although very little is known in respect to the circumstances and progress of the formation of the language into its present state, it is sufficiently obvious, that it has been developed from the conflict of its natural elements with the Latin and German idioms. Of the other Slavic dialects, the Bohemian is the only one which has exerted any influence upon the Polish tongue. The Italian and Turkish words introduced during the dominion of an Italian priesthood, and through the political relations of the Poles and the Turks, never entered deeply into the body of

[7] These statements seem to disagree with those of Hassel, which rest on the authority of the returns of 1820. He states that Austrian Poland has 4,226,969 inhabitants; Prussian Poland, 2,584,124. The population of the former consists however of a large proportion of Russniaks, and more especially of Jews; the latter has a similar proportion of German inhabitants.

[8] Other private estimates make them not more than seven millions.

the language; and might be easily exchanged for better Polish forms of expression.

Of all the Slavic dialects, the Polish presents to the foreigner the most difficulties; partly on account of the great variety and nicety of shades in the pronunciation of the vowels, and from the combination of consonants in such a way that only a Slavic tongue can conquer them, and cause the apparent harshness in some measure to disappear;[9] partly on account of its refined and artificial grammatical structure. In this latter respect it differs materially from the Russian language; which, although equally rich, is remarkable for its simplicity and perspicuity. The Polish and Bohemian idioms, in the opinion of the best judges, are above all others capable of faithfully imitating the refinements of the classical languages; and the Polish prose is modelled after the Latin with a perfection, which, in the golden age of Polish literature, was one of its characteristic features. It is therefore surprising, that the Polish language in poetry, although in other respects highly cultivated, does not admit the introduction of the classical prosody. We mean, the Polish language in its present state; for it is very probable, that in its original character it possessed, in common with all the other Slavic languages, the elements of a regular system of *long* and *short* syllables. So long, however, as there have existed Polish poets, they have not measured, but, in imitation of the French, have *counted* the syllables. With the exception of a few recent poets, who have written in blank verse, and a few weak attempts to adapt the Greek principles of accent to the Polish language, all Polish poetry is, like the French, in rhyme;

---

[9] We doubt whether any but Slavic organs would be able to pronounce the name of the place, to which the college of Zamosc was removed. It is written *Szczebrzeszyn.*

and the French Alexandrine is the favourite form of the Polish poets.[10]

FIRST PERIOD.

From the introduction of Christianity to Casimir the Great, A. D. 1333.

In dividing the early part of the history of the Polish literature into two periods, we follow the example and authority of Bentkowski; although it seems to be singular to pretend to give an account of a literature which did not yet exist. The history of the Polish literature does not indeed properly begin before the close of the second period; yet that of the *literary cultivation* of the nation commences with the beginning of that period; and a few slight traces of it are to be found even in the middle of the first. Of the language itself, nothing is left but the names of places and persons, and some Polish words scattered through the Latin documents of the time, written without orthographic rules, and therefore often hardly intelligible. There exists an ancient Polish war-song, the author of which is said to have been St. Adalbert, a Bohemian by birth, who was bishop of Prague at the end of the tenth century;[11] but even according to Rakow-

---

[10] Zaluski and Minasovrez wrote verses with *counted* not *measured* syllables, without rhyme; Przybylski's and Staszye's translations of Homer are in hexameters. That rhyme is not natural to the Polish language, is evident from the ancient popular poetry of the other Slavic nations; which are all without rhyme. The author of the work *Volkslieder der Polen,* assumes the absence of rhyme in some of them as a proof of their antiquity. Of Slavic popular songs only those of the Malo-Russians or Ruthenians are rhymed; and none of these lay claim to great antiquity.

[11] This song, called *Boga Rodzica,* can be named a war-song, only because the Poles used to sing it when advancing to battle. It is rather a prayer to the

iecki, a philologist who is more disposed than any other to find traces of an *early* cultivation of the Slavic nations, and especially of the Poles, this song, or rather hymn, is, in its present form, not older than the fourteenth century. All that is extant from this period is written in Latin. Besides some unimportant documents and an anonymous biography of Adalbert, there remain several historical works of the twelfth and thirteenth centuries.

Martin Gallus, a Frenchman, who lived in Poland between 1110 and 1135, is considered as the oldest Polish historian. Other chronicles of Poland were written by the bishops of Cracow, Matthew Cholewa, and Vincent, son of Kadlubec, who died in 1223; by Bogufal, bishop of Posen, some twenty years later; and by Godzislav Baszko, about thirty years later still. Strzembski wrote towards the middle of the thirteenth century a history of the popes and Roman emperors. In 1008 duke Boleslav, the son of Miecislav, invited Benedictine monks to Poland, who founded convents at Sieciechov and Lysagora, with schools attached to them. This example was followed at a later period by other orders; and in Poland, longer than in any other country, education was entirely in the hands of the ecclesiastics. For several hundred years the natives were excluded from all clerical dignities and privileges, and the numerous monasteries were filled only with foreign monks. Even as late as the fifteenth century, foreigners had decidedly the preference. In the year 1237 Pelka, archbishop of Gnesen, directed the institution of schools by the

---

Virgin, ending with a sixfold Amen. In a poetical respect it has no value. It is printed in Bowring's *Specimens of the Polish Poets*, p. 12; together with the music, copied from a manuscript which is said to be from the twelfth century. No translation is added. It is remarkable that this hymn is still sung, or at least was so in the year 1812, in the churches of the places where St. Adalbert lived and died, viz. at Kola and Gnesen. Niemcewicz, who published it, states that he himself heard it at that time at the latter place.

priests; but added the recommendation to the bishops, that they should employ as teachers only Germans who understood Polish. In A. D. 1285 at the synod of Leczyc, they went a step further in excluding all foreigners, who were ignorant of the Polish language, from the places of ecclesiastical teachers and instructors. But more than eighty years later, it was found necessary at the synod of Kalish in 1357 to repeat the same decree; and even a century after this time, in A. D. 1460, John Ostrorog complained that all the rich convents were occupied by foreign monks.[12] These ignorant men were wont to throw into the fire the few writings in the barbarian language, which they could discover; and, as instructors of the youth, were able to fill the heads of the young nobility with the most unnatural prejudices against the vernacular tongue of their own country Besides the clergy, many other foreigners also settled in Poland, as mechanics and traders, especially Germans. But as they all lived merely in the cities of Poland, they and their language had far less influence on the people, than was the case in Bohemia, where they mingled with all classes.

SECOND PERIOD.

From Casimir the Great to Sigismund I. A. D. 1333 *to A. D.* 1506.

Casimir is one of the few princes, who acquired the name of the Great not by victories and conquests, but through the real benefits of laws, national courts of justice, and means of education, which he procured for his subjects. His father, Vladislaus Lokietek, had resumed the royal title, which hitherto had been

[12] See Schaffarik's *Geschichte der Slav. Sprache,* p. 421.

alternately taken and dropped; and was the first who permanently united Great and Little Poland. Under Casimir, the present Austrian kingdom of Galicia, which, together with Lodomeria, the present Russian government Vladimir, was then called Red Russia, was added by inheritance. Lithuania became connected with Poland as a Polish fief in the year 1386, when queen Hedevig, heiress of the crown of Poland, married Jagello, duke of Lithuania; but was first completely incorporated as a component part of the kingdom of Poland only so late as the year 1569. Masovia had been thus united some forty years earlier. At the time of the marriage of Hedevig and Jagello, the latter caused himself to be baptized, and introduced Christianity into Lithuania, where he himself in many cases acted as an apostle.

As to the influence of Casimir the Great upon the literary cultivation of his subjects, it was more mediate than immediate. Whilst his cotemporary and neighbour, Charles IV of Bohemia, loved and patronized the language of that kindred nation, Casimir paid no attention whatever to the vernacular tongue of his country; nor was any thing done under his administration for the development of that rich dialect. This king indeed, as early as A. D. 1347, laid the foundation of the high school of Cracow; but the regular organization and influence of this institution dates only from half a century later.[13] But by introducing a better order of things, by providing his subjects with their earliest code of laws, by instituting the first constitutional diets, by fortifying the cities and protecting the tillers of the soil against a wild and oppressive nobility, he established a better tone of

[13] A History of the University of Cracow was recently published by Prof. Muczkowski, under the modest title: *Mieszkania i postepowanie, etc.* i. e. 'On the dwellings and the conduct of the Students of the University of Cracow in former centuries,' Cracow 1842. Vol. I. The work was planned for *ten* volumes.

moral feeling throughout the nation. A seed, sown in such ground, necessarily springs up slowly, but surely.

With Casimir the race of the Pjasts expired. His nephew, Louis of Hungary, a prince of the house of Anjou, was elected king; but his reign was spent in constant war, and left no trace of care for the internal cultivation of the country. The limitation of the power of the sovereign, and the exorbitant privileges of the Polish nobility, date from the reign of this prince; he resided mostly in Hungary, and granted to the Poles all their demands, in order to prevent the alienation of their crown from his house. After his death his second daughter, Hedevig, was preferred to the emperor Sigismund, who was married to the eldest, Mary; because this prince refused to subscribe the conditions demanded by the Polish Estates. Hedevig married Jagello of Lithuania; and under their descendants the Jagellons, who reigned nearly two centuries, Poland rose to the summit of its power and glory. With Siegmund I, the grandson of Jagello, but the fifth king after him, a new period of the Polish literature begins.

The history of the Polish language, as we have already said, properly commences only with the close, or at the utmost with the middle of the present period, when in the year 1488 the first printing office was erected at Cracow. Of the more ancient times, with a few exceptions, only weak and scattered traces are left. There was said to have existed a Polish translation of the Bible, made by order of queen Hedevig before the year 1390; but no copy had ever been seen; and there was reason to doubt whether it ever existed. There was extant however, an old manuscript of a Psalter, which the antiquarian Thadd. Czacki took to be a fragment of it; and other ancient manuscripts of portions of a Psalter were found at Saros Patak in Hungary, and seemed to belong to it. But no one of these codices bore any incontestable mark of its age. The Psalter of St. Florian, a convent near Linz in Austria, discovered in 1826 by the librarian Chmel, proved at last to be in reality the lost treasure. This important document, the origin of which could be philologically and historically traced back to the fourteenth century, after having given occasion to a passionate conflict in the Slavic literary world, was finally published by Kopitar in a complete and erudite edition, as the most ancient monument of the Polish language [14]

All other Polish manuscripts of those times are fragments; documents relating to suits of law, translations of statutes issued in Latin, the ten commandments in verse, a translation of one of Wickliffe's hymns, etc.

The orthography of the language, and especially the adoption of the Latin alphabet, seems to have troubled the few writers of this period exceedingly. They appear to have founded their principles alternately on the Latin, the Bohemian, and the German methods of combining letters; an inconsistency, which adds greatly to the difficulties of modern Slavic etymology.[15] In 1828 a remarkable manuscript was published under the title, *Pamientniki Janozara*, or Memoirs of a Janissary. It was the journal of a Polish nobleman, who had been induced by circumstances to enter the Turkish army during the siege and conquest of Constantinople, an event which took place A.D. 1453. This interesting document of a language, that is so remarkably poor in ancient monuments, was no longer intelligible to the common Polish reader. It was necessary to add a version in modern Polish in order to make it understood.

Annalists of Polish history, who wrote in Latin, were not wanting in this period. Sig. Rositzius, Dzierzva,[16] and more especially John Dlugosz, bishop of Lemberg, wrote histories and

---

[14] *Aelteste Denkmäler der Polnischen Sprache,* Wien 1838.

[15] Dobrovsky's *Slovanka,* Vol. II. p. 237.

[16] His *Chronicon Polonorum* was reprinted at Warsaw in 1824; together with Vincent Kadlubeck's *Res gestae principum ac regum Poloniae.*

chronicles of Poland; and the work of the latter is still considered as highly valuable.

THIRD PERIOD.

From Sigismund I, to the establishment of the schools of the Jesuits in Cracow. A. D. 1505 *to A. D.* 1622.

In northern climates, the bright and glowing days of summer follow in almost immediate succession a long and gloomy winter, without allowing to the attentive mind of the lover of nature the enjoyment of observing, during a transient interval of spring, the gradual development of the beauty of the earth. Thus the flowers of Polish literature burst out from their buds with a rapidity unequalled in literary history, and were ripened into fruit with the same prodigious celerity.

The university of Cracow had been reinstituted under Jagello in A. D. 1400, and organized after the model of that of Prague. Although the most flourishing period of this institution was the sixteenth century, yet it presented during the fifteenth to the Polish nobility a good opportunity of studying the classics; and it is doubtless through this preparatory familiarity with the ancient writers, that the phenomenon to which we have alluded must be principally accounted for. It was moreover now the epoch, when the genius of Christian Europe made the most decided efforts to shake off the chains which had fettered the freedom of thought. The doctrines of the German Reformers, although the number of their professed disciples was in proportion smaller than in Bohemia, had nevertheless a decided influence upon the general direction of the public mind. The wild flame of false religious zeal, which in Poland also under the sons and immediate successors of Jagello, had kindled the faggots in which the disciples of the new doctrines were called to seal the truth of their conviction with their blood, was extinguished before the milder wisdom of Sigismund I; although the early part of his reign was not free from religious persecution. The activity of the inquisition was restrained. But the new doctrines found a more decided support in Sigismund Augustus. Poland became, under his administration, the seat of a toleration then unequalled in the world. Communities of the most different religious principles formed themselves, at first under the indulgence of the king and the government, and finally under the protection of the law. Even the boldest theological skeptics of the age, the two Socini, found in Poland an asylum.[17]

The Bohemian language, which already possessed so extensive a

[17] Among these sects were the Unitarians, called also Anti-trinitarians, modern Arians, and afterwards Socinians. They called themselves Polish Brethren. Their principal school and printing office was at Racow; several of their teachers were distinguished for learning, their communities were wealthy and flourishing, and not a few of the highest families of Poland belonged to them. The doctrines of the two exiled Italians, Lelio and Fausto Socini, uncle and nephew, found among them only a conditional approbation; most of them were unwilling to receive Fausto, who developed his views more openly than his uncle, into their community. Internal dissensions were the result, and the establishment of new and smaller congregations. A disturbance among the students at Racow in 1638, gave to the Catholics and to the other Protestants a welcome pretext for persecuting them; in 1658 their denomination was ultimately suppressed, and the choice left to them between the adoption of the Roman Catholic religion or exile within three years. A part of them emigrated to Germany, where they were soon merged in other Protestant denominations; others went to Transylvania, where the Unitarians, about fifty thousand in number, belonged and still belong to the denominations acknowledged by the state, and enjoy all civil rights. They have two high schools, at Klausenburg and at Thoarda; but are far from being distinguished for learning. See Meusel's *Staatengeschicte*, p. 555. Lubienieci *Historia Reformationis Polonicae*, etc. etc.

literature, acquired during this period a great influence upon the Polish. The number of clerical writers, however, which in Bohemia was so great, was comparatively only small in Poland. Indeed it is worthy of remark, that while in other countries the diffusion of information and general illumination proceeded from the clergy, not indeed as a body, but from individuals among the clergy, in Poland it was always the highest nobility who were at the head of literary enterprises or institutions for mental cultivation. There are many princely names among the writers of this period; and there are still so among those of the present day. This may however be one of the causes, why education in Poland was entirely confined to the higher classes; while, even during this brilliant period, the peasantry remained in the lowest state of degradation, and *nothing* was done to elevate their minds or to better their condition. For it is to the clergy, that the common people have always to look as their natural and bounden teachers; it is to the clergy, that a low state of cultivation among the poorer classes is the most dishonourable. During this period, however, the opportunity was presented to the people of becoming better acquainted with the Scriptures, through several translations of them into the Polish language, not only by the different Protestant denominations, but also by the Romanists themselves. Indeed, with the exceptions above mentioned, all the translations of the Bible extant in the Polish language are from the sixteenth or the beginning of the seventeenth century.[18]

---

[18] An enumeration of the Polish versions of the Bible may be acceptable to the reader. The New Testament was first translated by the Lutheran Seklucyan, who was a Greek scholar, and printed at Königsberg 1551, three times reprinted before 1555. Afterwards for Catholics by Leonard, from the Vulgate, reviewed by Leopolita, Cracow 1556. Of the Old Testament, the Psalter alone was several times translated and repeatedly printed. The whole Bible was first translated for the Catholics by Leonard, from the Vulgate, and reviewed by Leopolita, Cracow 1561, reprinted in 1575 and 1577. Two years

We meet also, among the productions of the literature of this period, a few catechisms and postillae, written expressly for the instruction of the common people by some eminent Lutheran and reformed Polish ministers. But the want of means for acquiring even the most elementary information, was so great, that only a very few among the lower classes were able to read them. The doctrines of the Reformers, which every where else were favoured principally by the middle and lower classes, in Poland found their chief support among the nobility. Comparatively few of the people adhered to them. There was a time, between 1550 and 1650, when half the senate,[19] and even more

---

later by an anonymous translator from the original languages, for Calvinists, Brzesc 1563. Again from the original languages by Budny, an Unitarian clergyman, 1570, reprinted in 1572. From the Vulgate by the Jesuit Wuiek, Cracow 1599, reprinted at Breslau in 1740 in 8vo, and 1771 in 4to, with the Latin text. From the original languages by Paliurus, Wengierscius, and Micolaievius, for Calvinists, Dantzic 1632, the first Bible in 8vo, all the former being in fol. or 4to ; reprinted at Amsterdam 1660, at Halle 1726, at Königsberg 1738, 1779, and at Berlin 1810, by the Bible Society. See Ringeltaube's *Nachricht von den polnischen Bibeln,* Danz. 1744. Bentkowski's *Hist. liter. Pol.* Vol. II. p. 494. *Slovanka* Vol. I. p. 141. Vol. II. p. 228. Schaffarik's *Geschichte der Slav. Spr.* p. 424.

[19] The Polish senate was not a body, the members of which were elected for a certain term ; as those not acquainted with the Polish constitution might be disposed to believe. It was composed of all the archbishops and bishops, the waiwodes and castellans, i. e. the titled nobility, and the principal ministers of the king. It was thus in some measure the organ of the government and of the clergy, in opposition to the national representatives or the mass of the nobility. This body was not established until towards the close of the fifteenth century. Before 1466–70, every nobleman who chose, made his personal appearance in the senate at the summons of the king ; but Casimir, the son of Jagello, in his frequent want of money and men, repeated these summons so often, that the nobility found personal appearance inconvenient, and selected in their provincial conventions *nuntii,* to represent the nation, or rather the nobility; without however giving up the right of personal attendance. The

than half of the nobility, consisted of Lutherans and Calvinists. In the year 1570, these two denominations, together with the Bohemian Brethren, formed a union of their churches by the treaty of Sendomir for external or political purposes. In 1573, by another treaty known under the name of *pax dissidentium*, they were acknowledged by the state and the king, and all the rights of the Catholics were granted to the members of these three denominations, and also to the Greeks and Armenians. The want, however, of an accurate determination of their mutual relation to each other, occasioned repeatedly in the course of the following century bloody dissensions. The Protestants succeeded, nevertheless, in maintaining their rights, until the years 1717 and 1718, when their number having gradually yet considerably diminished, they were deprived of their suffrages in the diet. Their adversaries went still further; and, after struggling against oppression of all sorts, the dissidents had at length, in 1736, to be contented with being acknowledged as *tolerated sects*. After the accession of Stanislaus Poniatowsky to the throne in 1766, the dissidents attempted to regain their former rights. In this they were supported by several Protestant powers; but more especially by Russia, who thus improved the opportunity of increasing its influence in Polish affairs. In consequence of this powerful support, the laws directed against the dissidents were repealed; and in 1775 all their old privileges were restored to them, except the right of being eligible to the stations of ministers

---

nuntii, whose number was not fixed, were bound to appear, had the right to grant or to refuse duties, and to act as the advisers of the king. In 1505 the law was passed, that without their consent the constitution could not be changed. At the diet in A. D. 1652 it occurred for the first time, that a single *nuntius* opposed and annulled by his *liberum veto* the united resolutions of the whole convention. On this example a regular right was very soon founded and acknowledged. Deputies of cities were occasionally invited to the diet, but only in extraordinary cases.

of state and senators. In more recent times the Protestants have been admitted to all the rights of the Catholics; although the Roman Catholic is still the predominant religion of the kingdom of Poland.

We have permitted ourselves this digression, and anticipation of time; although we shall have an opportunity of again returning to this subject. The influence of Protestantism on the literature of Poland cannot be denied; although its doctrines and their immediate consequence, the private examination and interpretation of the Scriptures, have occupied the minds and pens of the Poles less than those of any other nation among whom they have been received. We now return to the sixteenth century.

The Polish language acquired during this period such a degree of refinement, that even on the revival of literature and taste in modern times, it was necessary to add nothing for its improvement; although the course of time naturally had occasioned some changes. Several able men occupied themselves with its systematic culture by means of grammars and dictionaries. Zaborowski, Statorius, and Januscowski wrote grammars; Macynski compiled the first dictionary. The first part of Knapski's *Thesaurus*, an esteemed work even at the present day, was first published in 1621, and may therefore be considered as a production of this period. But the practical use, which so many gifted writers made of the language for a variety of subjects, contributed still more to its cultivation. The point in which it acquired less perfection, and which appeared the most difficult to subject to fixed rules, was that of orthography. That the Latin alphabet is not fully adapted to express Slavic sounds, is evident in the Polish language. Indeed the reputed harshness of this language rests partly on the manner in which they were obliged to combine several consonants, which to the eye of the occidental European can only be united by intermediate vowels. On the other hand, it is just this system of letters which forms a connecting link between the Polish language and those of western Europe; and although most Slavic philologists regret that the Latin alphabet ever should have been adopted for any Slavic language in preference to the Cyrillic, yet Grimm (with whom we fully agree) thinks that "the adoption of the former, with appropriate additions corresponding to the peculiar sounds of each language and dialect, would have been beneficial to all European languages."[19]

Although the art of printing was introduced into Poland as early as 1488, when the first printing office was established at Cracow, yet printed books first became generally diffused between the years 1530 and 1540. The first work printed in Poland was a calendar for the year 1490; the first book printed in the Polish language was Bonaventura's life of Jesus, translated for the queen of Hungary, and published in 1522. In the second half of the sixteenth century nearly every city, which had a considerable school, had also its printing office.[20] The schools were unfortunately confined to the cities; nothing was done for the peasantry, who have remained even to the most recent times in a state of physical and moral degradation, with which that of the common people of no other country except Russia can be compared. A peasant who could read or write, would have been considered as a prodigy. So much the more, however, was done for the national education of the nobility. In the year 1579 the university of Wilna was instituted; in 1594, another university was created at Zamosc in Little Poland, by a private nobleman, the great chancellor Zamoyski; which however survived only a few years, and perished in the beginning of the

---

[19] Preface to Vuk's Servian Grammar, p. XXIII.

[20] See Schaffarik, *Geschichte*, p. 414. Bantkie's *Geschichte der Krakauer Buchdruckereyen.*

seventeenth century.[21] Numerous other schools of a less elevated character were founded at Thorn, Dantzic, Lissa, etc. most of them for Protestants.

So early as under Casimir, the son of Jagello, the Polish language began to be employed as the language of the court. Under his grandson Sigismund Augustus, the public laws and decrees were promulgated in the vernacular tongue of the country. But a language which thus issued from the court, was necessarily also dependent on the changes of the court. The influence of the French prince, Henry of Valois, successor of Sigismund Augustus, could not be considerable, as he occupied the throne only two months. But Stephen Bathory, prince of Transylvania, the brother-in-law of Sigismund Augustus, who was elected after Henry of Valois had deserted the country, was as a foreigner in the habit of interspersing his conversation and writings with Latin words, when the proper Polish words, of which language he had only an imperfect knowledge, did not occur to him. It is hardly credible that such a habit, or rather the imitation of it among his courtiers, could have had any influence on a language already so well established and cultivated, as the Polish idiom was at the close of the sixteenth century. The Polish literary historians, however, ascribe to Bathory's influence the fashion, which began at this time to prevail, of debasing the purity of the Polish language by an intermixture of Latin words and phrases.[22]

Although the Polish literature acquired during this period a kind of universality, and there were few departments of science, familiar to that age, which were not to some extent cultivated in it, yet it owes its principal lustre to the contributions made in it

---

[21] It was afterwards reinstated in the form of a large gymnasium by one of chancellor Zamoyski's descendants, and removed to Szczebrzeszyn. See Letters on Poland, Edinb. 1823, p. 95.

[22] See Schaffarik, *Geschichte*, p. 426.

to history, poetry and rhetoric. The didactic style did not reach the perfection of the historical; nor did Polish literature acquire any wide domain in purely scientific productions. In accordance with the national tendency, the mass of distinguished talents was devoted to those interests, which yield an immediate profit in life, or which are themselves rather the results of empirical knowledge, than of abstract contemplation, viz. to politics, to eloquence, and to poetry, in so far as this latter is considered not as a creative power, but as the most appropriate means for expressing and describing the emotions, passions, and actions of man. There have however always been not a few gifted Poles, who have cultivated the field of science for its own sake, without reference to the practical importance of their labours; and there are more especially at the present time many distinguished names among the Polish mathematicians, natural philosophers, and chemists. In Copernicus himself, born indeed of parents of German extraction, and in a city (Thorn) mostly inhabited by German colonists, but also born a Polish subject and educated in a Polish university, Poland and Germany seem to have equal rights.[23]

The principal reason why didactic prose did not acquire the same degree of cultivation as the historical style, is, that all

---

[23] Whether Copernicus is to be called a Pole or a German has been and is still a matter of dispute, and has been managed on the side of the Poles with the utmost bitterness and passion. The Poles have recently given expression to their claim upon him by erecting to him a monument at Cracow, and celebrating the third centennial anniversary of the completion of his system of the world, which took place in A. D. 1530. Let the question respecting Copernicus be decided as it may, Poland may doubtless lay claim to many other eminent natural philosophers as her sons; e. g. Vitellio-Ciolek, who was the first in Europe to investigate the theory of light, in the beginning of the thirteenth century; Brudzewski, the teacher of Copernicus; Martinus of Olkusz, the proper author of the new or Gregorian calendar, which was introduced sixty-four years after him, etc.

scientific works during this period, which was that of the formation of the language, were written by preference in Latin. Indeed, the authority of the classical languages did not suffer at all from the rising of the national literature. It is on the contrary a remarkable fact, that the cultivation of the vernacular tongue of the country, and the study of the Latin language in Poland, have ever proceeded with equal steps. The most eminent writers and orators of this period, who employed the Polish language, managed also the Latin with the greatest skill and dexterity. Even for common conversation, Latin and Polish were used alternately. Sigismund I, when separated from his first queen, Barbara Zapolska, maintained with her a correspondence in Latin; his second queen, Bona Sforza, used to employ that language in their most familiar intercourse.[24] Choisnin, in his Memoirs of the election of Henry of Valois, observes, that among a hundred Polish noblemen, there were hardly to be found two, who did not understand Latin, German, and Italian; and Martin Kromer goes so far as to state, that perhaps in Latium itself fewer persons had spoken Latin fluently than in Poland.[25] The reputation of the Latin poet Casimir Sarbiewski, in Latin Sarbievus, spread through all Europe. Most Polish poets were equally successful both in Polish and Latin verse. As the former language first developed itself in poetry, we therefore, in our enumeration of the principal writers of this time, begin with the poets.

Here the influence of the classics, and, above all, that of the Italian literature, is very distinctly perceived. Rey of Naglowic, ob. 1569, is called the father of Polish poetry. Most of his pro-

[24] See Macherszynski's *Geschichte der Lateinischen Sprache in Polen*, Cracow 1833. Dr. Connor in his History of Poland, 1698, speaking of the following period, says, that even the common people in Poland spoke Latin, and that his servant used to speak with him in that language. See Letters on Poland, Edinb. 1823. p. 108.

[25] De originibus et rebus gestis Polonorum, lib. XXX.

ductions are of the religious kind, chiefly in verse, but also orations and postillæ. His chief work was a translation of the Psalms.[26]

His principal followers were the Kochanowskis, a name of threefold lustre. John Kochanowski, ob. 1584, by far the most distinguished of them, published likewise a translation of David's Psalms, which is still considered as a classical work; in his other poems, Pindar, Anacreon, and Horace, were alternately his models, without diminishing the original value of his pieces.[27] Adam Mickiewicz compares him, in respect to the brevity, conciseness, and terseness of his expression, with the last named Roman poet; in reference to his treatment of the classic elements, to Goethe. His brother Andrew translated Virgil's Æneid; his nephew Peter, with more talent and success, the great epics of Tasso and Ariosto.

Rybinski maintains, as a lyric poet, in the opinion of several critics, the same rank with John Kochanowski; like him he wrote Polish and Latin verses, and was created poet laureate. Simon Szymonowicz, called Simonides, ob. 1629, obtained likewise the poetical crown from the pope Clement VIII; indeed his Latin odes secured him a lasting fame throughout all Europe, and procured him the appellation of the Latin Pindar. In Polish he wrote mostly idylls, after the model of Theocritus, Bion, and Moschus; but these, as their chief merit consists in the sweetness and delicacy of the language, only natives are able fully to appreciate.[28]

---

[26] *Psalterz Dawidow s modlitwami*, 1555.

[27] The Polish works of this poet, who is still considered as the chief ornament of the Polish Parnassus, were first collected in four volumes, Cracow 1584–90. After going through several editions, they have recently been printed at Breslau, 1824, in a stereotype edition. Bowring gives among his 'Specimens' some of the sweetest pieces of Kochanowski.

[28] The oldest edition extant of his Polish pastorals, was printed at Zamosc, 1614, under the title *Sielanki*. They were last printed, together with other

The productions of his friend and cotemporary Zimorowicz have the same general character, but are of less value in respect to diction. Other lyrical poets of merit may be named; e. g. the archbishop of Lemberg, Grochowski, a very productive writer; Czahrowski, Klonowicz, called also Acernus, and others.[29] As poets of a religious character we name here together, without reference to the denomination to which they belonged,—since most of the Polish poetical productions of this age were of a higher character than to suffer the intrusion of polemics,—Dambrowski, Bartoszewski, Miaskowski, whose hymns are considered as the finest of that period, Sudrovius, Turnowski, and others. The age was also rich in satires and epigrams, Polish as well as Latin. Productions of this class by the two Zbylitowskis, Pudlowski, Kraiewski, and a great many others, are still extant.

The facility of rhyme in a language so rich in rhymes as the Polish, seduced several writers to use verse as a vehicle for the most trivial thoughts, or for subjects the very nature of which is opposed to poetry. Thus Paprocki of Glogol, who is esteemed as a diligent historian and accurate investigator of the past, wrote his numerous works on genealogy and heraldry mostly in rhyme.[30] Other historical poems were also written, which perhaps would not have been utterly deficient in merit, had they been transferred into prose.

Eloquence, so nearly related to poetry, and which, nevertheless, perhaps on that very account, should be distinguished from it by the most definite limits, is a gift, the cultivation of which

---

eclogues, in the collection of Mostowski, *Sielanki Polskie,* Warsaw 1805. There are some specimens of his poetry in Bowring's work.

[29] This latter was honoured by his countrymen with the title of the Sarmatian Ovid; but his pieces, according to Bowring, are not only licentious, but also vulgar. See Specimen of the Polish Poets, p. 29.

[30] The same individual has been mentioned as a Bohemian writer; see above, p. 193.

may be expected above all in a republic. The Poles possess indeed all the necessary qualities for public orators; and eminent talents not only for poetical eloquence, but also for the pulpit, are not uncommon among them. Gornicki, ob. after 1591, Czarnkowski, Odachowski, and others, but especially the first named, were considered as the most distinguished orators of the age. The eloquence of the pulpit was exhibited in its highest eminence by Peter Skarga, court preacher of Sigismund III, whom his cotemporaries used to call the Polish Chrysostom; and by the learned Jesuit Wuiek, who also translated the Bible into Polish.[31] The sermons and orations of both of them, besides numerous other theological productions, were published at the time. Other theological writers of some distinction were, among the Catholics, Stanislaus Karnkowski, archbishop of Gnesen, Bierkowski, who was Skarga's successor, Bialobrzeski, Kuczborski, the Jesuit Rosciszewski, and others; among the Protestants, Seklucyan, the translator of the Polish Bible for Protestants;[32] Koszutski of Zarnowec, Radomski, Gilowski, and Budny, one of the leaders of the Unitarians, who also translated the Bible into Polish from the original languages.[33] We must remark, that the Polish theological literature of this period evinced much less of a polemical spirit than might have been expected, in an age when that of the neighbouring countries, Bohemia and Germany, abounded in controversial books and pamphlets, replete with unchristian bitterness and doctrinal rigidity. For productions of this character we have to look in Poland to the following period. The wise moderation of the two Sigismunds, and of Stephen Bathory, seems to have had a prodigious influence on the minds of the nation, to pacify them and keep them within appropriate limits.

History, especially national history, was justly considered as

---

[31] [32] [33] See above, p. 237, 238, n. 18.

one of the subjects most worthy of human attention. History is the great school, in which nations appear as the pupils, experience as the teacher; and the fate of mankind depends on a wise application of the great moral lessons which they daily receive. Most of the Polish historians of this age preferred however the Latin language; but their productions are too intimately connected with Poland to be separated from its literature, and may, therefore, be named here. The Polish chronicle written by Matthew of Miechow, body physician to Sigismund I, and published in 1521, was the first historical work printed in Poland. Martin Kromer, bishop of Ermeland or Warmia, called the Livy of Poland, Wapowski, Guagnini, an Italian, but naturalized and ennobled in Poland, and Piasecki, a Protestant, distinguished for his frankness, wrote works on Polish history; Koialowicz, on that of Lithuania. They all wrote in Latin. The first who published an historical work in Polish was Martin Bielski, ob. 1576. His chronicle of Poland, which is of value in every respect, is written in a style so beautiful, that it was called *le style d'or.* His son Joachim continued this work as far as to the reign of Sigismund III.[34] Another Polish chronicle, compiled with more erudition than taste, was written by Stryikowski, the author of numerous works on various subjects.

Other writers of merit, some of whom published original works on portions of history, while some translated the Latin volumes of their countrymen, or those of classic historical authors, were Wargocki, the Polish translator of Julius Cæsar, and other Roman writers; Orzechowski, also lauded as an orator; Januszowski, Blazowski, Paszkowski, Cyprian Bazylik, and others. Works on tactics were published by John Tarnowski, a general

[34] This work was first printed at Cracow in 1597, under the title *Kronika Polska.* The first part of it was republished at Warsaw in 1832, forming the sixth volume of the great collection of ancient Polish authors published by the bookseller Galezowski.

celebrated in his time; by Strubicz, and Cielecki. Collections of statutes and laws were made by Herbart, Sapieha, Groicki, Sarnicki, and others.

Several memoirs referring to this period, and written during it, have been first published in our days; since the value of cotemporary historical documents has begun to be sufficiently appreciated. One of these publications (Wilna, 1844) is a chronicle referring to the first half of the sixteenth century; and was written by John Tarnowski, the general mentioned above. The manuscript had been long considered as lost.

It still remains to note the progress made in the philosophical sciences. We remarked above, that scientific works in Poland were mostly written in Latin; and since the case with them is different from that of historical works,—because, as the results of scientific examination and discovery, they are independent of the country where they are written, and belong to the world,—we therefore mention here only those works which were published in the Polish language. Falimierz, in Latin Phalimirus, first ventured to use the vernacular tongue of the country for a scientific book. He published as early as 1534 a work on natural history, and especially *Materia medica.* The first medical work in the Polish language was written in 1541 by Peter of Kobylin; the first mathematical work by Grzebski. Their example was followed by Latosz, Rosciszewski, Andrew of Kobylin, Umiastowski, Spiczynski, Siennik, Oczko, Grutinius, Syrenski, in Latin Sirenius, and others, all physicians, astronomers, botanists, etc.[35]

[35] For more complete information respecting the writers of this period, see Bentkowski's *Hist. lit. Pol.* Vol. I. Schaffarik's *Geschichte,* etc.

FOURTH PERIOD.

From the erection of the Cracovian Jesuit Schools in A. D. 1622, *to the revival of science in A. D.* 1760.

The noble race of the Jagellons had become extinct on the death of Sigismund Augustus, in 1572.[36] Poland had become formally an elective monarchy. Henry of Valois was the first to subscribe the *pacta conventa*, the fundamental law of the national liberty ; the nation being understood to consist legally only of the nobility.[37] Stephen Bathory's strength kept the discordant elements together ; and while at home he took care to improve the administration of justice, and erected the high tribunals of Petricau, Lublin, and Wilna, his victorious arms in his contest with Russia raised Poland for a short time to the summit of its glory. But under his successor Sigismund III, a Swedish prince, and nephew of Sigismund Augustus and of Stephen, began that anarchy which is to be considered as the principal cause of Poland's final calamitous fate. For about fifty years the Poles still maintained with equal valour, though with alternate good

[36] We mean the direct male descendants of Jagello ; for descendants by the female and collateral lines occupied the throne after Stephen Bathory. Poland had never been by law an hereditary kingdom ; but in most cases one of the sons or brothers of the last king was elected.

[37] These *pacta conventa*, to which numerous articles were afterwards added, not only limited the king in his quality as king, but even also as a private man, in a degree to which no freeman would willingly submit. For example, he was not allowed to marry except with the consent of the diet ; and as each single nuntius had the right to oppose and render void the resolutions of the united estates by his *liberum veto*, the king could not marry whenever it occurred to any one of them to withhold his consent. In 1669 it was resolved, that no king should be allowed to abdicate.

and ill success, their warlike character abroad; even while internal dissensions and bloody party strife raged in their own unhappy country. But to such fundamental evils, combined with the rising power of Russia, with the revolt of the Kozaks in 1654, occasioned principally by religious oppression, and with the gradual but sure advancement of a new rival in the elector of Brandenburg, hitherto considered as a weak neighbour—to all these influences, the building thus sapped in its foundation could make no resistance, and its walls could not but give way, when they were suddenly shaken by the hands of avaricious and powerful enemies from without.

The perversion of taste, which at the beginning of the seventeenth century reigned in Italy, and thence spread over all Europe, with much more rapidity indeed than the true poetry and pure style of the fifteenth century had done, created also in the literature of Poland a new period; which, through the political circumstances above referred to, was protracted to a greater length than would have been expected in a literature already so rich in national models. To the remarkable activity of mind in the preceding period, there followed a literary lethargy. A very pernicious influence is also ascribed, by the literary historians of Poland, to the Jesuits; although this order is in general disposed to favour the cultivation of science. Under Sigismund III, they were shrewd enough to make themselves gradually masters of nearly all the colleges; and after a long and obstinate struggle, even the university of Cracow had to submit. According to Bentkowski, it was principally by their influence, that the tone of panegyric and of bombast was introduced, which for nearly a hundred and fifty years disgraced the Polish literature. The tastelessness of this style reached its highest point under John Sobieski; when the panegyrics with which this victorious captain was hailed by his courtiers, became the model for all similar productions. The fashion, first introduced at the close of the preceding period, of interspersing the Polish language with Latin words and phrases, became during the present more and more predominant; and was at length carried so far as to give even to Polish words a false Latin sound, by means of a Latin termination. French, German, and Italian forms of expression soon obtained the same right. But what was still worse, and what indeed affected the language most of all, was the fact, that even the natural structure and well established syntax of the Polish language had to give place to an injudicious imitation of foreign idioms. Thus the very circumstance of its great pliancy, one of its principal excellencies, became a source of its corruption.

Poland, moreover, at a time when the minds of the rest of Europe were tolerably pacified in a religious respect, became the scene of theological controversies full of sophistry and bitterness, the natural consequence of the incipient oppression of the dissidents. The literature was overwhelmed with pamphlets, stuffed with a shallow scholastic erudition, and written in a style both bombastic and vulgar. But the influence of the Jesuits was not limited to literature and science; it had a still more unhappy result in its active consequences. Poland became also during this century the theatre of a religious persecution, less authorized by even the semblance of law than any which had before, or has since, occurred in other countries. The Arians or Unitarians, after having been for more than sixty years tacitly included in the general appellation of *dissidents*, had to sustain between the years 1638 and 1658 the utmost rigour of oppression, and were finally banished from the country; and all this without having done any thing to forfeit their rights as dissidents, from which body they had to be formally expelled by the united hatred of the other Protestants and Catholics, before even a pretext could be devised of proceeding lawfully against them. Nor had the Lutherans, Calvinists, Greeks, and

Armenians, who, after the exclusion of the Unitarians, Quakers, and Anabaptists, were alone comprised under the name of dissidents, given any occasion for that gradual deprivation which they had to encounter of their lawful rights, in the possession of which they had been a hundred and fifty years undisturbed. The storm which threatened them, first manifested itself publicly in the diets of 1717 and 1718, and degenerated at last into open and shameless persecution. In the year 1724, a quarrel arose at Thorn, on occasion of a procession of the Jesuits, between the students of one of their schools and those of the Lutheran gymnasium. A Lutheran mob intermeddled and committed some excesses; in consequence of which the Jesuit Wolanski, in the name of his order, instituted a lawsuit against the Lutheran magistracy of the city. The result of this lawsuit was a tragedy, such as only the bloody pages of the books of the inquisition can exhibit, and unequalled as to its motives in the annals of the eighteenth century. All the perpetrators were punished with the utmost rigour; while Rösner, the president of the city, together with eleven other citizens, was publicly beheaded, and their property confiscated for the benefit of the order.

A body which acted in such a spirit, placed at the head of public education, could exert but a very injurious influence in a moral and religious respect; its influence on the literature and language has been described above. The general mental paralysis and lethargy, which reigned in Poland during this period, can indeed hardly be ascribed solely to their influence; but the latter served greatly to increase it. For more than twenty years *all* the schools in the whole country were in the hands of the Jesuits; and when in the year 1642 the congregation of the Piarists erected their first school in Warsaw, which soon was followed by several others founded by the same order, these seminaries had to struggle for nearly a century, watched and oppressed by the jealousy and despotism of the Jesuits, before they could acquire any influence consistent with the spirit in which they were founded. To the talents and firmness of Stanislaus Konarski, himself a Piarist, the Polish literary historians ascribe the principal merits of the final victory of his order. His endeavours indeed were favoured by a combination of fortunate circumstances. Literature and the fine arts found a friend and protector in a gifted and accomplished king, and in several high-minded noblemen of even more than regal authority. But the period of pedantry, perversion of taste, and deficiency of true criticism, had already lasted more than a hundred and thirty years. There was much to be done to cleanse the beds in the garden of literature from all the weeds which had luxuriated there, and to fertilize a soil which had so long lain fallow. The details of these endeavours belong however to the following period.

To the character of the theological literature of this age, we have above alluded. Among the Protestant writers were Andrew and Adalbert Wengierski. The works of the latter gave occasion to the polemical discussions of the Jesuit Poszakowski, himself the author of a history of the Lutheran and of the Calvinistic creed, and of several other books. Other works on subjects of theology and education, or collections of sermons and devotional exercises, were published by the Jesuits Szczaniecki, Koialowicz, Sapecki, Poninski, Zulkiewski, and others; and the Piarists Gutowski, Wysocki, Rosolecki, and others. The Jesuit Niesiecki wrote a comprehensive biblio-biographical work of great merit, which is considered as one of the best sources for the inquirer in Polish history and literature.[38] Another Jesuit, Wiiuk Koialowicz, translated Tacitus' Annals into Polish, and wrote in Latin a history of Lithuania. Knapski, also a Jesuit, published a large dictionary or "Thesaurus," which

---

[38] *Korona Polska,* Lemberg 1728–1743.

is still highly esteemed. Lubienski, archbishop of Gnesen, wrote in 1740 the first detailed geography in the Polish language. One of the most productive writers on various subjects of theology, history, and politics, was Starowolski, who died in 1656. Fourteen of his forty-seven works are written in Polish, the rest in Latin. We mention further, as geographical and historical writers of some merit, the Piarist Kola, professor Saltszowicz, Chodkiewicz, Niemir and Chwalkowski; and as a distinguished mathematician and scholar of general information, Broscius.

We conclude this period with the poets of that age; who, although perhaps they exhibited more talent than the cotemporary prose writers, must necessarily, from the nature of poetry, have suffered more from the predominant tastelessness of the time. Sam. Twardowski, ob. 1660, must be named first; a poet of fine gifts, but of an impure, bombastic, rhetorical style, the author of numerous lyrical and epic poems of very unequal value. After him came Vespasian Kochowski, the best lyric poet of the age; Gawinski, a very productive author, whose pastorals have been collected by Mostowski, together with those of Kochanowski, Simonides, and other classical poets; and Wenceslaus Potocki, the author of novels, poetry, and more especially epigrams, not without merit, but frequently licentious and indelicate. Among the poets of this age, who are in some measure distinguished by Polish critics, we find also a lady, Elizabeth Druzbacka, a poetess of high rank, but without a literary education or a knowledge of foreign languages, though not without natural gifts. Satires were written by Dzwonowski and Opalinski; historical and didactic poems by Bialabocki, prince Jablonowski, and by Leszczynski, father of king Stanislaus Leszczynski. Ovid was translated by Zebrowski and Otfinowski; Lucan's Pharsalia by Chroscinski, who versified also portions of the Bible; and again with more fidelity and skill by the Dominican monk Bardzinski

Other poets of this age were, prince Lubomirski, who on account of his wealth and wise sayings is styled the Polish Solomon; prince Wisniowiecki, who published whole poems without the letter *r*, because he could not pronounce that letter; Bratkowski, the author of a series of happy epigrams; Falibogowski, Szymonowski, the Jesuits Ignes and Poniatowski, and others.

FIFTH PERIOD.

From Stephen Konarski, A. D. 1760, *to the Revolution in* 1830.

The Polish language, at the beginning of this period, was in a melancholy state; it was, to use Schaffarik's expression, stripped of its natural gifts of perspicuity, simplicity, and strength, deformed by tastelessness, and grown childish and obsolete at the same time. An able work, *Memoirs*, referring to the period between 1750 and 1760, written by K. H. Kallontaj, and published a few years since by count E. Raczynski, gives a graphic picture of the miserable and illiterate state of society in Poland at that time; and shows clearly how the seeds of decay and destruction were already scattered with full hands on a susceptible soil. It was a fortunate circumstance, that, just at the time when several of the most powerful Polish noblemen began to feel an intense and patriotic interest in their neglected language,—the king Stanislaus Augustus and his uncle prince Czartoryski at their head,—there awoke a number of gifted minds, who began to plant with so much activity on the long deserted though still fertile soil, that the field of Polish literature soon flourished and bore fruit again. These fruits, however artificial and *un*national in their character, could only be compared to green-house productions. Various effective measures were taken for the revival of literature, and also for the promotion of science and art. But the new patrons could not afford to wait. The French literature of the day, with all its levity, shallowness, and splendour, seemed to be a material nearer at hand and more in harmony with the spirit of the court—the only school of revival for Polish literature—than their own national productions of former ages. In this way we may explain in part the frivolous tone, the shallow-mindedness, which prevail in all the Polish works of this age; during a period when vehement passions and furious contests already tore the country in pieces, and deep sorrow and grief reigned among all classes of society.

The establishment of the Monitor, a periodical work, to which the best and ablest men of Poland contributed, first exerted a superficial happy influence on the language.[39] Of still more importance in this respect was the establishment of a national stage, at the head of which were distinguished and well qualified men. But the measure which produced more effect than any other, was the appointment of a department of Education, resolved upon by the diet of 1775. Public instruction was thus made one of the great concerns of the government itself; and the power of the Jesuits, which had been for some time on the decline, was finally annihilated. The rich income of this order was henceforth entirely set apart for the benefit of learned institutions, to which free access was given. The provincial or departmental schools throughout the whole kingdom received a new organization on a different plan; and the university of Cracow resumed again its former rights. In respect to the instruction and melioration of the situation of the common people, we find as yet no attention whatever paid to these important subjects. It was not until 1807, or the foundation of the duchy of Warsaw under the administration of the king of Saxony,

---

[39] In 1764; it was the first periodical ever published in Poland.

that the lower classes obtained their rights as men; and unfortunately even then without the power of availing themselves of these rights. Stanislaus Augustus, however, and some of his advisers and counsellors, acted in this respect with an honest will and noble intention; and by promoting the general interests of mankind in literature and science, did much for the social improvement of their own country.

Meanwhile, this unhappy country was the scene of the most violent party struggles; during which the heads of the parties conducted themselves with the most revolting selfishness, and an entire forgetfulness of all political consequences and of their own moral responsibility. The fanaticism of the bishops of Cracow and Warsaw refused to the dissidents the restoration of their rights; and Russia thus acquired the first pretext for intermeddling with Polish affairs. In the course of a few years, Poland was reduced to that torn and broken state, which induced Catharine II to consider it as a country "where one needed only to stoop, in order to pick up something." For a short time this course of things even seemed to be favourable to literature. The minds of men were in a state of excitement, which gave them power to produce the greatest and most extraordinary things. But a reaction very naturally followed. After twenty years of mental and political struggles and combats, to sustain which claimed the whole united powers of mind and soul,—twenty years numerically productive in every department,—there followed a mental calm, an intellectual blank, of more than twelve years.

It was, as if with the political dissolution of the kingdom, with the annihilation of the unity of the nation, this latter had sunk back into a state of intellectual paralysis. The interval from A. D. 1795 to A. D. 1807, in comparison with the years which preceded and have followed, was remarkably poor in productions of value. The literature of translations rose in an undue proportion, and the purity of the language suffered considerably. The government of the duchy of Warsaw acted on wise and truly humane principles; and during the short period between 1807 and 1812, all was done for the improvement of the country, which the unfortunate circumstances of the case permitted. Under this administration the number of schools rose from 140 to 634; a commission was instituted for procuring the publication of appropriate books of instruction in the Polish language; and several similar measures were taken for advancing the best interests of the country. The constitution of the new kingdom of Poland, in 1815, entered essentially into the same views; and was in every respect favourable to the development of the mental faculties of the nation. The modern kingdom of Poland embraced, indeed, not much more than the sixth part of the vast territory, which under the Jagellons had constituted the kingdom of that name. Before the cessions at Andrussov in the year 1667, the ancient kingdom contained sixteen millions of inhabitants; the census of the modern kingdom in 1818, counted only 2,734,000. But that the population of this exhausted country increased during the Russian administration, —especially in consequence of the encouragement given to foreign colonists, the establishment of manufactures which furnished means of support for the lower classes, and other similar measures,—is apparent from the results of the census of 1827; according to which the kingdom then contained 3,705,000 inhabitants.[40]

In the field of science and literature, the nobility had at length found rivals among the free citizens; and the courts of these temples were now, through the erection of village schools, made accessible even to the peasant, who was, in name at least,

---

[40] See page 227 above.

no longer a degraded slave.[41] If the Russian government in Poland had been exercised in practice, according to the same principles on which it was founded; if Alexander's first intentions had been practically executed in the same spirit in which the happiness of his Polish subjects had been theoretically planned; perhaps it would have been less difficult to reconcile the minds of the Poles to the loss of their independence as a nation, which they justly consider as an inestimable good. We have here no concern with politics, except so far as they have a necessary influence on the state of general cultivation; or so far as they give birth to important occasional appearances in the republic of letters. Considered in the first point of view, it is not to be denied, that the Polish nation, since the foundation of the *constitutional* Russian kingdom of Poland in 1815, has made more progress towards social improvement, and has advanced more towards a state of equality in a mental and intellectual respect with the countries of middle Europe, viz. Germany, France and England, than during the whole vast period of their previous existence.

---

[41] The Polish serfs were indeed never regular slaves; but merely *glebae adscripti*, i. e. they could not be sold separately as mere things, but only with the soil they cultivated, which they had no right to leave. They were not reduced even to this state before the fifteenth or sixteenth century; for one of the statutes of Casimir the Great allows them the privilege of selling their property and leaving whenever they were ill treated. Of the present state of the Polish peasantry, the author of "Poland under the dominion of Russia," (Bost. 1834,) says: "The Polish peasant might perhaps be about as free as my dog was in Warsaw; for I certainly should not have prevented the animal from learning, had he been so inclined, some tricks by which he could earn the reward of an extra bone. The freedom of the wretched Polish serfs is much the same as the freedom of their cattle; for they are brought up with as little of human cultivation," etc. p. 165. And again: "The Polish serf is in every part of the country extremely poor, and of all the living creatures I have met with in this world, or seen described in books of natural history, he is the most wretched." p. 176.

For most of these improvements, however, the preparation had already been made, in the last ten years before the dissolution of the republic. The emancipation of the serfs, who comprised the whole peasantry, one of the fundamental laws of the duchy of Warsaw in 1807, was confirmed at the creation of the kingdom of Poland in 1815. In the diet of the kingdom, not only the nobility and the government, but also the cities and smaller communities, had their own representatives; and all Christian denominations acquired equal political rights. To the universities of Cracow, Wilna, and Lemberg,[42] there was added in 1818 a fourth at Warsaw. The kingdom of Poland contained in 1827, in each of its eight woiwodships, a palatine school, and besides this three other institutions for the higher branches of education; fourteen principal department schools, and nine for sub-departments; several professional seminaries for miners, teachers, agriculturists, and others; a military academy, a school for cadets, and a number of elementary schools, both private and public.[43] The Russian-Polish provinces, i. e.

---

[42] Lemberg indeed can hardly be called a Polish university. All its professors are Germans, and the lectures are delivered in Latin or German. It has only three faculties, viz. the philosophical, theological, and juridical. For medicine it has only a preparatory school, the course being finished at Vienna. Among the 65 medical students of 1832, there were 41 Jews. The university had in that year, in all, 1291 students. For the theological and juridical courses, which, according to law, comprise each four years, a previous preparation of two years spent in philosophical studies is required by the government. Thus the regular course of an Austrian student lasts six years. The same measures were taken to Germanize Cracow during the Austrian administration; but when in 1815 Cracow became a free city, it parted with all its German professors, and became again a genuine Polish university.

[43] From the account given of the state of the Polish common people in note 41 above, we must conclude that this number is very small. Mr. Ljach Szyrma, the author of Letters on Poland, (Edinb. 1823,) says: "The lower classes, unfortunately, do not enjoy the advantage of being proportionally benefited by

the part of Poland united with Russia in the three successive dismemberments of Poland, participate in all the means of education which the Russian empire affords; the province of West Prussia and the grand duchy of Posen, in those of the kingdom of Prussia, where an enlightened government has made, as is generally acknowledged, the mental improvement of the lower classes one of its principal objects. The Austrian kingdom of Galicia had in the year 1819 two lyceums, twelve gymnasiums, several other institutions for education of different names and for specific purposes, and also numerous elementary schools. The Catholic religion is here the only reigning one; although the Protestants, who here are still comprised under the name of dissidents, are tolerated.

The literary activity of the Polish nation occupied in 1827 not less than sixty printing offices and twenty booksellers. Of the latter, fifteen were in Warsaw, the rest scattered over all the province formerly belonging to Poland. At Warsaw alone five daily political papers and one weekly were published in the Polish language; besides these there existed only five, viz. one in each of the four larger cities, Cracow, Lemberg, Wilna, and Posen, and a fifth at St. Petersburg. There are other periodicals for scientific objects published at Warsaw; while in the other cities the German publications of that character are chiefly read. The periodical published by the national institution, called after count Ossolinski, at Lemberg, is however considered as the most important in the Polish language.

The high spirit of the Polish nation, and that glowing patriotism for which they are so distinguished, has induced them during the period of their unnatural partition and amalgamation

---

the learning requisite to their social condition. The parish schools are not sufficient to improve them in this respect; and the village schools, upon which their hopes chiefly rest, *are not numerous.*"

with foreign nations, to devote more zeal than ever to the sole national tie which still binds together the subjects of so many different powers—their language. There have been numerous learned societies founded; among them, above all, the society of the friends of science at Warsaw, to which the most eminent men of the nation belong, must be distinguished. Academies of arts and sciences have been established, and associations formed for various scientific purposes. The influence of all these institutions, more especially that of the above-mentioned society at Warsaw, has been very favourably employed in limiting that of the French and German languages, naturally induced by political circumstances.

The French language indeed, independently of the political events of modern times, had already acted powerfully on the Polish at the close of the preceding period. In poetry, the affected bombastic school of the Gongorists and Marinists had been supplanted throughout all Europe by the better taste of the cold, stiff, and formal French poets, whose defects it was much easier to imitate than their merits. For more than half a century the French language reigned with an uncontrolled and unlimited sovereignty over all the literary world. But its most absolute dominion was in Poland. In the manners of the nobility of this country, French gracefulness and ease were, in a peculiar and interesting manner, blended with the daring heroism of the knight and the luxuriousness of the Asiatic despot. French refinement and French witticism covered the rudeness and revelry characteristic of the middle ages. French teachers and governesses had inundated the whole country, and a journey to France was among the requisite conditions of an accomplished education. The Polish writers—all of them belonging to the nobility—to whom, from their youth, the French language was equally familiar with their own, unconsciously disfigured the latter by Gallicisms; since French forms of expression seemed to be the best adapted for the expression of French thoughts and French philosophy. A modern Polish author calls the Polish literature of this period a second edition of the French with inferior types and on worse paper.[44] Long after the rest of literary Europe had shaken off the yoke, the Polish poets, although the genius of their rich, creative, and pliant language was decidedly opposed to such a slavery, continued to submit to French rules and laws, and do so partly still.

We begin the enumeration of the distinguished writers of this period, with its principal founder, Stephen Konarski, mentioned above,[45] who was born A. D. 1700, and died in 1773. In his seventeenth year he entered the order of Piarists, and became later a professor in the college of this congregation at Warsaw. After a long stay in Italy and France, he returned to Poland; accompanied king Stanislaus Leszczynski to Lorrain; but again returned to his country and founded several institutions for education in Warsaw, Wilna, and Lemberg, on principles different from those of the Jesuits. In the year 1747 he went a third time to France, but returned after three years; and from that time devoted himself entirely to the literary and mental reform of his own country. Of his printed works, twenty-eight in number, fourteen are written in Polish. They embrace different topics in poetry, and a tragedy; but his principal merits lie in his writings on the subject of politics and education.[46]

After him we name the illustrious philosopher Stanislaus Leszczynski. Most of his works, on politics and ethics, were written in French; in the Polish language he wrote, besides one or two

---

44 Witwicki in *Wieczory pielgrzyma*, Paris 1837.

45 P. 254.

46 His works, which have never been collected, are enumerated in Bentkowski's History of Polish literature. Konarski was the first who ventured publicly to assail the *liberum veto*.

other works, a history of the Old and New Testaments in verse.[47] Zaluski, known more especially by the foundation of a large and celebrated library, in which he spent an immense fortune, and which he finally made over to his country,[48] was the friend of king Stanislaus and of Konarski. In possession of an uncommon amount of knowledge, and a very extensive erudition, which however he owed more to his remarkable memory than to any distinguished capacity, he wrote a large number of Latin and Polish books on literary and biographical subjects, and on poetry; in all which the genius of the preceding period still reigns.

Another nobleman of high rank, who distinguished himself by his patriotism and erudition, was Wenceslaus Rzewuski, woiwode of Podolia, and cotemporary with Zaluski, whom he surpassed however in critical taste and productive powers. His translation of the Psalms is highly esteemed. A still higher name as a patron of literature and the arts, is the uncle of king Stanislaus Augustus, prince Adam Czartoryski. He was marshal of the diet in 1764, when the ill-famed *liberum veto* was abolished, which gave to every deputy, singly, the right of overthrowing the otherwise unanimous resolutions of the diet, and thus was the principal cause of the lawless disorder which disgraced the sessions of that body. His merits as a statesman and a Mecænas are equal. Several historical works, designed to advance the honour of Poland, were published under his care and at his instigation. Amid all his numerous avocations, he found time to write several pieces for the national stage; which, as a promoter of the purity of the language, was a subject of his particular care and attention.[49]

---

[47] Nancy 1733.

[48] This celebrated library was transferred to St. Petersburg at the dismemberment of Poland, and has not yet been restored.

[49] The Czartoryskis may justly be called the Polish Medici, from the liberal patronage which the accomplished members of this family have ever given to talent and literary merit. Their celebrated seat, Pulawi, the subject of many

By the side of the name of Czartoryski, shines that of Potocki. More than one member of this illustrious family had in former times acquired the right of citizens in the republic of letters. Count Paul Potocki and his grandson Anthony, in the seventeenth and beginning of the eighteenth century, were both equally celebrated for their talents. The works of the former were published by count Zaluski, under the title of *Genealogia Potockiana ;* the speeches and addresses of the latter are partly printed in Daneykowicz' *Suada Polona*, and were in their time considered as models. But the most elevated rank in this family is occupied by the two brothers Ignatius and Stanislaus Kostka Potocki, whether as patriots and statesmen, or as writers and patrons of science. Ignatius, besides promoting several literary undertakings, and bearing the expenses of more than one journey for the purposes of science and learning, was himself a distinguished writer. He translated Condillac's work on logic, and introduced it into the Polish schools as a class book. His merits in respect to public education were great ; he was one of the most urgent promoters of the emancipation of the serfs ; and at his death in the year 1809, he left behind the reputation of a true friend of the people. His brother Stanislaus Kostka, although entertaining the same political principles, did not take the same active part during the struggles of the Poles for their expiring independence ; he retired to Austria after the king had joined the confederation of Targowicz, and there devoted himself entirely to his studies. In 1807 he returned to his country ; and there, as president of the department for schools and education, he found means to carry out his enlightened views and benevolent intentions for the good of his country. At the foundation of the

---

songs, and also of an episode in Delille's Jardins, was destroyed by the Russians in the late war, and its literary treasures are said to have been carried to St. Petersburg.

kingdom of Poland in 1815, he was made minister of public instruction, and was always found at the head of every noble and patriotic undertaking. From his oratorical powers, he was called *princeps eloquentiæ.* In respect to genius he was above his brother; although the latter seems to have surpassed him in energy of character. His principal work, "on Style and Eloquence," was published in 1815; another work of value is his translation of Winkelmann's book on ancient art, which he accompanied by illustrations and remarks, but did not finish. His influence on Polish literature was decided.[50] Another nobleman, distinguished as an orator and political writer, was Hugo Kollantay, count Sztumberg, who published, together with Ignatius Potocki, a history of the constitution.

At the head of the historical writers of this period stands Adam Naruszewicz, the faithful translator of Tacitus, whose style he adopted also in his original works. His history of the Polish nation is considered as a standard work; as a production, which in respect to erudition, philosophical conception, and style, is the *chef d'œuvre* of Polish literature. The six volumes published by himself comprise only the period between A. D. 965 and 1386, beginning with the second volume; as for the first, which was to have contained the earliest history of Poland, he intended to have executed it afterwards, and had indeed collected all the necessary materials, but was prevented by death. The Warsaw Society of Friends of Science published it thirty years after his death,

[50] The title of the former work is *O wymowie i stylu,* Warsaw 1815–16. Another work is *Pochwaly, mowy i rozprowy,* i. e. Eulogies, Speeches, and Essays, among which are nine on Polish literature, Warsaw 1816. Stanislaus Potocki was also the principal mover in the publication of the splendid work *Monumenta regum Poloniæ Cracoviensia,* Warsaw 1822. Stanislaus Kostka P. must not be confounded with Stanislaus Felix P. his cousin, one of the most obstinate advocates of the ancient constitution and its corruptions, who sold his country to Russia.

and endeavoured to engage the principal talents of Poland in the continuation of his work. This was done in such a way, that each writer was to undertake the history of the administration of a single king; and at last, after each part had appeared separately, the society was to make a collection of the whole, and, if necessary, cause it to be rewritten. Several able men have devoted themselves to this work. The plan of the society, which by its very nature excluded all unity of character, seems to have met with more approbation than, according to our opinion, it deserved. The Polish public is however indebted to it for more than one valuable work on history, to which it gave birth. Naruszewicz had collected for his undertaking a library of materials, in 360 folio volumes. He wrote also a history of the Tartars, a biography of the Lithuanian captain Chodkiewicz, and was admired as a poet. He died in 1796, it is said of grief at the fate of his unhappy country.

Naruszewicz was educated by the Jesuits, and was himself of that order until its dissolution. He died as bishop of Luck. In respect to time he stands as the first eminent writer of a new period, just on the verge of the past; and even his warmest admirers do not deny that he participated, in some slight degree, in the character of that past, by a certain inclination to panegyric and a flowery style. But in energy and richness of thought, he far surpasses all his predecessors, and has not yet been reached by any who have written after him.[51]

Another historical work of value on Poland, was edited by Joachim Lelewel. The history of Poland by Waga, in the want of any thing more suitable, had been in use as a class book in the Polish schools for more than fifty years. Lelewel, in order to

[51] His complete works are to be found in the great collection of count Mostowski, Warsaw 1804–5, 12 volumes. They appeared in 1824 at Breslau in a stereotype edition, in six volumes. Poetical works, Warsaw 1778.

improve its popularity, took this book as a foundation, but completely recast it, divided the history of Poland according to a plan perfectly new, completed the work, and published it under Waga's name. His rich additions regard chiefly the legislature, statistics, and the cultivation of the country. His very division of the history of Poland, into Poland conquering, Poland divided, Poland flourishing, and Poland on the decline, seems to indicate the political tendency of his work, and his desire to impress upon the Polish youth the great moral lessons which history presents.[52]

Another history of Poland of more extent was published by G. S. Bantkie. Lelewel said of the second edition of this book, which appeared in 1820, that "a more perfect work in this department did not exist."

One of the most remarkable writers of his time, on history and bibliography, was the Jesuit Albertrandy; who, besides being the author of several historical works and treatises, was indefatigable in collecting materials for the history of his country. He went to Italy, and here gathered during a stay of three years a hundred and ten folio volumes of extracts, entirely written with his own hand. He then went to Stockholm and Upsal, where the most important manuscripts relative to Poland are deposited. The Swedish government was narrow-minded enough, to allow him access to their libraries only on condition of his not

---

[52] Lelewel is the author of quite a number of historical productions of importance; and some others he published or translated. A catalogue of his works cannot be expected here. The most celebrated are his volume on the primitive Lithuanians (Wilna 1808); on the condition of Science and Arts in Poland before the invention of printing; on the Geography of the Ancients; on the Commerce of the Phœnicians, Carthaginians and Romans; on the history of the ancient Indians; on the discoveries of the Carthaginians and Greeks (Warsaw 1829), etc. Also a Polish Bibliography (Warsaw 1823–1826); Monuments of the language and constitution of Poland, Warsaw 1824, etc.

taking any written notes. But Albertrandy had so remarkable a memory, that he was able to make up for this disadvantage, by writing down every evening all that he had read during the day, and added in this way not less than ninety folio volumes to his library of manuscripts.

Portions of Polish history, or subjects belonging to it, were treated with success by the poet Niemcewicz; by Bentkowski, Kwiatkowski, Soltykowicz, Surowiecki, Lelewel, Onacewicz, the counts Ossolinski and Czacki, the former distinguished by learning and critical discernment, the latter the author of an esteemed history of the Polish and Lithuanian laws; by Maiewski, Siarczynski, and others. The princess Isabella Czartoryski intended her "Pilgrim of Dobromil," to be a book of historical instruction for the common people. Abridgments of Polish history were given by Miklaszewski and Falenski. The historical songs written by Niemcewicz, at the instigation of the Warsaw Society of Friends of Science, are also to be considered as belonging to history, as well as to poetry, since they are accompanied by valuable historical illustrations. The same author wrote Memoirs on ancient Poland. Turski translated the memoirs of Choisain on the administration of Henry of Valois; and the memoirs of Michael Oginski, *Sur la Pologne et les Polonais depuis* 1788 *jusqu'en* 1815, are a valuable contribution to the history of our time. Memoirs of J. Kilinski, a shoemaker by trade, but like the butcher Sierakowski, a successful revolutionary leader in 1795, were published in 1830. The modern periodicals likewise contain many well written historical essays, some of them of decided importance. This is especially true of the *Memoirs* of Warsaw, and also of Lemberg, the *Scientific Memoirs*, the Wilna and Warsaw *Journals*, the *Bee* of Cracow, the *Ant* of Poznania, and others.

We have remarked above, as a characteristic of the Polish literature, that although Poland was never poor in talents of various kinds, yet its literary contributions have aimed less at the advancement of science in general, than to exalt the glory of the Polish name, and thus have an immediate reflexive influence on the nation. In the same spirit, the history of other countries has received little attention, not excepting even ancient history. Poland indeed does not possess a single distinguished work on foreign history; and their Gibbons and Robertsons seem ever to have been absorbed in their own patriotic interests. As writers of merit on universal history and its auxiliary branches, we may mention Cajetan and Vincent Skrzetuski, count John Potocki, Bohusz, Jodlowski, Sowinski, prince Sapieha, count Berkowski, and above all Lelewel.[53] Several of his works have been translated into French and German. The German version of his History of the discoveries of the Carthaginians and Greeks (Berlin 1832), was accompanied by an introduction from the celebrated Ritter.

The Polish language, the purity of which at the beginning of the present period was an object of particular attention, has in our own century been the subject of numerous learned inquiries; some of which have added considerably to the light thrown in modern times by Slavic-German scholars upon the Slavic languages and Slavic history in general. Linde, besides several other philological and historical writings, has enriched Slavic literature with a comparative critical dictionary in six volumes, which is considered as one of the standard works of the language. G. S. Bantkie, the author of several historical and bibliographical works of great merit in the Polish, Latin, and German languages, has written a Polish grammar and Polish-German dictionary. Rakowiecki prepared a new edition of the *Jus Russorum*, introduced by a critical preface, and accompanied with many explanatory notes. We must, however, take this occasion to remark, that the Polish critics in general, even

[53] See the preceding note.

if in every other respect qualified as sagacious and impartial judges, are by no means infallible on subjects which have any relation to their own country. The glory and honour of their own nation are always with them the principal objects, to which not seldom the impartiality of a scientific inquirer, and even historical truth, is unscrupulously sacrificed. Maiewski wrote a book rich in ideas on the Slavi;[54] bibliographical works, and books on the literary history of Poland have been published by Chrominski, Sowinski, Juszynski, count Ossolinski, Szumski, and more especially by Bentkowski.[55] Count Stan. Potocki's works contain likewise a number of articles on Polish literature. In the previous periods, all bibliographical works were written in Latin.

The brilliant talent of the Poles for eloquence enjoyed, during the early part of this period and before the dissolution of the republic, the best possible opportunity for development, among the intellectual struggles and combats occasioned by the political circumstances of the country and the discussion of new political theories. The constitutional diet of 1788–1791 exhibited a rich store of oratorical talent. The names of the Potockis, Sapieha, Czartoryski, Kollantay, Matuszewicz, Niemcewicz, Soltyk, Kicinski, and others, were mentioned with distinction. The eloquence of the pulpit was of course much less cultivated in a nation which lives chiefly in politics. Lachowski, a Jesuit and court preacher of the last king, is by the Poles considered as an eminent preacher; although according to German judges he was shallow and voluble, and was surpassed by his cotemporary Wyrwicz, and above all by Karpowicz. Prazmowski, Jakubowski, Woronicz bishop of Warsaw, Szianawski,

---

[54] *O Slawianach i ich pobratymcach*, Warsaw 1816.

[55] Bentkowski's *Historya literatury Polsk.* Warsaw 1814, contains a catalogue of all works published on Polish literature, to 1814; see Vol. I p. 1—73.

Szweykowski, Zacharyaszewicz, and others, were esteemed as powerful preachers.

Besides the oratorical powers and the historical productions of the Poles, the reputation of their modern literature rests chiefly on poetry. Although the Polish poets adhered longer to the strict rules of Boileau than the rest of Europe, and have only in the most recent times chosen better models in the Germans and English,—without however having been able to free themselves entirely from their French chains,—yet the national genius of their language has sometimes conquered the artificial restraints of narrow rules and arbitrary laws. Naruscewicz, the celebrated historian, occupies also a distinguished rank as a poet. He translated Anacreon and some of Horace's odes; but wrote still more original pieces, odes, pastorals, epigrams, satires, and a tragedy entitled 'Guido.'

The most distinguished poet under Stanislaus Augustus was count Ignatius Krasicki, bishop of Ermeland or Warmia, and later of Gnesen, the Polish Voltaire. His principal works are an epic under the title of *Woyna Chocimska* or 'War of Chocim,' and three comic epics, one of which, *Monachomachia*, ridicules the monkish system and exhibits its absurdity in strong colours. He wrote this poem at the suggestion of Frederic the Great, to whose *coterie* of literary friends he belonged. His great heroic epic is considered by his countrymen as a standard work; while foreigners look at it as a valuable historical poem indeed, but as utterly deficient in true epic power and original invention. His smaller poems and prose writings are replete with wit and spirit; to see a bishop writing erotic songs and satirical epigrams was nothing extraordinary in his time. As a prose writer he appears as one of the few who were not blind to the defects and follies of their countrymen. Of his translations we mention Macpherson's Ossian and Plutarch. He belongs so decidedly to his age, i. e. to the age of the freezing, unpoetical,

13*

French influence, that our time, with its higher standard for a true poet, can no longer set a great value on his works.[56]

Trembecki, ob. 1812, as a lyric poet takes equal rank, according to some Polish critics, with Krasicki. His chief poem, *Zofiowka*, which has been translated into French by La Garde, is of that descriptive, contemplative kind, which was fashionable in his day. He had more imagination than other cotemporary Polish poets. Szymanowski, ob. 1801, a writer of pastorals, is distinguished for delicacy and sweetness. As to the beauty of his diction his countrymen are the best judges; but as for the character and real poetical value of his productions, we doubt whether the sounder taste of our day would relish the whole species so highly as was done at a time, when the forms of society had reached the very summit of artificial perversion. A certain longing after nature and its purity was the necessary result of such a state of things; but even nature itself they were unable to see, except in an artificial light. All the Polish productions of this species, in the present period, savour strongly of the French school; whilst the pastorals of the sixteenth century hover in the midst between the bucolics of the ancients and the Italian and Spanish eclogues.

There was the same decided influence of the French literature on Wengierski, who died in 1787; although less in respect to taste than to morals. Karpinski, also a writer of pastorals, approaches nearest the Greeks, and is on the whole a poet of uncommon talent. His original writings bear much more of a national stamp than those of other poets of this period. His translation of Racine's Athalia is considered as a masterpiece, and his version of the Psalms has not been surpassed in any language. Another distinguished poet is Dionysius Kniaznin, re-

---

[56] Krasicki's complete works were published by Dmochowski, Warsaw 1803–4. A stereotype edition appeared at Breslau in 1824.

markable for a certain external freshness, which imparts life to all his productions. He was educated in the college of the Jesuits at Witebsk; and it was during his whole life a matter of regret to him, that he "had lost the golden season of his youth, and wasted the labour of sleepless nights on irksome trifles." Notwithstanding this learned education, the author of the Letters on Poland finds between him and Burns a kind of analogy. Kniaznin's principal fame rests on a ludicrous heroic called the 'Balloon.' He spent a part of his life at Pulawy, the estate of prince Czartoryski, under the patronage of this nobleman; and is said to have become, like Tasso, the victim of a passion for one of his lady patronesses.

The following are further regarded among their countrymen as poets of the first rank, viz. Niemcewicz, Brodzinski, bishop Woronicz, and Mickiewicz. Julius Niemcewicz is also known by his political fortunes and influence, and is equally esteemed as an historian and for his poetical talents. The eloquence which he exhibited in the diet of 1788–92, as the *nuntius* or deputy of Lithuania, laid the foundation of his fame. When his country was lost, after having fought at the side of Kosciuszko and shared his fate as a prisoner, he accompanied this great man to America, where he associated with Washington, whose life he has since described. His eulogy on Kosciuszko is considered as a masterpiece. His principal works are his historical songs, his dramas, and his "Reign of Sigismund III." Whatever he writes evinces more than common talents; as to which his friends only deplore that he has scattered them so much, or, according to the expression of the author of the Letters on Poland, that "his genius was too eager in embracing at once so much within its potent grasp; and thus, instead of concentrating his powers, lessened their brilliant beams, by diffusing them over too wide a horizon.[57]

---

[57] P. 221. Niemcewicz's works have not yet been collected. Of his *Spiewy historycne*, or 'Historical Songs,' Warsaw 1819, Bowring gives

John Woronicz, bishop of Cracow, and afterwards of Warsaw, whom we have named above as one of the most eloquent preachers, is equally celebrated as a poet. His productions all have a character of dignity and loftiness; and, with the exception of some religious hymns, are devoted to the historical fame of his country. His "Sybil," in which he conjures up in succession the ancient Polish kings from their graves to behold the cruel state of their once triumphant country, and the "Lechiade," an epic, which Schaffarik considers as the best Polish production of this species, are his principal works. The inclination of the Polish poets to celebrate and exalt their own country and the heroic deeds of their ancestors, without even admitting the possibility of rivalship on the part of any other nation, can easily be accounted for; while to foreign critics the same poems, which inspire Polish readers with patriotic enthusiasm, often appear pompous and void of that simplicity, which is the true source of the sublime.

Casimir Brodzinski, ob. 1835, was an eminent original poet, and an excellent translator. His poetry is pervaded by a character of strong and decided nationality, and Bowring says of him: "If any man can be considered the representative of Polish feelings, and as having transfused them into his productions,

---

some specimens. These songs were set to music by distinguished Polish composers, especially ladies; and, on account of their deep patriotic interest, have reached a higher degree of popularity than any other Polish work. They were written at the instigation of the Warsaw Society of Friends of Science. Besides his two historical works, *Dzieie panowania Zygmunta III,* or Reign of Sigismund III, Warsaw 1819, and *Zbior pamietnikow,* etc. a collection of unprinted documents, Warsaw 1822; and his large historical novel *Jan z Teczyna,* Warsaw 1825; Niemcewicz published *Leyba i Szora,* or Letters of Polish Jews, Warsaw 1821, presenting an illustration of their situation. His most recent production, an elegiac poem, was published at Leipzig 1833. See below, p. 286.

Brodzinski is certainly the man." He translated Macpherson's Ossian; and first introduced Scott's masterpieces into the literature of Poland. He may be considered as one of the founders of the modern romantic school in Polish literature.

Adam Mickiewicz, born in 1798, whose name belongs, perhaps, more appropriately to the next period, owed his first reputation, as a poet of eminent talent, to three small volumes of miscellaneous poetry, first published in 1822–1828. A poetic tale, *Conrad Wallenrod*, a scene from the wars of the Poles with the Teutonic knights, was published shortly after.[58]

The series of Polish poets towards the end of this period, who have manifested some talent, is too long to permit us to enumerate them all; and even a complete catalogue of their names must not be expected in these pages, which are devoted merely to an historical review of the *whole* literature, and to individuals only so far as they go to form characteristic features of the physiognomy of the former. The "Dictionary of Polish poets," published in 1820 by Juszynski, describes the lives of not less than 1400 individuals, independently of course of their poetical worth. We confine ourselves to presenting some of the most distinguished names in addition to those above-mentioned, viz. Gurski, a very productive and popular writer; L. Osinski, still more esteemed as a critic: Molski, Tanski, Boncza Tomaszewski, Okraszewski, Tymowski, Szydlowski, and Kozmian, the author of a popular didactic poem.

The Polish literature of this time was particularly rich in translations, which are approved by their countrymen, although they perhaps will not satisfy the higher standard of German or English criticism. This is due partly to the richness and pliability of the language itself. Dmochowski, Przybylski, and

[58] The fourth volume appeared at Paris; where also his earlier poetry was reprinted in 1828 under the title *Poezye Adama Mickiewicza.*

Staszyc, translated Homer; and the first also Virgil. Dmochowski's translations are in rhymed verse; those of Przybylski, who also enriched Polish literature with translations of the Paradise Lost, the Lusiad, and of many other poems, are in the measures of the originals, and manifest both a profound knowledge of the foreign languages, and great dexterity in using his own. Staszyc has written valuable works on various subjects, and enjoys a high esteem as a literary man and patriot. Felinski, the translator of Delille and Racine, is considered as the most harmonious Polish versifier. Hodani, Osinski, Kicinski, Kruszynski, have likewise transplanted the productions of the French Parnassus into the Polish soil; Sienkiewicz, Odyniec, and others, devoted their talents to the English. Okrascewski translated the Greek tragic poets. Minasowicz, the author of fifty-three various works, and Nagurczewski, translated also several of the ancient authors; but according to the best critics, with more knowledge of the classic languages, than skill in the management of their own. Among all the distinguished poets mentioned above, there is hardly one, who, besides his original productions, did not likewise devote his talents to poetical translations; in which Karpinski, Naruscewicz, and Krasicki, were considered as eminently successful.

In the whole domain of poetry, there is no branch in which the Poles manifested a greater want of *original* power, than the dramatic. Here the influence of the French school was most decided, and indeed exclusive. We have seen above what pains were taken by the most distinguished men of the nation, to establish a national stage; to which they looked, not in the light of a frivolous amusement, but as a school for purifying and elevating the national language and literary taste, and also as a means of correcting vice by ridiculing it. In this view several clergymen wrote for the theatre. The Jesuit Bohomolec wrote the first original comedies in 1757; other comedies, valuable as pictures of the time, were written by bishop Kossakowski. Prince Czartoryski we have mentioned above as a writer of dramas. Zablocki, Lipinski, Osinski, Kowalski, and others, transplanted the French masterpieces to the Polish stage, or imitated them. The actors, Boguslawski, Bielawski, and Zolkowski, wrote original pieces. Tragedies, mostly on subjects of Polish history, were written by Niemcewicz, Felinski, Dembowski, Slowacki, Kropinski, Hofmann, and F. Wenzyk, whose "Glinski" is considered as the best Polish production of this kind. The most popular comedies in recent times are by count Fredro, who is called the Polish Molière. The Polish stage is still richer in melo-dramas, especially rural pictures in a dramatic form; of which Niemcewicz's piece, "John Kochanowski," is a fine specimen.

As it respects novels, tales in prose, and similar productions, the literature of Poland has been much less overwhelmed with this species of writing, in which mediocrity is so easy and perfection so rare, than that of their neighbours the Russians. We think this can easily be accounted for. They possess few, for the same reason that the English are so rich in them. Domestic life, the true basis of the modern novel, has no charms in Poland. The whole tendency of the nation is towards public life, splendour, military fame; theirs are not the modest virtues of private retirement, but the heroic deeds of public renown. The beauty, the spirit, the influence of their women, is generally acknowledged; but that female reserve and delicacy which draws the thread of an English novel through three volumes, would be looked for in vain in Poland. Niemcewicz, however, published in 1827 an historical novel, "John of Trenczyn," which is considered as a happy imitation of Scott. Others were written by count Skarbeck. Among the novels, which present a psychological development of character, and a description of fashionable life, "The Intimations of the Heart" is regarded as the principal work. It was written by the princess of Wirtemberg, daughter of Adam and Isabella Czartoryski. Another esteemed female writer is Clementina Hofmann, formerly Tanska.

The Poles, although from a feeling of pride and patriotism naturally disposed to overrate the productions of their own literature, are far from being deficient in critical judgment or in exalted ideas on the theory of the beautiful. The count Stanislaus Potocki and Ossolinski, L. Osinski, Golanski, and others, maintain a high rank in this department.

Philosophy, as an abstract science, independently of its immediate application to subjects of real life, has never found more than a few votaries among the Poles. In the beginning of the seventeenth century, Aristotle was translated into Polish by Petryci. For nearly two hundred years, the teachers of philosophy in the Polish universities stopped at Aristotle; and a few commentaries on his Ethics and Politics composed the whole philosophical literature of Poland. In the first years of our own century, Jaronski and Scianawski made an attempt to introduce the philosophy of Kant; but although the cause appeared to be in the best hands, they met with little success. Galuchowski, a German philosophical writer of merit, is a Pole by birth;[59] as also Trentovski and Cieszkowski, followers of Hegel, who prefer the German for their organ.[60]

For the study of polite literature and the Slavic languages during this period, Warsaw was the principal seat; for philology and the exact sciences, the university of Wilna. This learned institution had taken special pains in respect to the necessary elementary books for the study of the classical languages; and was distinguished by its able professors Groddek, Bobrowski,

---

[59] Author of the work *Die Philosophie in ihrem Verhältnisse zum Leben ganzer Völker*, Erlangen 1822.

[60] The first wrote *Grundlage der universellen Philosophie*, Karlsruh 1837; the second, *Prolegomena zur Historiosophie*, Berlin 1838.

and Zukowski. The former, a scholar of high reputation, in addition to several philological works, translated Buttman's Greek Grammar into Polish; the latter published also a Greek and a Hebrew Grammar. In the oriental languages Senkowski at St. Petersburgh is distinguished; and count Rzewuski at Vienna had great desert in connection with the periodical work, *Fundgruben des Orients*.

In consequence of the grand-duke Constantine's predilection for mathematics, an undue share of attention, after the erection of a kingdom of Poland under his administration, was paid in schools to the exact or empirical sciences; *undue* we call it, because on account of its excess, the moral and literary pursuits of the pupils were necessarily neglected. Mathematics, during this whole period, were taught by several eminent men; by John Sniadecki, who is at the same time considered as a model in respect to style and language; by Poczobut, Zaborowski, Czech, Rogalinski, and others. In the same departments the names of Twardowski, Polinski, and Konkowski, must be honourably mentioned. Count Sierakowski wrote a classical work on architecture; and the learned Polish Jew Stern is celebrated over all Europe as the inventor of arithmetical and agricultural machines. Count Chodkiewicz and Andrew Sniadecki are distinguished chemists. Natural philosophy, although less studied, had able professors in H. Osinski and Bystrzycki; natural history, more particularly botany and zoology, in Kluk and Jundzill. Medicine, until the middle of the last century, was in Poland exclusively in the hands of foreigners, especially Germans and French;[61] since then several gifted Poles have devoted

[61] See Dr. Connor's History of Poland, 1698. Even as late as the close of the seventeenth century, the Poles were barbarians enough to look upon the profession of a physician with contempt. They had however in earlier times some very celebrated physicians, as Martin of Olkusc, Felix of Lowicz, and Struthius, who was called to Spain to save the life of Philip II, and even to the Turkish sultan Suliman II.

themselves to this science, although they have not yet formed a national school. Lafontaine, body physician of the last king, Dziarkowski, Perzyna, Malcz, and others, must be mentioned here. The university of Wilna was the most celebrated school for medical science.

Among the reflecting statesmen of Poland, in the second decennium of our century, there began to be a great deal of attention bestowed on national economy and its various branches; more especially on studies connected with agriculture, as being the science most applicable to the present wants of the country. Poland being the most extensive plain in Europe, and for the most part of a very rich and fertile soil, the Poles would seem destined by nature to be an agricultural people. We cannot but observe here, that from this very circumstance, the wretched state of the labouring classes is placed in a still more striking light. The interests of agricultural science have been promoted by different societies, and several able treatises on those subjects have been published; although it does not appear that any new theory or principles have been started. Of all the branches of moral science, political economy has met in Poland with the most disciples. Valuable statistical works on Poland in the Polish language have been written by Staszyc, honourably mentioned above;[62] by Slawiarski, and others. Swiencki in his 'Geography of ancient Poland,' Surowiecki in his 'History of the Polish towns and peasantry,' give very valuable statistical notices; and the 'Journey to Constantinople and Troy' by count Raczynski, contains an exact statistical account of Podolia and the Ukraine.

The science of law must ever have been in a melancholy state in a country like Poland. Poland proper has always been governed by *statutes* and *constitutions*, sanctioned by the diet.

---

[62] Page 278.

These were either founded on ancient usages, *consuetudines*, or occasioned by particular circumstances. The towns were governed according to the code of Magdeburg. In Lithuania the ancient Lithuanian statutes, collected in 1529, prevailed and still prevail, if not in collision with any intervening *ukase*.[63] In the other provinces, the laws of the respective monarchies to which they are annexed, are in force. Thus the different portions of Poland are governed in accordance with seven different systems of law.[64] Under the administration of the last king of Poland, which was so rich in improvements, a general code of laws was also planned, and projects were prepared by able statesmen and lawyers; but they were all rejected by the diet of 1777. Under the Russian administration, preparation was made from the very beginning for the introduction of a new code; but the first project of a criminal code presented by the council of state, was likewise rejected by the diet of 1820. A portion of the civil code was accepted in A. D. 1825; but the complete code, which was ready for publication in the year 1830, had not, so far as we are informed, been introduced before the outbreak of the revolution. The administration of justice in Poland is about as bad as in Russia; being nothing but one great system of bribery and corruption. Of the judges of the lower courts, two thirds are elected; one third of these, and all the officers of the higher tribunals, are appointed by the government. In former times the profession of a lawyer, as well as that of a physician, was considered in Poland as degrading and unworthy of a nobleman. These two professions were not indeed prohibited by law, like that of traders,—for a nobleman who retailed "by yards or by pints," legally lost his rank,—but custom had made all those

[63] This code is frequently called the code of Leo Sapieha, the sub-chancellor of Lithuania, who in A. D. 1588 translated it from the White Russian into the Polish language.

[64] See *Revue Encyclopédique*, Oct. 1827, p. 219.

occupations which were the source of pecuniary profit, equally the objects of contempt. There was even a time, "when it was reckoned a matter of indifference for a nobleman *to understand arithmetic*."[65] In modern times the ideas on this subject have of course changed; the study of law is no longer despised, especially in its necessary connection with the administration of justice. Slotwinski in Cracow, Bantkie and Maciejowski in Warsaw, were esteemed as teachers of law. We shall hereafter have occasion to mention the valuable work of the latter on this subject. The Roman law, both civil and criminal, was studied in the universities, as well as the law of nature and nations; which latter, in the case of this unhappy country, has been for more than seventy years so cruelly violated.

It is a singular fact, that although, down to the year 1818 when the Russian government interfered to prevent it, foreign travel was one of the favourite means of education among the Polish nobility, their literature exhibits hardly any books of travels. A few were formerly written in Latin or French; among the latter we mention John Potocki's 'Travels for the purpose of discovering Slavic antiquities,' Hamb. 1795. In more modern times count Raczynski has published the 'Journal of his travels to Constantinople and the plain of Troy,' richly embellished with illustrations, mentioned above.[66] A view of Great Britain was given in 1828 by Ljach Szyrma, under the title *Anglia i Szkocya.*

---

[65] See Letters on Poland, p. 103.

[66] Breslau 1821. The same author published John Sobieski's Letters, a work read throughout all Europe in its French translation by count Plater and Salvandy. A whole series of *Memoirs,* among which are some of great importance for Polish history, for instance those of Passek, of Wybicki, of Kolontaj, etc. owe their publication to the generous liberality of this true nobleman.

SIXTH PERIOD.

From the Polish Revolution in 1830 *to the present time.*

We have thus brought down the history of Polish literature to the year 1830; an epoch of glorious, although most melancholy moment in the history of Poland. If the literature of a country could ever be regarded completely *in abstracto;* if it was not in intimate connection with the political fate and position of its country; we would have commenced this period with the first combats of the Romantic and Classical schools, that is, about fifteen years earlier.[67] But while these fifteen years may be considered in some measure as the time of the fermentation of that spirit, which broke out in 1830; this latter year—with its melancholy attempts on the part of Russia to crush all Polish nationality, by the annihilation of their higher seats of learning and the spoliation of all their libraries, as the principal means of cultivating it—forms only too distinctly an epoch, not only in Polish history in general, but specially in Polish literature.

The state of the country on the whole in the beginning of 1830 was not unprosperous. The cruel wrongs inflicted on the Poles since 1815 were all in express violation of a constitution, which met with the approbation of Kosciuszko and the best of the nation. A noble individual, or a high-spirited people, can more

---

[67] We do not know exactly from what point the Polish literary historians *after* Bentkowski date the period of the present literature; as we have not been able to get a view of Wiszniewski's *Historya literatury Polskiej*, Cracow 1840. We are even not certain, whether the works on literary history, which J. B. Rakowiecki and Prof. Aloys Osinski were said to be preparing about the same time, have ever appeared.

easily submit even to unjust laws, than to arbitrary despotism. *Legally* the Grand Duke had no right to keep a single Russian soldier in Poland; by the terms of the constitution they could be there only as foreign guests. *Legally* the press was free. *Legally* Poland could have defended herself by her charter against any arbitrary act of her sovereign or his viceroy. It would seem, however, that even the repeated infringements of the constitution, and the direct violation of the laws by the government, did not contribute so much to induce the Poles to insurrection, as the fierce and brutal behaviour of the Russian generalissimo, and of the Russian civil and military officers high and low, whose profligacy had long made them the objects of deep contempt. The annals of Warsaw indeed present, during the Russian administration, one of the most revolting pictures which history exhibits. And the idea, that it owes its darkest shades principally to the reckless despotism of one individual, serves only to make them appear still darker.

The war, which called into exercise all the mental faculties of the nation, put a stop of course to all literary activity; but even during the more quiet period which immediately succeeded it—the quietness of a cemetery—the dejected spirits of the nation, whose noblest sons an interval of two years had rendered prisoners, exiles, or corpses, are easily to be perceived in the results of their intellectual pursuits. A small volume, containing three poems by Niemcewiecz and Mickiewicz was printed in 1833 at Leipzig. It is the swan-like melody of the aged poet; whilst the younger celebrates the exploits of his valiant brethren. To the poems of the latter, (three volumes, Paris 1828,) a fourth volume was added, containing the riper productions of his manhood. The late vice president of Warsaw, Xavier Bronikowski, published at the same time *Polnische Miscellen* in the German language at Nuremberg. A number of Polish literati were gathered at Paris. A work, intended to contain about twelve volumes, with the title *Souvenirs de la Pologne, historique, statistique, et literaire*, was announced in that city; for the printing offices at home were of course closed against the expression of all patriotic feelings. The fifteen printing establishments at Warsaw issued in the year 1832, from March to December, only sixty-three works.

The universities of Warsaw and Wilna were broken up; and the rich libraries of these institutions were carried to St. Petersburgh. The emperor declared openly, that it should be his aim to annihilate all traces of *Polish* nationality, and to metamorphose it into a Russian people. Even the lower schools were in great part deprived of their funds, and changed to Russian government schools. After some years of utter privation as to all means of higher instruction, a new university for the Poles was founded at Kief; of course on a Russian model and in a Russian spirit. In a most consistent and energetic manner the language and the national peculiarities of the country were every where checked and persecuted; and attempts of every kind were made to replace them by Russian customs and the Russian language. The union of the Greek and Catholic churches was dissolved; and in that way thousands were compelled to join the Russian church. In the higher schools prizes were set forth for the best essays in the Russian language; and in 1833 a law was made, that after 1834 no Pole could hope for employment in the Russian service, without a complete knowledge of the Russian language. In the White Russian provinces, so called, that is in Lithuania, Podolia, and Volhynia,—countries which formerly had been under Russian dominion, and are still inhabited by a Lithuanian and Russian peasantry, while the nobility is Polish,—these severe and arbitrary measures were surprisingly successful in respect to the youth then in training; and the minister of the School department, Ouwarof, in his report of 1839, expressed his satisfaction in the strongest terms.

But Poland as a whole was far from giving satisfaction to the government. There was indeed a certain stoppage of mental life, which seemed to favour its views. Literary productions were few in proportion to the former productiveness. In the year 1837, not more than 118 books were published in the whole kingdom; and of these only 75 were Polish; the rest in Hebrew. The press and all other organs of public feeling were under the strictest control. Yet the very topics, which were chosen by the literati for their researches and commentaries, proved best of all that the love of their country was not extinguished. The history of Poland became more than ever a chosen study. Private libraries and archives were searched for materials; and detached parts of the past, and single branches of history, were made the subjects of a closer examination and research, than had ever before been devoted to such topics among this active and restless people. One of the most important works, issued immediately after the revolution, was Prof. Maciejowski's History of the Slavic Legislatures.[68] It was well received by the numerous German and Slavic scholars, who devote themselves to similar pursuits; but they soon found that it did not fully satisfy the claims of the deeper criticism of our days. It has come finally to be considered rather as a preparatory work, which was shortly afterwards partially completed by another production of the same author: "Contributions to the History of Slavic events, literature, and legislation."[69] A work by J. Hobe, "On the Slavic rights of inheritance," appeared

[68] *Historya prawodawstw Slowanskich,* Warsaw 1832–1835.

[69] *Pamietniki o djezach, pismiennictwie i prawodawstwie Slowian,* Warsaw 1838. A German translation appeared in 1842, at St. Petersburg: *Denkwürdigkeiten über die Begebnisse, das Schriftwesen, und die Gesetzgebung der Slaven.*—The same author published more recently a work on the ancient history of Poland and Lithuania: *Pierwotne dzieje Polski i Litwy,* etc. Warsaw 1846.

about the same time; also, a publication of the oldest Slavic documents relating to law by Prof. Kucharski.[70]

As valuable monographs must be mentioned, the history of queen Barbara Radzivil, from sources hitherto unknown, by M. Balinski, who wrote also a history of Wilna; the biographies of the Hetmans, by Zegota Pauli; a history of Posen, by Lukaszewicz; of Lithuania, by Th. Narbutt; of Poland in the first half of the sixteenth century, by Maraczewski; historical and topographical descriptions, relating also to language and manners, by Przezdziecki and by Kraszewski. We may also notice here the History of the Latin Language in Poland, by Dr. Macherzynski; a book considered as a mine of erudition and useful knowledge. To it is annexed a list of all the different editions of the Classics published in Poland. We learn from it, that Cicero's works have been edited there, either complete or in particular portions, not less than forty-five times; first as early as A. D. 1500, at Cracow. Horace also has appeared eight times, first in 1521; Ovid four times, first in 1529; Virgil six times, first in 1642.

The publication of early chronicles, for the purpose of rendering them more accessible to the public, was continued. That of Lemberg was edited by D. Zubrzycki in 1844; that of Cracow, by Macynski in 1845.[71] Archæological researches have continued to excite an interest. The dust of centuries has been shaken from many a valuable document; and there have been published in succession, A. Grabowski's Historical Antiquities of Poland,[72] the Antiquities of Galicia by Zegota Pauli,[73] and a

---

[70] *Najdawniejsze pomniki praw Slowianskich,* Warsaw 1838.

[71] Muczkowski's valuable History of the University of Cracow has been mentioned above, p. 232.

[72] *Starozytnoscisci historyczne Polskie,* Cracow 1840.

[73] *Starozytnoscie Gallicyiskie,* Cracow 1841.

work on Polish Archæology by count Eustace T.[74] Here belongs also the Collection of important historical Documents, edited in 1847;[75] and a series of numismatic publications, by Lelewel, who wrote in exile, by Poplinski, by Ig. Zagorski and E. Rastawiecki, and above all by count E. Raczynski.[76] The patriotic exertions of this nobleman, who has caused many a valuable old manuscript to be printed; and who has never seemed to be afraid of any sacrifice, when the promotion of science and literature is concerned; deserve the highest praise, and ought to serve as a model to others of noble name.

Church history also, a department hitherto entirely neglected, in Poland, has begun to receive some small degree of attention in the present period. Joseph Lukascewicz wrote a history of the Bohemian Congregations in Poland,[77] in 1835; and in 1846 a history of the Helvetian (Calvinistic) Confession in Lithuania. Count Valerian Krasinski, who found a home in England, has likewise published a history of the Reformation in Poland, in the English language.[78]

The history of recent times cannot be expected to be written in Poland; where the pen is chained, even if the mind keeps itself unfettered. The republic of Cracow, until about ten years ago, enjoyed a certain degree of liberty. It could have become the asylum of Polish literature and science; but it became only too soon the battlefield of political passions and combats. Some

---

[74] *Rzut okana zrodta Archæologii Krajowej*, Wilna 1842.

[75] Published at the same time in French: *Medailles de Pologne etc.* Posen 1838; a splendid work.

[76] *Kodex diplomatyczny Polski*, Warsaw 1847.

[77] This is the appellation of the Lutherans in Poland.

[78] Historical Sketch of the rise, progress, and decline of the Reformation in Poland, and of the influence which the Scriptural doctrines have exercised on that country in literary, moral, and political respects. By Count Valerian Krasinski. Vol. I. Lond. 1838.

of her scholars however kept themselves entirely aloof from the strife. Macherzinski's and Muczkowski's learned works, already mentioned above; a history of Polish Literature by Wisznewski; and a new Polish Dictionary, by Trajanski; were the immediate results.

New works of travels have been written by Kraszewski and Holawinski; the former describing the South of Russia, and the latter his pilgrimage to the Holy Land; both were published in 1845. A book of travels on Siberia, a land so seldom chosen for a tour of pleasure, had preceded them.[79]

Modern history, we have said, cannot be expected to be written in Poland. This remark leads us at once to the literature of Polish Emigrants, as it is generally called, which has sprung up in Paris. Since the revolution of 1830, this capital has been the principal seat of Polish literary activity. One of the first works of importance published there was Maurice Mochnacki's History of the Polish insurrection; which excited among his own countrymen a new and passionate feud. Mochnacki's name had been favourably known as the author of a work on the Polish literature of the nineteenth century;[80] and as the able editor of several periodicals. His political misfortunes, however, and especially the circumstance that he had been compelled to appear alternately as the tool of the grand duke Constantine, and as the victim of his hatred, made him a subject of distrust to his countrymen, although he had fought with bravery in the revolution. He died in France when not yet thirty years old. His scattered writings were published in 1836 by A. Jelowicki, one of the patriotic family of that name; who had been deeply implicated in the revolution, and lived as fugitives in Paris. A

---

79 *Wiadamosci o Syberyi przez I. K.* 1838.

80 *O Literaturze Polskiey w wieku dziewietnastym*, Warsaw 1830; published a few days before the outbreak of the Revolution.

printing office, which they have founded there, serves for the publication of Polish works.

Another work on the recent events was written by Wratnowski, who published a history of the insurrection in Volhynia, Paris, 1837. An animated picture of the time, which appeared three years ago, under the title, "Representation of the national spirit in Poland," by Ojczyczniak,[81] exhibits strong passions in the author; a glowing and certainly not unnatural hatred against the great powers; but a still more violent one against his *democratic* countrymen, to whom he imputes the perdition of the good cause. A history of the Polish insurrection, published by S. B. Gnorowski in the English language, Lond. 1839, is written in the same violent and prejudiced spirit.

The Slavic press in Paris has been especially productive in periodicals; all of them replete with passion and hatred against their oppressors; some of them conducted not without talent. The *Revue Slave*, the *Mlada Polska* (young Poland), the *Cronika Emigracyi Polskiej* (Polish Emigrant's Chronicle), and the *Polish Vademecum* edited by N. U. Hoffmann, may be named here. From the latter we learn, that, from 1831 to 1837 among the Polish emigrants in France, *nine* died in duels and *fourteen* by suicide.

Joachim Lelewel, whose *literary* activity belongs rather to the preceding period, while that now under consideration was partly the result of his *political* career, lives still at Brussels, where he has recently published (1849) a work on the civil rights of the Polish peasantry. He attempts to demonstrate, that the oppression and the debased condition of this class came upon them along with the introduction of Christianity; and represents the Romish clergy, whose advantage it was to keep up this state of things, as the principal enemies of the peasantry. Lelewel's

---

[81] *Wizerunki Duszy narodowej,* Paris 1847.

writings have wielded a more decided influence in Poland than those of any other modern author. The tendency of all his historical investigations, even when apparently without any such design, has been since the very beginning of the Russian dominion to undermine their power; and the great ability with which he contrived to veil hints, to disguise remarks, and to follow out under a harmless mask a certain and fixed purpose, had earned him twenty or thirty years ago the name of the "Jesuit of history."

It remains now to give a general survey of the progress of Polish *belles-lettres* during the last twenty years; and also of those mixed publications which excite a general interest. Here we must not omit to mention the "Evening Hours of a Pilgrim,"[82] a book which, in a sprightly style and a peculiarly interesting way, gives a good deal of information as to the literary and mental condition of Poland, and the much-lauded revival of letters during the reign of Stanislaus Poniatowski.

But perhaps the most interesting production of this period is Adam Mickiewicz's course of Lectures on Slavic literature and the condition of the Slavic nations, delivered in French at Paris, where he had found employment as a professor in the College de France.[83] The deep enthusiasm which pervades these lectures, the mental excitement by which they would seem to have been dictated from beginning to end, forbid us to consider them in the ordinary light of a mere course of instruction on the subject to which they relate. But there is no other work more full of ideas, or richer in thought; it is the reasoning of a poet, and a poet's way of viewing the world. The one great

---

[82] *Wieczory pielgrzyma,* Paris 1837.

[83] This work appeared at the same time in German, accompanied with a preface by the author, written expressly for the German edition. The German title is *Vorlesungen über Slavische Literatur und Zustände in den Jahren* 1840–1844. 4 vols. Leipzig 1843–44.

principle of these lectures again is *Panslavism*,—Panslavism spiritualized and idealized; and therefore in a shape which can inspire little fear to others in respect to their own nationality, although it can never excite their sympathies. Mickiewicz still idolizes Napoleon, and prophesies a revolution of the world; a new revolution, a torch to illumine the world; he himself is "a spark, fallen from that torch;" his mission is to prophesy to the world the coming events "as a living witness of the new revelation." Although these prophecies are not strictly political, we can see plainly, that in the expectation of the prophet this new revolution will consist in "the union of the *force* of Slavic genius, with the *knowledge* of the West" (France); by which of course the intermediate Teutonic principle must be crushed.

In purely poetical creations, this great poet shows his full power. In a beautiful tale, *Pan Tadeusz*, "Sir Thaddeus," (Paris 1834,) which, though in verse, may be considered as a novel, he very graphically described the civil and domestic life existing in Lithuania immediately before the war of 1812; and gave also further evidence of his genius by several smaller poems. He is, however, not very productive; a striking peculiarity of Slavic poets.

The principal poets of the modern romantic school in Poland, of which Mickiewicz must be considered the founder, are the following:

A. E. Odyniec and Julian Korssak, both chiefly known by happy translations from the English; but also not without creative power of their own. Anton Malczeski is the author of a poetical tale, *Maria*;[84] perhaps the most popular production of the

---

[84] *Marya*, first published at Warsaw 1825; afterwards in several different editions, among which may be mentioned here one prepared by Bielowski, Lemb. 1838; and one by Brockhaus and Avenarius, Leipz. and Paris 1844. A beautiful German translation appeared in the same year at Leipzig: *Maria*, aus dem Polnischen des A. Malczeski von K. R. Vogel.

Polish literature. It is a touching family legend, traditional in the noble house of Potocki in Volhynia; but transposed by Malczeski to the Ukraine, and connected in that way with graphic descriptions of this latter country. Malczeski lived a life of wild adventures; and died young, not yet 34 years old, in 1826.

The Ukraine appears to be, on the whole, one of the favourite theatres for the romantic school of Polish poets. Zaleski, Goszczynski, Grabowski, all of them poets of more than ordinary talents, give us pictures of this country, alternately sweet and rough, wild and romantic. There must necessarily be some mixture of attractive and repulsive elements here even for native poets; for the common people are Russians, and hate the Polish nobility as their oppressors. Nevertheless Thomas Padura, another of the young Polish school, chose even the dialect of the Ruthenian peasantry for his songs. Another Polish poet, who has selected the Ukraine for the theatre of most of his tales, is Michael Czaykowski; he too is considered as standing at the head of the novel writers of his country. His legends of the Kozaks,[85] his tales, *Wernyhora*,[86] *Kirdzali*, the Hetman of the Ukraine,[87] etc. manifest a more than common talent.

To the poetical literature of the Polish emigrants belong further the works of A. Gorecki, Garczinski, J. Slawacki, but, above all, of count Ignatius Krasinski; not the same individual who wrote a history of the Reformation in Poland in the English language.[88] He is by many of his countrymen considered as their greatest living poet. Most of his productions are enveloped

---

[85] *Powiesci Kosackie*, Par. 1837. A German translation by Minsberg, Glogau 1838.

[86] Paris 1838; a German translation, Leipz. 1841.

[87] The two latter appeared at Paris in 1838 and 1841, and were translated into French and German.

[88] See above, p. 290.

in a certain mystical atmosphere, which renders a commentary necessary in order to understand them. Two dramatic poems, one called, in contrast to Dante, "The Undivine Comedy;" the other, "Irydion," an illustration of Schiller's stern apothegm, that "the history of the world is the judgment of the world;"[89] are regarded as his most powerful productions.[90]

Meanwhile this department of literature, in Poland itself, has taken, in some of its branches, the same strictly national direction which characterizes the Russian and Bohemian tendencies of modern times. Many of the publications, which are reckoned under belles-lettres, are nothing better than drawing-room productions, so called, meant to satisfy the immediate wants of the reading world. Count Skarbek, J. Krascewski, F. Barnatowicz (ob. 1838), K. Korwell, Szabranski, and others, are popular novel writers. Among the poets we mention the same Szabranski, Nowasielski, Zialinski, Alex. Groza, Burski, and, above all, Lucian Siemienski and A. Bielowski. The latter, along with Kamienski, is the translator of Schiller. Count Vinzent Kicinski translated Victor Hugo; and Holawinski, Shakspeare. As successful dramatic writers are named, the counts Fredro, Korzeniowski, St. Jaozowski, etc.

Of an entirely national character are all the productions of Wladislas Woicicki, who devoted his life principally to the study of the antiquities of his country and its language. In 1838 he published an interesting collection of old Polish proverbs;[91] several historical tales, scattered in Annuals; a

---

[89] "Die Weltgeschichte ist das Weltgericht."

[90] *Nieboska Komedya,* Paris 1835; ed. 2, 1837; Germ. *Die ungöttliche Komödie,* aus dem Polnischen von K. Batornicki, Leipz. 1841.—*Irydion,* Par. 1836. This latter has been twice translated into German, Leipz. 1839, and Berlin 1846.

[91] *Starozytney wiessci z XI go XVI go i XVII go wieko.* The author

greater work, entitled "Domestic Sketches;" and another on Polish Woman;[92] all of them illustrations of Polish life and manners at certain times, and resting on an historical foundation. A rich collection of traditions and popular legends was published by the same scholar in 1839.[93] This important national feature has at last excited some attention among the Polish scholars. In 1838 a collection of the songs of the people in the country adjacent to the Bug was published.[94] Another appeared in the same year, prepared by the poets Siemienski and Bielowski (Prague 1838), with the title *Dumki*, i. e. Elegies,[95] being Polish translations of Malo-Russian popular songs. The great and simple beauty of this poetry of the Kozaks surprised the literary world. But Woicicki and Zegota Pauli were the first who gave their attention to the really Polish Lekhian popular songs, i. e. songs of the peasantry in Masuria and Podlachia, the grand duchy of Posen, the territory of Cracow, etc. of which, until then, the existence was hardly known.[96]

It would almost seem as if the Russian government, in placing all the evidences of the mental activity of its Polish subjects under its strictest guardianship, was ready to supply also the supposed want of popular poetry. There was recently published at Warsaw a collection of ballads, sixty-nine in number, devoted to the praise of all the sovereigns of Russia, from Rurik to Alexander. These ballads are in the popular tone, and were sold

had published a similar work before. Polish proverbs have also been collected by Knapski and Rysinski.

[92] *Zarysy domowe*, Warsaw 1841; and *Niewasty Polskie*, Wars. 1844.

[93] *Klechdy, Starozytnye powviesci i podania ludu Polskigo i Rusi*, Warsaw 1837.

[94] *Piesni ludu bielachrobatow, Mazurow i Rusiz nad Buga*, Lemb 1838.

[95] *Duma, Dumka*, means *thought*, and is the name of the elegiac, mostly historical, ballads of the Malo-Russian people.

[96] See more on this subject in Part IV.

cheap.[97] What degree of popularity they may have obtained, we are unable to say.[98]

---

[97] The title is *Spiewy historyczne Cesarstwa Rossyiskiego,* i. e. Historical songs of the Russian emperors.

[98] The English reader will find further information on Polish literature in Bowring's Introduction to his Polish Anthology, Lond. 1827 ; in Ljach Szyrma's Letters on Poland, published in London ; and in an article on Polish Literature in the Foreign Quarterly Review, Vol. XXV. No. 49. These are the only sources in the English language with which we are acquainted.

In grammatical and lexical works the Polish language is very rich; but the interest which the English have recently shown for the fate of the Poles seems not to extend to their language. The following are the principal works.

GRAMMARS: in German, Krumholz *Polnische Grammatik,* Breslau 1797, 6th edit. *Auszug aus Kopczynski's Grammatik,* von Polsfuss, Breslau 1794. Mrongovius *Poln. Sprachlehre,* Königsb 1794, and in several altered editions, under different titles; last edition Danzig 1836. Szumski's *Poln. Gramm.* Posen 1830. Vater's *Grammatik der Poln. Sprache,* Halle 1807. Bantkie *Poln. Grammatik* attached to his Dictionary, Breslau 1808–1824. Szrzeniawa *Wortforschungslehre der polnischen Sprache,* Lemberg and Lemgo 1842–43. Poplinski *Polnische Grammatik,* Lissa 1836; last edition 1840. Stostakowskiego *Polska Gramm.* Trzemeszne 1846. Schieweck *Grammatik der. Polnischen Sprache,* Fraustadt and Neustadt 1847. In French, Kopczynski *Essai d'une grammaire Polonaise,* Wars. 1807. Trambczynski *Grammatique raisonnée de la langue Polonaise,* new edit. Warsaw 1793.

DICTIONARIES, in German and French. The most useful are, Mrongovius *Handwörterbuch der Poln. Sprache,* latest edit. Danz. 1823. Troc *Franz-poln.-deutsches Wörterbuch,* in several editions from 1742 to 1821. J. V. Bantkie *Taschenwörterbuch der Poln. Sprache,* (German and French,) Breslau and Wars. in several editions from 1805 to 1819. Slownik *Francusko-Polski, Dictionaire Polonais Français,* Berlin and Leipzig 1839–45. *Dict. Polonais-Français,* 2 vols. 18mo. Paris 1844. J. A. E. Schmidt, *Nouveau Dictionaire portatif Français et Polonais,* Zerbst 1847. *Polnisch-Deutsches Taschenwörterbuch,* von Jordan, Leipzig 1845.—Standard works for the language are the etymological dictionaries: G. S. Bantkie *Slownik dokladny iez. pol. i. niem.* Breslau 1806, and Linde's *Slownik iez. pol.* Wars. 1807–14. For other philological works, see Schaffarik's *Geschichte der Slav. Spr.* p 410.

CHAPTER III.

LANGUAGES OF THE SORABIAN-VENDES IN LUSATIA, AND OF OTHER VENDISH TRIBES NOW EXTINCT.

THE north-eastern part of Germany, as far west as the Elbe and Saale, was, from the fifth to the tenth century, almost exclusively inhabited by nations of the Slavic race. Various Teutonic tribes—among them the Burgundians, the Suevi, Heruli, and Hermunduri—had before this taken up their temporary residence along the Baltic, between the Vistula and the Elbe. In the great migration of the Asiatic-European nations, which for nearly two centuries kept in motion all Europe from the Icy Ocean to the Atlantic, and extended even to the north of Africa, the warlike German nations moved towards the south-west, and Slavic tribes traversing the Danube and Vistula, in immense multitudes, took possession of the countries which they left. Those who came over the northern Vistula, settled along the coasts of the Baltic as far west as to the Elbe and Saale, and as far south as to the Erzgebirge (Ore Mountains) on the borders of Bohemia.

These Slavic tribes were called by the Germans, *Wenden*, Lat. *Venedi*, for which we prefer in English the form of *Vendes*, rather than that of Wends. It appears indeed that this name was formerly applied by the Germans indiscriminately to all the Slavic nations with which they came in contact; for the name *Winden*, Eng. *Vindes*, which is still, as we have seen, the German appellation for the Slovenzi, or the Slavic inhabitants of Southern Germany, is evidently the same in a slightly altered form. The name of *Wenden*, Vendes, became, however, in the course of time, a specific appellation for the northern German-Slavic tribes; of which, at the present day, only a few meagre remnants are left. They were nevertheless once a powerful nation. Five independent branches must be distinguished among them.

We first name the *Obotrites*, the former inhabitants of the present duchies of Mecklenburg, and the adjacent country, west, north, and south. They were divided into the Obotrites proper, the Wagrians in Holstein, and the Polabæ and Linones on the banks of the Elbe and Leine; but were united under a common chief or king. They and their eastern neighbours the Wiltzi, (Germ. *Wilzen*, Lat. *Veletabæ*,) with whom they lived in perpetual warfare, were the most warlike and powerful among the Vendish tribes. The Wiltzi or Pomeranians lived interspersed with the Kassubes, a Lekhish tribe, between the Oder and the Vistula, and were subjugated by the Obotrites in A. D. 782. It was however only by the utmost exertions, that these latter could maintain their own independence against their western and southern neighbours, the Germans. Conquered by Charlemagne, they regained their independence under his successors, and centuries passed away in constant and bloody conflicts and alternate fortunes. In the middle of the twelfth century, however, they were completely subjugated by Henry the Lion, duke of Saxony and Bavaria. He laid waste their whole country, destroyed most of the people, and compelled the few remaining inhabitants and their prince, to accept Christianity from his bloody hands. In A. D. 1167 he restored to this latter, whose name was Pribislaus, a part of his kingdom, and gave his daughter Matilda in marriage to the son of Pribislaus, who, a few years later, was made a prince of the empire, and was thus gained over to the German cause. His descendants are the present dukes of Mecklenburg; and it is a memorable fact, that these princes are at the present day the only sovereigns in Europe of the Slavic race. German priests and German colonists introduced the German language; although we find that Bruno, the chief missionary among the Obotrites, preached before them in their own language. The Slavic dialect spoken by them expired gradually; and probably without ever having been reduced to writing, except for the sake of curiosity when very near its extinction. The only documents of it, which have come down to us, are a few incomplete vocabularies, compiled among the Polabæ and Linones, i. e. the inhabitants adjacent to the Elbe, in Slavic *Labe*, and to the Leine, in Slavic *Linac*.

Long after the whole region was perfectly Germanized, a few towns in the eastern corner of the present kingdom of Hanover, were still almost exclusively inhabited by a people of Slavic race, who in the seventeenth century, and even to the middle of the eighteenth, had preserved in some measure their language and habits. But, since the Germans were strongly prejudiced against the Vendish name,—the nations of this race, especially those in the western part of the German territories, being despised as subjugated tribes, and inferior in general knowledge and information,—they gradually renounced their national peculiarities. Towards the close of the seventeenth century, when Hennings, German pastor at Wustrow, took great pains to collect among them historical notices and a vocabulary of their language, he found the youth already ignorant of the latter, and the old people almost ashamed of knowing it, or at least afraid of being laughed at by their children. They took his inquiries, and those of other intelligent persons, in respect to their ancient language and usages, as intended to ridicule them, and denied at first any knowledge of those matters. We find, however, that preaching in the Vendish language of this region was still continued for some time later. Divine service was held in it for the last time at Wustrow, in the year 1751. According to the vocabularies which Hennings and a few others collected, their dialect, like that spoken in Lower Lusatia, was nearly related to the Polish language; partaking however in some peculiarities of the Bohemian, and not without some of its own.[1]

The second great Vendish tribe, the Wiltzi or Pomeranians (Germ. *Wilzen*), also called Veletabæ, were, as we said above, subjugated in A. D. 782 by the Obotrites; and the country between the Oder and the Vistula formed for more than a hundred and fifty years a part of the great Vendish kingdom. They regained, however, even before the final dissolution of this latter in A. D. 1026, the partial independence of their own dukes; who attached themselves to Germany, and afterwards, under the name of the dukes of Pomerania, became princes of the empire. In the year 1124 the first Pomeranians were baptized by Otho, bishop of Bamberg; and the place where this act was performed, Ottosbrunnen (Otho's Well), which five hundred years ago was encircled by four lime-trees, is still shown to the traveller. As they received religion and instruction from Germany, the influence of the German language can easily be accounted for. German colonists aided in spreading it throughout the whole country. The last person who understood the old Pomeranian language, is said to have died in the year 1404. No trace of it remains, excepting only the names of places and persons, the Slavic origin of which can be recognized throughout all north-eastern Germany by the terminations in *itz*, *enz*, *ik*, or *ow*. In

[1] Herder, in his *Volkslieder,* communicated a popular ballad from this dialect. See *Literatur und Kunst,* Vol. VII. p. 126, edit. of 1827–30.

A. D. 1637 the line of the old Pomeranian dukes expired, and the country fell to Brandenburg, with the exception of that part which Sweden usurped at the peace of Westphalia. The island of Rügen, which till A. D. 1478 had its own native princes, belonged to this latter. It is the principal seat of German-Slavic antiquities. The ancient Rugians and their gods are mentioned by Tacitus, and described by Saxo Grammaticus. The old chronicles and legends, founded on still older traditions, speak of a large and flourishing city named Vineta on the small island Wollin, south-east of Rügen, once the principal seat of the western Slavic commerce, and, as Herder calls it, the Slavic Amsterdam. This city is said by some to have been destroyed by the Danes; by others to have been ingulfed in the sea by the sinking of the ground beneath it. Modern inquirers, however, have doubted whether it ever existed; and, hard as it is to renounce the many poetical associations attached to such a subject,—so similar to those which fill the mind in thinking of Pompeii and Herculaneum,—their objections have not yet been satisfactorily refuted.

The third separate branch of the Vendish stem were the Ukrians, or Border-Vendes, Germ. *Ukern*, from *Ukraina*, border. They lived in the territory which afterwards became the margravate of Brandenburg, and were divided into several tribes, as the Hevelli on the banks of the Havel, the Retarians, etc. Their situation was such, that constant conflicts between them and the guardians or watch of the German frontiers, the Saxon margraves on the other side of the Elbe, were unavoidable. These served gradually to extend the German *marches* or frontiers further and further, until in the year 1134 Albert the Bear, count of Ascania, finally conquered the Vendes. The Slavic inhabitants of this region were cruelly and completely destroyed; the country was repeopled by German and Dutch colonists, and given as a fief by the emperor to Albert the Bear, the first margrave of Brandenburg. Brandenburg was the German form for *Brannibor*, the most considerable of the Vendish cities, after which the country was called. The names of places, many of them altered in a similar manner, are indeed the only weak traces of the Vendish language once spoken in this part of Germany. No tribe of the Vendes seems to have been so completely extinguished; the present inhabitants of Brandenburg being of as pure a German origin, as those of any other part of Germany.

The descendants of only two Vendish tribes have preserved their language; and even these, from powerful nations spread over the surface of at least 4800 geographical square miles, have shrunk into the comparatively small number of scarcely two hundred thousand individuals, now inhabitants of Upper and Lower Lusatia. Nearly all of them are peasants; for the higher classes, even if Slavic blood perhaps runs in their veins, are completely Germanized. These tribes are the Sorabians, Lat. *Sorabæ*, Germ. *Sorben*, in Lusatia, divided into two different branches. They call themselves to this very day *Servians*, or rather (as also their brethren on the Danube) *Serbs;* their language, the *Serbish* language. Although in fact two distinct tribes, and speaking different dialects, yet their early history cannot well be separated. After the dissolution of the great kingdom of Thuringia by the Francs and Saxons in the year 1528, the Sorabians, or Sorbæ, took possession of the countries left by the Hermunduri, viz. the territory between the Harz mountains, the Saale, and the Erzgebirge, and extended their dominion in a northern direction to the seats of their brethren, the Ukrians, and towards the east as far as to the region in which their near relations, the Lekhes, about the same time had settled. They made slaves of the few German inhabitants whom they found scattered through this country; and, according to their industrious habits, began immediately after their arrival to cultivate the soil, to build cities, and to trade in the productions of the country. Although not strictly a warlike people, they were able for several centuries to defend their frontiers against the frequent attacks of their German neighbours on the other side of the Saale, and to give them trouble in return. But they yielded before the arms of Charlemagne; and after a short interval of renewed independence, they were completely subjugated and made tributary by Henry I. Their country, according to the German custom, was divided into *marches*, and populated with German settlers. These latter more especially occupied the towns, and built villages among the woods and mountains; whilst the Vendes, chiefly addicted to agriculture, continued to occupy the plains. But even on the plains, there soon arose the castles of German knights, their masters and oppressors; and the Vendish population was by degrees reduced to the miserable condition of serfs.

In the year 968, the first attempt was made to convert them to Christianity, partly by the sword of the conqueror, partly by the instruction of Christian missionaries. But more than one century passed away, before the Christian religion was fully introduced among them. Benno, bishop of Meissen, who died in A. D. 1106, at the age of ninety-six, acquired by his activity in the work of converting the Vendes, the name of the apostle of the Slavi. The obstinate resistance with which the Christian religion had been rejected by them, can easily be explained by the unjudicious, nay flagitious way, in which it was presented to them by the Germans; who came among them, the sword in one hand and the cross in the other; and exacted moreover from them the sacrifice of their language, their customs, their whole nationality in exchange. The naturally childlike and submissive disposition of the Slavi rendered them in all other regions, as we have seen, willing to receive the Christian doctrines, more especially when their superiors themselves acted as their apostles, as was in some measure the case with the Russian Vladimir, Jagello in Lithuania, etc.[2] But the mode described above, which was adopted by the German heroes, not only among the Vendes, but also some centuries later among the old Borussians, could not but rouse all their feelings of pride and nationality to a decided resistance. Even when the Germans refrained from force, their means of conversion were equally opposed to the spirit of Christianity. Bishop Otho of Bamberg, for instance, was accustomed, when on his missionary travels, to have fifty or more wagons in his train loaded with cloth, victuals, and other supplies, in order to reward on the spot those who submitted to baptism.[3]

But the holy light of Christianity, even after the Vendish tribes had embraced its doctrines, did not clear up the darkness of their fate. The whole humiliating relation between masters and serfs in Germany, which still degraded the last century, was unknown to the free ancient Germans, among whom only the prisoner of war was a slave; and is derived from the period of the submission of the Vendes. The Germans indeed seem to have considered them as an inferior race, and treated them accordingly. The contempt with which the old historians speak of them, is revolting to every liberal and unprejudiced mind, and can hardly be explained. For the Sorabians seem to have been at the time of their submission, superior on the

---

[2] "On a certain day all the inhabitants of Kief were assembled on the banks of the Dnieper, and on a signal from the monarch, all plunged into the river, some to the waist, others to the neck; parents held their children in their arms while the ceremony was performed by the priests in attendance. Thus a nation received baptism, not only without murmuring, but with cheerfulness; for all were convinced that a religion, embraced by the sovereign and boyards, must necessarily be the best in the world." Foreign Quart. Review, Art. on Karamsin's History of Russia, Vol. III. p. 160. Compare Henderson's Travels in Russia, p. 191.

[3] See Cramer's *Pommersche Kirchen-Historie*, L. I. c. 29.

whole to the Germans in respect to civilization; although in consequence of this contemptuous treatment, they in the course of time fell far behind them. Despised and oppressed, they were kept for centuries in a state of ignorance and neglect; from which, it seems, they could only escape by renouncing their Slavic peculiarities, and above all their language. The use of this latter before courts of justice was in the fourteenth century forbidden by law throughout most of the country. In the beginning of the same century, the Vendish language was still sometimes heard at Leipzig, but not afterwards. In the villages also it became wholly extinct fifty or a hundred years later; and only single words passed over into the German language. But this was not the case with their usages and other national peculiarities; there are still several tribes, nay the peasants of whole provinces in this part of Germany, in whom the Slavic origin can be distinctly traced.[4] Their language however was driven into the remotest eastern corner of their former extensive territory; and is there, and only there, still to be heard. We speak of the province called Lusatia, situated between Saxony, Bohemia, Silesia, and Brandenburg, of which the greatest part is at present under the Prussian dominion, and the smallest but richest portion under that of Saxony.

Lushitze, Lusatia, Germ. *Lausitz*, signifies in Slavic, a low marshland. This name was formerly applied only to the north-eastern part of this province, or Lower Lusatia, which is, or was at least at the time of the Vendish settlement, a country of that description. At a later period, the name was carried over very

[4] Among others the peasants of the duchy of Altenburg, who are highly respectable through a certain degree of cultivation rare among German peasants, and distinguished for their wealth and prosperous condition. Although long since perfectly Germanized, certain Vendish usages have been kept up among them, more especially at weddings and similar festivals, the details of which are very interesting.

improperly to the south-western part, or Upper Lusatia, a beautiful and mountainous region. Lusatia was given by Henry I, as a fief, to the margrave of Meissen. In the course of the following centuries, its two parts were repeatedly separated and reunited, alternately under the dominion of the last named margrave, of Poland, or of Bohemia, without however belonging to the German empire. In the fourteenth century it was at length incorporated with Bohemia, and remained so for nearly three hundred years. To this circumstance alone the partial preservation of the Vendish language is to be ascribed. At the peace of Prague, A. D. 1636, it was allotted to Saxony. At the congress of Vienna in 1815, it was assigned, with the exception of the smaller half of Upper Lusatia, to Prussia, to which monarchy it still belongs.

1. *Language of the Sorabians in Upper Lusatia.*

The cities of Bautzen, Zittau, Kamenz, Löbau, and their districts, form the Saxon part of Upper Lusatia. Of its 195,000 inhabitants, about the fourth or fifth part still speak the Vendish language. In the north-eastern part of Upper Lusatia, which belongs to Prussia, there is about the same proportion of Vendish inhabitants In both territories the whole number of Vendes is about 100,000. Their language is very nearly related to the Bohemian; where the Sorabians of Lower Lusatia and the Poles pronounce the letter *h*, the Upper Lusatians and Bohemians give the sound of *g*. Both Lusatian dialects have of course lost very many of their original peculiarities; thus both have adopted the article from the German language.

The Reformation exhibited here, as every where, its favourable influence on the vernacular language. The bishops of

Meissen, to whose diocese Lusatia belonged, had indeed repeatedly admonished the priests and curates, to whose care the spiritual welfare of the poor Slavic Lusatians was intrusted, to learn the language of the people; but no particular pains was taken; and the Romish clergy, who spoke of the natives with the utmost contempt, were quite satisfied to hear the people say *Amen* and *Kyrie Eleison* after their own Latin prayers. As Lusatia lies near to the scene of Luther's earliest influence, the Gospel was preached early to the Slavic inhabitants by some of his followers; and it had the natural consequence, that the Romish clergy also began to give some attention to the vernacular language. In 1550, if not before, a Sorabian translation of the New Testament, the manuscript and perhaps the autograph of which is preserved in the library of Berlin, was completed; but it was never printed; probably because during the melancholy period of the "Interim" so called, which commenced about that time, the energies of the Protestants were in some measure paralyzed. Towards the end of the century Luther's smaller Catechism, and several other religious and doctrinal tracts, were translated from the German, mostly by clergymen, and introduced into the schools; chiefly the village schools; for the cities were steadily becoming more and more Germanized.

The neglect and decline of the Sorabian population was however always painfully felt by some patriotic individuals; and the very injudicious and tyrannic attempts of their German rulers, during the seventeenth century, to eradicate the language and supplant it by the German, found in all places only a reluctant and forced submission. But the effect of appointing every where German magistrates and German pastors was irresistible. The language was gradually forgotten by the rising generation; and hardly a Vendish book was printed during the first three quarters of the seventeenth century. Indeed hardly any one knew how to write in a language, the orthography and grammar of which had not yet been subjected to any rules or principles.

In 1679 the Jesuit Jacob Ticinus, a native of Lusatia, in a little Latin pamphlet, advised his countrymen to adopt the rules of orthography current in the Bohemian language, so nearly related to their own.[5] But the Protestants among them, who constituted the principal part in number and respectability, rejected his advice; and preferred to adopt the rules established shortly afterwards by a German clergyman, Z. J. Bierling.[6] This was a system between the Bohemian and the German, and is still observed. It was probably a sense of the approaching danger of an ultimate total extirpation of their language, that roused the slumbering Vendes again to some efforts. Parts of the Gospels were published towards the close of the same century by Michael Frenzel; and in 1706 the whole New Testament appeared in a Vendish translation, conformed to Luther's German one.

A translation of the whole Bible, made by several Protestant clergymen, was first published in 1729; and has been twice reprinted. A version for Catholics, by A. Swotlik, is extant in manuscript. A German hymn-book for the latter already existed in 1696; and in 1710 the Protestants were likewise supplied with one. In the former the orthography of Ticinus was followed; while the latter was printed according to the system of Bierling. Thus this handful of people, surrounded by German adversaries and underminers of their nationality, and who would have had hard work enough even if they had stood as one man in their own defence, were split into parties, even in things the most indifferent; and thus made their own weakness still weaker.

The Protestants succeeded at last in the establishment of a

---

[5] *Principia linguae Vandalicae seu Wendica,* Prague 1679–1682.

[6] *Didascalia sive Orthographia Vandalica,* Bautzen 1689.

seminary for the education of Vendish ministers at Leipzig in 1716. Another was instituted at Wittenberg, A. D. 1749. Their literature continued to be almost exclusively of a religious kind; and consisted mostly of translations from the German. Another *Wendische Grammatica* was written by G. Matthei, one of the translators of the Vendish Bible. A dictionary was prepared by Frencel.[7] Both works can now only be considered as curiosities. The latter proceeds upon the firm conviction, that the Slavi were originally Hebrews; and contrives to point out in all the substantives or nouns of the Sorabian language a certain degree of analogy. The only philological works, which will be of use to those who may wish to study this Slavic dialect in our day, is a short grammar by Seiler,[8] and a more modern one by J. P. Jordan. The latter has adopted the system of orthography best adapted to the language, viz. that introduced by Dobrovsky for the Bohemian.[9]

The Upper Lusatian dialect has acquired in this way a degree of cultivation, which of course, since most of those who speak and read it are of the common people, comparatively few are able to appreciate. In religious hymns, there is no deficiency; and several cantos of Klopstock's Messiah have been translated into it by Möhn, in the measure of the original. In regard to the popu-

---

[7] *De Originibus linguae Sorabicae* M. Abrah. Frencelii, Budiss. et Zwickau 1693–96.

[8] *Kurzgefasste Grammatik der Sorben-Wendischen Sprache*, Bautzen 1828.

[9] *Grammatik der wendisch-sorbischen Sprache in der Ober Lausitz. Im Systeme Dobrovsky's abgefasst*, von J. P. Jordan, Prague 1841. Here may be mentioned also, *Maly Sserb*, i. e. *der kleine Serbe, wendische-deutsche Gespräche etc. mit einem wendisch-deutschen und deutsch-wendischen Wörterbuch, etc.* von J. E. Schmaler, Bautzen 1841.—There exists besides this only one Sorabian Dictionary, and this in Latin, *Vocabularium latino-sorbicum*, by G. A. Swotlik, Bautzen 1721.

lar songs of the Sorabians, a kind of poetry in which most Slavic nations are so rich, no pains was taken until recently to discover whether they had any or not. But when on the publication of the remarkable Servian ballads, the interest of the German public in this species of poetry became strongly excited, the Saxon minister of state, baron Nostitz, himself an esteemed German poet, turned his attention particularly to this subject; and succeeded in collecting several little songs full of that sweet, half pensive, half roguish feeling, which characterizes Slavic popular poetry in general. They were translated by him and communicated in manuscript to his friends; but whether they have ever been printed we are not informed.

This subject, however, was not long suffered to rest. Two societies have been formed within the last twelve years, one at Breslau among the students of the university natives of Lusatia; the other at Bautzen among the scholars of the Gymnasium or High School; for the promotion of their native language and extending the knowledge of the antiquities of their country. Both these societies of the rising generation are favoured and assisted by gentlemen who take a general interest in Slavic affairs. Another learned society, called "The Scientific society of Upper Lusatia," a union of scholars, had been founded previously. In 1836, this society offered a premium for collecting a certain number of genuine songs with their melodies, still extant among the common people. The result has been a very valuable collection. The first numbers appeared in 1841; and the whole will form a standard work in the literature of popular poetry. It was an agreeable surprise to find, that even these isolated Slavic tribes, who have been so long separated from other nations related to them, were still in possession of a store of genuine Slavic ballads and ancient melodies; while, on the other hand, many other ballads were found among them, in which the influence of their German neighbours, or perhaps their own influence on the latter, could be distinctly traced. Ballads and ditties, known to have been sung centuries before in Hessia or on the Rhine, rose suddenly from the night of an unheeded existence; disguised, indeed, but easily recognized, in a Slavic dress, which bore indications of the same antiquity.[10]

2. *Language of the Sorabians in Lower Lusatia.*

Lower Lusatia, or the north-eastern part of the Lusatian territory, together with the adjacent circle of Cotbus in Brandenburg, has about the same number of Vendish inhabitants as the upper province. The dialect they speak has a strong affinity with the Polish; but is, like that of their brethren in Upper Lusatia, corrupted by German interpolations, and even in a still greater degree. It is obviously on the decline; and we can only expect, that after the lapse of a hundred years or less, no other vestige of it will be left than written or printed documents.

The first book known to have been printed in this dialect, which is written according to a peculiar combination of the German letters, is Möller's Hymns, Catechism, and Liturgy, Bautzen 1574. Their present literature, like that of Upper Lusatia, is confined to works for religious instruction, grammars, and dictionaries. Of the former they possess no small number. They have also a complete version of the Bible. The New Testament was translated for them as early as 1709, by Fabricius, and printed together with the German text. It has been repeatedly reprinted; and

[10] *Volkslieder der Wenden in der Ober und Nieder Lausitz, und mit den Sangweisen, deutsher Uebersetzung, etc.* herausgegeben von Leopold Haupt und J. E. Schmaler, Grimma 1841, 2 vols. The second volume contains the songs in the dialect of Lower Lusatia.

in the year 1798 a translation of the Old Testament by Fritze was added.[11]

---

[11] Philological works on this dialect are the following: Hauptmann's *Wendische Sprachlehre,* Lübben 1761. *Kurze Anleitung zur Wend. Sprache,* 1746. Megiseri *Thesaurus Polyglottus,* Frankf. 1603; including the Lower Lusatian. Several vocabularies of this dialect are extant in manuscript; see Schaffarik's *Geschichte,* p. 486.

PART IV.

SKETCH OF THE POPULAR POETRY OF THE SLAVIC NATIONS.

In the preceding view of the literature of the Slavic nations, we have abstained from giving any specimens of their poetry. A *few* would not have satisfied the reader, and could not have done justice to poets, who each for himself has a literary character of his own; and *many* would have at least doubled the size of this volume. Shukovsky, Pushkin, Mickewicz, Brodzinski, Krasinski, Kollar—each, as we said, has an individual poetical character of his own, of which the reader could have gathered no just idea without a whole series of their productions; and these even then would have lost half their value in a translation. Yet they all have little of that peculiar *Slavic* character, which belongs still in some degree to all Slavic nations; and which is so strikingly expressed in their Popular Poetry.

Our remark respecting the loss of the principal charms which all poetical productions have to undergo, when clothed in a foreign dress, applies as well to popular poetry as to the works of literature, and even more. Indeed, if any kind of poetry must needs lose half its beauties in a translation, the truth of the Latin saying, *Dulcius ex ipsa fonte bibuntur aquæ*, will never be more readily acknowledged, than in respect to the idiomatic peculiarities of popular ballads. This holds good principally of merely lyric productions, the only kind of songs which are left to some of the Slavic tribes. They are grown into the very bone and marrow of the language itself; and a congenial spirit can at the utmost imitate, but never satisfactorily translate them. And yet they are the most essential features in the physiognomy of a people; or, as Görres expresses it, they are like pulse and breath, the signs and the measure of the internal life. "While the great *epic* streams," as this ingenious writer justly says, "reflect the character of a whole wide-spread river-district, in time and history, these lyric effusions are the sources and fountains, which, with their net-work of rills, water and drain the whole country; and, bringing to light the secrets of its inmost bowels, pour out into lays its warmest heart's blood."[1] We therefore give the specimens of Slavic popular poetry, which we here present to the reader, not merely as poems to be admired, but rather as characteristic features of the mental condition of the respective nations, and of their manner of thinking and feeling.

This is the age of utilitarianism. The Genius of poetry still lives indeed, for he is immortal; but the period of his living power is gone. His present dwelling is the study; the sphere of his operations the parlour; the scene, where his exhibitions are displayed in a dress of morocco and gold, is the centre table of the rich and the genteel. *Popular poetry*,—we do not mean that divine gift, the dowry of a few blessed individuals; we mean that general productiveness, which pervades the mass of men as it pervades Nature,—popular poetry, among all the nations of Europe, is only a dying plant. Here and there a lonely relic is discovered among the rocks, preserved by the invigorating powers of the mountain air; or a few sickly plants, half withered in their birth, grow up in some solitary valley,

---

[1] *Volks und Meisterlieder*, Frankf. a. M. 1817.

hidden from the intrusive genius of modern improvement and civilization, who makes his appearance with a brush in his hand, sweeping mercilessly away even the loveliest flowers which may be considered as impediments in his path. Twenty years hence, and a trace will not be left, except the dried specimens which the *amateur* lays between two sheets of paper, and the copies preserved in cabinets.

Among the nations of the Slavic race alone is the living flower still to be found, growing in its native luxuriance; but even here, only among the Servians and Dalmatians in its full blossom and beauty. For centuries these treasures have been buried from the literary world. Addison, when he endeavored to vindicate his admiration of the ballad of "Chevy-Chace," by the similarity of some of its passages with the epics of Virgil and Homer, had not the remotest idea, that the immortal blind bard had found his true and most worthy successors among the likewise blind poets of his next Hyperborean neighbours. The merit of having lifted at last the curtain from these scenes, belongs to Germany, chiefly to Herder. But only the few last years have allowed a more full and satisfactory view of them.

In laying before our readers a sketch of Slavic popular poetry, we must renounce at once any attempt at chronological order. Slavic popular poetry has yet no history. Not that a considerable portion of it is not very ancient. Many mysterious sounds, even from the gray ages of paganism, reach us, like the chimes of distant bells, unconnected and half lost in the air; while, of many other songs and legends, the colouring reminds us strongly of their Asiatic home. But the wonderful tales they convey, have mostly been only confined to tradition; especially there, where the fountain of poetry streamed, and streams still, in the richest profusion, namely, in Servia. Handed down from generation to generation, each has impressed its mark upon them. Tradition, that wonderful offspring of reality and imagination, affords no safer basis to the history of poetry, than to the history of nations themselves. To dig out of dust and rubbish a few fragments of manuscripts, which enable us to cast one glance into the night of the past, has been reserved only for recent times. Future years will furnish richer materials; and to the inquirer, who shall resume this subject fifty years after us, it may be permitted to reduce them to historical order; while we must be contented to appreciate those, which are before our eyes, in a moral and poetical respect.

The Slavi, even when first mentioned in history, appear as a singing race. Procopius, relating the surprise of a Slavic camp by the Greeks, states that the former were not aware of the danger, having lulled themselves to sleep by singing.[2] Karamzin, in his history of the Russian empire, narrates, on the authority of Byzantine writers, that the Greeks being at war with the Avars, about A. D. 590, took prisoners three Slavi, who were sent from the Baltic as ambassadors to the Khan of the Avars. These envoys carried, instead of weapons, a kind of guitar. They stated, that, having no iron in their country, they did not know how to manage swords and spears; and described singing and playing on the guitar as one of the principal occupations of their peaceful life.[3] The general prevalence of a musical ear and taste among all Slavic nations is indeed striking. "Where a Slavic woman is," says Schaffarik, "there is also song. House and yard, mountain and valley, meadow and forest, garden and vineyard, she fills them all with the sounds of her voice. Often, after a wearisome day spent in heat and sweat, hunger and thirst, she animates, on her way home, the silence of the

---

[2] *De Bello Gothico*, lib. iii. c. 14.

[3] Vol. I. p. 69.

evening twilight with her melodious songs. What spirit these popular songs breathe, the reader may learn from the collections already published. Without encountering contradiction, we may say, that among no other nation of Europe does natural poetry exist to such an extent, and in such purity, heartiness, and warmth of feeling, as among the Slavi."[4]

Although we recognize in the last sentence the voice of a Slavic enthusiast, we copy the whole of his remarks as perfectly true; and would only add, that we do not consider "heartiness and warmth of feeling" more a characteristic feature of Slavic than of Teutonic popular poetry. As for the purity and universality with which popular poetry is preserved among the Slavic nations, we strongly fear, that the chief cause of these advantages lies in the barrenness of their literature, and in the utter ignorance among the common people even of its elements.

Before we attempt to carry our reader more deeply into this subject, we must ask him to divest himself as much as possible of his personal and national feelings, views, and prejudices, and to suffer himself to be transported into a world foreign to his habitual course of ideas. Human feelings, it is true, are the same every where; but we have more of the artificial and factitious in us than we are aware of. And in many cases, we hold, that it is not the worst part of us; for we are far from belonging to the class of advocates of mere nature. The reader, for instance, must not expect to find in all the immense treasure of Slavic love-songs, adapted to a variety of situations, a single trace of *romance*, that beautiful blossom of Christianity among the Teutonic races. The love expressed in the Slavic songs is the natural, heartfelt, overpowering sensation of the human breast, in all its different shades of tender affection and glowing sensuality; never elevating but always natural, always unsophis-

[4] *Geschichte der Slavischen Sprache und Literatur,* p. 52.

ticated, and much deeper, much purer in the female heart, than in that of man. In their heroic songs, also, the reader must not expect to meet with the chivalry of the more western nations. Weak vestiges of this kind of exaltation, with a few exceptions, are to be found among those Slavic nations only, who, by frequent intercourse with other races, adopted in part their feelings. The gigantic heroism of the Slavic Woiwodes and Boyars is not the bravery of honour; it is the valour of manly strength, the valour of the heroes of Homer. The Servian hero, Marko Kralyewitch, was regarded by Goethe as the personification of *absolute* heroism; but even Marko does not think it beneath him to flee, when he meets one stronger than himself. These are the dictates of nature, which only an artificial point of honour can overcome.

But, for the full enjoyment of Slavic popular poetry, we must exact still more from the reader. He must not only divest himself of his habitual ideas and views, but he must adopt foreign views and prejudices, in order to understand motives and actions; for the Oriental races are far from being more in a state of pure nature than ourselves. He will have to transport himself into a foreign clime, where the East and the West, the North and the South, blend in wonderful amalgamation. The suppleness of Asia and the energy of Europe, the passive fatalism of the Turk and the active religion of the Christian, the revengeful spirit of the oppressed, and the child-like resignation of him who cheerfully submits,—all these seeming contradictions find an expressive organ in Slavic popular poetry. Even in respect to his moral feelings, the reader will frequently have to adopt a different standard of right and wrong. Actions, which a Scotch ballad sometimes shields by a seductive excuse,—as for instance in the case of "Lady Barnard and Little Musgrave," where we become half reconciled to the violation of congujal faith by the tragic end of the transgressors,—are detestable crimes in the eyes of the Servian poet. On the other hand, he relates with applause deeds of vengeance and violence, which all feelings of Christianity teach us to condemn; and even atrocious barbarities, which chill our blood, he narrates with perfect composure. This latter remark refers, in fact, chiefly to the ancient epics of the Servians. Much less of barbarism and wild revenge meets us in their modern productions, namely, the epic poems relating to the war of deliverance in the beginning of the present century; although their oppressors had given them ample cause for a merciless retaliation. In the shorter and more lyric songs, of which a rich treasure is the property of most Slavic nations, and in which their common descent is most strikingly manifested, there prevails a still purer morality, and the most tender feelings of the human breast are displayed.

It was on account of this decidedly exotic character of Slavic popular poetry, that, when the author of the present work first published a German version of the Servian popular songs, Goethe considered it as an advantage, that the work of translation had fallen into the hands of a lady. Only a female mind, the great poet thought, was capable of the degree of accommodation requisite to clothe the "barbarian poems" in a dress, in which they could be relished by readers of nations foreign to their genius. Even the love-songs, although "of the highest beauty," he thought could only be enjoyed *en masse.* But this last remark applies in a certain measure to all popular poetry; for these little songs are like the warblings of the wood-birds; and a single voice would do little justice to the whole. The monotonous chirping of one little feathered singer is tedious or burdensome; while we enjoy their full concert as the sweetest music of nature. One swallow does not make a summer. But the whole blissful sense of nature waking from her wintry sleep comes over you, when you hear the full, mixed chorus of the little songsters of the grove; and the monotonous cry of the cuckoo seems to belong just as much to the completeness of the concert, as the enchanting solo of the nightingale.

If we attempt to characterize Slavic popular poetry as a whole, we have chiefly to consider those shorter songs, which are common to all Slavic tribes, and which alone can be compared to the ballads of other nations. For, among the Slavi, only the Servians, including the Dalmatians, Montenegrins, and Croats, who speak the same language,—and indeed among all other modern nations they alone,—possess long popular epics, of a heroic character. What of this species of poetry still survives among the other Slavic nations, or indeed in any other country of Europe, is only the echo of former times. The endlessly protracted "Storie" of the Italians are, indeed, often longer than the Servian heroic tales; but in no other respect do they afford a point of comparison with them.

The Slavic popular songs have nothing, or very little, of the bold dramatic character which animates the Scotch, German, and Scandinavian ballads. Even dialogues occur seldom, except in some narrative form; as for instance:

> To her brother thus the lady answered;

or,

> And the bonny maiden asked her mother.

A division into epic and lyric ballads would also be difficult. A considerable portion, especially of the Russian and Servian songs, begin with a few narrative verses; although the chief part of the song is purely lyric. These introductory verses are frequently allegorical; and if we do not always find a connection between them and the tale or song which follows, it is because one singer borrows these introductions from another, and adds an extemporaneous effusion of his own. These little allegories, however, frequently give a complete picture of the subject. They are, also, not always confined to the introduction, but spun out through the whole poem. The following Russian elegy on the death of a murdered youth, may illustrate our remarks. We translate as literally as possible. The Russian original, like the translation, has no rhymes.[5]

ELEGY.

O thou field! thou clean and level field!
O thou plain, so far and wide around!
Level field, dressed up with every thing,
Every thing; with sky-blue flowerets small,
Fresh green grass, and bushes thick with leaves;
But defaced by one thing, but by one!

For in thy very middle stands a broom,
On the broom a young gray eagle sits,
And he butchers wild a raven black,
Sucks the raven's heart-blood glowing hot,
Drenches with it, too, the moistened earth.
Ah, black raven, youth so good and brave!
Thy destroyer is the eagle gray.

Not a swallow 't is, that hovering clings,
Hovering clings to her warm little nest;
To the murdered son the mother clings.
And her tears fall like the rushing stream,
And his sister's like the flowing rill;
Like the dew the tears fall of his love:
When the sun shines, it dries up the dew.

---

[5] This song is among the few, which Russian critics think as ancient as the sixteenth century. See Karamzin's *History of Russia*, Vol. X. p. 264.

Servian songs begin also frequently with a series of questions, the answers to which form mostly a very happy introduction to the tale. For instance:

What's so white upon yon verdant forest?
Is it snow, or is it swans assembled?
Were it snow, it surely had been melted;
Were it swans, long since they had departed.
Lo! it is not swans, it is not snow, there,
'T is the tents of Aga, Hassan Aga, etc.[6]

In Russian songs, on the other hand, a form of expression frequently occurs, which we venture to call a negative antithesis. It is less clear than the Servian, but just as peculiar. A preceding question seems to be frequently supposed; as we have also seen in the piece adduced above. "It is not a swallow," the poet says, "that clings to her nest; it is a mother who clings to her son." In other songs we hear:

Not a *falcon* floateth through the air,
Strays a *youth* along the river's brim, etc.

or,

Not a cuckoo in the forest cool doth sing,
Not in the gardens sings a nightingale;
In the prison dark a brave youth sighs,
He sighs and pours out many parting tears.

The frequency of standing epithets, characteristic more or less of all popular poetry, is particularly observable among the Slavic nations. The translator will be troubled to find corresponding terms; but whatever he may select, it is essential always

---

[6] Bowring's translation.

to employ the same; for instance, he must not translate the far-extended idea of *bjeloi*, white, alternately by *white*, *bright*, *snowy*, *fair*. In Slavic, not only things really white are called so, but every thing *laudable* and *beautiful* is called white; as, the *white* God, i. e. the *good* God; the *white* Tzar, i. e. the monarch of *white*, or great and powerful, Russia. In most cases the poet himself no longer thinks of the signification and original meaning of the word. Yards, walls, bodies, breasts, hands, etc. are invariably *white;* even the breast and the hand of the tawny Moor. The sea is seldom mentioned without the epithet *blue;* Russian heroes have *black* hair, but the head of the Servian hero is called *Rusja glava*, fair-haired, with a reddish shade. Russian youths, together with their steeds, are invariably *dobroe*, that is, good or brave; the heart is in the poetry of the same nation *retivoe*, cheerful, rash, light. The sun is in Servian *yarko*, bright; in Russian *krasnoi*, which signifies fair and red. Doves are in both languages *gray*. How much the poets are accustomed to these epithets, and how heedlessly they use them, appears from a Servian tale, called "Haykuna's Wedding," a charming poem, and even much more elaborated than is common, where the breasts of a beautiful girl are compared to two gray doves. To remind our readers of the father of popular poetry, Homer, and of the like use by him of stereotype epithets, is unnecessary.

The Slavic popular ballads, like the Spanish, very seldom lay any claim to completeness. They do not pretend to give you a whole story, but only a *scene*. They are, for the most part, little pictures of isolated situations, from which it is left to the imagination of the hearers to infer the whole. The narrative part is almost always descriptive, and, as such, eminently *plastic*. If the picture represented has not the dramatic vivacity of the ballads of the Teutonic nations, it has the distinctness, the prominent forms, and often the perfection of the best executed bas-reliefs of the ancients. Like these, the Slavic poems seldom represent wild passions or complicated actions; but, by preference, scenes of rest, and mostly scenes of domestic grief or joy. When we look at the celebrated Greek bas-relief, which represents an affianced maiden the evening before her wedding, weeping, or bashfully hiding her fair face, while a servant girl washes her feet,[7] we cannot help being impressed with just the same feelings, which seize us when we hear or read one of the numerous Slavic songs devoted to similar scenes. To illustrate our remarks, and to make our readers understand exactly what we call the *plastic* character of Slavic popular songs, we insert here the following Servian love-scene. We add, that it was one of Goethe's favourites, worthy, in his opinion, to be compared with the Canticles.[8] There is a melody in the language of this song, not to be imitated in any translation. We confess that Frederic Schlegel's definition of architecture, " frozen music," occurs to us when we read it in the original.

JOVO AND MARIA.

'Cross the field a breeze it bore the roses,
Bore them far into the tent of Jovo ;
In the tent were Jovo and Maria,
Jovo writing and Maria broidering.
Used has Jovo all his ink and paper,
Used Maria all her burnished gold-thread.
Thus accosted Jovo then Maria ;
" O sweet love, my dearest soul, Maria,
Tell me, is my soul then dear unto thee ?
Or my hand find'st thou it hard to rest on ?"
Then with gentle voice replied Maria ;
" O, in faith, my heart and soul, my Jovo,

[7] The piece to which we allude was in the possession of the Cardinal Albani, at Rome ; but has since been carried to England. A fine copy in plaster is in the Museum at Paris ; from which numerous drawings have been taken, now scattered all over Europe.

[8] *Kunst und Alterthum,* Vol. II. p. 49.

Dearer is to me thy soul, O dearest,
Than my brothers, all the four together.
Softer is thy hand to me to rest on,
Than four cushions, softest of the soft ones." [9]

The high antiquity of Slavic popular poetry is manifest among other things, in the frequent mythological features which occur. In the ballads of the Teutonic nations, we recollect very few instances of talking animals. As to those which talk in nursery tales, we are always sure to discover in them enchanted princes or princesses. In one Scotch ballad, "The Gray Goshawk," a horse speaks; and, in a few other instances, falcons and nightingales. In Spanish popular poetry we do not meet with a single similar example. In the songs of all the Slavic nations, conversing, thinking, sympathizing animals are very common. No one wonders at it. The giant Tugarin Dragonson's steed warns him of every danger. The great hero Marko's horse even weeps, when he feels that the death of his master approaches. Nay, life is breathed even into inanimate objects by the imagination of Slavic girls and youths. A Servian youth contracts a regular league of friendship and brotherhood with a bramble-bush, in order to induce it to catch his coy love's clothes, when she flees before his kisses. Even the stars and planets sympathize with human beings, and live in constant intercourse with them and their affairs. Stars become messengers; a proud maiden boasts to be more beautiful than the sun; the sun takes it ill, and is advised to burn her coal-black in revenge. The moon hides herself in the clouds when the great Tzar dies. One of the most interesting Servian tales, called "The Heritage," is the fruit of the moon and the morning star's gossiping with each other. It begins thus:

---

[9] *Narodne Srpske Pjesne skup. i izd. Vuk* etc. Leipz. 1824. Vol. I. p. 55. *Volkslieder der Serben, von Talvj,* Halle 1825. Vol. I. p. 46.

To the morning star the moon spake chiding;
"Morning star, say where hast thou been wandering?
Where hast thou been wandering and where lingering,
Where hast thou three full white days been lingering?"

To the moon the morning star has answered;
"I've been wandering, I've three days been lingering,
O'er the white walls of the fortress Belgrade,
Gazing there on strange events and wonders."

The events which the star had witnessed, it now proceeds to relate to the moon; and these make the subject of this beautiful tale.

After having touched upon these general features, did our limits permit, we should speak more at large of those mythological beings of a more distinct character, which belong to the individual Slavic races; for example, the Vila of the Servians, the Russalki of the Malo-Russians, and the like; at least so far as this belief is interwoven in their poetry, the only respect in which it concerns us here. But we must confine ourselves to a few brief remarks.

The strong and deeply-rooted superstitions of the Slavic nations are partly manifest in their songs and tales; these are full of foreboding dreams, and good or bad omens; witchcraft of various kinds is practised; and a certain oriental fatalism seems to direct will and destiny. The connection with the other world appears nevertheless much looser, than is the case with the Teutonic nations. There is no trace of spirits in Russian ballads; although spectres appear occasionally in Russian nursery tales. In Servian, Bohemian, and Slovakian songs, it occurs frequently, that the voices of the dead sound from their graves; and thus a kind of soothing intercourse is kept up between the living and the departed. The superstition of a certain species of blood-sucking spectres, known to the novel-reading world under the name of *vampyres*, a superstition retained chiefly in Dalmatia, belongs also here. In modern Greek, such a spectre is called *Brukolacas* in Servian *Wukodlak.* We do not however recollect the appearance of a vampyre, in any genuine production of modern Greek or Servian poetry. It seems as if the sound sense of the common people had taught them, that this superstition is too shocking, too disgusting, to be admitted into poetry; while the oversated palates of the fashionable reading world crave the strongest and most stimulating food, and can only be satisfied by the most powerful excitement.

In the whole series of Slavic ballads and songs, which lie before our eyes, we meet with only one instance of the return of a deceased person to this world, in the like gloomy and mysterious way, in which the Christian nations of the North and West are wont to represent such an event. This is in the beautiful Servian tale, "Jelitza[10] and her Brothers." As it is too long to be inserted here entire, we must be satisfied with a sketch of it. Jelitza, the beloved sister of nine brothers, is married to a Ban on the other side of the sea. She departs reluctantly, and is consoled only by the promise of her brothers to visit her frequently. But "the plague of the Lord" destroys them all; and Jelitza, unvisited and apparently neglected by her brothers, pines away and sighs so bitterly from morning to evening, that the Lord in heaven takes pity on her. He summons two of his angels before him;

"Hasten down to earth, ye my two angels,
To the white grave where Jován lies buried,
The lad Jován, Jelitza's youngest brother;
Into him, my angels, breathe your spirit,

[10] Pronounced *Yelitza.*

Make for him a horse of his white grave-stone,
Knead a loaf from the black mould beneath him,
And the presents cut out from his grave-shroud;
Thus equip him for his promised visit."

The angels do as they are bidden. Jelitza receives her brother with delight, and asks of him a thousand questions, to which he gives evasive answers. After three days are past, he must away; but she insists on accompanying him home. Nothing can deter her. When they come to the church-yard, the lad Jován's home, he leaves her under a pretext and goes back into his grave. She waits long, and at last follows him. When she sees the nine fresh graves, a painful presentiment seizes her. She hurries to the house of her mother. When she knocks at the door, the aged mother, half distracted, thinks it is "the plague of the Lord," which, after having carried off her nine sons, comes for her. The mother and daughter die in each other's arms.[11]

This simple and affecting tale affords, then, the only instance, in Slavic popular poetry, of a regular apparition; but even here that apparition has, as our readers have seen, a character very different from that of a Scotch or German ghost. The same ballad exists also in modern Greek; although in a shape perhaps not equal in power and beauty to the Servian.[12]

---

[11] The whole of this tale is translated in Bowring's little volume of "Servian Popular Poetry."

[12] The Greek ballad is entitled "The Journey by Night," and begins thus:

Μάννα, μὲ τοὺς ἐννεά σου υἱούς, καὶ μὲ τὴν μιά σου κόρη.

'O mother, thou, with thy nine sons, and with thine only daughter.'

A Russian ballad also begins very similarly:

"At Kief, in that famous town,
Resided a rich widow;
Nine sons the widow of Kief had,
The tenth was a daughter dear.

The story however is essentially different.

But the very circumstance that its subject is so isolated among the Slavic nations, who are so ready to seize other poetical ideas and to mould them in various ways, leads us to believe, that the Servian poet must have heard somehow or other the Greek ballad, or a similar one; and that the subject of the Servian ballad, although this is familiar to all classes, was originally a stranger in Servia. Nowhere indeed, in the whole range of Slavic popular poetry, do we meet with that mysterious gloom, with those enigmatical contradictions, which are peculiar to the world of spirits of the Teutonic North; and which we think find their best explanation in the antithesis between the principles of Christianity, and the ruins of paganism on which it was built.

It is true, that, wherever Christianity has been carried, similar contradictions must necessarily have taken place; but the mind of the Slavic nations, so far as it is manifest in their poetry, seems never to have been perplexed by these contradictions. History shows, that the Slavic nations, with the exception of those tribes who were excited to headstrong opposition by the cruelty and imprudence of their German converters, received Christianity with childlike submission; in most cases principally because their superiors adopted it.[13] Vladimir the Great, to whom the Gospel and the Koran were offered at the same time, was long undecided which to choose; and was at last induced to embrace the former, because "his Russians could not live without the pleasure of drinking."[14] The wooden idols, it is true, were solemnly destroyed; but numerous fragments of their altars were suffered to remain undisturbed at the foot of the cross; and the passion-flower

---

[13] See above p. 306, n. 2.

[14] This remarkable fact is mentioned by all Russian historians, on the good authority of the ancient annalist Nestor.

grew up in the midst of the wild broom, the branches of which, tied together, the Tshuvash considers, even at the present day, as his tutelary spirit or Erich.[15] No struggle seems ever to have taken place, to reconcile these contradictory elements; while the more philosophical spirit of the Teutonic nations, and their genius for meditation and reflection, could not be so easily satisfied. The character of the Teutonic world of spirits is the reflex of this struggle. The foggy veil which covers their forms, the mysterious riddles in which their existence is wrapped, the anxious pensiveness which forms a part of their character, all are the results of these fruitless and mostly unconscious endeavours to amalgamate opposing elements. We cannot approach the region of their mysterious existence without an awful shuddering; while the few fairies, which Slavic poetry and superstition present us, strike us by the distinctness and freshness of their forms, and give us the unmingled impression either of the ludicrous or of the wild and fantastic.

It remains to speak of the moral character of Slavic popular poetry. If, in respect to its decency, we may judge from the printed collections, we must be struck with the purity of manners among the Slavic nations, and the unpollutedness of their imagination. Hacquet, speaking of the Slovenzi or Vindes, the Slavic inhabitants of Carniola, states, that the songs with which they

---

[15] "The Tshuvashes have a Penate, which they call Erich. This Erich is nothing but a bundle of broom, *cytisus*, tied together in the middle with the inner bark of the linden. It consists of fifteen branches of equal size, about four feet long; above is a piece of tin attached to it. Each house has such an Erich, which usually stands in a corner of the entry. Nobody ventures to touch it. When it becomes dry, a new Erich is tied together, and the old one placed in running water with great reverence." See *Stimmen des Russ. Volks*, von P. v. Goetze, Stuttg. 1828, page 17.—The

accompany their dances are often indecent.[16] But there is little dependence to be placed on judgments of this description. Sometimes expressions and ideas are rashly called indecent, which only differ from the conventional forms of decency without really violating its laws. Hacquet moreover only half understood those songs of the Slovenzi. We will at least not condemn them without having seen them. Among the Russian songs, there are some of a certain wanton and equivocal character, displaying with perfect *naïveté* a scarcely half-veiled sensuality. The boldness, with which these songs are sung in chorus by young peasant women, has often excited the astonishment of foreigners. The number of ballads of this description, however, so far as we are informed, is not considerable; and the character of Russian love-ballads in general is pure and chaste. As for the Servians, they have in fact a great multitude of songs of a very marked levity and frivolity; and Goethe, when these first appeared in the German version of Gerhardt, could not help finding it remarkable, that two nations, one half-barbarous, the other the most practised of all, (*die durchgeübteste*, meaning the French,) should meet together on the step of frivolous lyric poetry.[17] But these Servian songs are pure in comparison with many Grub-Street ballads and German *Zotenlieder*. The spirit of roguery and joviality, which prevails in them all, proves that they are more the overflowings of wild and unrestrained youth, than the fruits of dissoluteness of manners. They are often coarse, but never vulgar; they are indelicate, but they are not impudent. At any rate, we never meet in them that confounding of virtuous and vicious feelings, which has so often struck us

---

Tshuvashes, however, are not a Slavic, but a Finnish race, living under the Russian dominion.

[16] Dobrovsky's *Slavin*, 1834, p. 113.

[17] *Werke, Ausgabe letzter Hand*, Vol. XLVI. p. 332.

painfully even in the best Scotch and German ballads. We refer the reader here to our previous remarks on the measure of right and wrong, to be applied in our judgment of nations foreign to us in habits and pursuits. The heroes of the Servian epics are always represented as virtuous, often to harshness. Marko Kralyewitch is always ready to punish young women for any trespass against female modesty, by severing their heads from their shoulders; and even to his own bride, when he thinks her too obliging towards himself, he applies the most ignominious names, and threatens her with the sword.

Love and heroism, the principal subjects of all poetry, are also the most popular among the Slavi. But one of the peculiarities of their poetry is, that these two subjects are kept apart more than among other nations. While in the exploits of the Spanish heroes, which the popular Romances celebrate, love is so interwoven with heroism, and heroism with love, that we are not able to separate this two-fold exaltation of a generous mind, love is almost excluded from the heroic poems of the Slavi; or, at least, admitted only about in the same degree as in the epics of the ancients. It is seldom, if ever, the motive of the hero's actions. We need then add nothing more, to describe the character of Slavic heroism. It is never animated by romantic *love;* although sometimes, in the more modern epics of the Servians, by romantic *honour*. In one of the modern Servian tales, perhaps about a century old, which describes a duel between a Dalmatian Servian and a Turk, a scene of the most perfect chivalry occurs. The young Dalmatian captain, Vuk Jerinitch, having just reached manhood, inquires of the older captains, which of the Turks had most injured their country during the last invasion, while he was a child. The old captains name to him Zukan, the Turkish standard-bearer. Vuk consequently challenges him, proposing at the same time, in true Oriental character, that, himself having a beautiful sister and the Turk a wife of equal beauty, both shall belong to the victor. Zukan of course accepts the challenge. Their meeting is in the best chivalric style; they demand of each other no pledge or oath of faith, but meet in Vuk's tent with perfect confidence; they embrace and kiss each other, and make friendly inquiries after each other's health. The first hour of their meeting flies away in conviviality, and in admiration of the ladies. At last the desire to gain the Christian girl induces the Turk to interrupt their drinking. But, before they begin the fight, "they kiss each other on the cheeks, and forgive each other mutually their blood and death." This scene indeed has a decidedly Oriental costume; but the feelings, from which it results, are produced by as much of romantic exaltation as any Spanish romance could exhibit.

Goetze, in the introduction to his German translation of Russian popular ballads, observes: "In the Russian love songs we meet with more *softness* of feeling than romantic delicacy." We do not perceive any marked difference in that respect, between the character of Russian and of other Slavic erotic songs; and apply therefore his remark to the whole race. *Romantic* delicacy we must not, in fact, expect to find; but often all the natural delicacy of warm, tender, devoted love; all the freshness of youthful, unsophisticated feelings; all the burning passion of Spanish love, with the same strong tincture of sensuality; though seldom, very seldom, that depth, that infiniteness of the same feeling, so affectingly expressed in more than one popular ballad of the Scandinavians, Germans, and British,—that love which reaches far beyond the grave, and chains souls to each other even in different worlds. Russian lovers, who are compelled by circumstances to leave their mistresses, give frequently the following or similar advice:

Weep not, weep not, O sweet maid!
Choose, O choose another love!
Is he better, thou'lt forget me;
Is he worse, thou'lt think of me,
Think of me, sweet soul, and weep!

Love, among the Slavi, more than among any other Christian race, seems to be a *dream of youth*. Among unmarried persons of both sexes, free and easy intercourse is kept up. But nothing can favour less a free and lasting affection, than the national mode of contracting marriages. Among those Slavic nations, who have lived long in connection with the Teutonic races, the national manners have of course partly changed in this respect, as in others; especially among the higher classes. But among the Servians, the old Asiatic custom, according to which a marriage is agreed on by the parents of the parties, often without these knowing each other, is kept up in its fullest extent; and, even among all Slavic nations, strong traces of this custom are still left. Affianced Slavic girls often do not see their intended husbands before the wedding-day. Thus a girl, even in attaching herself to a youth, must early familiarize herself with the thought, that the time may come when she will have to take back her heart at her parent's bidding. Illegitimate love is rare; and is considered as the highest crime. Of the Russian popular songs, no small portion describe lovers taking leave of each other, because the youth or the maid must marry another; in another considerable portion, young married women are represented lamenting their miserable fate. The following popular ballad will afford the reader a characteristic specimen of the whole tenderness of such a Russian parting scene.

THE FAREWELL.

Brightly shining sank the waning moon,
And the sun all beautiful arose;

Not a falcon floated through the air,
Strayed a youth along the river's brim.
Slowly strayed he on and dreamingly,
Sighing looked unto the garden green,
Heart all filled with sorrow mused he so:
"All the little birds are now awake,
All, embracing with their little wings,
Greeting, all have sung their morning songs.
But, alas! that sweetest doveling mine,
She who was my youth's first dawning love,
In her chamber slumbers fast and deep.
Ah! not even her friend is in her dreams,
Ah! no thought of me bedims her soul,
While my heart is torn with wildest grief,
That she comes to meet me here no more."

Stepped the maiden from her chamber then;
Wet, O! wet with tears her lovely face,
All with sadness dimmed her eyes so clear,
Feebly drooping hung her snowy arms.
'T was no arrow that had pierced her heart,
'T was no adder that had stung her so;
Weeping, thus the lovely maid began:
"Fare thee well, beloved, fare thee well,
Dearest soul, thy father's dearest son!
I have been betrothed since yesterday;
Come, to-morrow, troops of wedding-guests;
To the altar, I, perforce, must go!
I shall be another's then; and yet
Thine, thine only, thine alone till death."

P.[18]

[18] In those four of our Russian specimens marked P, the translation is by J. G. Percival.

But the warm and tender hearts of the Slavic women, nevertheless, find means to satisfy that natural want of the female breast, to pour out on certain objects the whole blessing of love. *Family* connections are among no other race regarded as so holy, the ties of relationship are nowhere so cherished, as among the Slavi. Maternal tenderness is the subject of very many songs; and is set by comparisons in the most shining light. In the Russian ballad above adduced,[19] we have seen how slightly the poet thinks of the love of the wife; her tears are dried up by the sun, like the morning dew; while the mother's tears gush out incessantly like the waters of the mountain stream. In a Servian ballad, a youth wounds his hand. The Vila, a malicious mountain-nymph, offers to cure him. But she exacts a high price,—from his mother, her right hand; from his sister, her hair; and from his wife, her necklace of pearls. The mother willingly gives her right hand, and the sister her hair, but the wife refuses the necklace. The love of a mother is often described by the image of swallows, clinging to their own warm nest; or of tender doves, bereft of their young ones. The rights of a mother are respected with true filial piety, even by the barbarian hero Marko, who never fails to pay his aged mother filial respect.

More remarkable, however, in Slavic popular poetry, is the peculiar relation of the sister to the brother. This remark holds especially good of Servia. Sisters cling to their brothers with a peculiar warmth of feeling. These are their natural protectors, their supporters. They swear by the head of their brothers. To have no brother is a misfortune, almost a disgrace. A mourning female is represented in all Slavic poetry under the constant image of a cuckoo; and the cuckoo, according to the Servian legend, was a sister who had lost her brother. Numerous little

---

[19] Page 323.

songs illustrate the great importance which a Servian girl attaches to the possession of a brother. Those who have none, think even of artificial means for procuring one. This is exhibited in a pretty little ballad, where two sisters, who have no brother, make one out of white and pink silk wound around a stick of box-wood; and, after putting in two brilliant black stones as eyes, two leeches as eyebrows, and two rows of pearls as teeth, put honey in his mouth, and entreat him "to eat and to speak." In another ballad, of a more serious description, "George's young wife" loses at once in battle her husband, her brideman (*paranymphos*, in Servia a female's legitimate friend through life), and her brother. The gradations of the poetess in her description of the widow's mourning are very characteristic, and give no high idea of conjugal attachments in Servia.

For her husband, she has cut her hair;
For her brideman she has torn her face;
For her brother she has plucked her eyes out.
Hair she cut, her hair will grow again;
Face she tore, her face will heal again;
But the eyes, they'll never heal again,
Nor the heart, which bleedeth for the brother.

After having thus attempted to point out to the reader what we consider as the *general* characteristic features of Slavic popular poetry, we proceed to add a few remarks on the *distinguishing* traits of the different nations of the Slavic race individually, so far as our limits permit.

And here it is among the nations of the Eastern Stem that we must look for our principal harvest. We follow the same order as in the former parts of this work.

The Russians have very few ballads of high antiquity; and, even in this small number, hardly any one has reference to the heroic prose tales, which are the delight of Russian nurseries.

The Russians have indeed nursery tales (*skazki*) of all descriptions; and we have often heard, that, during the first decennium of the present century, still many an old-fashioned country squire, many a country gentlewoman brought up among her female slaves like an oriental princess, were in the habit of having themselves lulled to sleep by them. They are almost invariably told in the same words; and as much as possible with the same intonation of voice. One *Skazkochnik*, or *Skazkochnitza*, adopts this manner from another. The traditions of Vladimir and his giant heroes are the favourite, but not the exclusive subjects of these tales. They are also printed and sold separately; with a coarse woodcut on the upper part of every page, representing the scene described, and the back of the page empty. We are told that they are mostly got up by "Deacons," a class of the lower clergy, in their leisure hours. It is probable that these traditions formerly existed also in the shape of popular ballads; but no trace has been left of them. In the beginning of this century the work of Kirscha Danilof, of which we have spoken in our view of Russian literature,[20] was first published, containing the ancient traditions; written in the national prosodic measure, but without any poetical spirit; replete with anachronisms and absurdities, without the *naïveté* which can alone make these latter tolerable. They were, besides, full of interpolations; and were evidently the productions of a man from the people who had acquired half an education. For this reason they have never gained popularity in this shape.

The more modern heroic ballads of the Russians are of a remarkably tame character. Lawless and rebellious deeds are sometimes their subjects; but they end mostly with an act of retributive justice. We shall give a specimen of this species before we part with the Russians.

---

[20] See above, p. 64.

By far the largest portion of Russian popular songs is of the erotic kind. According to Russian authorities, even their oldest ballads, to judge from the language,[21] cannot be traced further than to the last quarter of the sixteenth century; and the number even of these is very small. Most of those now current among the people are derived from the beginning of the middle of the last century. According to Goetze, the reign of Peter the First was very favourable to popular poetry.[22] His daughter, the empress Elizabeth, was a successful poetess herself; and her ditties had a perfectly popular character. If we may draw a conclusion from the frequency with which modern historical events have given birth to popular ballads, one must suppose that many ancient ones are lost. The victories of Peter the First are celebrated in many popular ballads, some of which are of no inconsiderable merit; as the reader will judge for himself from the specimen we give below. The French invasion also, of 1812, which aroused the Russian nation so powerfully, gave rise to not a few patriotic songs, of many of which the authors were peasants and common soldiers.

There are, however, various indications, which seem to justify the belief, that several of the Russian ballads still current among the people are, in fact, more ancient than they appear, or perhaps even than they actually are in their present shape. We have not room here to dwell on this subject. We remark only, that from one circumstance alone we may draw the safe conclusion, that the Russians have ever been a *singing* race. We allude to their custom of attaching verses full of allusions and sacred meaning to every festival, nay, to every extraordinary event of

---

[21] We say, 'to judge from the language.' But their coincidence with Bohemian ballads of the thirteenth century, and various other indications (e. g. their frequent mention of the Danube), seem to vindicate, for their groundwork at least, a very high antiquity.

[22] *Stimmen des Russischen Volkes,* von P. v. Goetze, Stuttg. 1848.

human life, and thus of fettering the flying hours with the garland chains of poetry and song. They have to this very day their wedding songs, Pentecost and Christmas carols, and various other songs, named after the different occasions on which they are chanted, or the game which they accompany. Although these songs, also, have been modernized in language and form, they seem always to have been regarded with a kind of pious reverence, and appear to have been altered as little as possible. Most of their allusions are, for that reason, unintelligible at the present day. That their groundwork is derived from the age of paganism, is evident from the frequent invocations of heathen deities, and from various allusions to heathen customs.

Nearly related to these songs are the various ditties of a social kind, which peasant girls and lads are in the habit of singing on certain stated occasions; for instance, walking songs, dancing songs, and the like. They consist mostly of endless repetition, often of words or single syllables, apparently without meaning; and the tune, in which these fragmentary poems are sung, is after all the best part of it. Yet not seldom a spark of real poetry shines through that melodious tissue of unmeaning words. What is most remarkable in these songs, which have now been more than a century the exclusive property of the common people, is the utter absence of coarseness and vulgarity, even in the wedding songs.

The Russian songs, like the Russian language, have a peculiar tenderness, and are full of caressing epithets. These are even frequently applied to inanimate objects. A Russian postilion, in a simple and charming song, calls the tavern, which he never can make up his mind to pass without stopping, "his dear little mother." The words *Matushka*, *Batushka*, *Starinka*, which we may venture to give in English by *motherling*, *fatherling*, *oldling*, are in Russian favourite terms of endearment. The postboy's song may stand here as eminently characteristic of the cheerful, childlike, caressing disposition of the nation. It is translated in the measure of the original, as nearly as it could be imitated in English.

THE POSTILION.

Tzarish Tavern, thou
Our good motherling,
So invitingly
Standest by the way!
Broad highway, that leads
Down to Petersburg;
Fellows young as I,
As they drive along,
When they pass thee by,
Always will turn in.

Ah, thou bright sun-light,
Red and bright sun-light,
O'er the mountain high,
O'er the forest oaks;
Warm the youngster's heart,
Warm, O warm me, sun;
And not me alone,
But my maiden, too.

Ah, thou maiden dear,
Fairest, dearest maid,
Thou my dearest child,
Art so kind and good!
Black those brows of thine,
Black thy little eyes,
And thy lovely face
All so round and white;
Without painting, white,
Without painting, red!

To thy girdle rolls
Fair and braided hair;
And thy voice is soft,
Full of gentle talk.

P.

Russian lovers are quite inexhaustible in fondling and caressing expressions. "My shining moon, my bright sun, my nourisher (*Kormiletz*), my light, my hope, my white swan," together with all those epithets common to all languages, as, *dove*, *soul*, *heart*, etc. are current terms in Russia. Especially favourable to this affectionate manner of address is the abundance of diminutives which the language possesses. Not only "little soul," "little heart," *Dushinka*, *Serdzinka*, etc. are favourite expressions of Russian lovers; but we find even *Yagodka*, "little berry," and *Lapushka*, "little paw," etc. Love is ingenious in inventing new diminutives for the beloved object.

This exquisite tenderness in the Russian love-songs is united with a deep, pensive feeling, which indeed pervades the whole Russian popular poetry. Were we to describe the character of this in one expression, we should call it *melancholy-musical*. Even the more frivolous and equivocal songs have a tincture of this pensiveness. While the Servian songs of this description are the ebullitions of merry and petulant youth, the Russian are frequently not without a spice of sentimentality. Girls are often represented painting the unhappy consequences of their weakness with a very suspicious mixture of penitence and pleasure; so that the hearer remains undecided, whether the former or the latter is predominant.

In perfect harmony with this melancholy is the Russian national music. The expressive sweetness of the Russian melodies has long been the admiration of those foreign composers, to whom circumstances had made them known. The history of these melodies is just as uncertain as that of the verses; they seem always to have been united; no one knows where they came from. In respect to popular tunes and songs, the answer which the Ashantees gave to Mr. Bowditch has often occurred to us: "They were made when the country was made." The Russian tunes are richer and more varied than are popular airs in general. Of most of the songs only the first two verses are set to the melody; all the following being repeated in the same tune. But there are some which extend further. Some of these airs include more than a whole octave in their notes; while the national melodies of most other nations move in general among a few notes.

To account for the melancholy character of the Russian music and poetry, and to reconcile it with the well-known cheerful disposition of the nation, has been attempted by several Russian critics. "The peculiarities of a nation," Karamzin remarks, "may always be explained by the circumstances which have operated on it; although the grandchildren may have some of the virtues and some of the vices of their ancestry, even if they are differently situated. Perhaps the present character of the Russians may exhibit faults, which it contracted during the barbarism of the Mongolian subjugation." The pensiveness which pervades the Russian songs has also been considered as a remnant of that gloom, necessarily impressed on the Russian character during two centuries of the most cruel oppression. There is no doubt that the Russians before, during, and after their subjugation by the Mongols, had a thousand causes of discouragement and disasters; bloody civil wars, the most barbarian despotism, the plague, slavery,[23] and the like. But it is just as certain, that notwithstanding all the causes of sorrow, the Russians are still the most cheerful and light-hearted people on earth; with all their hearts and senses enjoying the scanty plea-

[23] Slavery in Russia is comparatively of modern date.

sures of life; though deprived of all civil privileges, and even of many social rights. The truth is, that it is with nations as with individuals. Neither in the one case nor in the other must we expect always to see them deposit their *habitual* feelings in their poetry. It is a well-known fact that Molière was a man of a most serious disposition. Cowper, immediately before writing his "John Gilpin," was in a mood bordering on despair. Young, while composing his melancholy Night Thoughts, enjoyed his life as well as any man. The Russians do not sing their every-day sentiments, but their holiday feelings. That sweet pensiveness, which thrills so affectingly through their music and poetry, is to them a species of luxury. A soft, melancholy emotion, not deep enough indeed to cause suffering, and slumbering in every-day life in the recesses of the poet's soul, awakes in the hour of inspiration and spreads a gentle shadow over his habitual sunshine. The peculiar melancholy *resignation* of Slavic lovers we have already attempted to explain. Indeed, it is to their love songs, principally, that the general remark on the pensiveness of Russian songs and airs is applicable.

We here subjoin some specimens of them. The first is extant in a great many versions, differing somewhat from each other. We choose the one we like best, as given by Sacharof:[24]

A PARTING SCENE.

"Sit not up, my love, late at evening hour,
Burn the light no more, light of virgin wax,

[24] *Pjesni Russkawo Naroda,* St. Petersb. 1837–39, Vol. IV. p. 29.—We would remark here, that all our specimens are translated, not by means of the German, but from the original languages, and that all the originals are (or have been) in our possession. It would have been easy to embellish these simple songs by little additions or omissions, the rhymeless ones by rhyme, and the rhymed ones by more regularity; but we could not possibly have done it without impairing the fidelity of such a version.

Wait no more for me till the midnight hour;
Ah, gone by, gone by is the happy time!
Ah, the wind has blown all our joys away,
And has scattered them o'er the empty field.
For my father dear, he will have it so,
And my mother dear has commanded it,
That I now must wed with another wife,
With another wife, with an unloved one!
But on heaven high two suns never burn,
Two moons never shine in the stilly night;
And an honest lad never loveth twice!
But my father shall be obey'd by me,
And my mother dear I will now obey;
To another wife I'll be wedded soon,
To another wife, to an early death,
To an early death, to a forced one."

Wept the lovely maid many bitter tears,
Many bitter tears, and did speak these words:
" O beloved one, never seen enough,
Longer will I not live in this white world,
Never without thee, thou my star of hope!
Never has the dove more than one fond mate,
And the female swan ne'er two husbands has,
Neither can I have two beloved friends."

No more sits she now late at evening hour,
But the light still burns, light of virgin wax;
On the table stands the coffin newly made;
In the coffin new lies the lovely maid.

THE DOVE.

On an oak tree sat,
Sat a pair of doves;

And they bill'd and coo'd
And they, heart to heart,
Tenderly embraced
With their little wings;
On them, suddenly,
Darted down a hawk.

One he seized and tore,
Tore the little dove,
With his feather'd feet,
Soft blue little dove;
And he poured his blood
Streaming down the tree.
Feathers too were strew'd
Widely o'er the field;
High away the down
Floated in the air.

Ah! how wept and wept;
Ah! how sobb'd and sobb'd
The poor doveling then
For her little dove.

"Weep not, weep not so,
Tender little bird!"
Spake the light young hawk
To the little dove.
"O'er the sea away,
O'er the far blue sea,
I will drive to thee
Flocks of other doves.
From them choose thee then,
Choose a soft and blue,
With his feathered feet,
Better little dove."

"Fly, thou villain, not,
O'er the far blue sea
Drive not here to me
Flocks of other doves.
Ah! of all thy doves
None can comfort me;
Only he, the father
Of my little ones."

P.

The following little elegy we translate from a Russian Annual; the editor of which, Baron Delvig, took it down from the lips of a peasant girl.

THE FAITHLESS LOVER.

Nightingale, O nightingale,
Nightingale so full of song,
Tell me, tell me, where thou fliest,
Where to sing now in the night?
Will another maiden hear thee
Like to me, poor me, all night
Sleepless, restless, comfortless,
Ever full of tears her eyes?
Fly, O fly, dear nightingale,
Over hundred countries fly,
Over the blue sea so far;
Spy the distant countries through,
Town and village, hill and dell,
Whether thou find'st any one,
Who so sad is, as I am?

O, I bore a necklace once,
All of pearls like morning dew;
And I bore a finger-ring,
With a precious stone thereon;

And I bore deep in my heart
Love, a love so warm and true.
When the sad, sad autumn came,
Were the pearls no longer clear;
And in winter burst my ring,
On my finger, of itself! [25]
Ah! and when the spring came on,
Had forgotten me my love.

There is one trait in the Russian character, which we recognize distinctly in their poetry, namely, their peculiar and almost Oriental veneration for their sovereign, and a blind submission to his will. There is indeed somewhat of a religious mixture in this feeling; for the Tzar is not only the sovereign lord of the country and master of their lives, but he is also the head of the orthodox church. The *orthodox* Tzar is one of his standing epithets. The following ballad, which we consider as one of the most perfect among Russian popular narrative ballads, exhibits very affectingly the complete resignation with which the Russian meets death, when decreed by his Tzar. In its other features, also, it is throughout natural. Its historical foundation is unknown. There are several versions of it extant, slightly differing from each other; which seems to prove that it has been for a long time handled by the people.

THE BOYAR'S EXECUTION.

"Thou, my head, alas! my head,
Long hast served me, and well, my head;
Full three-and-thirty summers long;
Ever astride of my gallant steed,
Never my foot from its stirrup drawn.
But alas! thou hast gained, my head,

[25] Both these are bad omens for a Russian girl.

Nothing of joy or other good ;
Nothing of honours or even thanks."

Yonder along the Butcher's street,
Out to the fields through the Butcher's gate,[26]
They are leading a prince and peer.

Priests and deacons are walking before,
In their hands a great book open ;
Then there follows a soldier troop,
With their drawn sabres flashing bright.
At his right, the headsman goes,
Holds in his hand the keen-edged sword ;
At his left goes his sister dear,
And she weeps as the torrent pours,
And she sobs as the fountains gush.

Comforting speaks her brother to her :
" Weep not, weep not, my sister dear !
Weep not away thy eyes so clear,
Dim not, O dim not thy face so fair,
Make not heavy thy joyous heart !
Say, for what is it thou weepest so ?
Is 't for my goods, my inheritance ?
Is 't for my lands, so rich and wide ?
Is 't for my silver, or is 't for my gold ?
Or dost thou weep for my life alone ?"

" Ah, thou, my light, my brother dear,
Not for thy goods or inheritance,
Not for thy lands, so rich and wide,
Is 't that my eyes are weeping so ;
Not for thy silver and not for thy gold,
'Tis for thy life, I am weeping so."

---

[26] Names of the street and gate in Moscow, through which formerly criminals were led to execution.

" Ah, thou, my light, my sister sweet!
Thou mayest weep, but it won't avail;
Thou mayest beg, but 't is all in vain;
Pray to the Tzar, but he will not yield.
Merciful truly was God to me,
Truly gracious to me the Tzar,
So he commanded my traitor head
Off should be hewn from my shoulders strong."

Now the scaffold the prince ascends,
Calmly mounts to the place of death;
Prays to his Great Redeemer there,
Humbly salutes the crowd around;
" Farewell world, and thou people of God;
Pray for my sins that burden me sore!"

Scarce had the people ventured then
On him to look, when his traitor head
Off was hewn from his shoulders strong.[27] P.

We add another more modern heroic ballad, composed, perhaps, by one of the soldiers, who was present at the exploit. The first siege of Azof took place in 1695. The fortress was, however, not taken by storm, although repeated assaults were made; but the garrison capitulated in the following year. The great white Tzar is of course Peter I.[28]

---

[27] *Buinaya golowushka,* that is, the *fierce, rebellious, impetuous head,* and *mogutshiya pletsha,* or *strong shoulders,* are standing expressions in Russia, in reference to a young hero; the former, especially, when there is allusion to some traitorous action.

[28] Sacharof's Collection, Vol. IV. p. 218; see p. 346.

THE STORMING OF AZOF.

The poor soldiers have no rest,
Neither night nor day !
Late at evening the word was given
To the soldiers gay ;
All night long their weapons cleaning,
Were the soldiers good,
Ready in the morning dawn,
All in ranks they stood.

Not a golden trumpet is it,
That now sounds so clear;
Nor the silver flute's tone is it,
That thou now dost hear.
'Tis the great white Tzar who speaketh,
'Tis our father dear.
Come, my princes, my Boyars,
Nobles, great and small !
Now consider and invent
Good advice, ye all !
How the soonest, how the quickest,
Fort Azof may fall ?

The Boyars, they stood in silence.—
And our father dear,
He again began to speak
In his eye a tear :
Come, my children, good dragoons,
And my soldiers all,
Now consider and invent
Brave advice, ye all,
How the soonest, how the quickest,
Fort Azof may fall ?

Like a humming swarm of bees,
So the soldiers spake,

With one voice at once they spake:
"Father, dear, great Tzar!
Fall it must! and all our lives
Thereon we gladly stake."

Set already was the moon,
Nearly past the night;
To the storming on they marched,
With the morning light;
To the fort with bulwark'd towers
And walls so strong and white.

Not great rocks they were, which rolled
From the mountains steep;
From the high, high walls there rolled
Foes into the deep.
No white snow shines on the fields,
All so white and bright;
But the corpses of our foes
Shine so bright and white.
Not up-swollen by heavy rains
Left the sea its bed;
No! in rills and rivers streams
Turkish blood so red!

Different dialects are spoken, and different ballads are sung by the population of Malo-Russia[29] and of those Polish-Russian and Polish-Austrian provinces, where the peasantry is of the Ruthenian race. The musical element is still more prevalent among them; and their ditties are rhymed. The few very ancient ones, which are still extant, alone make an exception.

[29] That is, the Russian governments Kief, Pultava, Tshernigof, Kharkof, and Yekatrinoslav. The latter, the cradle of the present population of Malo-Russia, belongs, according to the present geographical division of the Russian empire, to Southern Russia.

These have the form and the spirit of the ballads of the Great Russians, and can in no way be discerned from them; while the great mass has a different character. Indeed, such an immense number of ballads have originated in the rich and fertile steppes of the Ukraine, that it would seem as if each bough of their forest trees must harbour a singer, and each blade of grass on these endless blooming plains whisper the echo of a song.[30] The pensive character of the Great Russian popular poetry becomes, in that of the Malo-Russian and Ruthenian, a deep melancholy, that finds vent in a great variety of sweet, elegiac, melodies. According to the author of a little collection of their popular songs, published first in a German translation, "these are the after-pains of whole generations; these are the sorrows of whole centuries, which are blended in one everlasting sigh!"[31] If we look back to the history of these regions, we cannot doubt that it is the spirit of their past, that breathes out of these mournful strains. The cradle of the Kozak stood in blood; he was rocked to the music of the clashing of swords. For centuries the country on both banks of the Dnieper as far as to the north-western branch of the Carpathian mountains, the seat of this race, was the theatre of constant warfare and aggression; there was no time for the blessings of a peaceful development. Their narrative ballads have, therefore, few other subjects than the feuds with Poles and Tartars; the Kozak's parting with his beloved one; or his lonely death on the border, or on the bloody

---

[30] The Polish poet Bogdjanski is said to have collected in the government of Pultava alone towards 8000! A great many of these consist, of course, only in variations of the same theme, owing to the failing memory of the singer. Maximovitch's Collection contains several thousand pieces.

[31] *Volksleider der Polen gesammelt und übersezt, von W. P.* Leipzig 1833. It ought to have been called *Songs of the Ruthenian people in Poland.*

battle field! No wonder that their little lyric effusions have imbibed the same melancholy spirit.

These vast level regions were the principal thoroughfares of the hordes of Mongols and Tartars, who from the thirteenth to the fifteenth century overspread Russia, and penetrated as far as Silesia. In Northern Russia, at least, a shade of the old forms and constitutions was preserved; and native princes reigned under Mongol dominion; but in the South every thing was broken up, and the country laid completely waste. Fugitives, reduced to a life of plunder and booty, congregated here and there; the country on the Lower Don, near the entrance of this river into the sea of Azof, was one of their strongholds; another portion found refuge on the islands of the Dnieper, just below the present site of Yekatrinoslav. Here they fortified themselves in little rude castles; while, after all, their situation out of the track of the wild barbarians was their best shelter.

The first named region was principally the asylum for fugitives from Great Russia; deserters and exiles from other parts of the country joined them; and the Tartar population, which they found on the spot, and the neighbouring Kalmuk tribes, mingled with them. These are the Kozaks of the Don; of whom the Kozaks of Grebensk, of Yaitzk, and of the Ural, are branches. They are Russians, and sing the songs of their brethren, the Russians. The river Don, or, as it is familiarly and at the same time respectfully called, *Don Ivanovitch*,[32] plays a prominent part in their ballads. They have a touching child-like love for that noble river, so majestic and yet so gentle, that once gave shelter on its banks to their forefathers. Father Don, the stilly (*tikho*) Don, Don Ivanovitch, are its constant epithets. The scene of a considerable number of their ballads is in the vessels which glide upon the 'stilly' Don.

---

[32] The origin of this polite appellation is its rise in the Ivanovskoi Lake.

The fugitives who had congregated on the Dnieper were also Russians; but the mixture of other nations, which they received, would appear to have come principally from the Circassians of the Caucasus, as the still beautiful shape and countenance of the Tshernomorski seem to indicate;[33] and also in part from the Ruthenian tribes of the Carpathian mountains, as their language proves. These are the Zaporoguean Kozaks; so called from having their principal seats beyond the *porogues*, or waterfalls of the Dnieper. Both sections of the Kozaks founded a kind of military democratic government; and tried to shelter themselves against their enemies in those rude castles called *Sicza*, best protected by thick woods and the surrounding water. They soon began to spread out in the small towns called *Groazisko*, fortified also indeed, but built so slightly that they were almost as soon erected as destroyed. The Kozaks of the Don, after the deliverance of Russia in the second half of the fifteenth century, acknowledged in some degree the sovereignty of the Russian Tzar; and aided Ivan II to conquer Siberia. They were used by his successors as border guardians against the wild Asiatic hordes; whom they partly chased from their homes in the Ural mountains, and settled there in their stead. Thus they spread all over Siberia; always looking back with a pensive and languishing feeling to their "dear fatherling," their gentle "nourisher," their "stilly Don Ivanovitch."[34]

From the Zaporoguean Kozaks, meanwhile, had issued the

[33] Towards the close of the eighteenth century, Catharine II induced great numbers of the Zaporoguean Kozaks to move to the northern shore of the Kuban, east of the Black Sea or *Tshernayamora*, in order to protect the border against the Circassians. They are hence called Tshernomorskĭi, or Black Sea Kozaks.

[34] These affectionate feelings were gradually extended towards all the rivers of their ancient establishments. Their ballads express a tender attachment to Mother Wolga, Mother Kamyshenka, Mother Tsarytzina, etc.

population of the Ukraine. Their first establishment consisted of a strict republic of warriors; no female was admitted into their strongholds on the islands of the Dnieper. By degrees they relaxed; and began with keeping their families in villages in the vicinity, where they spread with incredible rapidity. Then a line of separation was drawn between the inhabitants of the settlements, and the Zaporogueans in the castles; none of these latter were allowed to marry. Thus their youth were always ready for the enemy; and the distinction was only dropped in more peaceful times. They kept themselves independent of Russia until the latter part of the seventeenth century; but their more dangerous enemies had long been the Poles, their north-western neighbours. It was the period of Poland's glory. The Poles were conquerors in the North and in the East. At last the Kozaks, after a century of struggles, acknowledged the authority of the Polish sovereign Stephan Bathori (ob. 1586); moved partly, it is said in their traditions, by the personal grandeur of that chevaleresque monarch. But now the Polish nobility overspread the Ukraine. They became land-owners and oppressors; and their stewards, their still more detested assistants. They were followed by the Jesuits; who alternately by persuasion and compulsion attempted to entice the natives, who all belonged to the Greek church, to come under the dominion of the Pope. A war of religious persecution and resistance arose. The Kozaks ultimately revolted in 1648; and a few years after (in 1654) their Hetman Chmielnitzky submitted himself and the whole Ukraine to Tzar Alexeï, the father of Peter I.

The struggles of this insurrection, their previous feuds with the Poles their oppressors, and afterwards their repeated revolts from the Russians, who tried to undermine their liberties, have given birth to a great number of simple ballads, the bold spirit of which presents a noble relief to the habitual melancholy of Malo-Russian poetry in general. They have professional singers, who are called *Bandurists;* and who, with a kind of simple guitar in their hand, ramble through the country, sure to find a willing audience in whatever village they may stop. Their ballads are of course not confined to the scenes of the earlier centuries; the more recent wars with the Turks and Tartars also, and the campaigns made in modern times in the service of Russia, present subjects enough of interest; for their productiveness is still alive, although the race of the professional bards is growing more and more scarce. They call their historical ballads *Dumi*, or *Dumki*, an appellation for historical elegies, which has recently been adopted by Polish literati.[35]

We give here a few characteristic specimens of their poetry; serving to illustrate their warlike spirit, as well as their domestic relations; their skill in narrative ballads, as well as their power of expressing in lyric strains the unsophisticated feelings of a tender heart. We begin with two genuine Kozak elegies.

ON THE MURDER OF YESSAUL TSHURAÏ.[36]

O eagle, young gray eagle,
  Tshuraï, thou youth so brave,
In thine own land, the Pole,
  The Pole dug thee thy grave!

The Pole dug thee thy grave,
  For thee and thy Hetman;
They killed the two young heroes,
  Stephen, the valiant Pan.

---

[35] See above, p. 297.

[36] Yessaul is the name of that officer among the Kozaks, who stands immediately under the Hetman. The ballad refers to an incident which happened before 1648. It is from Sreznevski's *Starina Zaporoshnaya*, i. e. *History of the Zaporoguean Kozaks*, Kharkof 1837.

O eagle, young gray eagle,
Thy brethren are eagles too;
The old ones and the young ones,
Their custom well they knew!

The old ones and the young ones
They are all brave like thee,
An oath they all did take
Avengéd shalt thou be!

The old ones and the young ones,
In council grave they meet;
They sit on coal black steeds,
On steeds so brave and fleet.

On steeds so brave and fleet
They are flying, eagle like;
In Polish towns and castles
Like lightning they will strike.

Of steel they carry lances,
Lances so sharp and strong;
With points as sharp as needles,
With hooks so sharp and long.

Of steel they carry sabres,
Two edged, blunted never;
To bring the Pole perdition
For ever and for ever!

LAMENT FOR YESSAUL PUSHKAR.

There flows a little river,
And Worskla is its name;
And of the little river
Know old and young the fame.

And on the little river,
 They know good songs to sing;
And on the little river,
 They like good thoughts to think.

O thoughts, ye manly thoughts,
 Ye call up sorrow and woe;
O thoughts, ye manly thoughts,
 From you strong deeds can grow!

Where are you, brave Kozaks?
 Where are you, valiant lords?
Your bones are in the grave,
 In the deep moor your swords!

Where art thou, O Pushkar?
 Where art thou, valiant knight?
Ukraina weeps for thee,
 And for her fate so bright.

His bones are in the grave,
 Himself with God is now;
O weep, O weep, Ukraina,
 An orphan left art thou.

Ukraina, thy bright fate
 Destroy'd Wihowski's spell;[37]
He with the heart of stone,
 And with the mind of hell!

The following melancholy song expresses the general hatred against the Pole, the oppressor, in a manner not less strong. *Haidamack* is another name for the Ruthenian peasant under

---

[37] Probably John Wihowski, Hetman after Chmielnicki. After the death of this latter, he fell off from Russia, and led the Kozaks back to Poland. It seems it was he who occasioned Pushkar's death.

Polish dominion, and was formerly, as well as *Burlak*, also applied to the Malo-Russian Kozaks in general.

SONG OF THE HAIDAMACK.[38]

Gladly would I to the war,
    To the war so full of prey,
    Pleasure of the Haidamack!
    But the steward bids me stay,
    Lest the proud Pole's cows should stray!

Gladly to the merry dance
    Would I on the gusli play,
    Pleasure of the rosy maid!
    But the steward bids me stay,
    Lest the proud Pole's sheep should stray!

Gladly I would hunting go,
    With the bobtailed dog so fleet,
    Pleasure of a good brave youth!
    But the steward bids me stay,
    Lest the proud Pole's steeds should stray!

O farewell, thou rosy maid,
    Rattle gently, rusty sabre!
    Quick on horseback, Haidamack!
    Stray may steeds, sheep, cows and all;
    Perish may the haughty Pole!

We finish with a few Ruthenian ballads, having no political reference. The first is interesting as illustrating a peculiar popular superstition. The Leshes are a kind of Satyrs; covered like them with hair, and of a very malicious nature. They steal

---

[38] Manuscript.

children and young women. Their presence has a certain benumbing influence; a person whom they visit cannot move or stir; although, in the case of our ballad, we have some suspicion that "the brandy, the wine, and the mead," had some preparatory influence.

The second exhibits the whole plaintive, yielding mood of a Russian loving maid; and may be considered as a *characteristic* specimen.

SIR SAVA AND THE LESHES.[39]

With the Lord at Nemirov
  Sir Sava dined so gladly;
Nor thought he that his life
  Would end so soon and sadly.

Sir Sava he rode home
  To his own court with speed;
And plenty of good oats
  He bids to give his steed.

Sir Sava behind his table
  To write with care begun;
His young wife she is rocking
  In the cradle her infant son.

'Holla! my lad, brisk butler,
  Bring now the brandy to me;
My well-beloved lady,
  This glass I drink to thee.

'Holla! my lad, brisk butler,
  Now bring me the clear wine;
This glass and this, I drink it
  To this dear son of mine.

---

[39] From Czelakowski's Collection; see above, p. 216, n. 58.

'Holla! my lad, brisk butler,
  Now bring me the mead so fast;
My head aches sore; I fear
  I've rode and drunk my last!'

Who knocks, who storms so fiercely?
  Sir Sava looks up to know;
The Leshes stand before him,
  And quick accost him so:

'We bow to thee, Sir Sava,
  How far'st thou, tell us now!
To thy guests from the Ukraina,
  What welcome biddest thou?'

'What could I bid you, brethren,
  To-day in welcome's stead?
Well know I, ye are come
  To take my poor sick head!'

'And tell us first, Sir Sava,
  Where are thy daughters fair?'
'They are stolen by the Leshes,
  And wash their linen there.'

'Now to the fight be ready!
  Sir Sava meet thy lot!
Thy head is lost! one moment,
  Death meets thee on the spot.'

The sabre whizzes through the air
  Like wild bees in the wood.
The young wife of Sir Sava
  By him a widow stood!

THE LOVE-SICK GIRL.[40]

Winds are blowing, howling,
Trees are bending low;
O my heart is aching,
Tears in streams do flow.

Years I count with sorrow,
And no end appears;
But my heart is lighten'd,
When I'm shedding tears.

Tears the heart can lighten,
Happy make it not;
E'en one blissful moment
Ne'er can be forgot.

Some there are who envy
E'en my destiny;
Say, 'O happy flow'ret
Blooming on the lea.'

On the lea so sandy,
Sunny, wanting dew!
O without my lover
Life is dark to view.

Nought can please without him,
Seems the world a jail;
Happiness exists not,
Peace of mind doth fail.

Where, dark-browed belov'd one,
Where, O may'st thou be?
Come and see, astonished,
How I weep for thee!

---

[40] From Sacharof's Collection, St. Petersb. 1839. Vol. IV. p. 427.

Whom shall I now lean on,
  Whose caress receive ?
Now that he who loves me
  Far away doth live ?

I would fly to thee, love,
  But no wings have I ;
Withered, parch'd, without thee,
  Every hour I die.

The following little elegy, heard and written down in Galicia, we have always considered as one of the gems of poetry. It is a sigh of deep, mourning, everlasting love.

THE DEAD LOVE.

White art thou, my maiden,
  Can'st not whiter be !
Warm my love is, maiden,
  Cannot warmer be !

But when dead, my maiden,
  White was she still more;
And, poor lad, I love her,
  Warmer than before.[41]

Of still greater importance in respect to our subject are the SERVIANS. We have seen already in this work, that the inhabitants of the Turkish provinces of Servia and Bosnia, of Monte-

[41] The reader will find an elaborate essay on the popular poetry of the Ukraine in the Foreign Quarterly Review, Vol. XXVI. No. 51. It was evidently written by one of the Polish exiles in England. In it, however, a singular mistake is made as to the derivation of the appellation of the Zaporoguean Kozaks. *Porog* does not mean " Island " in any Slavic language.

negro, of the Austrian kingdom of Slavonia, of Dalmatia and Military Croatia, speak essentially the same language; which is likewise the vernacular dialect of numerous Servian settlements in Hungary, along the south-western shore of the Danube. Of this language, which has been alternately called Illyrian, Servian, Morlachian, Bosnian, Croatian, Rascian, and perhaps by still other different appellations, it may be truly said, that it has more names than dialects; and even the few of these latter differ so slightly, that the difference would scarcely be perceived by a foreigner. It is also true, that, on account of the various systems of writing which have been adopted by the different sections of this race, the foreigner will sometimes find it more difficult to understand the language as written than as spoken.

The inexhaustible mine of Servian popular poetry belongs then to the whole nation; although, of course, neither the productiveness is every where the same, nor the power and opportunity of preservation. For its favourite home we must look to those regions where modern civilization has least penetrated; viz. to Turkish Servia, Bosnia, Montenegro. There also the vernacular language is spoken with the greatest purity.

An intelligent Italian traveller, Abbate Fortis, published about a hundred years ago an interesting description of the Morlachians, that is, the Croatian Servian inhabitants of Dalmatia, a tribe distinguished by wild passions and proud contempt of civil life; but full of poetical feeling, and much attached to old usages and the recollections of their ancestors. He printed for the first time some of their beautiful ancient ballads; but although they were much admired in the German versions which Herder and Goethe gave of them (through the French), the region of their birth remained a *terra incognita.* To a few literati only it was known, that many of these ballads, although in a spurious shape, had been collected by the Franciscan monk, Andreas Cacich Miossich; and also that a great many fragments of remarkable popular heroic songs were scattered, as illustrations, through the Croatian and Dalmatian dictionaries of Belloszteneez, Jambressich, and Della Bella. It was known, too, but only by a few, that even ancient Servian historians referred to similar songs.

Vuk Stephanovitch Karadshitch must therefore be called the true discoverer of this mine of beauty; and the judiciousness, patience, and conscientious honesty, with which his collection was got up, deserves the highest praise. Many of the remarkable songs first communicated to the literary public were the reminiscences of his own youth; for he was born and brought up in Turkish Servia. Many more he was only able to find after years of careful and indefatigable research. His large collection —four volumes with at least five or six hundred pieces of poetry —was formed upon the principle, that no piece should be admitted, for the genuineness of which he could not be personally responsible, by having himself heard it from one of the people. Nearly the third part of these poems consists of epic tales; some of them from five to seven hundred verses long; one, more than twelve hundred.

The poetry of the Servians is most intimately interwoven with their daily life. It is the picture of their thoughts, feelings, actions, and sufferings; it is the mental reproduction of the respective conditions of the mass of individuals, who compose the nation. The hall where the women sit spinning around the fireside; the mountains on which the boys pasture their flocks; the square where the village youth assemble to dance the *kolo*;[42] the plains where the harvest is reaped; the forests through which the lonely traveller journeys,—all resound with song. Song accompanies all kinds of business, and frequently relates to it. The Servian *lives* his poetry.

[42] See a description of this national dance in Wilkinson, *Dalmatia and Montenegro*, I. p. 399.

The Servians are accustomed to divide their songs into two great portions. Short compositions in various measures, either lyric or epic, and sung without instrumental accompaniment, they call *shenske pjesme*, or *female songs*, because they are mostly made by females. The other portion, consisting of long epic tales in verses of five regular trochaic feet, and chanted to the *Guslé*, a kind of simple violin with one chord, they called *Yunatchke pjesme*, that is, *heroic* or *young men's songs;* for it is an interesting fact, that the ideas of a *young man* and of a *hero*, are expressed in Servian by one and the same word, *Yunak*. The first are, in a very high degree, of a domestic character. They accompany us through all the different relations of domestic life; as well through its daily occupations, as through the holidays and festivals which interrupt its ordinary course. Much has been said, and more could be said, in praise of these harmonious effusions of a tender, fresh, and unsophisticated feeling; but, as we have already dwelt at large upon their general character, we must be satisfied here with adding only that which distinguishes Servian lays from other Slavic songs.

And this distinction we find principally in the *cheerfulness*, which is the fundamental element of Servian poetry,—a serenity clear and transparent like the bright blue of a southern sky. The allusions to the misfortunes of married life alone, gather sometimes in heavy clouds on this beautiful sky. The fear of being chained to an *old* man, or of a grim mother-in-law, or the quarrelling of the sisters-in-law, or the increasing cares of the household,—for, in the true patriarchal style, married sons remain in the house of the parents, and all make together only one family,—all these circumstances disturb sometimes the inexhaustible serenity of the Servian women, and call forth gentle lamentations, or perhaps still oftener horrible imprecations, from their humble breasts. Indeed the songs not made for particular occasions also bear strongly and distinctly the stamp of domestic life, and are full of allusions to family relations.

A spirit of graceful roguery is very prevalent among Servian girls. Their social spinning meetings are especially productive of little witty ballads, in which men and women are represented as disputing, and the former, of course, are always outwitted; just as is the case in numerous English and German popular ballads. But love is also among them the grand and prevailing theme. To judge from these songs, Servian girls and youths keep up a frequent and tender intercourse with each other. The youth bears carefully in memory the hour when the girls go to fetch water; and the frequent festivities, where the dance is not permitted to fail, give the best opportunity for mutual intercourse. Further to the south, and between the mountains, the customs are more strict, and love-songs are less frequent.

Among the ancient songs, recited on certain stated occasions, the wedding songs, adapted to all the various ceremonies of Slavic marriage, are the most remarkable. And here we meet again with one of those various contradictions of the mental world, which puzzle philosophy. While all the symbolic ceremonies are strongly indicative of the shameful state of servitude and humiliation, to which the institution of marriage subjects the Slavic woman;[43] (for Slavic *maidens* are in a certain measure free and happy, and, if beautiful and industrious, even honoured and sought after;) the *songs*, the mental reproductions of these coarse, rough, humiliating *acts*, are delicate, sprightly, and almost gallant. There are various indications, that, like the Russian

---

[43] A Servian woman never would sit down in the presence of her husband. At table she stands behind him, and waits on him and his guests. Even the wife of prince Milosh did so; only with the restriction that she confined her services to her husband. The Morlachians—who seem indeed to be the *rudest* part of the Servian population—do not mention their wives to a stranger without adding: "With your permission."

songs of this description, which they strongly resemble, they are derived from a very early period. Like them they have no allusion to church ceremonies.[44]

The feeling expressed in their love-songs is in general gentle and often playful, indicating more of tenderness than of passion. If, however, they are excited to anger, their hatred becomes rage; and is poured forth in imprecations, of which no other language has a like multitude. But these imprecations are not stereotype, as is the case with most other nations. They are composed often, with astonishing ingenuity, by the offended persons themselves. Sometimes we see curses invoked upon the satisfying of the common wants of life. Thus when the lad curses his faithless love: "As much bread as she eats, so much pain may she suffer! as much water as she drinks, so many tears may she shed!"

We subjoin a few of these Servian ballads as specimens, just as they happen to come to hand.

PARTING LOVERS.

To white Buda, to white castled Buda
Clings the vine-tree, cling the vine-tree branches;
Not the vine-tree is it with its branches,
No, it is a pair of faithful lovers.
From their early youth they were betrothed,
Now they are compelled to part untimely;
One addressed the other at their parting:
"Go, my dearest soul, and go straight forward,
Thou wilt find a hedge-surrounded garden,
Thou wilt find a rose-bush in the garden,
Pluck a little branch off from the rose-bush,
Place it on thy heart, within thy bosom;
Even as that red rose will be fading,

[44] The reader will find a description of a Morlachian wedding in Wilkinson, Vol. II. p. 164 sq. For a fuller account, see *Volkslieder der Serben, von Talvj*, Vol. II. Introduction.

Even so, love, will my heart be fading."
And the other love this answer gave then ;
"Thou, dear soul, go back a few short paces,
Thou wilt find, my love, a verdant forest,
In the forest stands a cooling fountain,
In the fountain lies a block of marble ;
On the marble stands a golden goblet,
In the goblet thou wilt find a snowball.
Dearest, take that snowball from the goblet,
Lay it on thy heart within thy bosom ;
Even as the snowball will be melting,
Even so, love, will my heart be melting."

RENDEZVOUS.

Sweetheart, come, and let us kiss each other !
But, O tell me, where shall be our meeting ?
In thy garden, love, or in my garden ?
Under thine or under mine own rose-trees ?
Thou, sweet soul, become thyself a rose-bud ;
I then to a butterfly will change me ;
Fluttering I will drop upon the rose-bud ;
Folks will think I'm hanging on a flower,
While a lovely maiden I am kissing !

ST. GEORGE'S DAY.

To St. George's day the maiden prayed ;
" Com'st thou again, O dear St. George's day !
Find me not here, by my mother dear,
Or be it wed, or be it dead !—
But rather than dead, I would be wed !"[45]

---

[45] Servian popular poetry has properly no rhymes ; but wherever a rhyme occasionally occurs, it appears to be welcome ; so in this little piece, which is faithfully conformed to the original. All our specimens of the Servian "female" songs are taken from the first volume of Vuk's Collection. See above, p. 115.

UNITED IN DEATH.

Two young lovers loved each other fondly,
And they washed them at the self-same water,
And they dried them with the self-same napkin.
One year passed, their love was known by no one;
Two years passed, and all the world did know it,
And the father heard it and the mother;
And their love the mother would not suffer,
But she parted the two tender lovers.

Through a star the youth sent to the maiden:
"Die, O love, on Saturday at evening,
I, thy youth, will die on Sunday morning."
And they did as they had told each other;
Died the maiden Saturday at evening,
Died the youth on Sunday morning early;
Close together were the two then buried;
Through the earth their hands were clasped together;
In their hands were placed two young green apples.

Little time had passed since they were buried;
O'er the youth sprang up a verdant pine-tree,
O'er the maid a bush with sweet red roses;
Round the pine-tree winds itself the rose-bush,
As the silk around a bunch of flowers.

But not all the female Servian songs exhibit so much tenderness. That their usual gentleness and humility does not always prevent these poor oppressed beings from sometimes taking the lead in domestic affairs, one would be apt to conclude from the following ballad:

HOUSEHOLD MATTERS.

Come, companion, let us hurry
That we may be early home,
For my mother-in-law is cross.
Only yestreen she accused me,
Said that I had beat my husband;
When, poor soul, I had not touched him.
Only bid him wash the dishes,
And he would not wash the dishes;
Threw then at his head the pitcher,
Knocked a hole in head and pitcher;
For the head I do not care much;
But I care much for the pitcher,
As I paid for it right dearly;
Paid for it with one wild apple,
Yes, and half a one besides.[46]

Objects of still higher admiration the Servians afford us in their *heroic* poems. Indeed, what epic popular poetry is, how it is produced and propagated, what powers of invention it naturally exhibits,—powers which no art can command,—we may learn from this multitude of simple legends and complicated fables. The Servians stand in this respect quite isolated; there is no modern nation, that can be compared to them in epic productiveness; and a new light seems to be thrown over the grand compositions of the ancients. Thus, without presumption, we may pronounce the publication of these

[46] For more specimens see Bowring's *Servian Popular Poetry*, Lond. 1827. These little songs are there made much more attractive by giving them an English dress with *rhymes*, and accommodating them to the English way of feeling and expressing feelings; a proceeding which we have purposely avoided, because our only object is a *faithful* translation. Dr. Bowring has moreover translated mainly from our German translation.

poems one of the most remarkable literary events of modern times.

The general character of the Servian tales is the *objective* and the *plastic*. The poet, in most cases, is in a remarkable degree *above* his subject. He paints his pictures not in glowing colours, but in distinct, prominent features; no explanation is necessary to interpret what the reader thinks he sees with his own eyes. If we compare the Servian epics with those, which other Slavic nations formerly possessed, we find them greatly superior. In the Russian *Igor*, the whole narrative is exceedingly indistinct; you may read the whole of it five times, without being able clearly to follow out the composition. Not a single character stands out in relief. The mode of representation has more of the lyric than of the epic. The ancient Bohemian poems have more distinctness and freshness. No obscurity disturbs us. But the passions of the poet break forth so often, as to give the whole narration something of the subjective character; while the Servian, even when representing his countrymen in combat with their mortal enemies and oppressors, displays about the same partiality for the former, as Homer for his Greeks.

The introductions, not only to the tales themselves, but even to new situations, are frequently allegorical. A distinct image is placed before the eyes at once. A tale, describing a famous sanguinary deed of revenge, commences thus:

What's that cry of anguish from Banyani?[47]
Is 't the Vila? is 't the hateful serpent?
Were 't the Vila, she were on the summit;
Were 't the serpent, it were 'neath the mountain;
Not the Vila is it, nor a serpent;

[47] A mountainous region in the vicinity of Montenegro.

Shrieked in anguish thus Perovitch Batritch
In the hands of Osman, son of Tchorov.[48]

Ravens are the messengers of unhappy news. The battle of Mishar begins with the following verses:

Flying came a pair of coal-black ravens
Far away from the broad field of Mishar,
Far from Shabatz, from the high white fortress;
Bloody were their beaks unto the eyelids,
Bloody were their talons to the ankles;
And they flew along the fertile Matshva,
Waded quickly through the billowy Drina,
Journey'd onward through the honoured Bosnia,
Lighting down upon the hateful border,
'Midst within the accursed town of Vakup,
On the dwelling of the captain Kulin;
Lighting down and croaking as they lighted.

Three or four poems, of which courtships or weddings are the subjects, begin with a description of the beauty of the girl. Especially rich and complete is the following:

Never since the world had its beginning,
Never did a lovelier flow'ret blossom,
Than the flow'ret in our own days blooming;
Haikuna, the lovely maiden flower.

She was lovely, nothing e'er was lovelier!
She was tall and slender as the pine-tree;
White her cheeks, but tinged with rosy blushes,
As if morning's beam had shone upon them,
Till that beam had reached its high meridian.
And her eyes, they were two precious jewels,

---

[48] See the similar beginning of "Hassan Aga," p. 324 above.

And her eyebrows, leeches from the ocean,
And her eyelids they were wings of swallows ;
And her flaxen braids were silken tassels ;
And her sweet mouth was a sugar casket,
And her teeth were pearls arrayed in order ;
White her bosom, like two snowy dovelets,
And her voice was like the dovelet's cooing;
And her smiles were like the glowing sunshine ;
And her fame, the story of her beauty,
Spread through Bosnia and through Herz'govina.

We should never end, if we continued thus to extract all the beautiful and striking passages from the Servian popular lyrics; although their chief merit by no means consists in beautiful passages, but, in most cases, in the composition of the whole, and in the distinct, graphic, and plastic mode of representation. In respect to their style, we add only a single remark. Slavic popular poetry in general has none of the vulgarisms, which, in many cases, deface the popular ballads of the Teutonic nations. Yet *dignity* of style cannot be expected in any popular production. Those whose feelings, from want of acquaintance with the poetry of nature, are apt to be hurt by certain undignified expressions interspersed unconsciously sometimes in the most beautiful descriptions, will not escape unpleasant impressions in reading the Servian songs. The pictures are always fresh, tangible, and striking; but, although not seldom the effects of the sublime, and of the deepest tragic pathos, are obtained by a perfect simplicity, nothing could be more foreign to them than the dignified stateliness and scrupulous refinement of the French stage.

The number and variety of the Servian heroic poems is immense The oldest legendary cycle is formed by their great Tzar Dushan Nemanyitch and his heroes; by the pious prince

Lazar, their last independent chief, who was executed by the Turks after having been made prisoner in battle; and by the death of his faithful knights on the field of Kossovo. The two battles fought here, in 1389 and 1447, put an end to the existence of the Servian empire. In immediate connection with these epic songs are those of which Marko Kralyewitch, i. e. Marko the king's son, the Servian Hercules, is the hero; at least thirty or forty in number. The pictures, which these ballads exhibit, are extremely wild and bold; and are often drawn on a mythological ground. Indeed both the epic and the lyric poetry of the Servians are interwoven with a traditional belief in certain fanciful creatures of Pagan superstition, which exercise a constant influence on human affairs. Witches (*Vjashtitzi*), veiled women who go from house to house, carrying with them destruction; the plague, personified as an old horrible looking female; and also the saints, and among them the *thunderer* Elias and the *fiery* Mary who sends lightning; these all appear occasionally. But the principal figure is the Vila, a mountain fairy, having nearly the same character as the northern elementary spirits; though the malicious qualities predominate, and her intermeddling is in most cases fatal.

There are various features which serve to allay the extreme wildness and rudeness of the oldest Servian poems. As one of the principal of these we consider the solemn institution of a contract of brotherhood or fraternal friendship, which the Servians seem to have inherited from the Scythians.[49] Two men or two women promise each other before the altar, and under solemn ceremonies, in the name of God and St. John, eternal friendship. They bind themselves by this act to all the mutual duties of brothers and sisters. Similar relations exist also between the

---

[49] See an account of this remarkable custom, from the Abbate Fortis, in Wilkinson, II. p. 178 sq.

two sexes, when a maid solemnly calls an old man her "father in God," or a young one her "brother in God;" or when a man calls a woman his "mother or sister in God." This is mostly done in cases of distress. When a person, thus appealed to, accepts the appellation, they are in duty bound to protect and to take care of the unfortunate, who thus give themselves into their hands; according to the prevailing notion, a breach of this contract is severely punished by Heaven. Marko Kralyevitch was united in such an alliance with the Vila; in modern times we find it sometimes between Turks and Servians in the midst of their most bitter feuds.

The traditional ballads of the Servians, referring to the heroes of their golden time, are undoubtedly in their groundwork of great antiquity; but as until recently they have been preserved only by tradition, it cannot be supposed, that they have come down in their present form from the original time of their composition; which was perhaps nearly cotemporary to the events they celebrate. In most of them frequent Turcisms show, that the singer is familiar with the conquerors and their language. According to Vuk, very few are in their present form older than the fifteenth century.

The more modern heroic ballads—for the productiveness of this remarkable people is still alive—are essentially of the same character. They may be divided into two parts. One division, probably composed during the last two centuries and down even to the present time, is devoted to a variety of subjects, public and private. Duels, love stories, satisfaction of blood-revenge, domestic quarrels and reconciliation, are alternately related. The variety of invention in these tales is astonishing; the skill of the combinations and the final development surpasses all that hitherto has been known of popular poetry. One of the most remarkable of them is a narrative of 1227 lines; which relates to the marriage of a young man, Maxim Tzernovitch, son of

Ivan Tzernovitch, a wealthy and powerful Servian. The father goes to Venice to ask in marriage for his son the daughter of the Doge. He describes him as the handsomest of young men; but, when he comes home, he finds him metamorphosed by the small-pox into the ugliest. By the advice of his wife, he substitutes another handsome young man to fetch home the bride with the procession of bridal guests; promising him the principal share in the bridal gifts; for he commits the fraud less from covetous views than from pride, being afraid of being put to shame as unable to keep his word before the haughty Venetians. They succeed in bringing away the bride; but the cheat is discovered on the road; a contest arises, and the whole affair ends in a horrible slaughter.

Vuk Stephanovitch has heard this tale repeatedly, and with several variations; but the principal features, for instance a rich and elaborate description of the bridal gifts, were always recited exactly in the same words. It was chanted in the most perfect manner by an old singer, named Milya, whom prince Milosh often had to sing it before him; and from whose lips Vuk at last took it down.

Another section of more modern ballads narrates events from the latest war between the Servians and Turks, between 1801 and 1815. Who of our readers has not heard of Kara George? His companions, Yanko Katitch, Stoyan Tchupitch, Milosh of Potzerye, are in Servia as well known and admired as Kara George himself. They and their comrades are the heroes of these ballads. The gallant Tchupitch rewarded the blind poet Philip, who chanted to him a long and beautiful poem of his own composition, with a white horse. The subject of his narrative was the battle of Salash; where Tchupitch himself had been the Servian commander.[60]

---

[60] This beautiful poem see in Vuk, III. p. 299 sq. Transl. by Talvi, II. p. 245.

The same ballad singer Philip is the author of most of the modern heroic poems. Of others the authors are not known. Little stress is laid on the art of poetry, exercised with such extraordinary power. These productions of our day are by no means inferior to the ancient. There is indeed no essential difference, either in their diction or in their conception; and it is easy to be perceived, that old and young have been nursed from their infancy on tales of "the days of yore." Some passages of Philip's ballads are really Homeric.[61] Fortunately, the period is past when our admiration for hyperborean poetry needed to be justified by its similarity with the classics. We have learned that real poetry is not spell-bound to names, nor to any nation or age; and the *beautiful* has obtained in our time an independent existence, no longer subject to certain forms and conditions, but resting on itself and its divine gifts.

The difficulties Vuk Stephanovitch met with in collecting these wonderful ballads, were not small. He was often hardly able to prevail on the young men and girls to recite, still less to sing them before him; partly from a natural shyness to exhibit themselves before a stranger; partly because his search after effusions which had so little value in their eyes, and his attempt to fix them by writing, seemed to them an idle and useless occupation. The only reason which they could conceive for it was, that the learned idler meant to ridicule them; and his request was frequently answered by the words: "We are no blind men to sing or recite songs to you."

Of the heroic poems, he tells us, that they are not only chanted, but often recited, as *we* are accustomed to *read;* and that in this latter way, old people teach them by preference to the

---

[61] As the best illustration of this remark we recommend, among other examples, the poem on the death of Meho Orugditch, Vuk, III. p. 333 sq. Transl. by Talvi, II. p. 279 sq.

children. His own father, grandfather, and uncle, were wont to recite and to sing them; and the two latter even composed not a few. Among those from whose lips he took down the present collection, were lads, peasants, merchants, as also hayduks, i. e. highwaymen, in Servia a mode of life less disreputable than with us, and somewhat approaching to heroism. Further, at least seven or eight were blind men; all of them professional bards, and almost the only persons willing to satisfy him. The *shenske pjesme*, or female poems, he had to catch by chance; and short as they are, it was easy to keep them in memory after having heard them once or twice.

While these latter poems are mostly sung without any instrumental accompaniment in the spinning-rooms, in the pastures, or at the village dances; on the other hand the tavern, the public squares, the festive halls of the chiefs, are the places where the Guslè is heard which accompanies the heroic ballads. The bard chants two lines; then he pauses and gives a few plaintive strokes on his primitive instrument; then he chants again, and so on. He needs these short pauses for recollection, as well as for invention. Although these ballads are chiefly sung by blind men, yet no hero thinks it beneath him to chant them to the Guslè. Pirch, a Prussian officer, who travelled in Servia some twenty years ago, tells us, that the Knjas, his host, took the instrument from the hands of the lad, for whom he had sent to sing before his guest, because he did not satisfy him, and played and chanted himself with a superior skill. Clergymen themselves are not ashamed to do it. Nay, even Muhammedan-Bosnians, more Turks than Servians, have preserved this partiality for their national heroics. The great among them would not, indeed, themselves sing them; but they cause them to be chanted before them; and it happened, that a Christian prisoner in Semendria obtained his liberty by their intercession with the Kadi, which he owed merely to their fondness for his ballads. A considerable number of fine songs are marked in Vuk's collection as having been first heard from Muhammedan singers.

Although the same ballads are not heard every where, yet the poetical feeling and productiveness seem to be pretty equally distributed over all the region inhabited by the Servian race. The heroic ballads originate mostly in the southern mountains of Servia, in Bosnia, Montenegro, and its Dalmatian neighbourhood. Towards the North-East the productiveness diminishes; the songs are still *known* in the Austrian provinces, but the recitation of them, and the Guslè itself, are left to blind men and beggars. Pirch heard, nevertheless, the ballads of Marko Kralyevitch in the vicinity of Neusatz, in Hungary. On the other hand, the amatory Servian ballads, and all those comprised under the name of female songs,—although by no means exclusively sung by women,—originate chiefly in those regions, where perhaps a glimpse of occidental civilization has somewhat refined the general feeling. The *villages* of Syrmia, the Banat, and the Batchva, are the home of most of them; in the Bosnian towns also they are heard; while in the *cities* of the Austrian provinces they have been superseded by modern airs of less value, perhaps, and certainly of less nationality.

It remains to remark, that while in all the other Slavic popular poetry, the *musical* element is prominent, it is in the Servian completely crowded into the background. Even the little lyric pieces, or female ballads, are not only in a high degree monotonous, but even without the peculiar sweetness of most popular airs. They also are chanted rather than sung.

The Bulgarian language is said to be particularly rich in popular ballads; and it would hardly be credible, that the numerous nations with which they mixed for centuries, should not have influenced their poetry as well as their language. Nevertheless, those ballads we have met with are not distinguished in any way from the Servian; especially from those Servian ones sung in the provinces where intercourse with a Turkish population is more frequent. One specimen will be sufficient.

THE SLAVE GANGS.[52]

O thou hill, thou high green hill !
Why, green hill, art thou so withered ?
Why so withered and so wilted ?
Did the winter's frost so wilt thee ?
Did the summer's heat so parch thee ?
Not the winter's frost did wilt me,
Nor the summer's heat did parch me,
But my glowing heart is smothered.
Yesterday three slave gangs crossed me;
Grecian maids were in the first row,
Weeping, crying bitterly :
"O our wealth ! art lost for ever !"
Black-eyed maidens from Walachia
Weeping, crying in the second :
"O ye ducats of Walachia !"
Bulgar women in the third row,
Weeping, crying, "O sweet home !
O sweet home ! beloved children !
Fare ye well, farewell for ever !"

The Slovenzi or Vindes, that is, the Slavic inhabitants of Carniola and Carinthia, have of course their own ballads, which have been recently collected. That the influence of the German population, with whom they live intermingled, has been very great, even in these songs, cannot be matter of surprise. It is, however, chiefly discernible in the melodies they sing; which are said to be the same familiar to the German mountaineers of Styria and Tyrol. Several narrative ballads of some length are

[52] From Czelakowsky's Collection ; see above, p. 216, n. 58.

still extant among them, similar to the Servian, but rhymed. These have been communicated to the German public in a translation by their poet Anastasius Grün. They are all too long to be given here as specimens; we therefore confine ourselves to the following pretty little song:

THE DOVELET.[53]

" Where were you, and where have you stray'd
In the night?
Your shoes are all with dew o'erlaid;
In the night, in the night."

I strayed there in the cool green grove,
In the night.
There flutters many a turtle dove,
In the night, in the night.

They have such little red cheeks, they all,
In the night;
And bills so sweet, and bills so small,
In the night, in the night.

There I stood, lurking on the watch,
In the night;
Till one little dovelet I did catch,
In the night, in the night.

It had of all the sweetest bill,
In the night;
Red rose, its cheeks were redder still,
In the night, in the night.

---

[53] From *Slowanske narodnj pjsne sebran. F. L. Czelakowskym*, Prague 1822–27. The collection of Carniolan ballads by Achazel and Korytko, which appeared in 1839, we have not yet seen.

That dovelet now caresses me
In the night;
And kissing each other we'll ever be,
In the night, in the night.

The field of popular poetry, which the Slavic nations of the WESTERN STEM present to us, promises a gleaning of a comparatively inferior value.

It appears from the Königshof manuscript, that five centuries ago the BOHEMIANS *had* a treasure of popular poetry. This document exhibits also the extraordinary fact, that almost the same ballads were sung in Bohemia in the thirteenth century, which are now heard from the lips of Russian and Servian peasant girls. The reader may compare the following songs, all of them faithfully translated.

ANCIENT BOHEMIAN SONGS.[54]

I.

O my rose, my fair red rose,
Why art thou blown out so early?
Why, when blown out, frozen?
Why, when frozen, withered?
Withered, broken from the stem!

Late at night I sat and sat,
Sat until the cocks did crow;
No one came, although I waited
Till the pine-torch all burned low.

Then came slumber over me;
And I dreamed my golden ring

[54] From *Rukopis Kralodworsky, etc. wydan od W. Hanky,* Prague 1835, p. 106.

Sudden slipp'd from my right hand;
Down my precious diamond fell.
For the ring I looked in vain,
For my love I longed in vain!

II.[55]

O, ye forests, dark green forests,
Miletinish forests!
Why in summer and in winter,
Are ye green and blooming?
O! I would not weep and cry,
Nor torment my heart.
But now tell me, good folks, tell me,
How should I not cry?
Ah! where is my dear good father?
Wo! he deep lies buried.
Where my mother? O good mother!
O'er her grows the grass!
Brothers have I not, nor sisters,
And my lad is gone!

SERVIAN SONG.[56]

O my fountain, so fresh and cool,
O my rose, so rosy red!
Why art thou blown out so early?
None have I to pluck thee for!
If I plucked thee for my mother,
Ah! poor girl, I have no mother;
If I plucked thee for my sister,
Gone is my sister with her husband;
If I plucked thee for my brother,

---

[55] Ibid. pp. 107 sq. 197 sq. 131 sq.

[56] Taken down by Vuk from the lips of a peasant girl.

To the war my brother 's gone.
If I plucked thee for my lover,
Gone is my love so far away!
Far away o'er three green mountains,
Far away o'er three cool fountains!

PASSAGES FROM SEVERAL RUSSIAN BALLADS,

current at the present day.

I.

Last evening I sat, a young maid,
I sat till deep in the night;
I sat and waited till day-break,
Till all my pine-torch was burnt out.
While all my companions slept,
I sat and waited for thee, love!

II.

No good luck to me my dream forebodes;
For to me, to me, fair maid, it seemed,
On my right hand did my gold ring burst,
O'er the floor then rolled the precious stone.

The Bohemians preserved their nationality, and very probably with it their ancient popular songs, down to the seventeenth century. During the thirty years' war, of which Bohemia was in part almost uninterruptedly the seat, a complete revolution in manners, institutions, and localities, took place. Whole villages emigrated, or were driven into the wide world, wandering about in scattered groups as fugitives and mendicants. Most of the ancient songs may have died at that time. The German influence increased rapidly during the remainder of the seventeenth century, mostly by force and reluctantly; still more during the eighteenth century by habit, intermarriages, education, etc. The Bohemians, the most musical nation in the world, are still a singing people; but many of their ditties are evidently borrowed from the German; in others, invented by themselves, they exhibit a spirit entirely different from that of their ancestors. These modern songs are mostly rhymed. The following specimen of songs still current among the peasantry of Bohemia, will show well the harmless, playful, roguish spirit that pervades them.

THE FORSAKEN MAIDEN.

Little star with gloomy shine,
If thou couldst but cry!
If thou hadst a heart, my star,
Sparks would from thee fly,
Just as tears fall from mine eye.

All the night with golden sparks
Thou wouldst for me cry!
Since my love intends to wed,
Only 'cause another maid
Richer is than I.

LIBERAL PAY.

Flowing waters meet each other,
And the winds, they blow and blow;
Sweetheart with her bright blue eyes
Stands and looks from her windów.

Do not stand so at the window,
Rather come before the door;
If thou giv'st me two sweet kisses,
I will give thee ten and more.

HAPPY DEATH.

In a green grove
Sat a loving pair;
Fell a bough from above,
Struck them dead there.
Happy for them,
That both died together;
So neither was left,
To mourn for the other.

THE LYING BIRD.

What chatters there the little bird,
On the oak tree above?
It sings, that every maid in love
Looks pale and wan from love.

My little bird, thou speak'st not true,
A lie hast thou now said;
For see, I am a maid in love,
And am not pale, but red.

Take care, my bird; because thou liest,
I now must punish thee;
I take this gun, I load this gun,
And shoot thee from the tree.

In the following fine ballad the German influence is manifest. It is extant in two different texts. We give it in Bowring's version, which has less of amplification and embellishment than is usual in English translations.

THE DEAD LOVE.

I sought the dark wood where the oat grass was growing;
The maidens were there and that oat grass were mowing.

And I called to those maidens: "Now say if there be
The maiden I love 'midst the maidens I see?"

And they sighed as they answered: "Ah no! alas no!
She was laid in the bed of the tomb long ago."[57]

"Then show me the way where my footsteps must tread,
To reach that dark chamber, where slumber the dead."

"The path is before thee, her grave will be known,
By the rosemary wreaths her companions have thrown."

"And where is the church in church-yard, whose heaps
Will point out the bed where the blessed one sleeps?"

So twice to the church-yard in sadness I drew,
But I saw no fresh heap and no grave that was new.

I turned, and with heart-chilling terror I froze,
And a newly made grave at my feet slowly rose.

And I heard a low voice, but it audibly said,
"Disturb not, disturb not the sleep of the dead!

"Who treads on my bosom? what footsteps have swept
The dew from the bed where the weary one slept?"

"My maiden, my maiden, so speak not to me,
My presents were once not unwelcome to thee!"

"Thy presents were welcome, but none could I save,
Not one could I bring to the stores of the grave.

"Go thou to my mother, and bid her restore
To thy hands every gift which I valued before.

"Then fling the gold ring in the depth of the sea,
And eternity's peace shall be given to me.

---

[57] In the original, *she was buried last week*. The lover could hardly expect to find a *new* grave, if she had been buried *long ago*.

"And sink the white kerchief deep, deep in the wave,
That my head may repose undisturbed in the grave!"

The SLOVAKS, the Slavic inhabitants of the north-western districts of Hungary, are considered, as we have seen above, as the direct descendants of the first Slavic settlers in Europe. Although for nearly a thousand years past they have formed a component part of the Hungarian nation, they have nevertheless preserved their language and many of their ancient customs. Their literature, we know, is not to be separated from that of the Bohemians. Their popular effusions are original; although, likewise, between them and the popular poetry of their Bohemian brethren, a close affinity cannot be denied. The Slovaks are said to be still exceedingly rich in pretty and artless songs, both pensive and cheerful; but the original Slavic type is now very much effaced from them. The surrounding nations, and above all the Germans, have exercised a decided and lasting influence upon them.

The following ballads are still heard among the Slovaks. The first of them is also extant in an imperfect German shape. As the coarse dialect, in which the German ballad may be heard, is that of the "Kuhländchen," a small district of Silesia, where the Slavic neighbourhood has not been without influence, we have no doubt that the more complete Slavic ballad is the original.

THE MOTHER'S CURSE.

The maiden went for water,
To the well o'er the meadow away;
She there could draw no water,
So thick the frost it lay.

The mother she grew angry;
She had it long to bemoan;

" O daughter mine, O daughter,
  I would thou wert a stone ! "

The maiden's water-pitcher
  Grew marble instantly ;
And she herself, the maiden,
  Became a maple tree.

There came one day two lads,
  Two minstrels young they were ;
" We've travelled far, my brother,
  Such a maple we saw no where.

" Come let us cut a fiddle,
  One fiddle for me and you ;
And from the same fine maple,
  For each one, fiddlesticks two."

They cut into the maple,—
  There splashed the blood so red ;
The lads fell on the ground,
  So sore were they afraid.

Then spake from within the maiden :
  " Wherefore afraid are you ?
Cut out of me one fiddle,
  And for each one, fiddlesticks two.

" Then go and play right sadly,
  To my mother's door begone,
And sing : Here is thy daughter,
  Whom thou didst curse to stone."

The lads they went, and sadly
  Their song to play began ;
The mother, when she heard them,
  Right to the window ran :

"O lads, dear lads, be silent,
Do not my pain increase;
For since I lost my daughter,
My pain doth never cease!"

SUN AND MOON.

Ah! if but this evening
Would come my lover sweet,
With the bright, bright sun,
Then the moon would meet.

Ah! poor girl this evening
Comes not thy lover sweet;
With the bright, bright sun,
The moon doth never meet.

The reader will perceive that these Slovakian songs are rhymed. There are however also rhymeless verses extant among them; the measure of which seems to indicate a greater antiquity, and brings them nearer to the nations of the Eastern stock.[58]

Of all the Slavic nations, the Poles, as we have already remarked, had most neglected their popular poetry. There were indeed several collections of popular ballads published, partly by Polish editors, with the title of popular poetry in Poland. But they all, without exception, so far as we know, refer to the Ruthenian peasantry in Poland, who use a language different from the Polish, and essentially the same as the Malo-Russian. These tribes, inhabitants of Poland for centuries, may indeed be

[58] All our Bohemian and Slovakian specimens are taken from Czelakowsky's Collection, as we happened not to be in possession of Kollar's and Erben's later work of that kind. For the full title see p. 385, note.

called *Poles* with perfect propriety. Yet this name is in a more limited sense applied to the Lekhian race exclusively; and it is in respect to them that we remarked above, that their songs had been collected for the first time only a few years ago.[59]

That they also had national ballads of their own could hardly be a matter of doubt: and the neglect may easily be explained, in a nation among whom all that has any reference to mere boors and serfs has always been regarded with the utmost contempt. Their beautiful national dances, however, known all over the world, the graceful Polonaise, the bold Masur, the ingenious Cracovienne, are just as much the property of the peasantry, as of the nobility. Their dances were formerly always accompanied by singing; just as it was customary in olden times every where, and as it is still the usage among the Russian and Servian peasantry, to dance to the music of song instead of instruments. But these songs are always extemporized; and in Poland probably were never written down. The early refinement of the language secured to the upper classes a greater or lesser share in their national literature, which gave them apparently better things; although we have seen above, that, far from developing itself from its own resources, their literature was alternately ingrafted on a Latin, Italian, or French stock. Among the country gentry, and even at the convivial parties of the nobility, the custom of extemporizing songs, probably full of national reminiscences, continued even down to the beginning of our own century. Very little stress was naturally laid upon them; since the interest for all that is national, historical, or in any way connected with the people, belongs only to the most recent times. In our day, the local scenes of Lithuania have excited some interest, and the Ukraine has become the favourite theatre of Polish poets.

---

[59] See above p. 297.

The Polish nation has an ancient hymn, which may be said to belong in some measure to popular poetry. It is known under the name of *Boga Rodzica*, or God's Mother; and is said to have been composed by St. Adalbert, who lived at the end of the tenth century. According to Niemcewicz, the Polish poet, it was still chanted in the year 1812 in the churches of Kola and Gnesen, the places where St. Adalbert lived and died. It is a prayer to the Virgin, ending with a sixfold Amen; and was formerly sung by the soldiers when advancing to battle. For that reason probably we find it frequently called a war song.

The popular ballads, published by Woicicki and Zegota Pauli, are not distinguished in any way from those still extant among the Slovakians, Bohemians, and Lusatian Sorabians. It can only be matter of surprise, that they have imbibed no more of the wild and romantic character of the ballads sung by the Ruthenians, with whom they live intermingled in several regions. They are ruder in form; and alternately rhymed, or distinguished from prose only by a certain irregular but prosodic measure, sometimes trochaic, but mostly dactylic. With the classical beauty of the Servian songs they can bear no comparison; in which latter the perfect absence of *vulgarity* may perhaps be partly accounted for, by their having been produced among a people where no privileged classes exist. Only in their wedding songs, and other similar ones, is there a striking affinity; it is in general in these relics of ancient times, that the popular poetry of the nations of the Eastern and of the Western Stems meet in one distinct and fundamental accord.

Many of the more ancient ballads extant among the Poles we find also in one or other of the Western Slavic languages. For example, the following; which exists in the Vendish language in a shape more diffuse and twice as long; and also in Slovakian, still more sketchlike. That the Polish ballad is derived from a time, when the horrid invasions of the Tartars were at least still distinctly remembered, we may safely conclude. In the Slovakian ballad the invaders are called Turks; in the Vendish ballad, probably the latest of the three, they have lost all individual nationality, and have become merely "enemies," or "robbers."

THE INVASION OF THE TARTARS.[60]

Plundering are the Tartars,
Plundering Jashdow castle.

All the people fled,
Only a lad they met.

"Where's thy lord, my lad?
Where and in what tower
Is thy lady's bower?"

"I must not betray him,
Lest my lord should slay me."

"Not his anger fear,
Thou shalt stay not here,
Thou shalt go with us."

"My lord's and lady's bower
Is in the highest tower."

Once the Tartars shot,
And they hit them not.

Twice the Tartars shot,
And they killed the lord.

---

[60] *Pjesni ludu Bialo Chrobatow, Mazurow i Russinow z nad Bugu zebr. przez K. W. Wojcickiego*, i. e. Songs of the White Chrobatians, Masovians, and Russinians on the Bug, collected by K. W. Woicicki, Warsaw 1836. Vol. I. p. 85. See above, p. 297.

Thrice the Tartars shot—
They are breaking in the tower,
The lady is in their power.

Away, away it goes,
Over the green meadows,
Black, black the walls arose !

" O lady, O turn back,
To thy walls so sad and black.

" O walls, ye dreary walls !
So sad and black are you,
Because your lord they slew !

" Because your lord is slain,
Your lady is dragged away
Into captivity !
A slave for life to be,
Far, far in Tartary !"

Among the ballads of almost all nations we find some that illustrate the mournful and destitute state of *motherless orphans.* There seems to be hardly any feeling, which comes more directly home to the affectionate compassion of the human heart, than the pitiable and touching condition of helpless little beings left to the tender mercies of a *stepmother ;* who, with her traditional severity, may be called a kind of standing bugbear of the popular imagination. The Danes have a beautiful ballad, in which the ghost of a mother is roused by the wailings and sufferings of her deserted offspring, to break with supernatural power the gravestone, and to re-enter, in the stillness of the night, the neglected nursery, in order to cheer, to nurse, to comb and wash the dear seven little ones, whom God once intrusted to her care. It is one of the most affecting pieces of popular poetry we ever have met with. The Slavic nations have nothing that can be compared with it in *beauty;* but most of them have several ballads on the same subject; and in a general collection, the "Orphan Ballads" would fill a whole chapter.[61] The simple ditty which we give here as another specimen of Polish popular poetry, exceedingly rude as it is in its form, and even defective in rhyme and metre, cannot but please and touch us by its very simplicity.

POOR ORPHAN CHILD.[62]

Poor little orphan is wandering about,
Seeking its mother and weeping aloud.

Jesus Christ met it, mildly to it spake:
"Where art thou roaming, poor little babe?

"Go not, go not, babe, too far thou wilt roam,
And goest e'er so far, not to thy mother come.

"Now turn and go, dear babe, to the green cemetery,
From out her deep grave thy mother will speak to thee."

"Wo! at my grave who's knocking so wild?"
"Mother! dear mother! it's I, thy poor child!

"Take me to thee, take me,
Ill I fare without thee!"

"Go home, my babe, and thy strange mother tell,
She'll wash thy tattered shirt and comb and clean thee well!"

"When my shirt she washes,
Sprinkles it with ashes.

---

[61] We have also two most exquisite Lithuanian ballads which treat of the same subject; one of them being the lament of a *fatherless* boy.

[62] *Pjesni ludu Polskiego w Galicyi zebr. Zegota Pauli*, Lemberg 1838, p. 57. See above, p. 297.

"When she puts it on to me,
Scolds so grim and bitterly!

"When she combs my head,
Runs the blood so red.

"When she braids my hair,
Pulls me here and there!"

"Go thee home, my babe, the Lord thy tears will dry!"
And the babe went home, laid her down to cry.

Laid her down to cry, one day only cried;
Groaned the second day, and the third day died.

From his heaven our Lord did two angels send,
With the poor babe they did to heaven ascend.

From the hell our Lord did two devils send;
They took the bad stepmother and down to hell they went.

Of all the surviving Slavic tribes, we have seen that the nationality of the VENDES of Lusatia is most endangered. If formerly, as a race, they suffered from persecution and oppression, they have now for several centuries shared all the advantages of an enlightened education and wise institutions with their German countrymen; and it would therefore be erroneous to consider them still in the light of an oppressed or subjugated nation. Although their language cannot be said to be *favoured* by the government, they have their schools, their worship, their courts of justice, and, above all, their ballads, without let or hinderance; and if nevertheless the statistics of each year, especially in the plains of Lower Lusatia, show a diminution of the Slavic speaking population, we must attribute it rather to the natural and irresistible effect of time and circumstances, than to any despotic or arbitrary measures of the government. The Vendish villages are flourishing; the costumes of the peasants are heavy and rich; and to their general welfare the *cheerful* merry character of their ballads seems to bear testimony. Their melodies resemble the Bohemian, as much as their ballads do those of their neighbours; but German melodies also are frequently heard among them, and many translations of German popular ballads have become perfectly naturalized. That the language of Upper Lusatia approaches very near to the Bohemian, we have stated above. It is, however, much more interspersed with German words; although not to such a degree as the Lower Lusatian dialect.

Of all the Slavic popular ballads, we find in those of the Lusatians least of that chaste feeling, which is in general characteristic of Slavic love songs. The pleasures of illicit intercourse and their consequences, which make also a favourite theme of the common English and German ballads, are often grossly described; and we may conclude that the talent of extemporizing, or in general making pretty verses, has forsaken the female villagers in this German neighbourhood, and passed over to the men.

We give here two characteristic ballads of the Upper Lusatian language.

THE ORPHAN'S LAMENT.[63]

Far more unhappy in the world am I,
Than on the meadow the bird that doth fly.

Little bird merrily flits to and fro,
Sings its sweet carol upon the green bough.

[63] *Pjesnicki hornich i delnich Luziskich Serbow*, i. e. Songs of the Servians of Upper and Lower Lusatia, published by L. Haupt and J. E. Schmaler, Grimma 1844. Comp. p. 304, above.

I, alas, wander wherever I will,
Every where I am desolate still!

No one befriends me, wherever I go,
But my own heart full of sorrow and woe!

Cease thy grief, oh my heart, full of grief,
Soon will a time come that giveth thee relief.

Never misfortune has struck me so hard,
But I ere long again better have fared.

God of all else in the world has enough;
Why not then widows and orphans enough?[64]

GOOD ADVICE FOR LADS.

Let him who would married be,
Look about him and take care,
That he does not take a wife,
  Take a wife;
He'll repent it all his life.

If thou shouldst make up thy mind,
And shouldst take too young a wife,
Youthful wife has boiling blood,
  Boiling blood;
No one thinks of her much good.

If thou shouldst make up thy mind,
And shouldst take too old a wife,

---

[64] A similar *naïveté* we find in a little Servian elegy. A poor girl sings: "Our Lord has of every thing his fill; but of poor people he seems to have greater plenty than of any thing else!"

In the house she'll creep about,
Creep about ;
And will frighten people out.

If thou shouldst make up thy mind,
And shouldst take a handsome wife,
Nought but trouble she will give,
Trouble give ;
Others' visits she'll receive.

If thou shouldst make up thy mind,
And shouldst take too short a wife,
Lowly thou must stoop to her,
Stoop to her,
Wouldst thou whisper in her ear.

If thou shouldst make up thy mind,
And shouldst take too tall a wife,
Ladders thou to her must raise,
Ladders raise,
If thou wouldst thy wife embrace.

If thou shouldst make up thy mind,
And shouldst take a snarling wife,
Thou wilt want no dog in the house,
Dog in the house ;
Thy wife will be the dog in the house.

As for poor ones, let them be,
Nothing they will bring to thee,
Every thing will wanting be,
Wanting be ;
Not a soul will come to thee.

If thou shouldst make up thy mind,
And shouldst take a wealthy wife,

Then with patience thou must bear,
    Thou must bear,
If the breeches she should wear.

Pretty, modest, smart, and neat,
Good and pious she must be ;
If thou weddest such a wife,
    Such a wife,
Thou'lt not repent it all thy life.

Merry ballads like these are usually sung at wedding feasts, where several of the old Slavic ceremonies are still preserved ; among other things the bringing home of the bride in solemn procession. Many old verses, mostly fragments of half forgotten ballads, familiar to their ancestors, are in like manner occasionally recited. But the poetical atmosphere, which still weaves around the Russian or Servian maiden a mystical veil, through which she gazes, as in a dream full of golden illusions and images, into that condition of new existence feared and desired by her at once—that atmosphere is destroyed by the lights of the surrounding civilization, which show the sober reality of things in full glare. The flowers are withered that were wound around the chains; but the chains themselves have become lighter. The ancient wedding songs, full of pagan allusions, have been supplanted by glees mostly composed by their half German pastors; the only educated men who still speak their language. Indeed, not a few of their most popular ballads are written by their curates. How soon these will be superseded by German songs, no one can say; but it requires no great stretch of prophetic power to predict, that the time is near at hand.

ADDITIONS AND CORRECTIONS.

Page 2 sq. note 5, at the end.—According to Schaffarik's later opinion, as expressed in his *Antiquities*, the appellation Slavi, Slaveni, or Slovenians, is derived from one of their seats, that is, the country on the Upper Niemen, where the *Stloveni* or *Sueveni* of Ptolemy lived. It is said to be called by the Finns *Sallo* (like every woodland) ; by the Lithuanians, *Sallawa, Slawa;* in old Prussian, *Salava;* by the neighbouring Germans, *Schalauen;* in Latin, *Scalavia.* But it seems a more natural conclusion, that *vice versa* the name of the district was rather derived from Slavic settlers living in the midst of a German, Russian, and Finnish population.—For the derivation from *slovo*, word, speech, the circumstance seems to speak, that in most Slavic languages the appellation for a German (and formerly for all foreigners) is *Njemetz*, i. e. one dumb, an impotent, nameless, speechless person. What more natural, in a primitive stage of culture, than to consider only those as speaking, who are *understood;* and those who seem to utter unmeaning sounds, as dumb, impotent beings?

Page 10. l. 7.—The national name of the Montenegrins, here given as *Czernogortzi*, is better written *Tzernogortzi;* see p. 119, n. 17. Their number is given by Sir J. G. Wilkinson at 80,000, or more.

Page 12. l. 8, 22 —For *Leckian* read *Lekhian.*

Page 59. l. 2 from bott.—For *dialect* read *language.*

Page 107. n. 3.—The name of the German traveller in Servia is *O. von Pirch*, not *Birch.*

Page 280. l. 17.—For *Scianawski* read *Szianiawski.*

Page 289.—Note 72 should read: *Starozytnosci historycne Polskie*, Cracow 1840.—Also Note 73 should read: *Starozytnosci Gallicyiskie*, Lemberg 1840.

Page 293.—As the author of the " Evening Hours of a Pilgrim," Witwicki should have been named.

Page 297. l. 15.—For *Masuria* read *Masovia.*

Page 323.—The signature P. should follow the Elegy ; see p. 337, note.

Page 327. n. 9.—For *Pjesne* read *Pjesme.*

Page 355. n. 31.—For *Volksleider* read *Volkslieder.*

INDEX.

NAMES OF SLAVIC AUTHORS MENTIONED IN THE PRECEDING WORK.

L.

M.

N.

T.

U.

V.*

W.

---

* There is only one letter in the Slavish Alphabet for *V* and *W*. In the personal names of those nations, which use the Cyrillic alphabet, we have written it V, according to the English pronunciation; in those belonging to nations which have adopted the Latin alphabet, we of course did not feel justified in making any alteration. The Slavic *W* is always pronounced like the English *V*.

FINIS.

Travels, Adventures, &c.--Europe.

The Genius of Italy;

Being Sketches of Italian Life, Literature, and Religion.

BY REV. ROBERT TURNBULL,

Author of "The Genius of Scotland."

Third edition. 1 vol. 12mo, $1 ; illustrated edition, cloth, gilt, $2.

The edition with extra illustrations, handsomely bound, will be ready in the autumn.

"Mr. Turnbull gives us the orange groves, and the fountains, and the gondolas, and the frescoes and the ruins, with touches of personal adventure, and sketches of biography, and glimpses of the life, literature, and religion of Modern Italy, seen with the quick, comprehensive glances of an American traveller, impulsive, inquisitive, and enthusiastic. His book is a pleasant record of a tourist's impressions, without the infliction of the tiresome minutiæ of his everyday experience." —*Literary World.*

"At a moment when Italy is about to be regenerated—when the long-slumbering spirit of the people is about assuming its ancient vigor, a work of this kind is desirable. * * * The country, its people, and prominent features are given with much truth and force."—*Democratic Review.*

Views A-Foot;

Or, Europe seen with Knapsack and Staff.

BY BAYARD TAYLOR.

New edition, with an additional Chapter of Practical Information for Pedestrians in Europe, and a Sketch of the Author in Pedestrian Costume, from a Drawing by T. Buchanan Read. 12mo., cloth, $1 25.

——— The same, fancy cloth, gilt extra, $1 75.

"There is a freshness and force in the book altogether unusual in a book of travels. * * * As a text-book for travellers the work is essentially valuable; it tells how much can be accomplished with very limited means, when energy, curiosity, and a love of adventure are the prompters; sympathy in his success likewise, is another source of interest to the book. * * * The result of all this is, a wide-spread popularity as a writer, a very handsomely printed book, with a very handsome portrait of the author, and we congratulate him upon the attainment of this and future honors."—*Union Magazine.*

The Spaniards, and their Country.

BY RICHARD FORD.

12mo, green cloth. $1 00.

"The best English book, beyond comparison, that ever has appeared for the illustration, not merely of the general topography and local curiosities, but of the national character and manners of Spain."—*Quarterly Review.*

"This is a very clever and amusing work."—*Louisville Exam.*

"The style is light, dashing, and agreeable."—*N. Y. Mirror.*

*** Washington Irving commends this as the best modern popular account of Spain.

Scenes and Thoughts in Europe.

BY AN AMERICAN.

(Geo. H. Calvert, Esq., Baltimore.) 12mo. 50 cts.

"This book is a delightful instance of the transforming and recreative power of the mind upon every thing it touches. The most hackneyed ground of Europe, persons and objects that have been the theme for the last half dozen years of every literary remittance from abroad, appear to us clothed with new charms and meanings, because examined with a finer penetration than they have been by any other English or American traveller."—*Tribune.*

THE LIBERTY OF ROME;

A HISTORY.

With an Historical account of the Liberty of ancient Nations.

BY SAMUEL ELIOT, ESQ.

2 vols. 8vo, cloth, and illustrated with 12 Plates. $4 50.

LIST OF PLATES.

1. Allegorical.
2. Homer singing on the Chian strand.
3. Bust of Socrates.
4. Imaginary View of Early Rome.
5. Bust of Pythagoras.
6. The Secession of the People to Mons Sacer.
7. The meeting of Camillus and Manlius after the retreat of the Gauls.
8. Bust of Marcus Tullius Cicero.
9. The Triumph of Quintus Fabius.
10. Caius Gracchus weeping before his Father's Statue.
11. Cicero denouncing Catiline.
12. Bust of Lucius Junius Brutus.

OPINIONS OF THE PRESS.

"Mr. Eliot's aim is an important one It is to indicate the kind and amount of liberty enjoyed by the ancient Romans. He has formed a just conception of what is meant by the word liberty, which is too often confounded with mere forms of government, at best but its guards and supports. * * * The scale of the work is so extensive, that details necessarily disappear in any abridged statement of its contents, nor is it possible by extracts to convey an idea of the value and interest of the book. To be appreciated it must be taken as a whole. There are few salient passages. But its general impression is in the highest degree healthy, conducive to the expansion of the mind, and calculated to enrich it with new and important ideas. We are glad to receive from an American hand such a welcome contribution to our best order of Literature."—*London Examiner.*

"A work of high character and distinguished merit. The author has brought to the performance of a task of such magnitude and difficulty, vast stores of erudition, a highly cultivated taste, a comprehensive and penetrating intellect, and a grave and sober judgment; qualities indispensable to one who would write such a history, and rarely to be found combined to the same extent in the same ndividual."—*John Bull.*

"We have had histories of Rome written by the scholar, by the credulous, and lately a history of it by the great historic skeptic, Niebuhr We had not yet one by a philosopher; we thank Mr. Eliot for having undertaken, and we may add, succeeded in his task. This is a good and new book to the classic student and thinker."—*Daily News.*

"This remarkable book presents us with a view of liberty in a different and truer light than has been laid before us by any writer. Extensive reading, a well balanced and philosophical mind, above all prejudice, could alone have fitted its author for producing a work which must take a high rank in American Literature, in its style as well as in its subject."—*Providence Journal.*

"The present volumes exhibit the evidence of many qualities essential to so large an enterprise in their accomplished author. They are in the highest degree creditable to the conscientious fidelity of his researches, to his industry and power of persistent labor, to his acquaintance with the most authentic sources of ancient and modern learning, and to the extent and variety of his erudition, which is free from any tincture of pedantry or ostentation.—*New-York Tribune.*

Travels, Adventures, and Discoveries---In the East.

CONTINUED.

Egypt and its Monuments;

Or, Egypt a Witness for the Bible.

BY FRANCIS L. HAWKS, D. D., LL. D., &c., &c.

Illustrated with Engravings from the works of Champollion, Rosellini, Wilkinson, and others; and Architectural Views of the principal Temples, &c. 1 vol. 8vo, uniform with "Layard's Nineveh," cloth, $3; half morocco, gilt edges, $4.

SECOND EDITION, REVISED AND ENLARGED.

"It will have a lively interest; not for the Bible student only, but for all who take interest in historical research."—*N. Y. Com. Advertiser.*

"A valuable contribution to our Sacred Literature."—*Newark Daily Advertiser.*

"It supplies a desideratum in the Literature of the Bible."—*Buffalo Commercial.*

"An intelligible, true, and readable book on Egypt, beyond what the experiences of a single traveller could furnish the materials of."—*Boston Transcript.*

"The volume will constitute a valuable addition to Christian Literature."—*N. Y. Recorder.*

"The volume of Dr. Hawks will be welcomed by many readers as a valuable contribution to the stock of information, hitherto to be obtained only in the costly volumes of Wilkinson and others. There probably exists no other volume of the same size containing so much information on Egypt."—*Cambridge Chronicle.*

"The volume is intensely interesting, and will abundantly repay a careful perusal."—*Christian Alliance.*

"The entire work is filled with most instructive facts, gathered from recent discoveries in monumental literature, valuable alike to the theological student and general reader."—*Universalist Review.*

"In the treatment of this subject, Dr. Hawks's admirable faculty of lucid arrangement and distinct statement has full play; and he proceeds, too, with a calm confidence of the strength of his positions, that cannot fail to inspire his readers—such of them especially as have been somewhat startled by the bold assertions of the infidel school of Egyptologists and their train of ignorant imitators—with a similar confidence."—*Methodist Quarterly Review.*

The East;

Or, Sketches of Travel in Egypt and the Holy Land.

BY REV. J. A. SPENCER, M. A.,

Editor of the New Testament in Greek, with English Notes. Member of the New-York Historical Society, &c., &c.

Splendidly Illustrated with Original Drawings. 8vo, pp. 500. Uniform wi "Layard's Nineveh," "Hawks's Monuments of Egypt," &c

CONTENTS.

EGYPT.—Alexandria.—The Nile and the Pyramids.—The Pyramids and their Builders.—Life on the Nile.—Philae, Syene, Elephantine, Esneh.—Necropolis of Thebes.—Luxor and Karnak.—Dendera, Es-siout, Beni-hassan.—The Metropolis of Egypt.—Mosks, Citadel, Heliopolis.—Coptic Church, Public Men and Events.

THE HOLY LAND.—Life in the Desert.—Palestina, the Hill Country.—The Holy City.—Gethsemane, the Mount of Olives.—Calvary and the Holy Sepulchre.—Bethlehem and its Vicinity—The Dead Sea and the Jordan.—Judea, Samaria, Jacob's Well, Nabulus.—Sebaste, Tabor Tiberias, Nazareth.—Mount Carmel, St. Jean d'Acre, Tyre.—Sidon, Beirut and its Vicinity—Appendix, Notes, &c.

Anglo-Saxon.

Anglo-Saxon Course of Study.

A Compendious Anglo-Saxon and English Dictionary.

By the Rev. JOSEPH BOSWORTH, D.D., F.R.S., &c., &c. 1 vol., 8vo, cloth, $3.

A Grammar of the Anglo-Saxon Language.

By LOUIS F. KLIPSTEIN, A.M., LL.M., and Ph. D., of the University of Giessen. 12mo, cloth, $1 25.

Tha Halgan Godspel on Englisc.

The Anglo-Saxon Version of the Holy Gospels. Edited by BENJAMIN THORPE, F.S.A. Reprinted by the same. 12mo, cloth, $1 25.

Analecta Anglo-Saxonica,

With an Introductory Ethnological Essay, and Notes, Critical and Explanatory. By LOUIS F. KLIPSTEIN, A.M., LL.M., and Ph. D., of the University of Giessen. 2 vols., 1200 pages, $3 50.

Natale Sancti Gregorii Papæ.

Ælfric's Homily on the Birthday of St. Gregory, and Collateral Extracts from King Alfred's Version of Bede's Ecclesiastical History and the Saxon Chronicle, with a full Rendering into English, Notes Critical and Explanatory, and an Index of Stems and Forms. By LOUIS F. KLIPSTEIN, A.M., LL.M., and Ph. D., of the University of Giessen. 12mo, 50 cts.

A Glossary to the Analecta Anglo-Saxonica,

With the Indo-Germanic and other Affinities of the Language. By LOUIS F. KLIPSTEIN, A.M., LL.M., and Ph. D., of the University of Giessen. *In preparation.*

"There is no doubt that a few years hence, the persevering and ill-rewarded toils of this learned scholar will be looked back upon with sincere gratitude, by all who love the study of our incomparable language, in its better and more sinewy part. If Dr. K. is, as we suppose, a foreigner. he has acquired a mastery of English which is marvellous, and which, by the by, shows the advantage to be derived from Anglo-Saxon. These volumes, taken in connection with the grammar, and the forthcoming glossary, will make it easy for any private student to make himself acquainted with that delightful old tongue, to which we owe almost all our words of endearment, such as *home, father mother, brother, sister;* almost all our names of English flowers, as *daisy, cowslip, primrose, nosegay;* and abundance of the short, monosyllabic, pungent nouns, which half-learned folks would barter away for sesquipedalian latinisms. We mean such as *dell, dale, wrath, wealth, knave, thrust, churl, wreath,* and *soul.* The preliminary essay prepares the way, by tracing very clearly the lineage of the Anglo-Saxon language: it is a valuable contribution to Ethnology."—*Presbyterian.*

"Surely it is a matter of concern to know and understand well our own tongue. How much better then would it be, if in our public and private schools, as much attention at least were given to the teachings of English as of Greek and Latin, that our youths might bring home with them a racy idiomatic way of speaking and writing their own language, instead of a smattering of Greek and Latin, which they almost forget and generally neglect in a few years' time. * * * For this, a study of the Anglo-Saxon is absolutely needful; for after all, it has bequeathed to us by far the largest stock of words in our language."—*Loudon.*

"The most valuable portion of our language comes to us directly through the Anglo-Saxon; and to make the study of it a part of our general system of education, would be to administer the most powerful antidote to the deteriorating influence of would-be fine speakers and writers, which is gradually robbing our English speech of much of its native energy and precision.—*Lit. World.*

www.ingramcontent.com/pod-product-compliance
Lightning Source LLC
LaVergne TN
LVHW021143110826
845150LV00005B/1114

* 9 7 8 1 4 2 5 5 4 7 6 4 6 *